sweetness &lightning

2

Gido Amagakure

c o n t e n t s

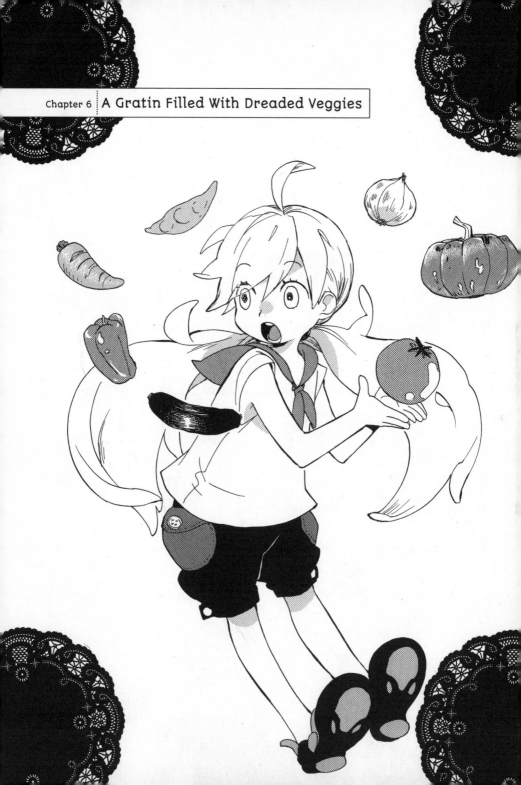

Chapter 6 A Gratin Filled With Dreaded Veggies

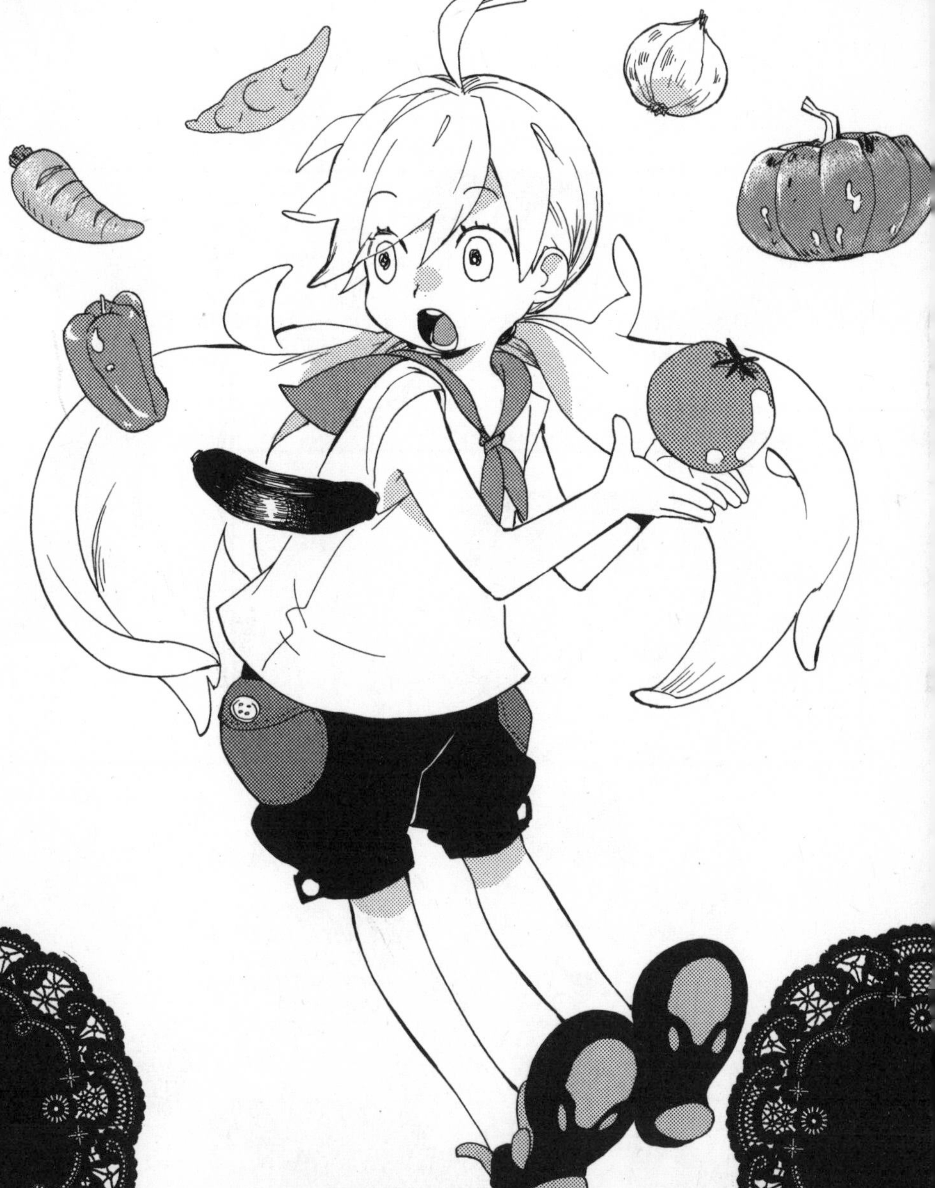

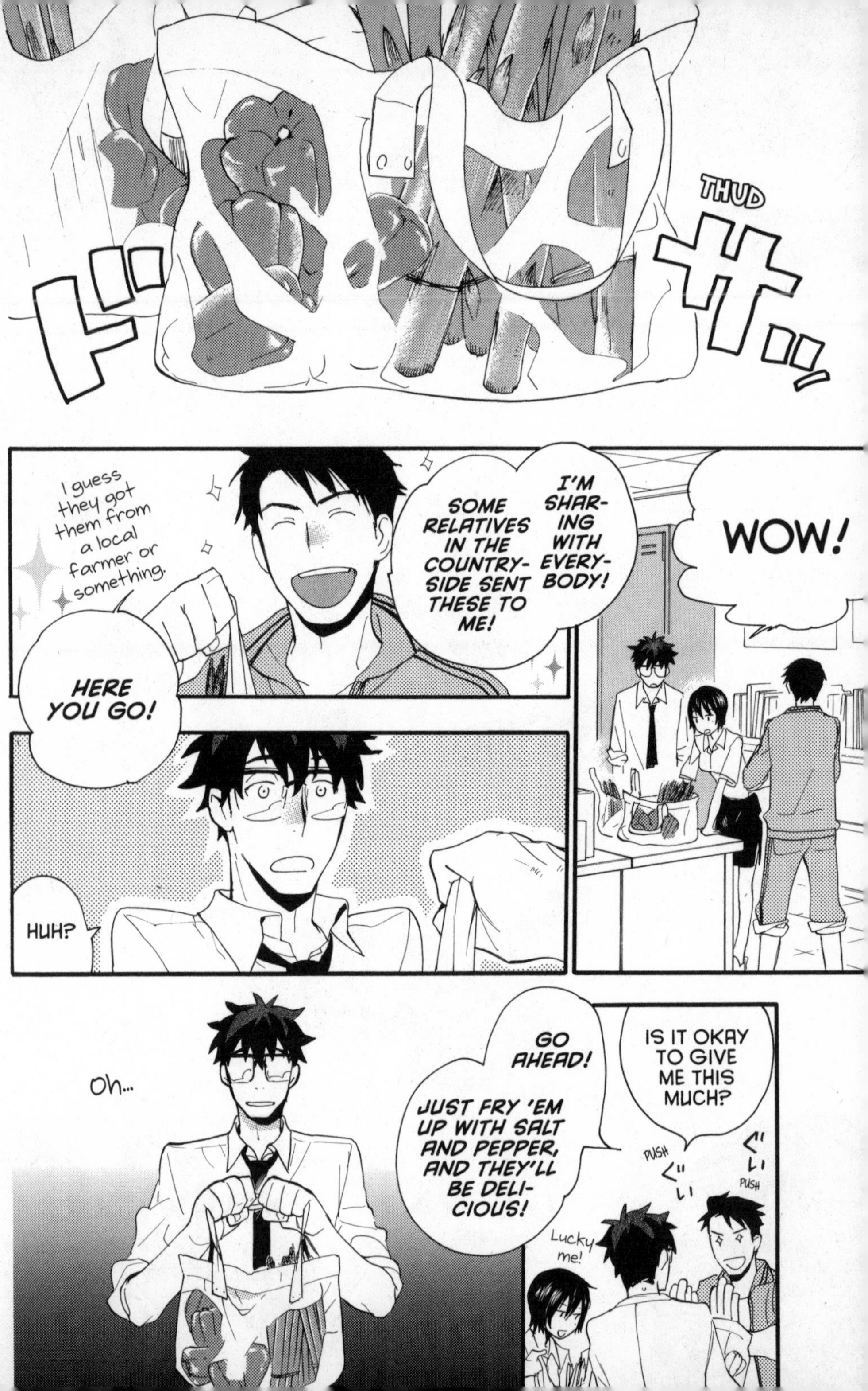
THUD
ドサッ
WOW!
I'M SHARING WITH EVERYBODY!
SOME RELATIVES IN THE COUNTRYSIDE SENT THESE TO ME!
I guess they got them from a local farmer or something.
HERE YOU GO!
HUH?
IS IT OKAY TO GIVE ME THIS MUCH?
GO AHEAD!
JUST FRY 'EM UP WITH SALT AND PEPPER, AND THEY'LL BE DELICIOUS!
ぐい PUSH
ぐい PUSH
Lucky me!
Oh...

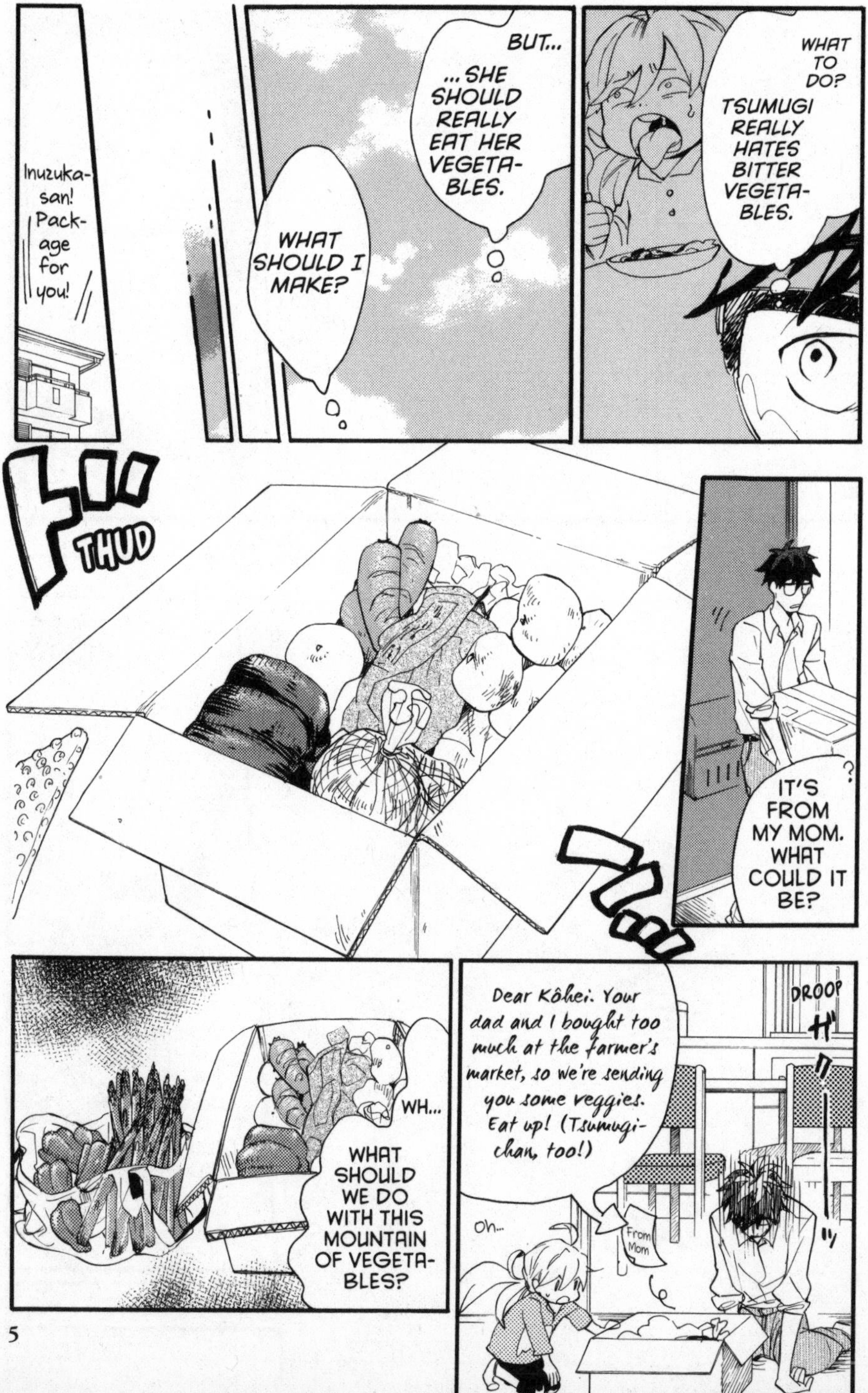
WHAT TO DO? TSUMUGI REALLY HATES BITTER VEGETABLES.
BUT... ...SHE SHOULD REALLY EAT HER VEGETABLES.
WHAT SHOULD I MAKE?
Inuzuka-san! Package for you!
IT'S FROM MY MOM. WHAT COULD IT BE?
THUD
DROOP
Dear Kôhei. Your dad and I bought too much at the farmer's market, so we're sending you some veggies. Eat up! (Tsumugi-chan, too!)
From Mom
Oh...
WH...
WHAT SHOULD WE DO WITH THIS MOUNTAIN OF VEGETABLES?

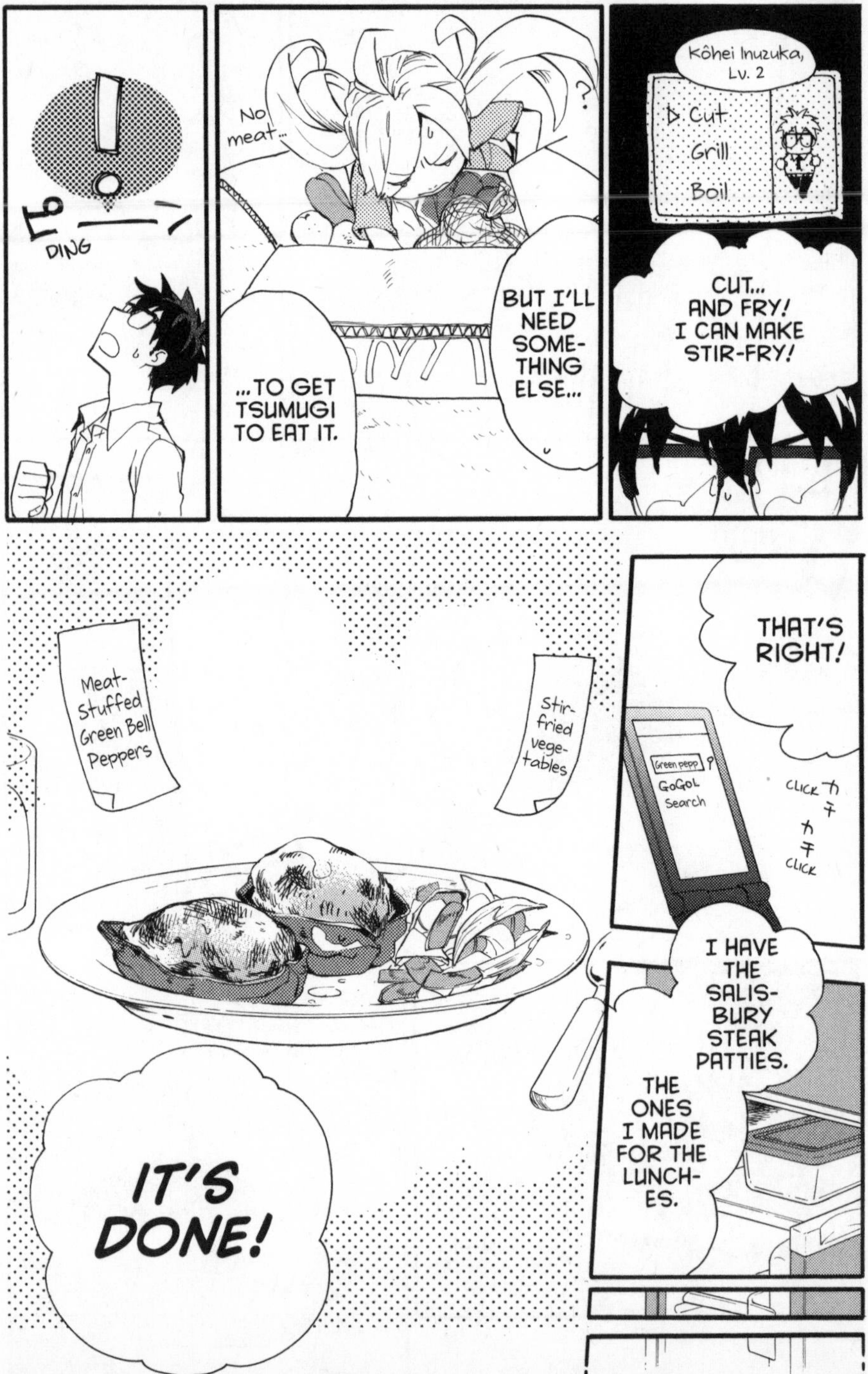
Kôhei Inuzuka, Lv. 2
Cut
Grill
Boil
CUT... AND FRY! I CAN MAKE STIR-FRY!
No meat...
?
BUT I'LL NEED SOME-THING ELSE...
...TO GET TSUMUGI TO EAT IT.
!
DING
THAT'S RIGHT!
Green pepp
GoGoL Search
CLICK
CLICK
I HAVE THE SALIS-BURY STEAK PATTIES.
THE ONES I MADE FOR THE LUNCH-ES.
Meat-Stuffed Green Bell Peppers
Stir-fried vege-tables
IT'S DONE!

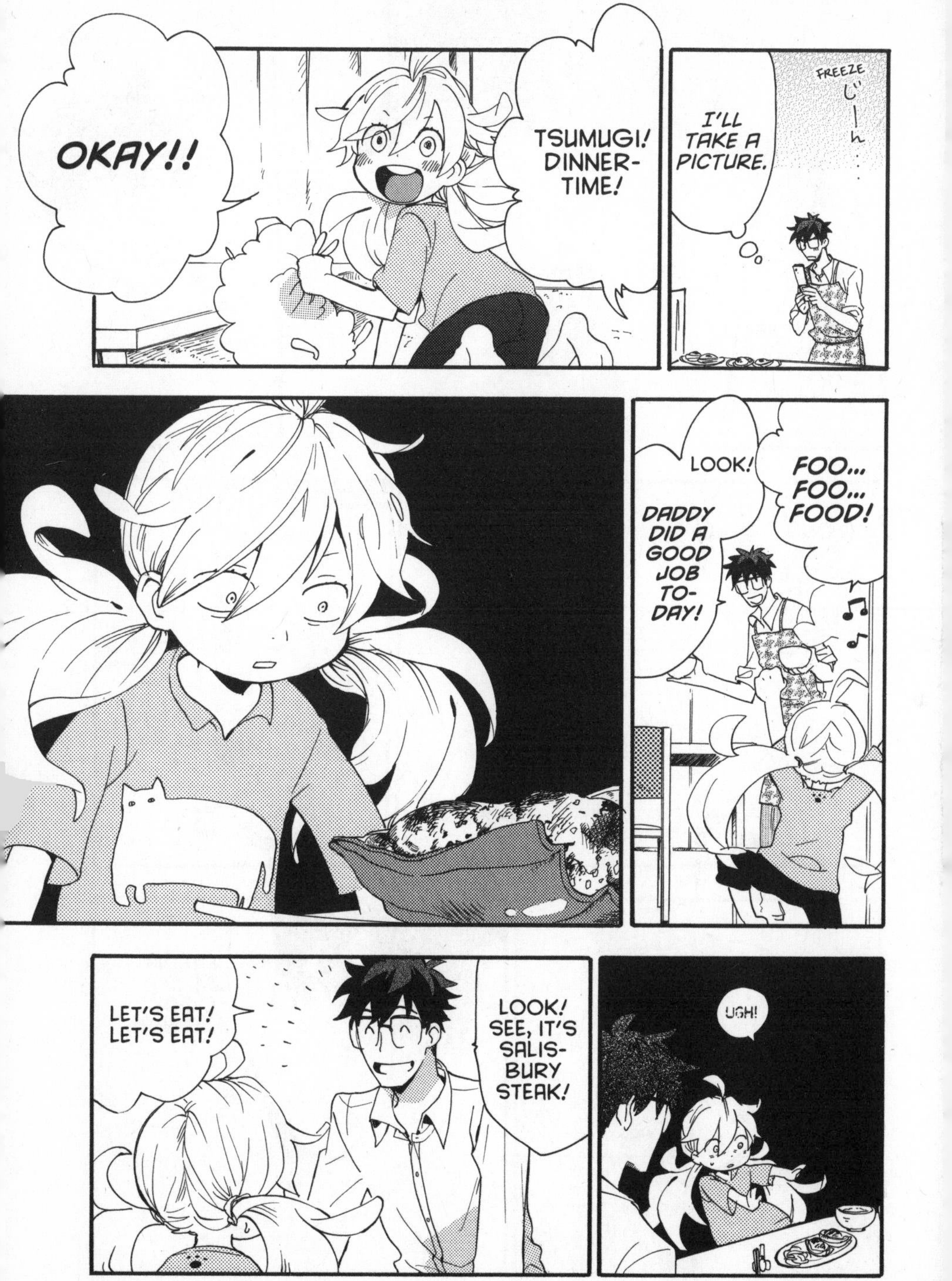
FREEZE
じーん…
I'LL TAKE A PICTURE.
TSUMUGI! DINNER-TIME!
OKAY!!
FOO... FOO... FOOD!
LOOK!
DADDY DID A GOOD JOB TO-DAY!
UGH!
LOOK! SEE, IT'S SALIS-BURY STEAK!
LET'S EAT! LET'S EAT!

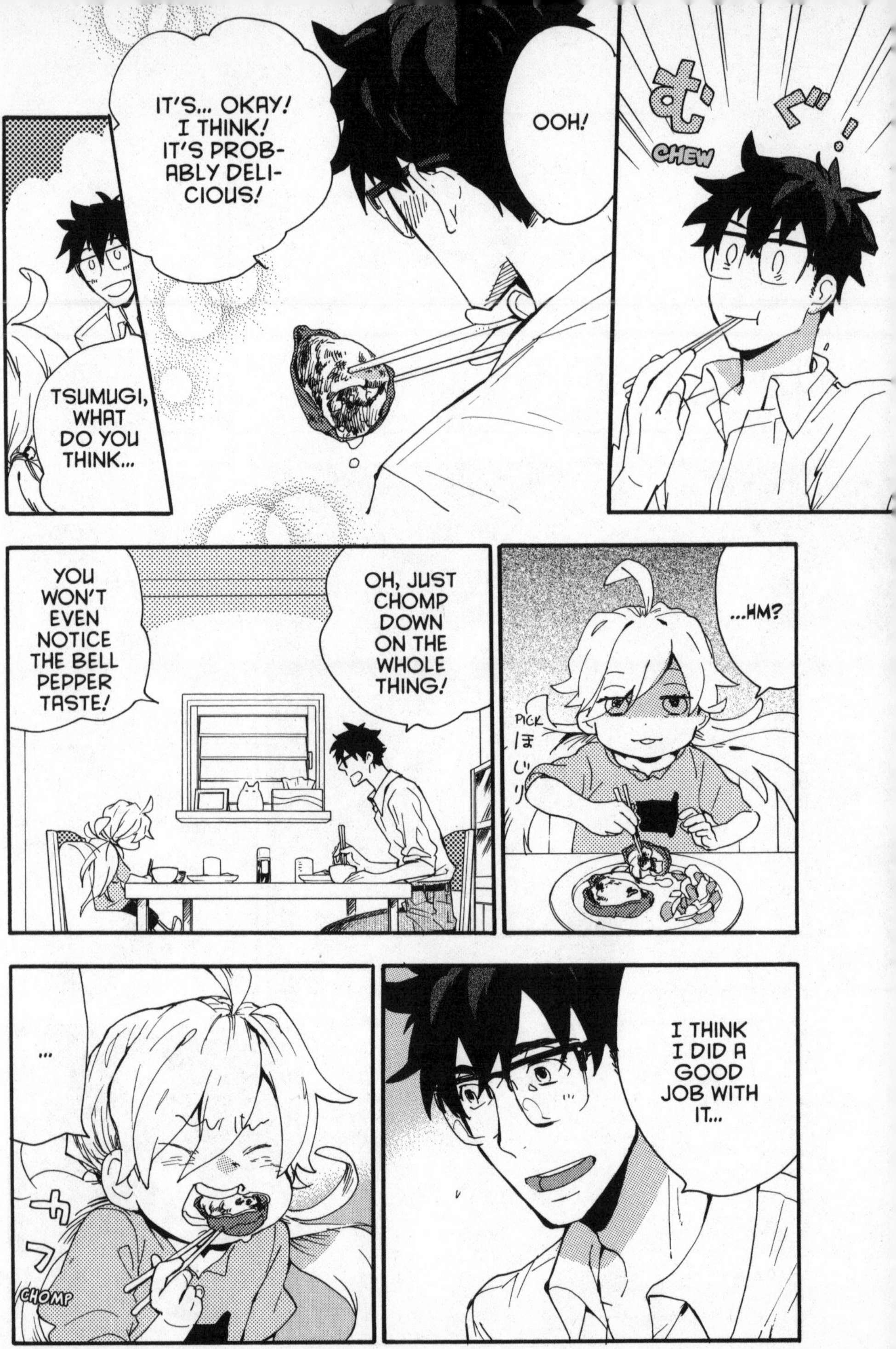

むぐ!
CHEW
OOH!
IT'S... OKAY! I THINK! IT'S PROBABLY DELICIOUS!
TSUMUGI, WHAT DO YOU THINK...
...HM?
PICK
ほじり
OH, JUST CHOMP DOWN ON THE WHOLE THING!
YOU WON'T EVEN NOTICE THE BELL PEPPER TASTE!
I THINK I DID A GOOD JOB WITH IT...
...
カプ
CHOMP

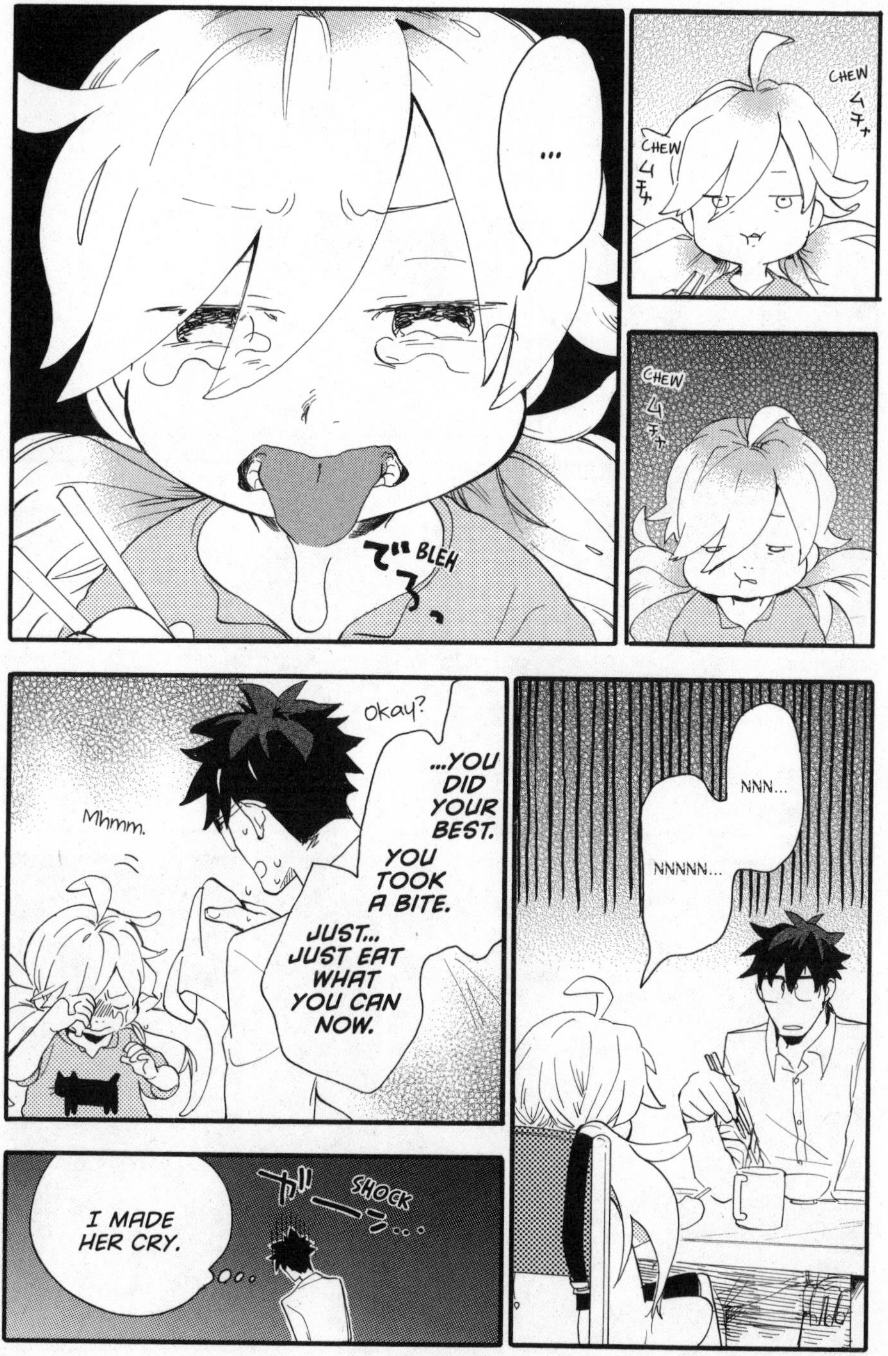
CHEW
ムチャ
CHEW
ムチャ
CHEW
ムチャ
...
でろ
BLEH
NNN...
NNNNN...
Okay?
...YOU DID YOUR BEST. YOU TOOK A BITE. JUST... JUST EAT WHAT YOU CAN NOW.
Mhmm.
I MADE HER CRY.
ガーン
SHOCK

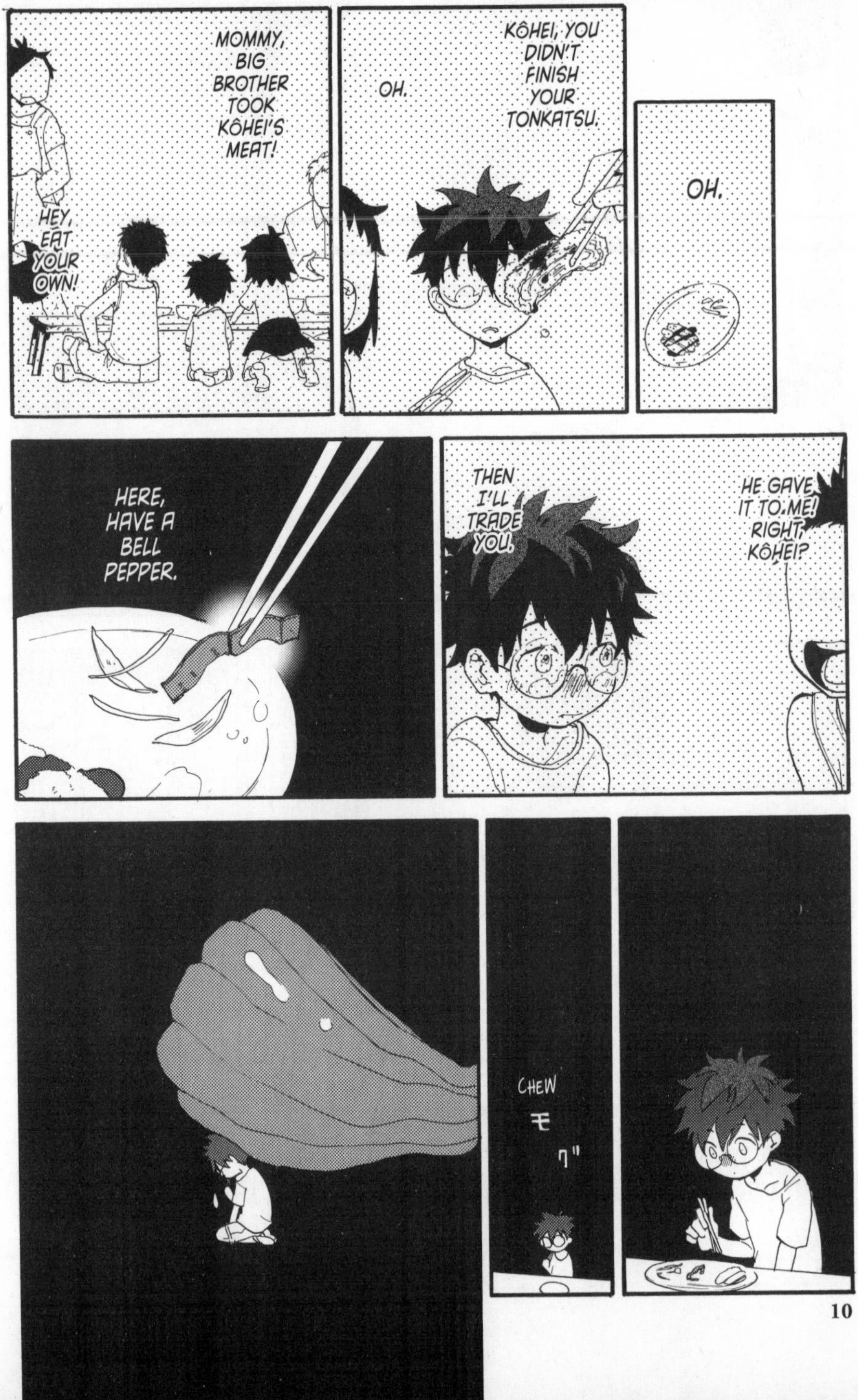
OH.
KÔHEI, YOU DIDN'T FINISH YOUR TONKATSU.
OH.
MOMMY, BIG BROTHER TOOK KÔHEI'S MEAT!
HEY, EAT YOUR OWN!
HE GAVE IT TO ME! RIGHT, KÔHEI?
THEN I'LL TRADE YOU.
HERE, HAVE A BELL PEPPER.
CHEW
モグ

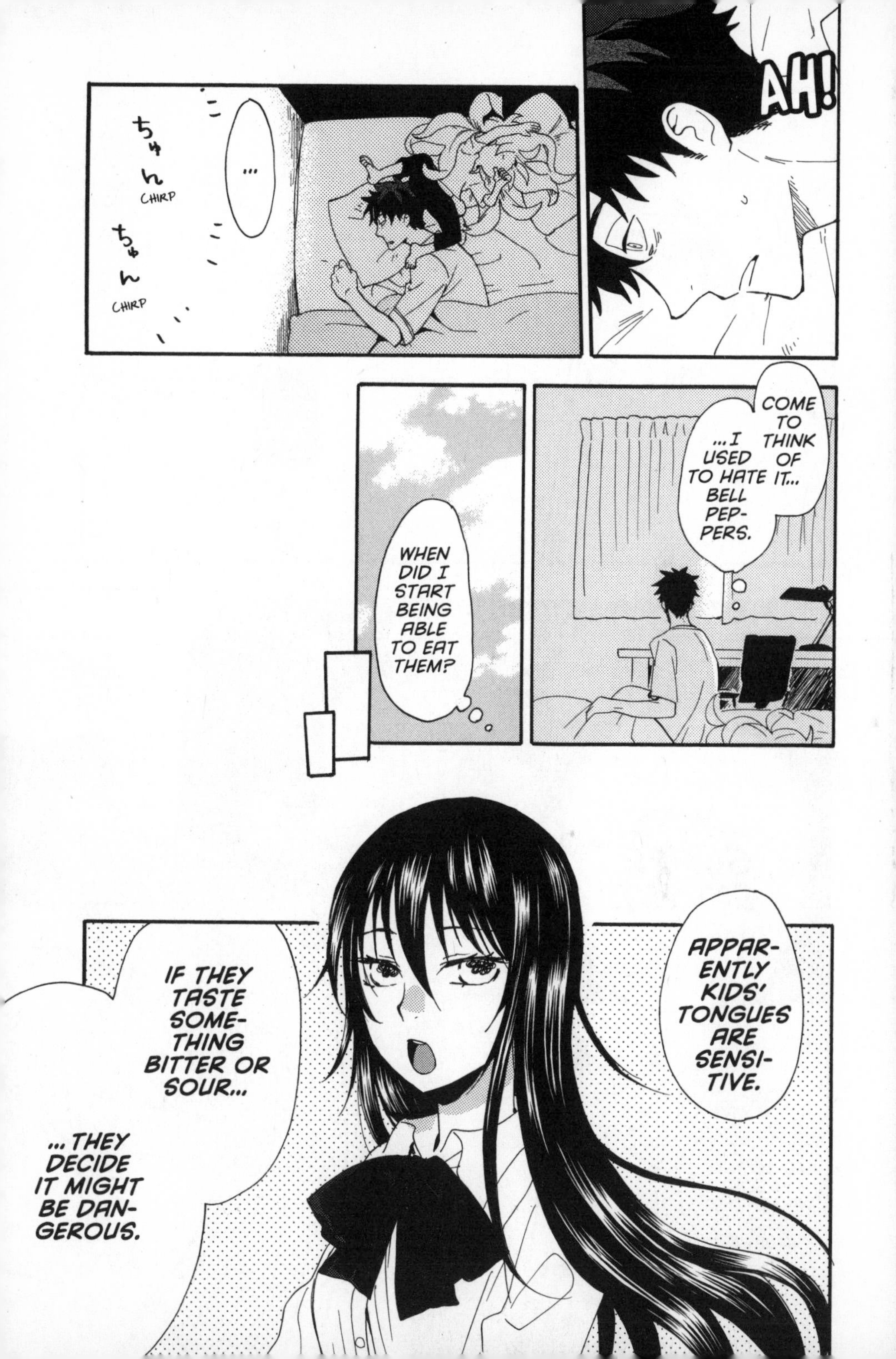
AH!
ちゅん
CHIRP
ちゅん
CHIRP
...
COME TO THINK OF IT...
...I USED TO HATE BELL PEP-PERS.
WHEN DID I START BEING ABLE TO EAT THEM?
APPAR-ENTLY KIDS' TONGUES ARE SENSI-TIVE.
IF THEY TASTE SOME-THING BITTER OR SOUR...
...THEY DECIDE IT MIGHT BE DAN-GEROUS.

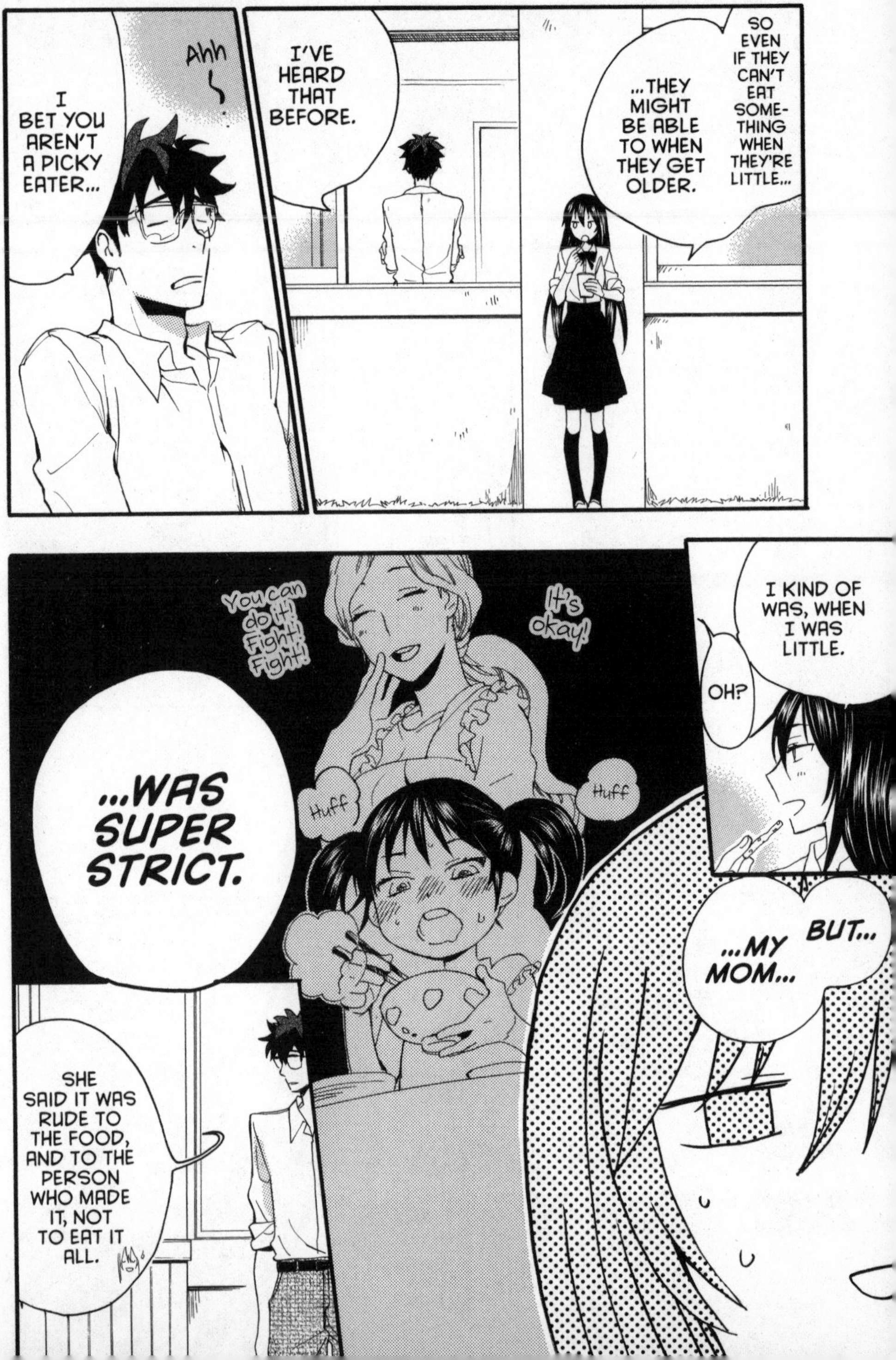
SO EVEN IF THEY CAN'T EAT SOMETHING WHEN THEY'RE LITTLE...
...THEY MIGHT BE ABLE TO WHEN THEY GET OLDER.
I'VE HEARD THAT BEFORE.
Ahh
I BET YOU AREN'T A PICKY EATER...
I KIND OF WAS, WHEN I WAS LITTLE.
OH?
BUT...
...MY MOM...
...WAS SUPER STRICT.
It's okay!
You can do it! Fight! Fight!
Huff
Huff
SHE SAID IT WAS RUDE TO THE FOOD, AND TO THE PERSON WHO MADE IT, NOT TO EAT IT ALL.

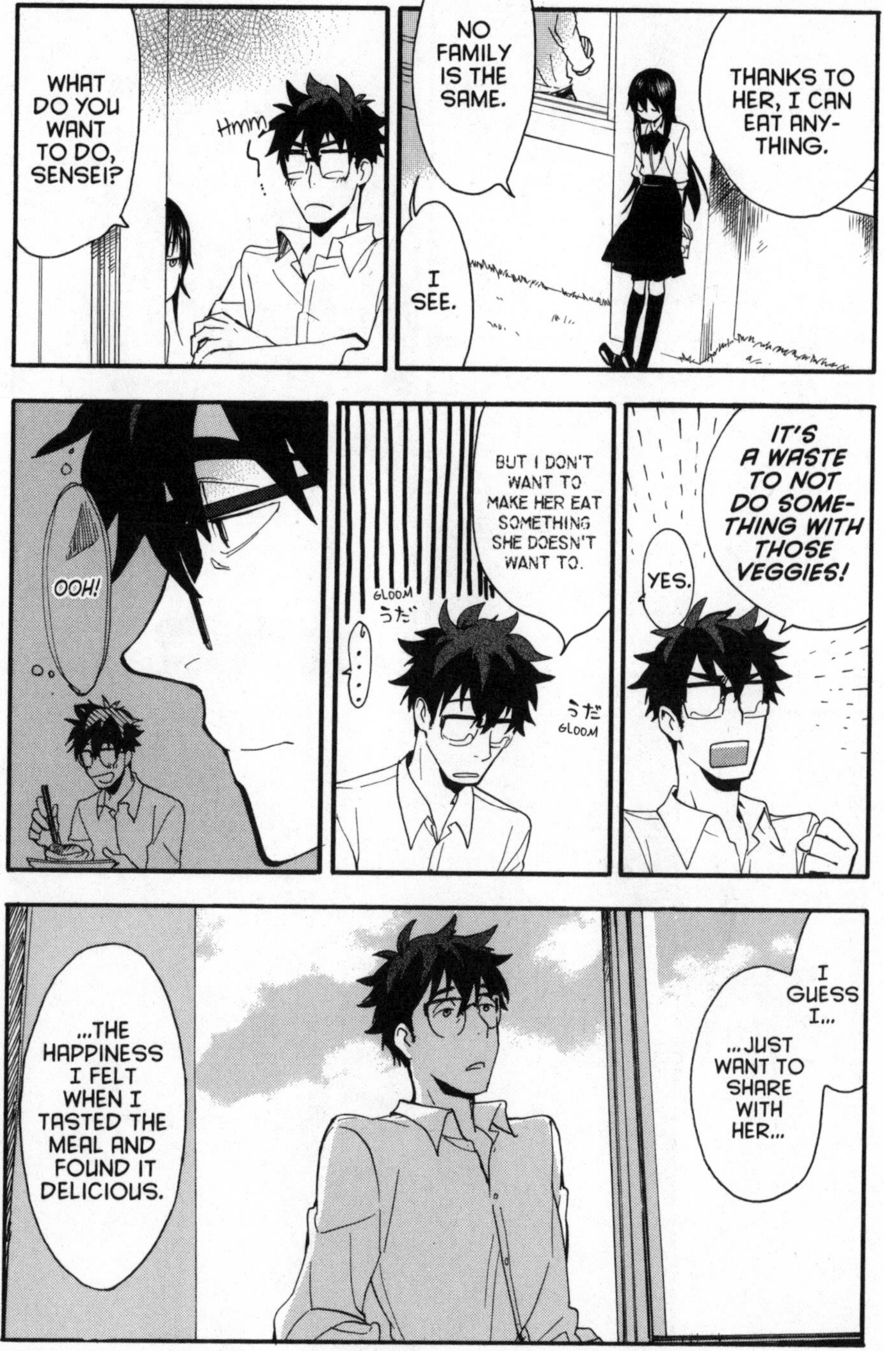
THANKS TO HER, I CAN EAT ANYTHING.
NO FAMILY IS THE SAME.
I SEE.
Hmm
WHAT DO YOU WANT TO DO, SENSEI?
IT'S A WASTE TO NOT DO SOMETHING WITH THOSE VEGGIES!
YES.
BUT I DON'T WANT TO MAKE HER EAT SOMETHING SHE DOESN'T WANT TO.
GLOOM うだ
うだ GLOOM
OOH!
I GUESS I...
...JUST WANT TO SHARE WITH HER...
...THE HAPPINESS I FELT WHEN I TASTED THE MEAL AND FOUND IT DELICIOUS.

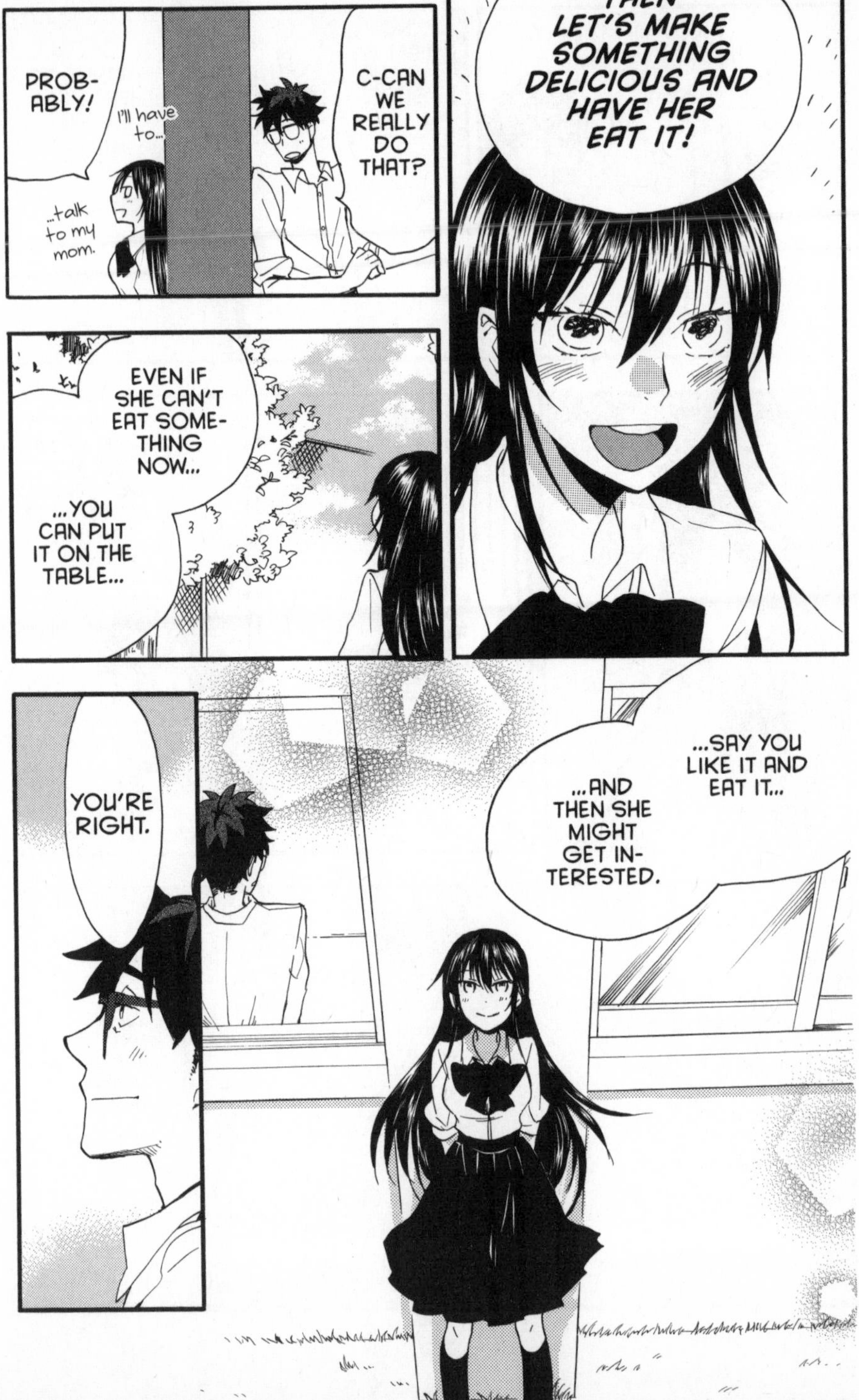

THEN LET'S MAKE SOMETHING DELICIOUS AND HAVE HER EAT IT!
C-CAN WE REALLY DO THAT?
PROB-ABLY!
I'll have to...
...talk to my mom.
EVEN IF SHE CAN'T EAT SOME-THING NOW...
...YOU CAN PUT IT ON THE TABLE...
...SAY YOU LIKE IT AND EAT IT...
...AND THEN SHE MIGHT GET IN-TERESTED.
YOU'RE RIGHT.

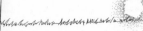

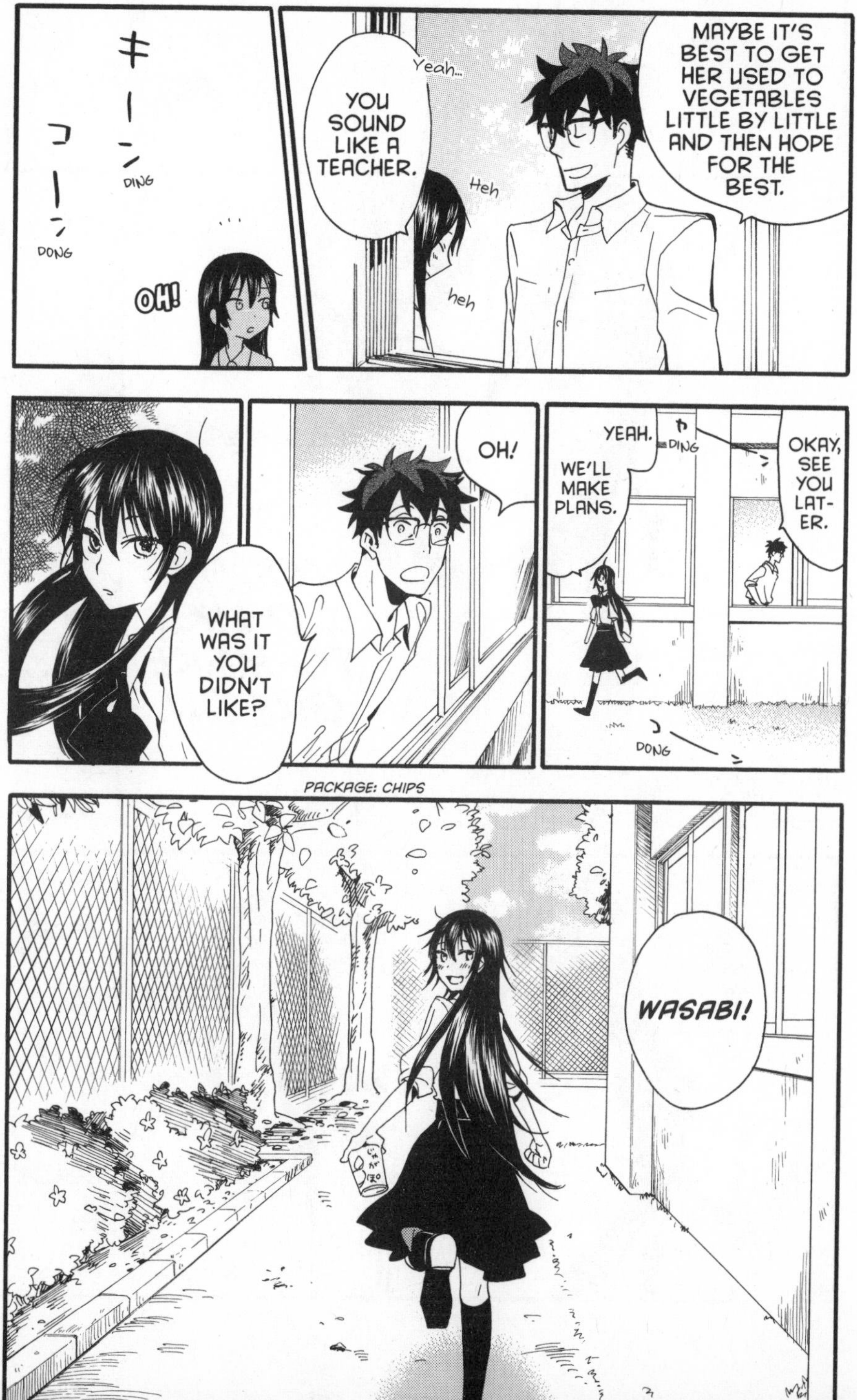
MAYBE IT'S BEST TO GET HER USED TO VEGETABLES LITTLE BY LITTLE AND THEN HOPE FOR THE BEST.
Yeah...
YOU SOUND LIKE A TEACHER.
Heh
heh
キーン
DING
コーン
DONG
...
OH!
OKAY, SEE YOU LATER.
DING
YEAH. WE'LL MAKE PLANS.
DONG
OH!
WHAT WAS IT YOU DIDN'T LIKE?
PACKAGE: CHIPS
WASABI!

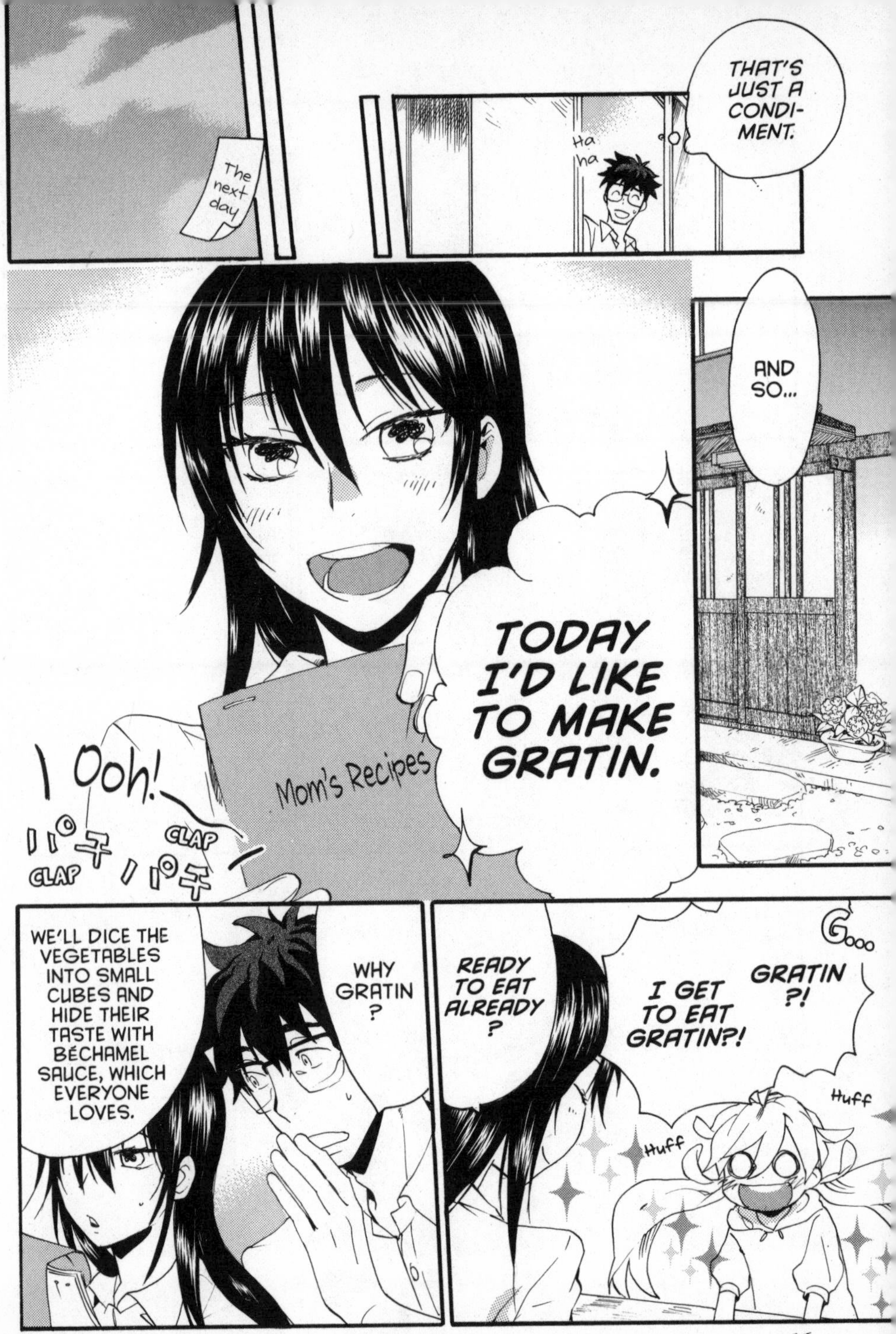

Ha ha
THAT'S JUST A CONDIMENT.
The next day
AND SO...
TODAY I'D LIKE TO MAKE GRATIN.
Mom's Recipes
Ooh!
パチパチ
CLAP CLAP
Gooo
GRATIN?!
I GET TO EAT GRATIN?!
Huff
Huff
READY TO EAT ALREADY?
WHY GRATIN?
WE'LL DICE THE VEGETABLES INTO SMALL CUBES AND HIDE THEIR TASTE WITH BÉCHAMEL SAUCE, WHICH EVERYONE LOVES.

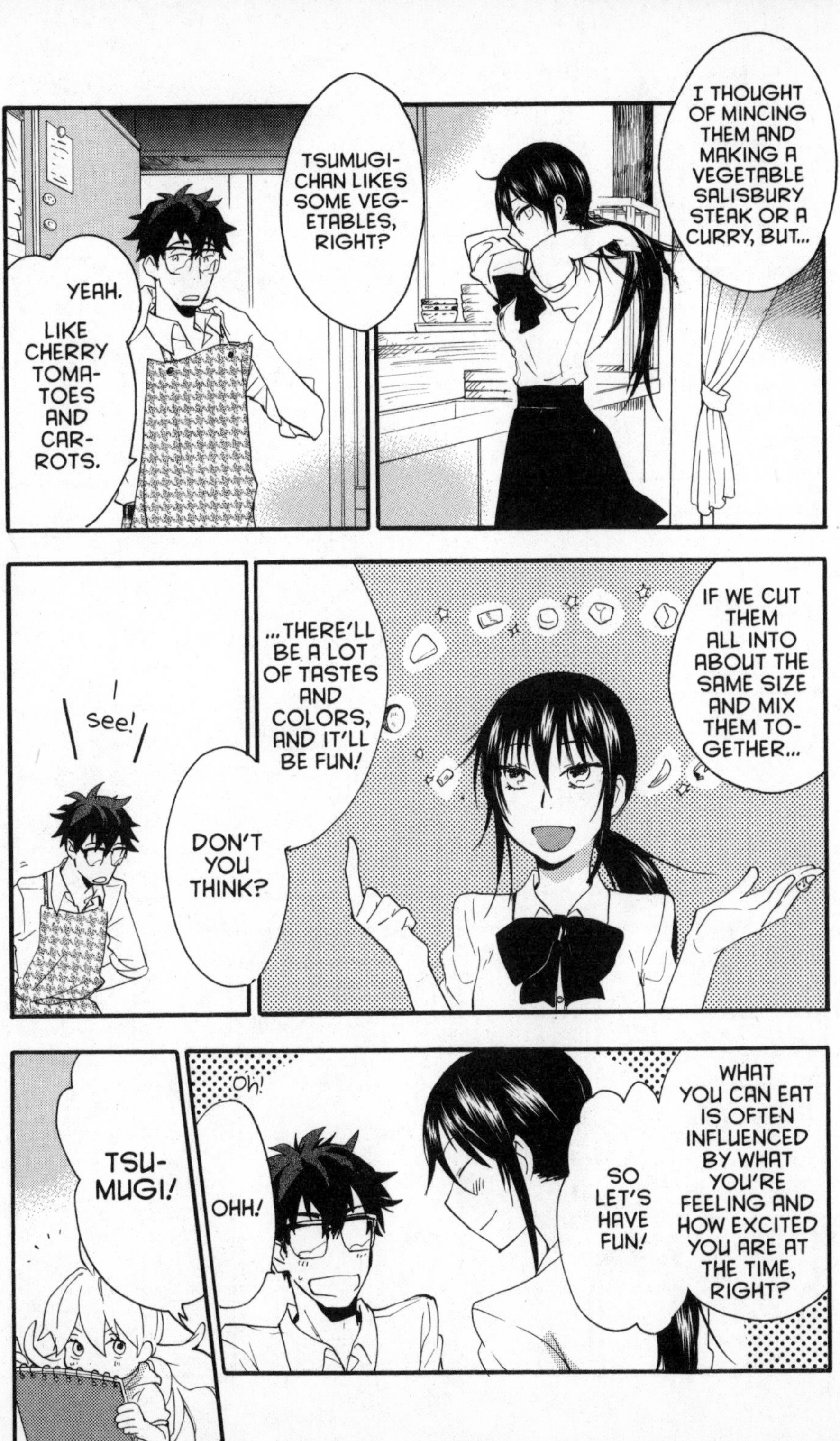
I THOUGHT OF MINCING THEM AND MAKING A VEGETABLE SALISBURY STEAK OR A CURRY, BUT...
TSUMUGI-CHAN LIKES SOME VEGETABLES, RIGHT?
YEAH.
LIKE CHERRY TOMATOES AND CARROTS.
IF WE CUT THEM ALL INTO ABOUT THE SAME SIZE AND MIX THEM TOGETHER...
...THERE'LL BE A LOT OF TASTES AND COLORS, AND IT'LL BE FUN!
DON'T YOU THINK?
I see!
WHAT YOU CAN EAT IS OFTEN INFLUENCED BY WHAT YOU'RE FEELING AND HOW EXCITED YOU ARE AT THE TIME, RIGHT?
SO LET'S HAVE FUN!
Oh!
OHH!
TSUMUGI!

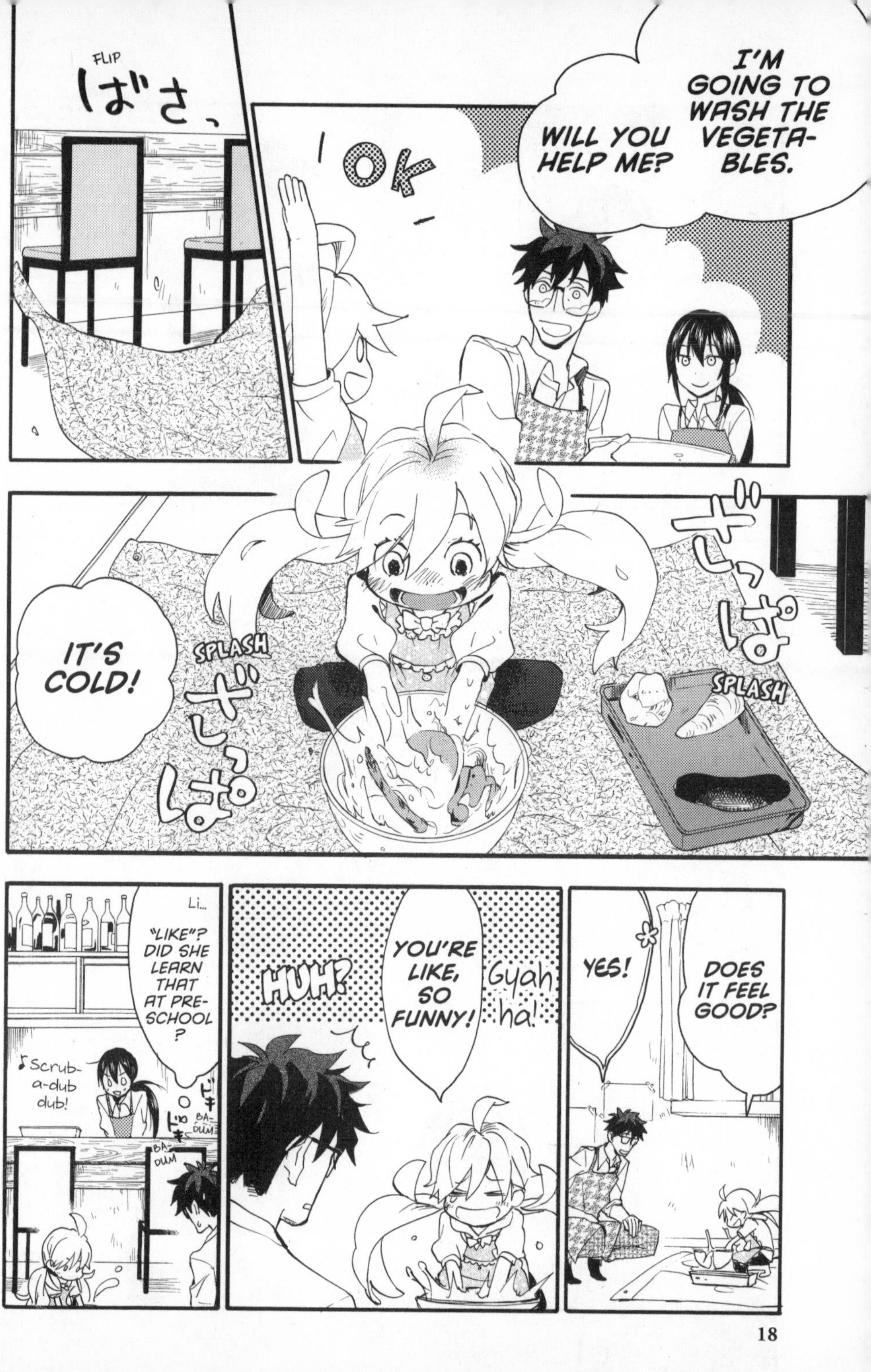
I'M GOING TO WASH THE VEGETA-BLES.
WILL YOU HELP ME?
OK
FLIP
ばさ、
ざっぱ
SPLASH
SPLASH
ざっぱ
IT'S COLD!
DOES IT FEEL GOOD?
YES!
Gyah ha!
YOU'RE LIKE, SO FUNNY!
HUH?
Li...
"LIKE"? DID SHE LEARN THAT AT PRE-SCHOOL?
ドキ BA-DUM
ドキ BA-DUM
♪Scrub-a-dub dub!

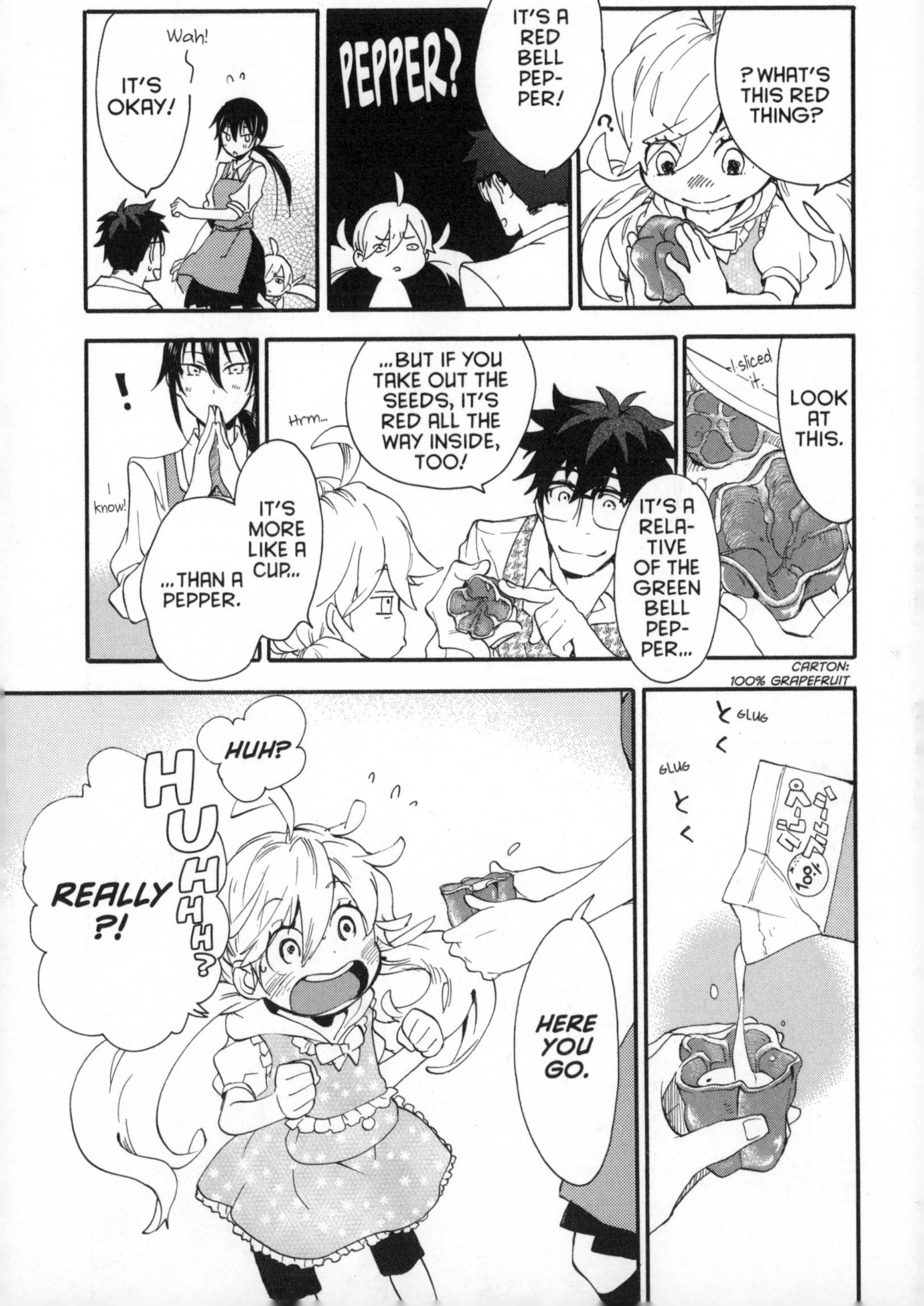
? WHAT'S THIS RED THING?
IT'S A RED BELL PEP-PER!
PEPPER?
Wah!
IT'S OKAY!
I sliced it.
LOOK AT THIS.
IT'S A RELA-TIVE OF THE GREEN BELL PEP-PER...
...BUT IF YOU TAKE OUT THE SEEDS, IT'S RED ALL THE WAY INSIDE, TOO!
Hrm...
IT'S MORE LIKE A CUP...
...THAN A PEPPER.
!
I know!
CARTON: 100% GRAPEFRUIT
GLUG
GLUG
HERE YOU GO.
HUH?
HUHHHH?
REALLY?!

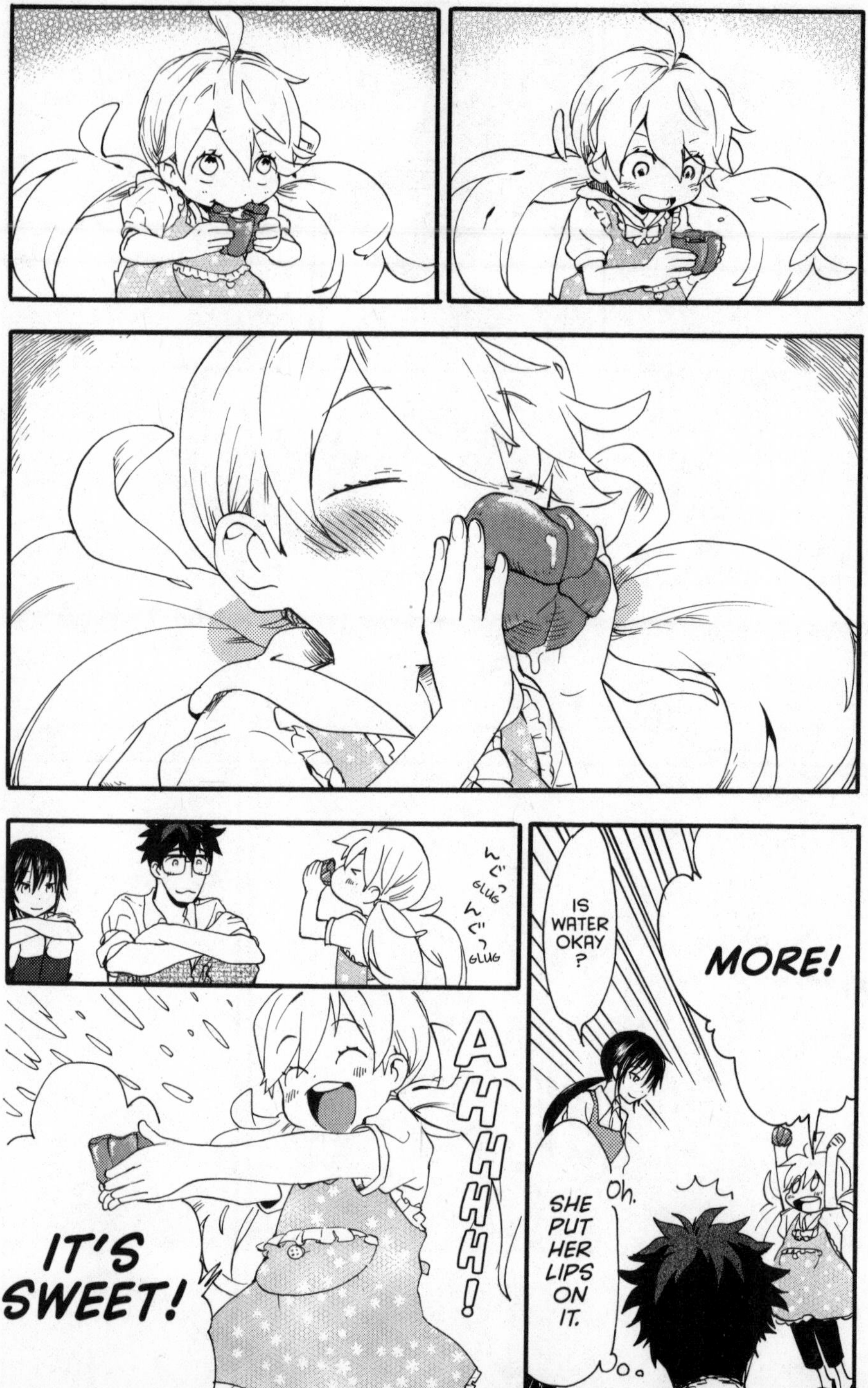
MORE!
IS WATER OKAY?
Oh.
SHE PUT HER LIPS ON IT.
んぐっ
GLUG
んぐっ
GLUG
AHHHHHH!
IT'S SWEET!

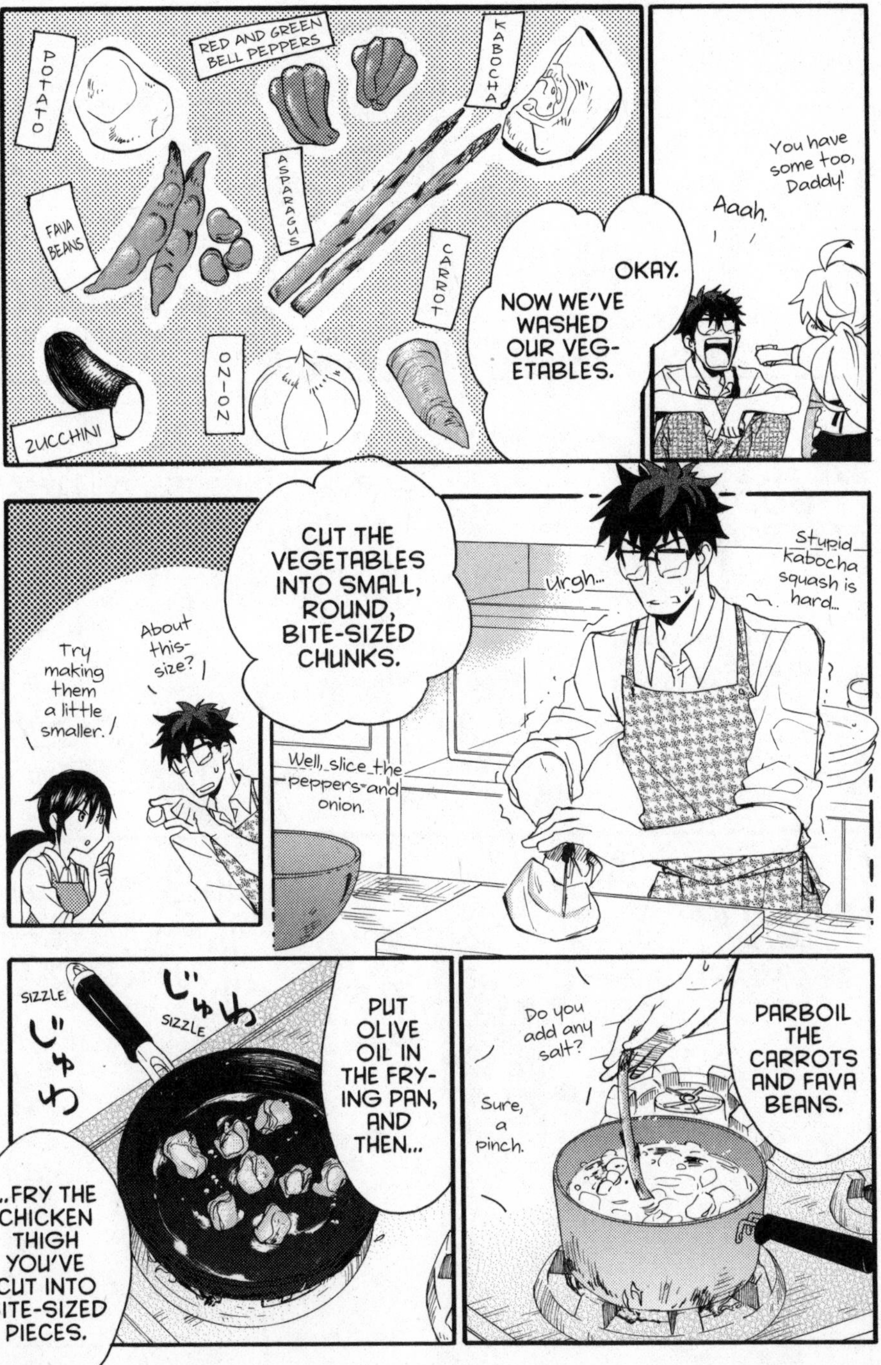
You have some too, Daddy!
Aaah.
OKAY. NOW WE'VE WASHED OUR VEG-ETABLES.
KABOCHA
RED AND GREEN BELL PEPPERS
POTATO
ASPARAGUS
CARROT
FAVA BEANS
ONION
ZUCCHINI
Stupid kabocha squash is hard...
Urgh...
CUT THE VEGETABLES INTO SMALL, ROUND, BITE-SIZED CHUNKS.
Well, slice the peppers and onion.
About this-size?
Try making them a little smaller.
PARBOIL THE CARROTS AND FAVA BEANS.
Do you add any salt?
Sure, a pinch.
PUT OLIVE OIL IN THE FRY-ING PAN, AND THEN...
じゅわ
SIZZLE
じゅわ
SIZZLE
...FRY THE CHICKEN THIGH YOU'VE CUT INTO BITE-SIZED PIECES.

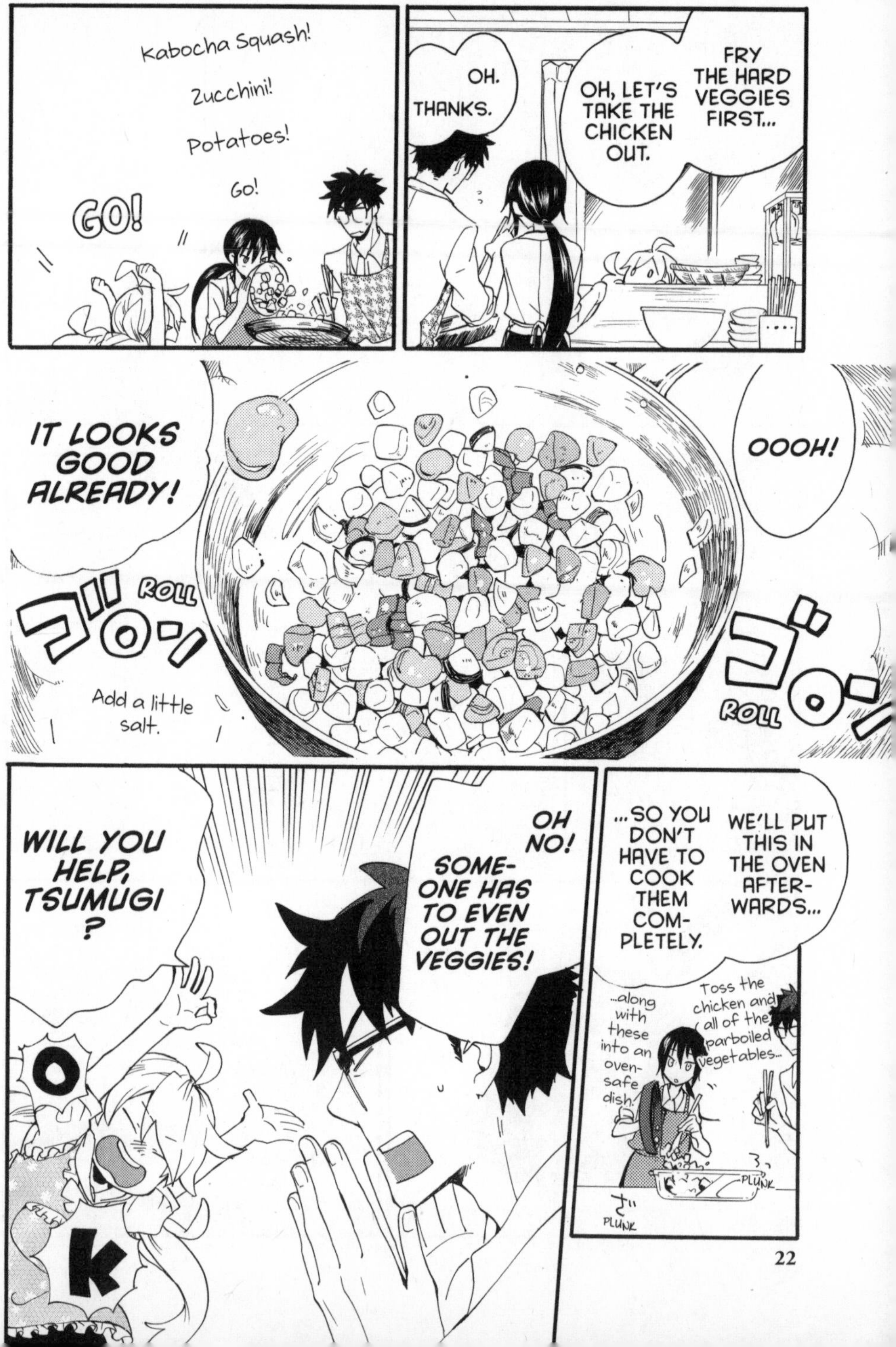
FRY THE HARD VEGGIES FIRST...
OH, LET'S TAKE THE CHICKEN OUT.
OH. THANKS.
Kabocha Squash!
Zucchini!
Potatoes!
Go!
GO!
OOOH!
ROLL
ROLL
IT LOOKS GOOD ALREADY!
Add a little salt.
WE'LL PUT THIS IN THE OVEN AFTER-WARDS...
...SO YOU DON'T HAVE TO COOK THEM COM-PLETELY.
Toss the chicken and all of the parboiled vegetables...
...along with these into an oven-safe dish.
PLUNK
PLUNK
OH NO! SOME-ONE HAS TO EVEN OUT THE VEGGIES!
WILL YOU HELP, TSUMUGI?
O
K

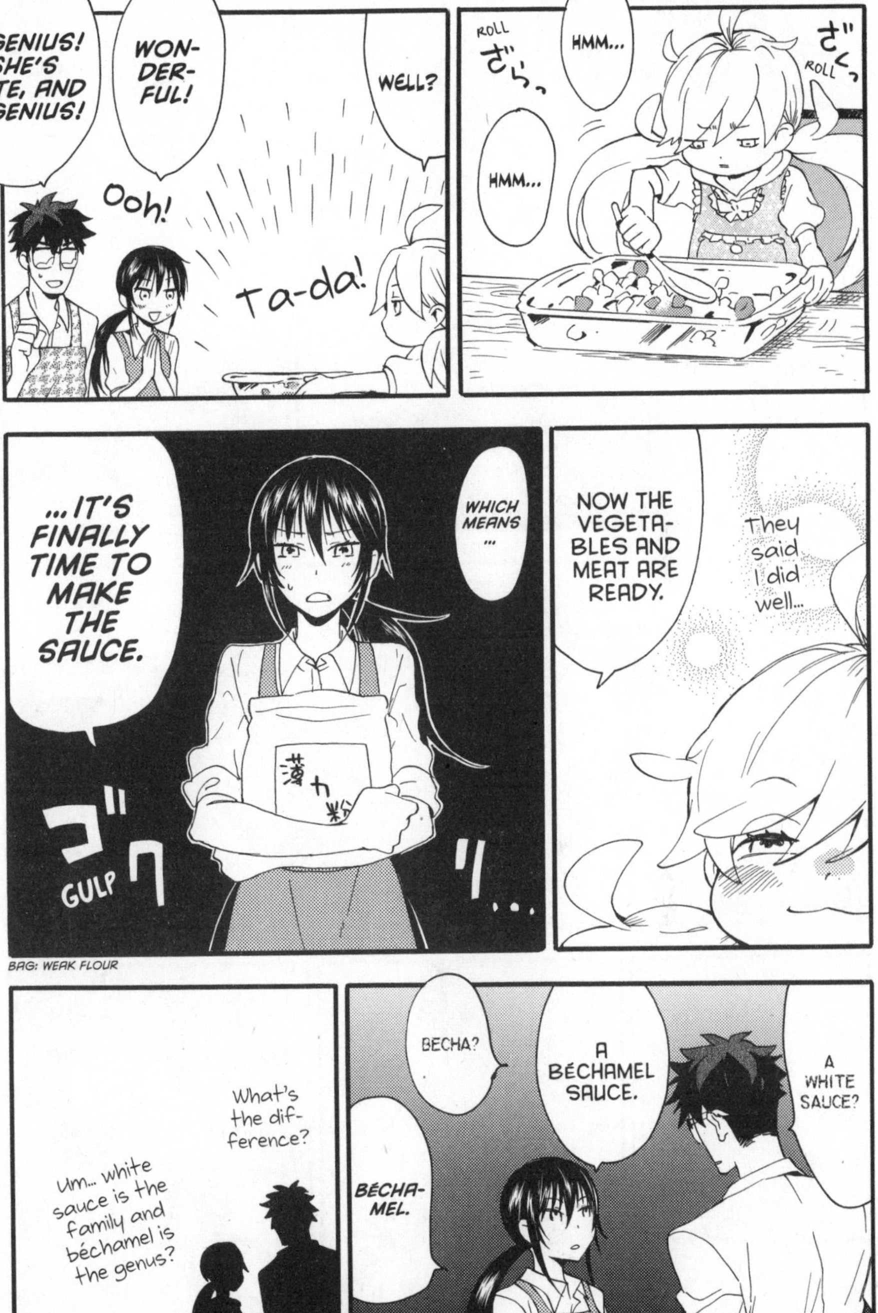
ざくっ ROLL
HMM...
ROLL ざらっ
HMM...
WELL?
WON-DER-FUL!
A GENIUS! SHE'S CUTE, AND A GENIUS!
Ooh!
Ta-da!
They said I did well...
NOW THE VEGETA-BLES AND MEAT ARE READY.
WHICH MEANS ...
...IT'S FINALLY TIME TO MAKE THE SAUCE.
薄力粉
ゴクリ GULP
...
BAG: WEAK FLOUR
A WHITE SAUCE?
A BÉCHAMEL SAUCE.
BECHA?
BÉCHA-MEL.
What's the dif-ference?
Um... white sauce is the family and béchamel is the genus?

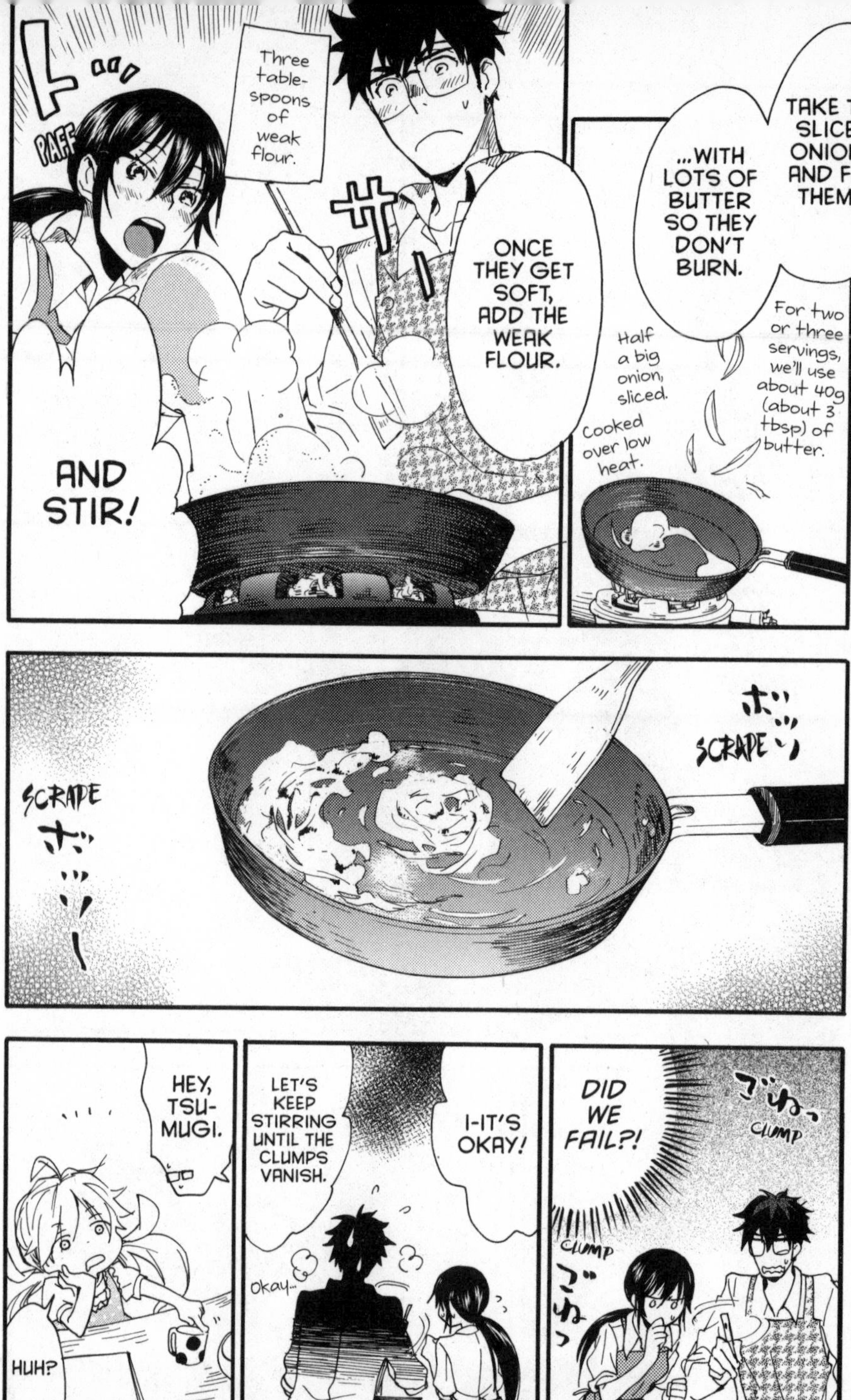
TAKE THE SLICED ONIONS AND FRY THEM...
...WITH LOTS OF BUTTER SO THEY DON'T BURN.
For two or three servings, we'll use about 40g (about 3 tbsp) of butter.
Half a big onion, sliced.
Cooked over low heat.
ONCE THEY GET SOFT, ADD THE WEAK FLOUR.
Three table-spoons of weak flour.
PAFF
AND STIR!
SCRAPE
SCRAPE
DID WE FAIL?!
CLUMP
CLUMP
I-IT'S OKAY!
LET'S KEEP STIRRING UNTIL THE CLUMPS VANISH.
Okay...
HEY, TSU-MUGI.
HUH?

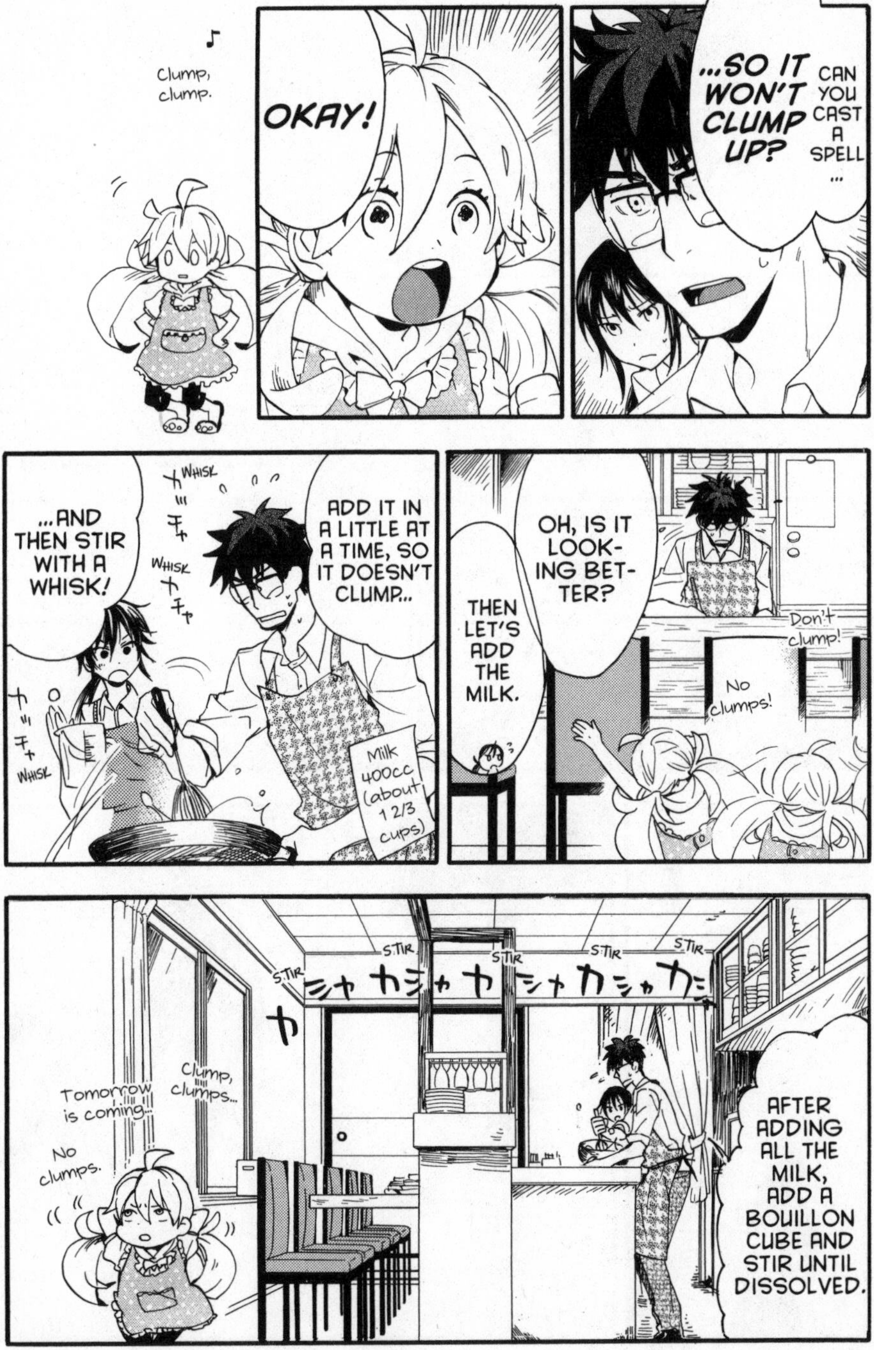
CAN YOU CAST A SPELL ...
...SO IT WON'T CLUMP UP?
OKAY!
♪
Clump, clump.
OH, IS IT LOOKING BETTER?
THEN LET'S ADD THE MILK.
Don't clump!
No clumps!
ADD IT IN A LITTLE AT A TIME, SO IT DOESN'T CLUMP...
WHISK
WHISK
...AND THEN STIR WITH A WHISK!
Milk 400cc (about 1 2/3 cups)
WHISK
STIR
STIR
STIR
STIR
AFTER ADDING ALL THE MILK, ADD A BOUILLON CUBE AND STIR UNTIL DISSOLVED.
Clump, clumps...
Tomorrow is coming...
No clumps.

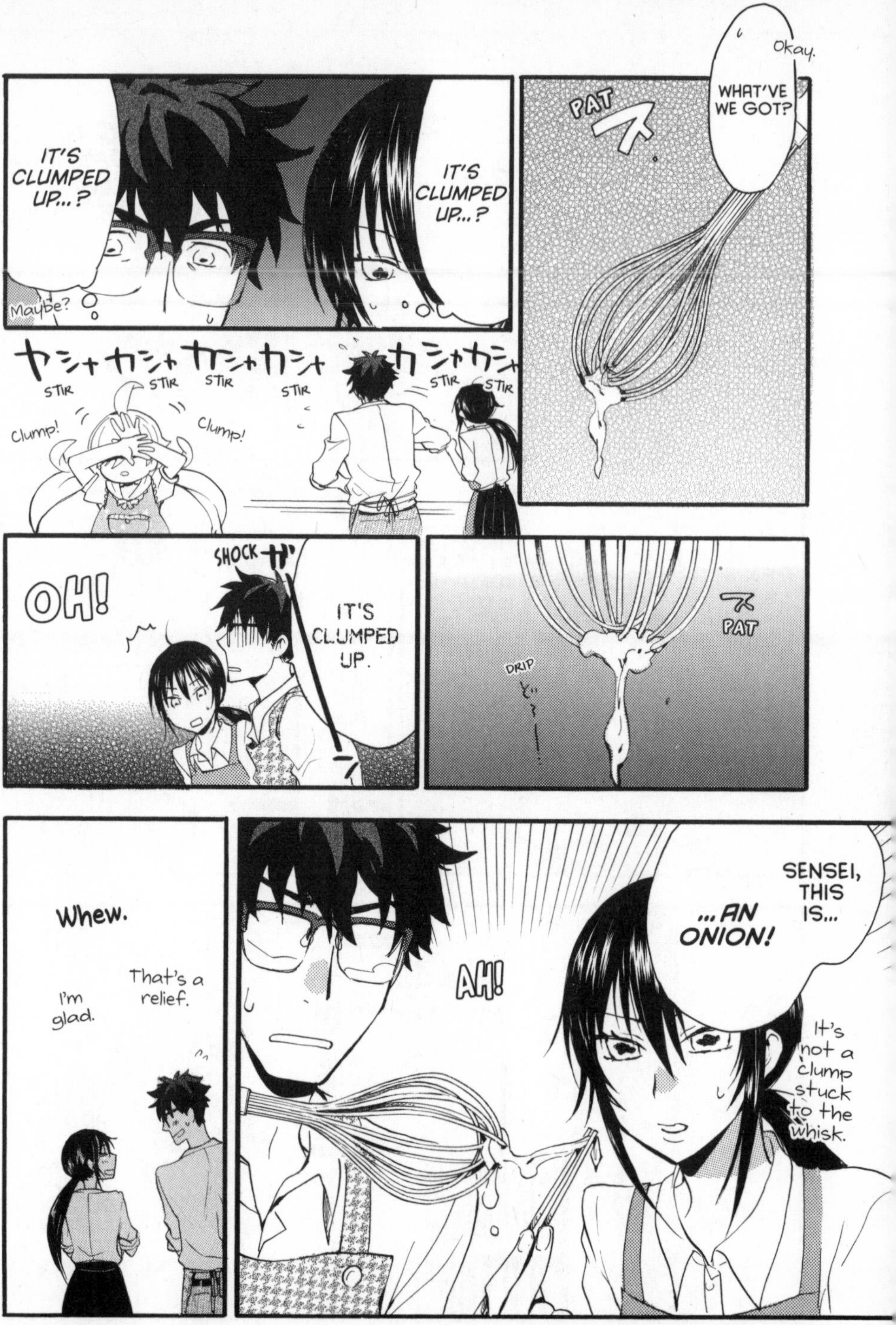
Okay.
WHAT'VE WE GOT?
PAT
IT'S CLUMPED UP...?
IT'S CLUMPED UP...?
Maybe?
カシャカシャ カシャカシャ カシャカシャ
STIR STIR STIR STIR STIR STIR
Clump!
Clump!
PAT
DRIP
SHOCK
IT'S CLUMPED UP.
OH!
SENSEI, THIS IS...
...AN ONION!
AH!
It's not a clump stuck to the whisk.
That's a relief.
Whew.
I'm glad.

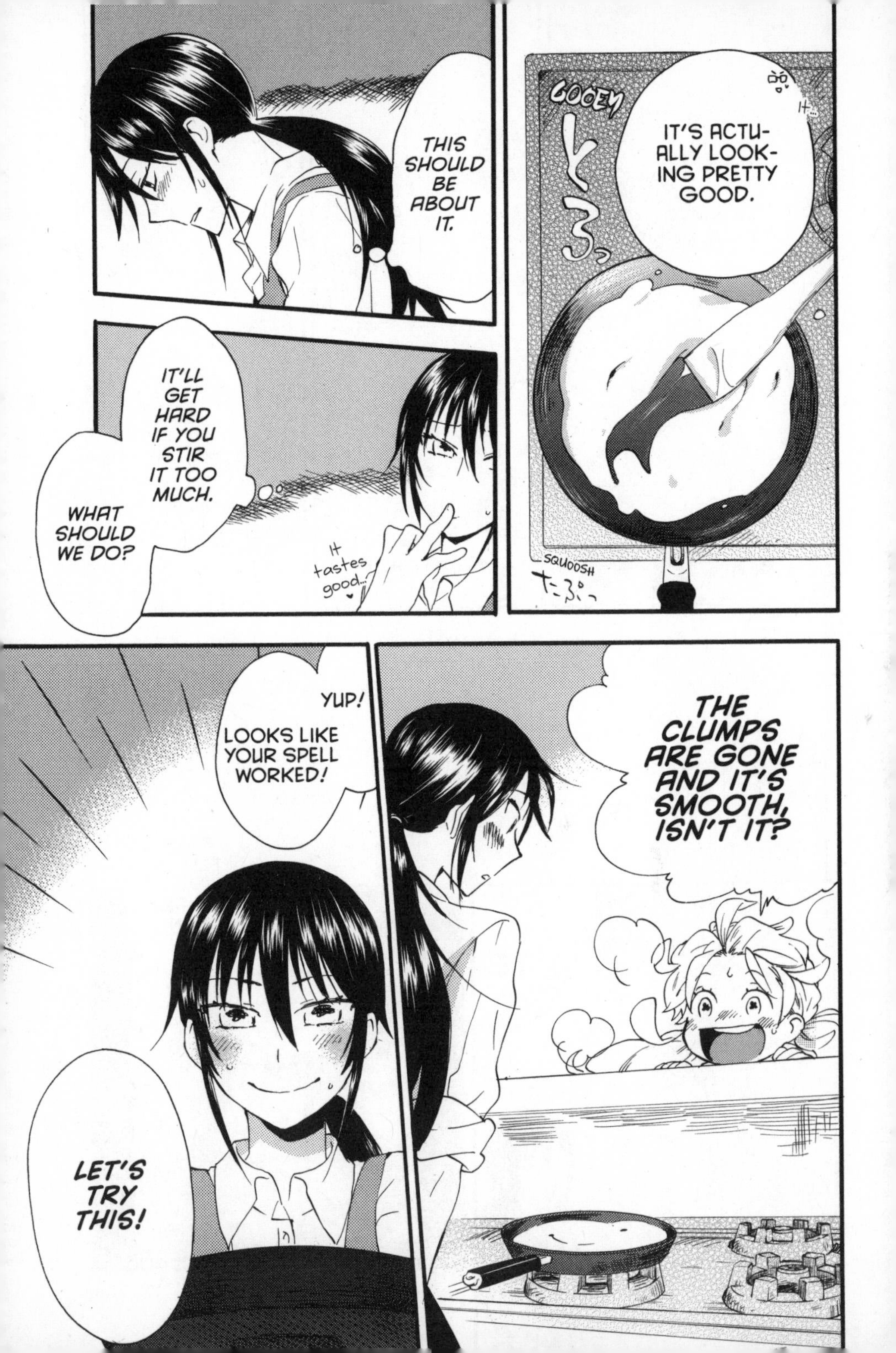
GOOEY
It...
IT'S ACTUALLY LOOKING PRETTY GOOD.
SQUOOSH
THIS SHOULD BE ABOUT IT.
IT'LL GET HARD IF YOU STIR IT TOO MUCH.
WHAT SHOULD WE DO?
It tastes good...
THE CLUMPS ARE GONE AND IT'S SMOOTH, ISN'T IT?
YUP!
LOOKS LIKE YOUR SPELL WORKED!
LET'S TRY THIS!

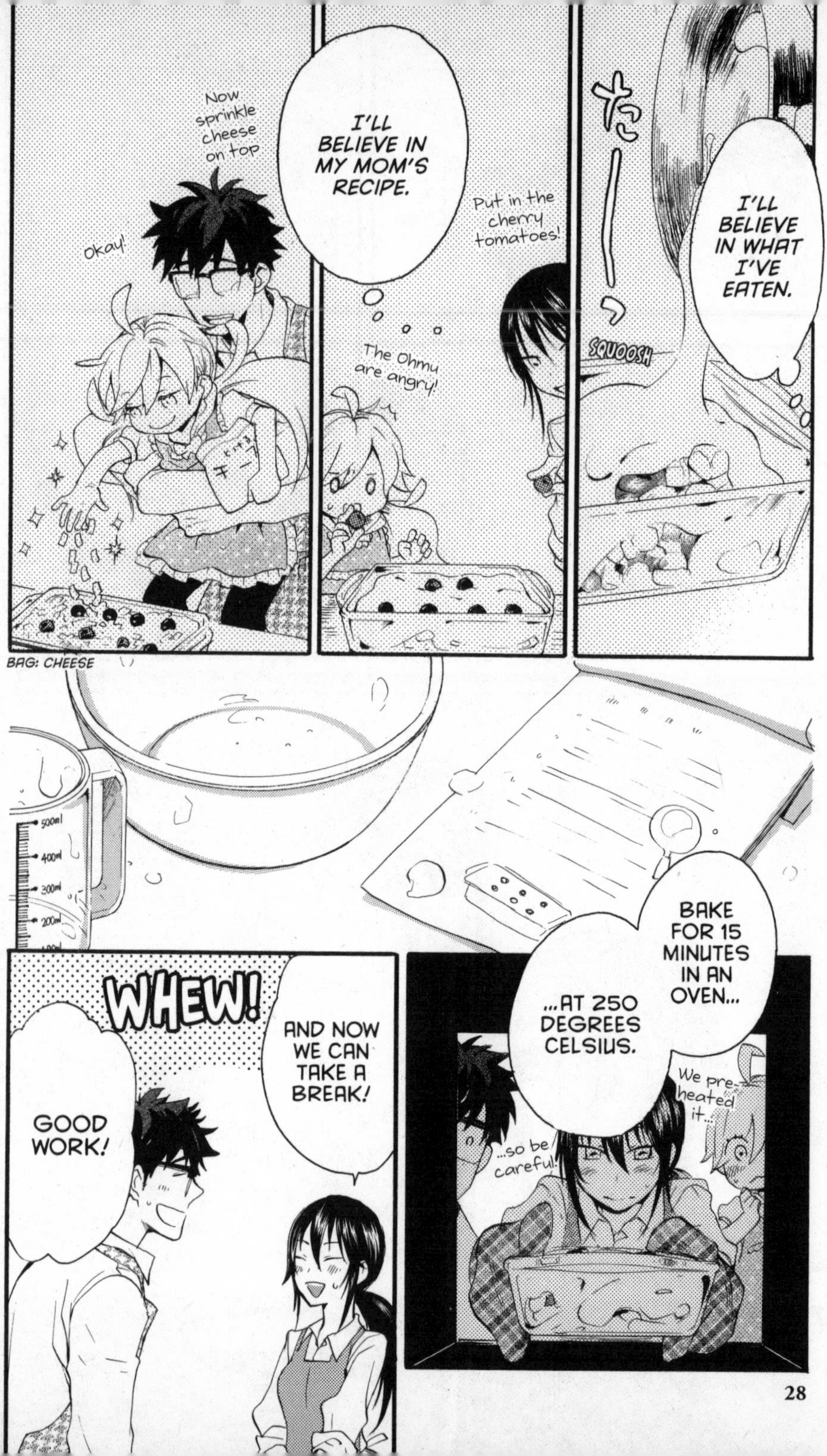
I'LL BELIEVE IN WHAT I'VE EATEN.
SQUOOSH
I'LL BELIEVE IN MY MOM'S RECIPE.
Put in the cherry tomatoes!
The Ohmu are angry!
Now sprinkle cheese on top
Okay!
BAG: CHEESE
BAKE FOR 15 MINUTES IN AN OVEN...
...AT 250 DEGREES CELSIUS.
We pre-heated it...
...so be careful!
WHEW!
AND NOW WE CAN TAKE A BREAK!
GOOD WORK!

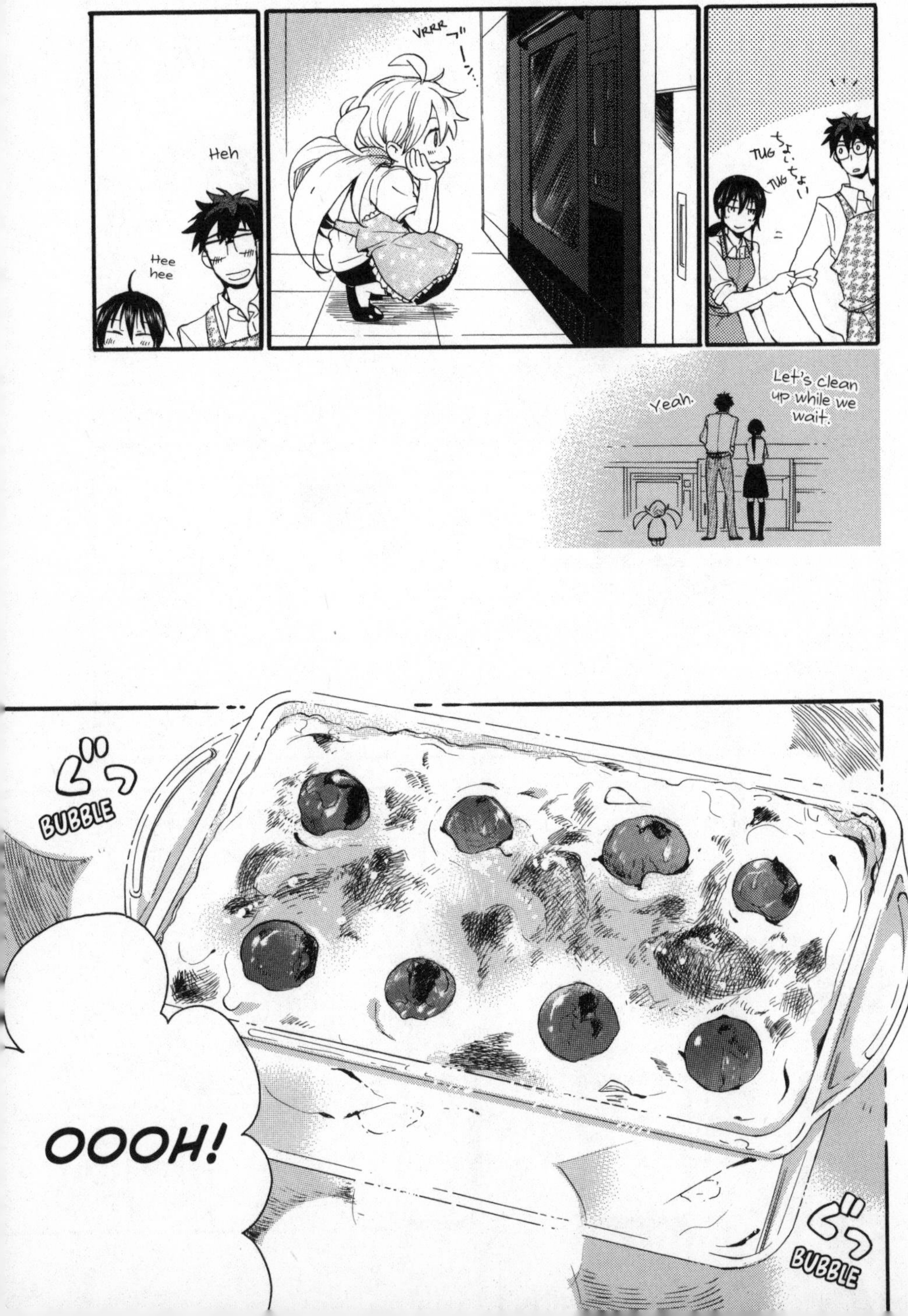

TUG
TUG
ちょい ちょい
VRRR
Heh
Hee hee
Let's clean up while we wait.
Yeah.
ぐつ
BUBBLE
OOOH!
ぐつ
BUBBLE

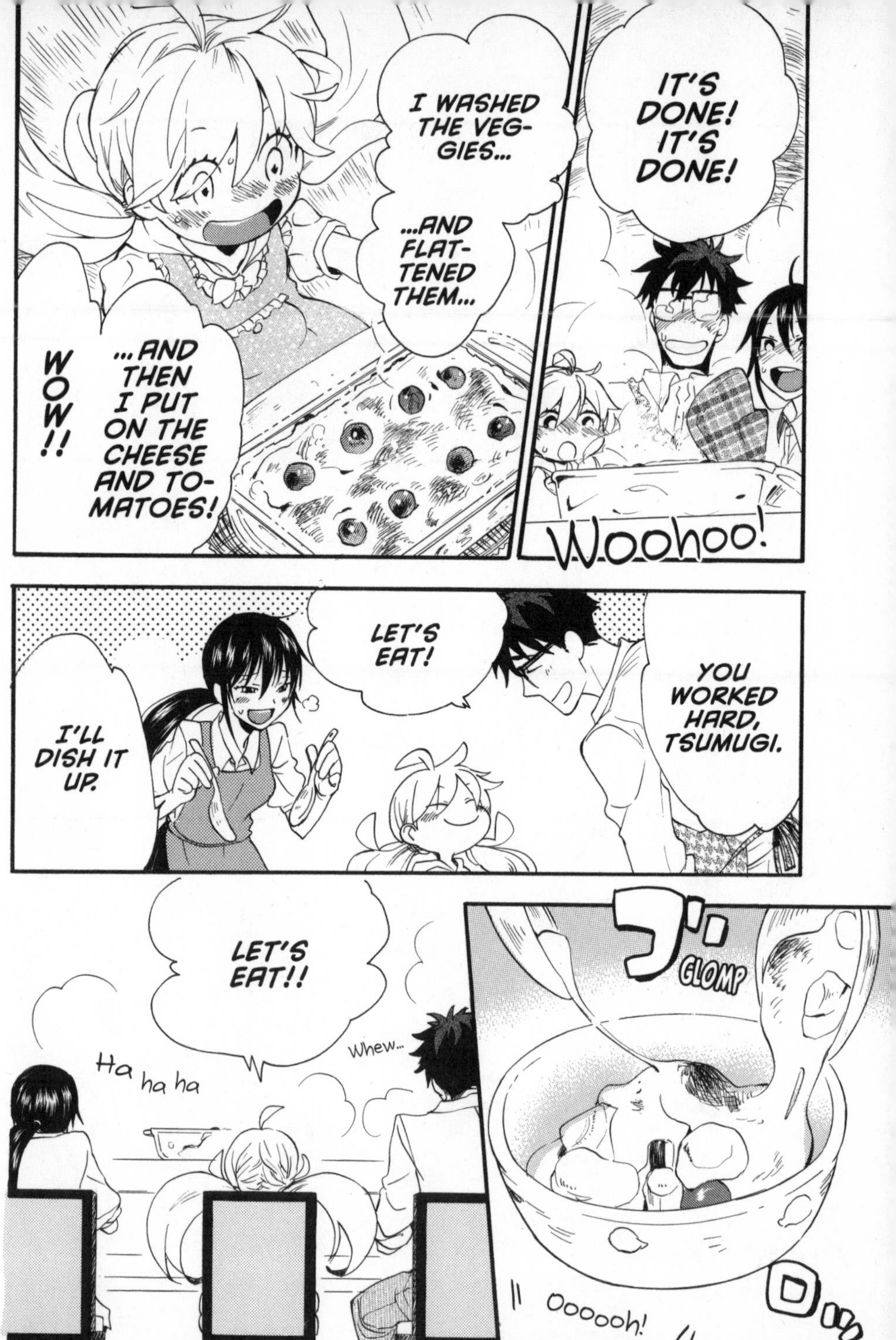
IT'S DONE! IT'S DONE!
Woohoo!
I WASHED THE VEG-GIES...
...AND FLAT-TENED THEM...
...AND THEN I PUT ON THE CHEESE AND TO-MATOES!
WOW!!
YOU WORKED HARD, TSUMUGI.
LET'S EAT!
I'LL DISH IT UP.
GLOMP
Oooooh!
LET'S EAT!!
Whew...
Ha ha ha

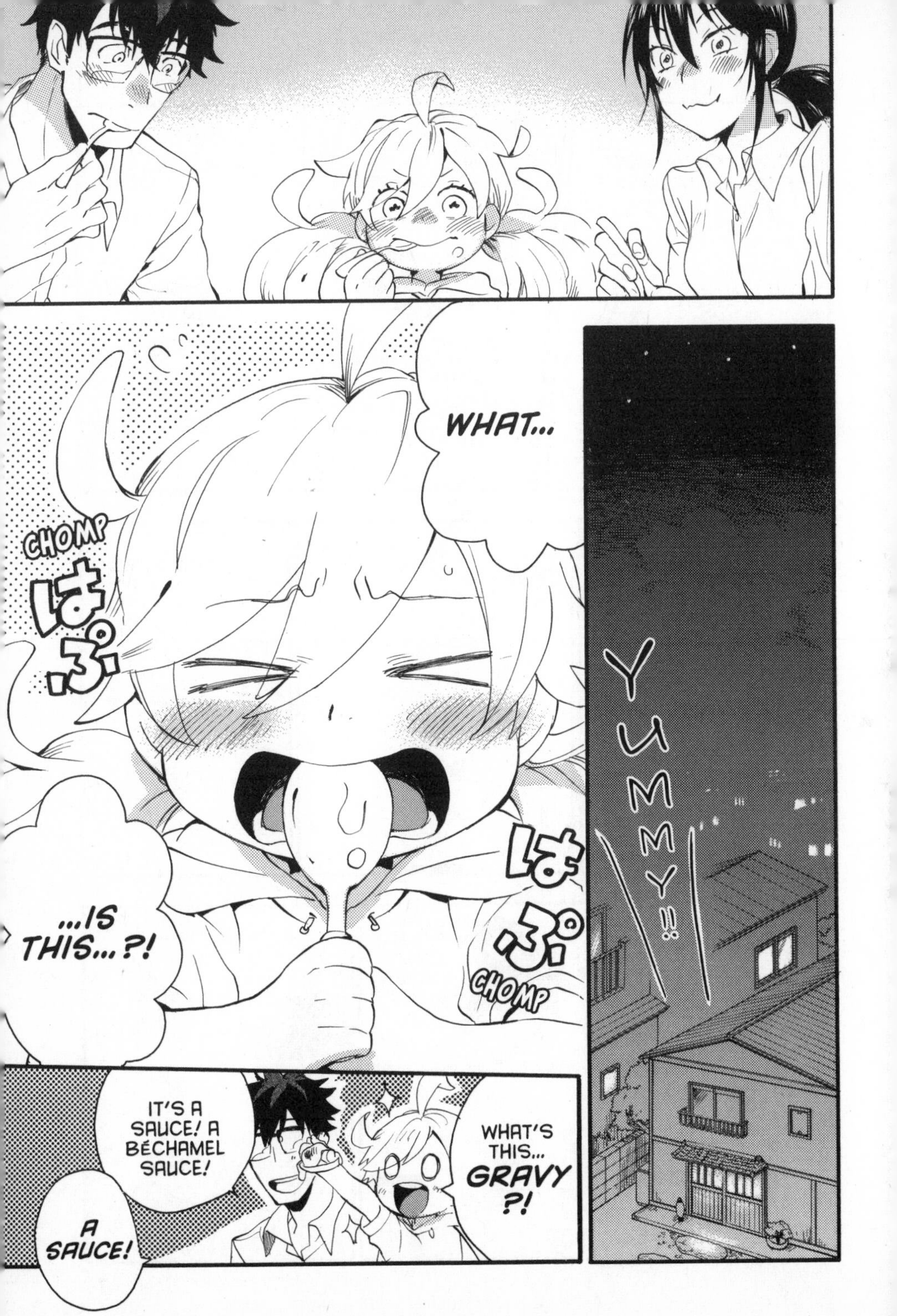
YUMMY!!
WHAT...
CHOMP
はぷ
はぷ
CHOMP
...IS THIS...?!
WHAT'S THIS... GRAVY?!
IT'S A SAUCE! A BÉCHAMEL SAUCE!
A SAUCE!

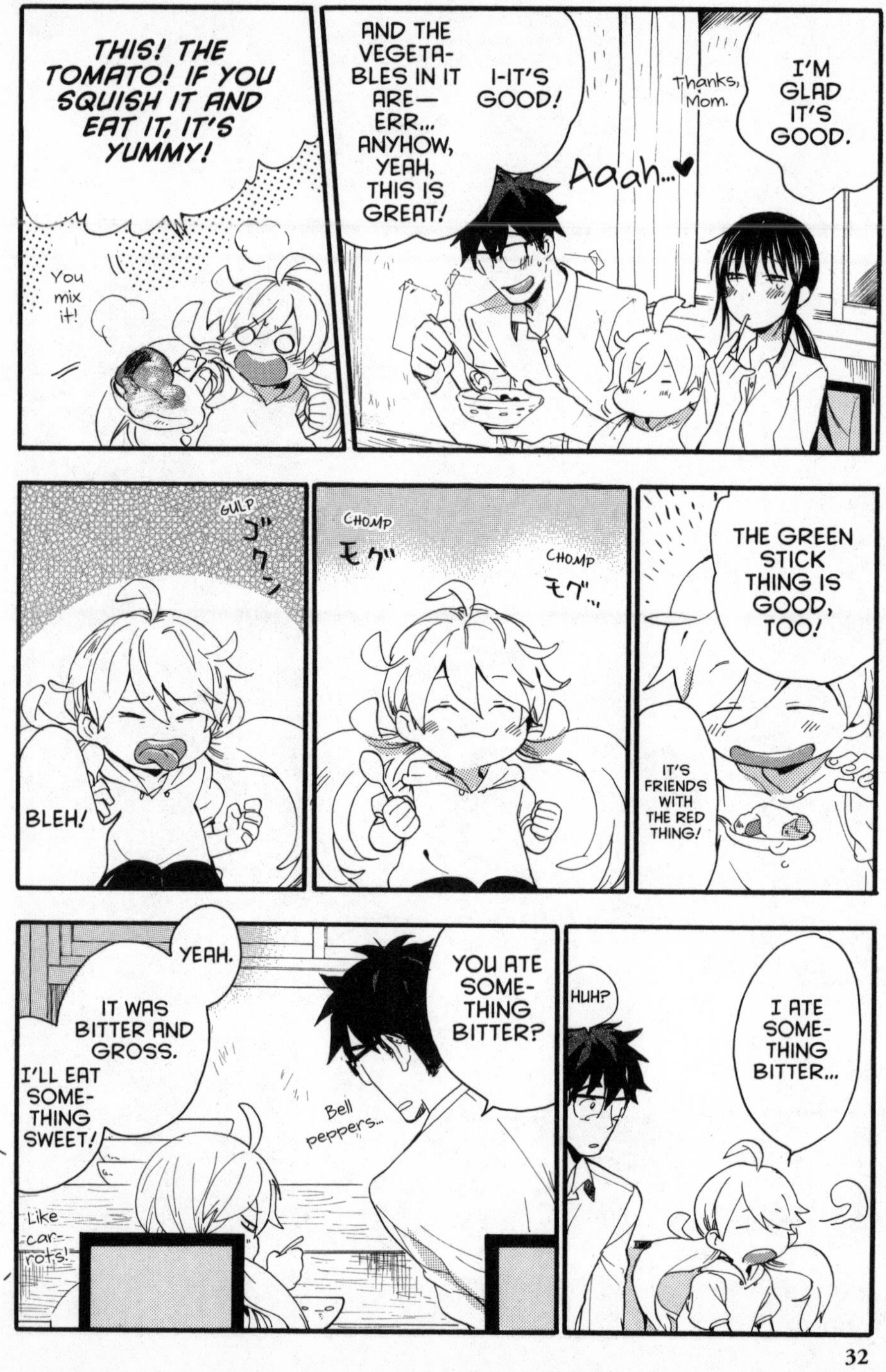
I'M GLAD IT'S GOOD.
Thanks, Mom.
I-IT'S GOOD!
AND THE VEGETA-BLES IN IT ARE— ERR... ANYHOW, YEAH, THIS IS GREAT!
Aaah...♥
THIS! THE TOMATO! IF YOU SQUISH IT AND EAT IT, IT'S YUMMY!
You mix it!
THE GREEN STICK THING IS GOOD, TOO!
IT'S FRIENDS WITH THE RED THING!
CHOMP
モグ
CHOMP
モグ...
GULP
ゴクン
BLEH!
I ATE SOME-THING BITTER...
HUH?
YOU ATE SOME-THING BITTER?
YEAH.
IT WAS BITTER AND GROSS.
I'LL EAT SOME-THING SWEET!
Bell peppers...
Like car-rots!

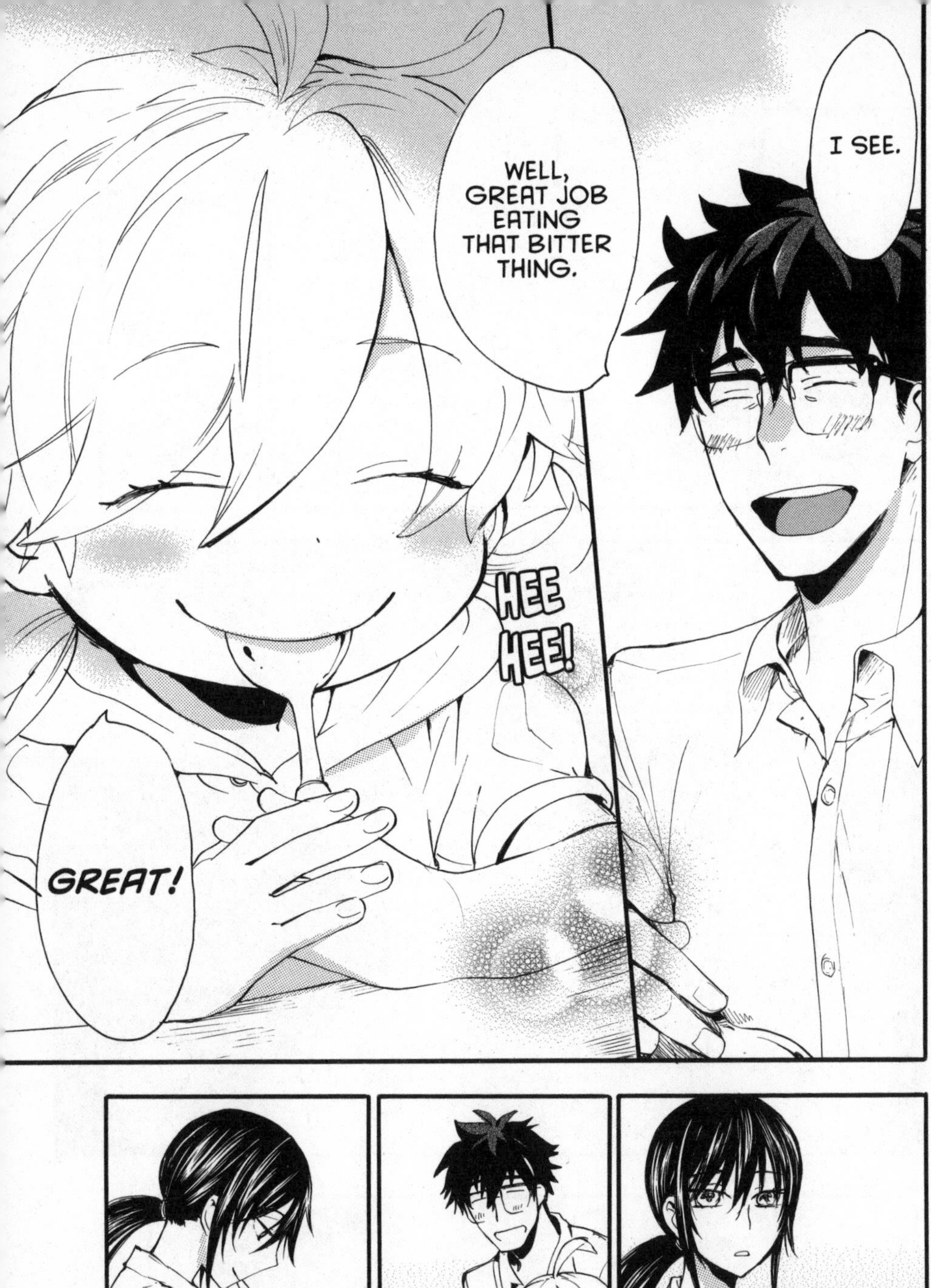
I SEE.
WELL, GREAT JOB EATING THAT BITTER THING.
HEE HEE!
GREAT!

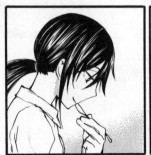

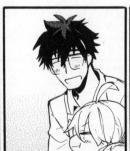

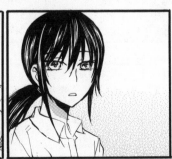

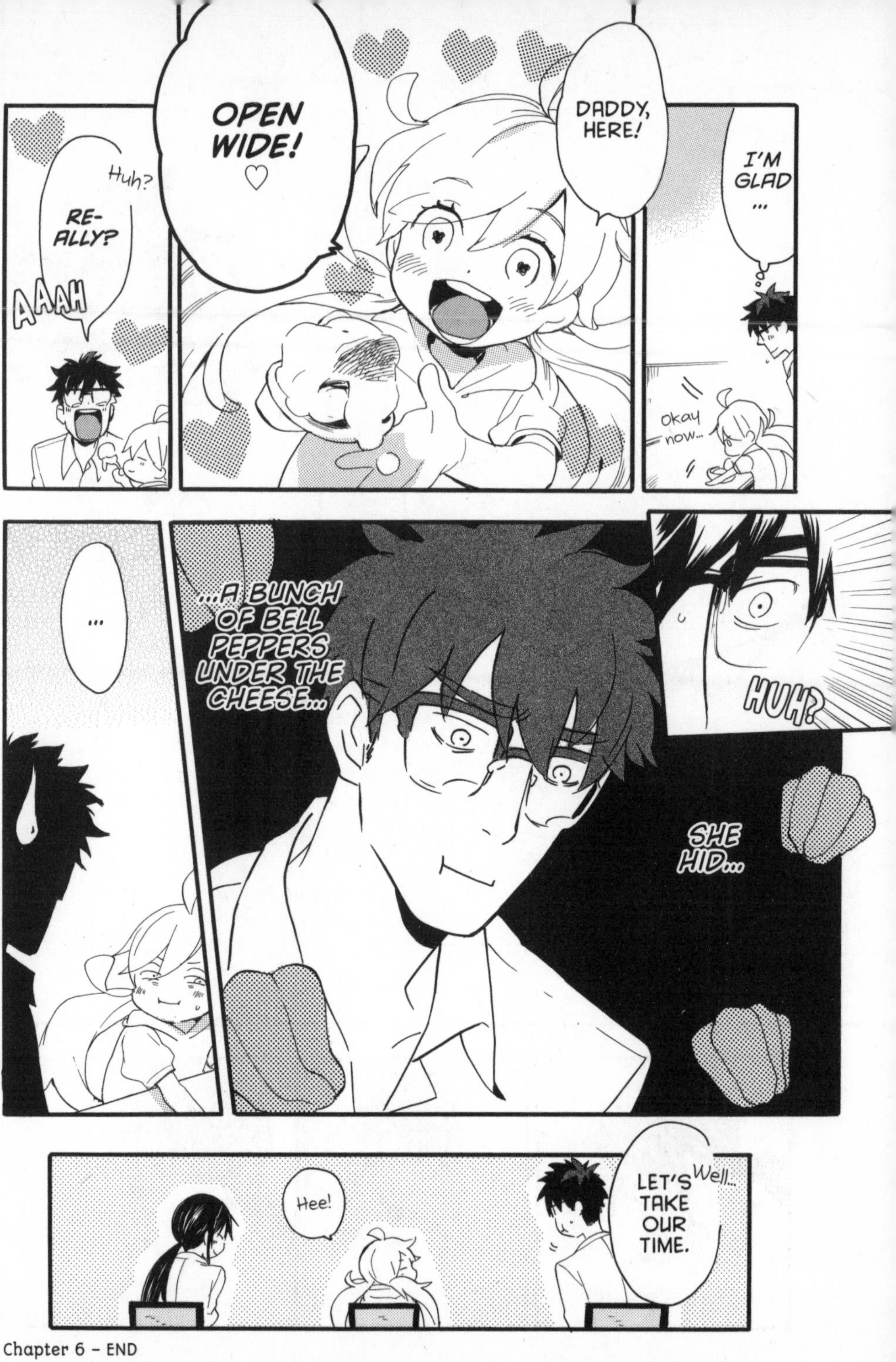
I'M GLAD ...
Okay now...
DADDY, HERE!
OPEN WIDE! ♡
Huh?
RE-ALLY?
AAAH
HUH?
SHE HID...
...A BUNCH OF BELL PEPPERS UNDER THE CHEESE...
...
Well...
LET'S TAKE OUR TIME.
Hee!

Chapter 6 - END

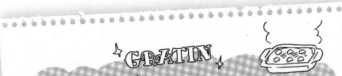

GRATIN

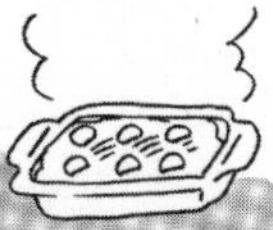

Ingredients Serves 4

(A) 1 potato, 1/16 kabocha squash, 1 zucchini
150 g chicken thighs, 4-5 stalks of asparagus, 1/2 carrot

(B) 2 bell peppers (1 red, 1 green) 1 onion
some cherry tomatoes 50 g grated cheese

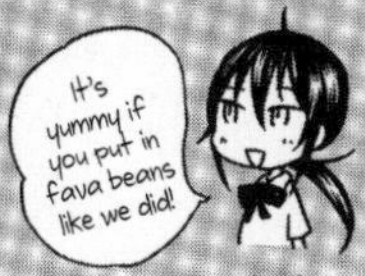
It's yummy if you put in fava beans like we did!

Béchamel Sauce

40 g butter, 40 g weak flour

(C) 600 cc milk, 1 boullion cube (dissolve in a small amount of hot water)

(D) about 1 Tbsp salt, dash of pepper

Steps

1. Chop the ingredients in **A** into 1-2 cm chunks. Parboil **carrots**. Julienne the **B** ingredients.

2. Put the **butter** into a frying pan and add the following ingredients in this order: **potatoes, onions, zucchini, chicken thigh, squash, asparagus, bell peppers**. Use low heat so the mixture doesn't burn.

POINT You're going to cook the gratin in the oven, so it's okay if the mixture isn't fully cooked.

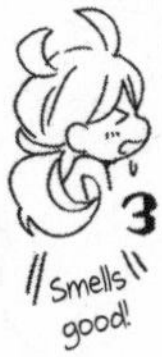
Smells good!

3. Add the **weak flour** to **2** and continue to cook. Once the flour is mixed in, add **C**. Mix and stir until smooth, then reduce the sauce for a few minutes. Add **D** to taste, and the carrots from **1**, before placing in an oven-safe baking dish.

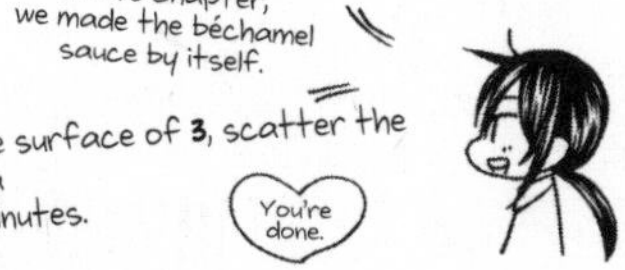
In this chapter, we made the béchamel sauce by itself.
You're done.

4. Sink the **cherry tomatoes** into the surface of **3**, scatter the **grated cheese**, and then place in a preheated oven at 200°C for 15 minutes.

CONVERSION NOTES:
150 G CHICKEN = ABOUT 1/3 LB, 50 G CHEESE = 1 3/4 OZ, 40 G BUTTER = 2 2/3 TBSP, 40 G FLOUR = 1/3 CUP
600 CC MILK = ABOUT 2.5 CUPS, 200°C = ABOUT 400°F

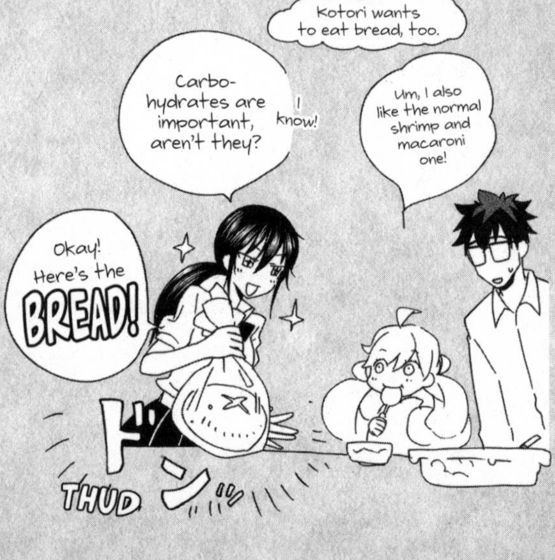
Kotori wants to eat bread, too.
Um, I also like the normal shrimp and macaroni one!
Carbo-hydrates are important, aren't they?
I know!
Okay! Here's the BREAD!
ドン
THUD

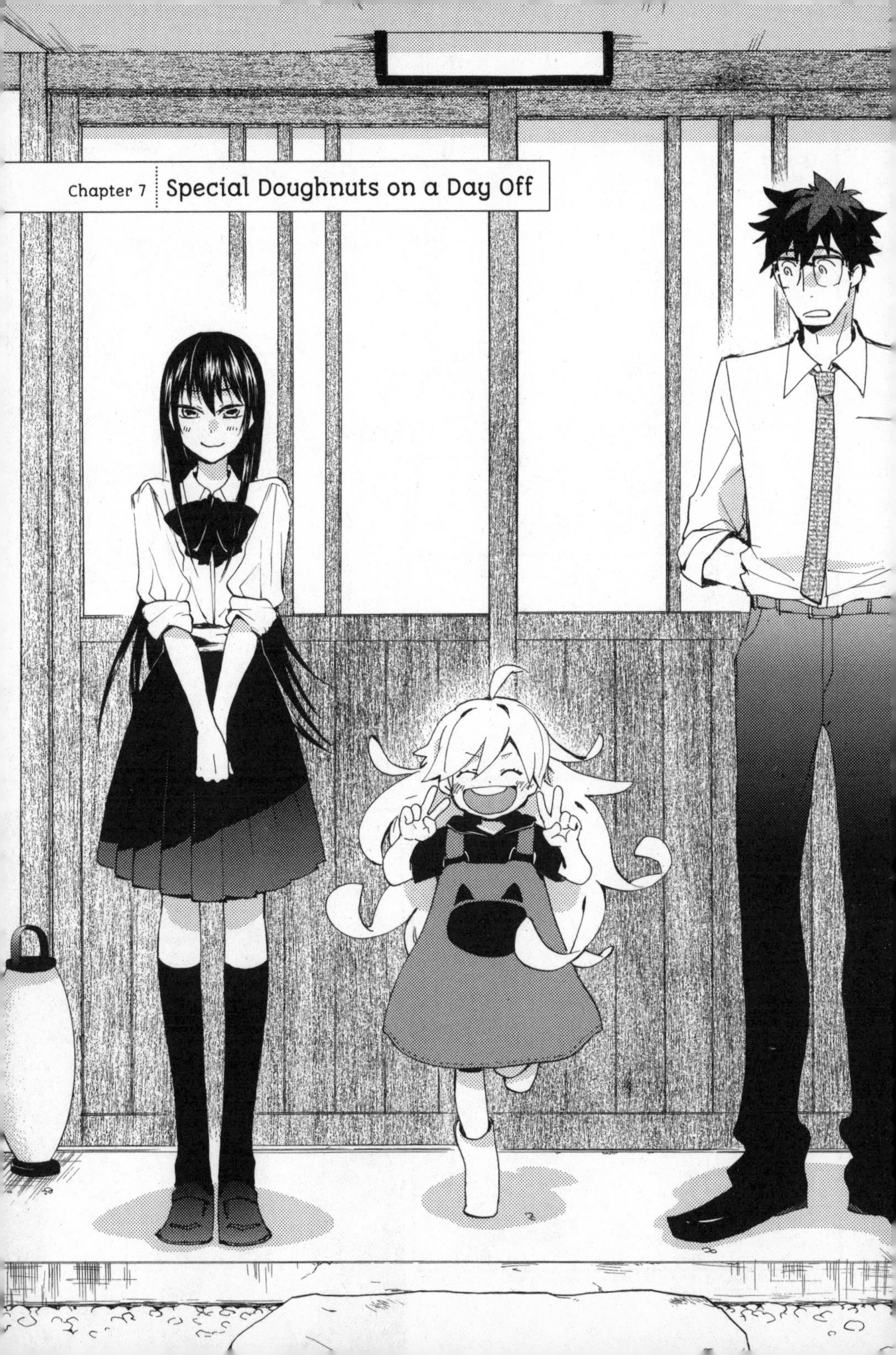
Chapter 7
Special Doughnuts on a Day Off

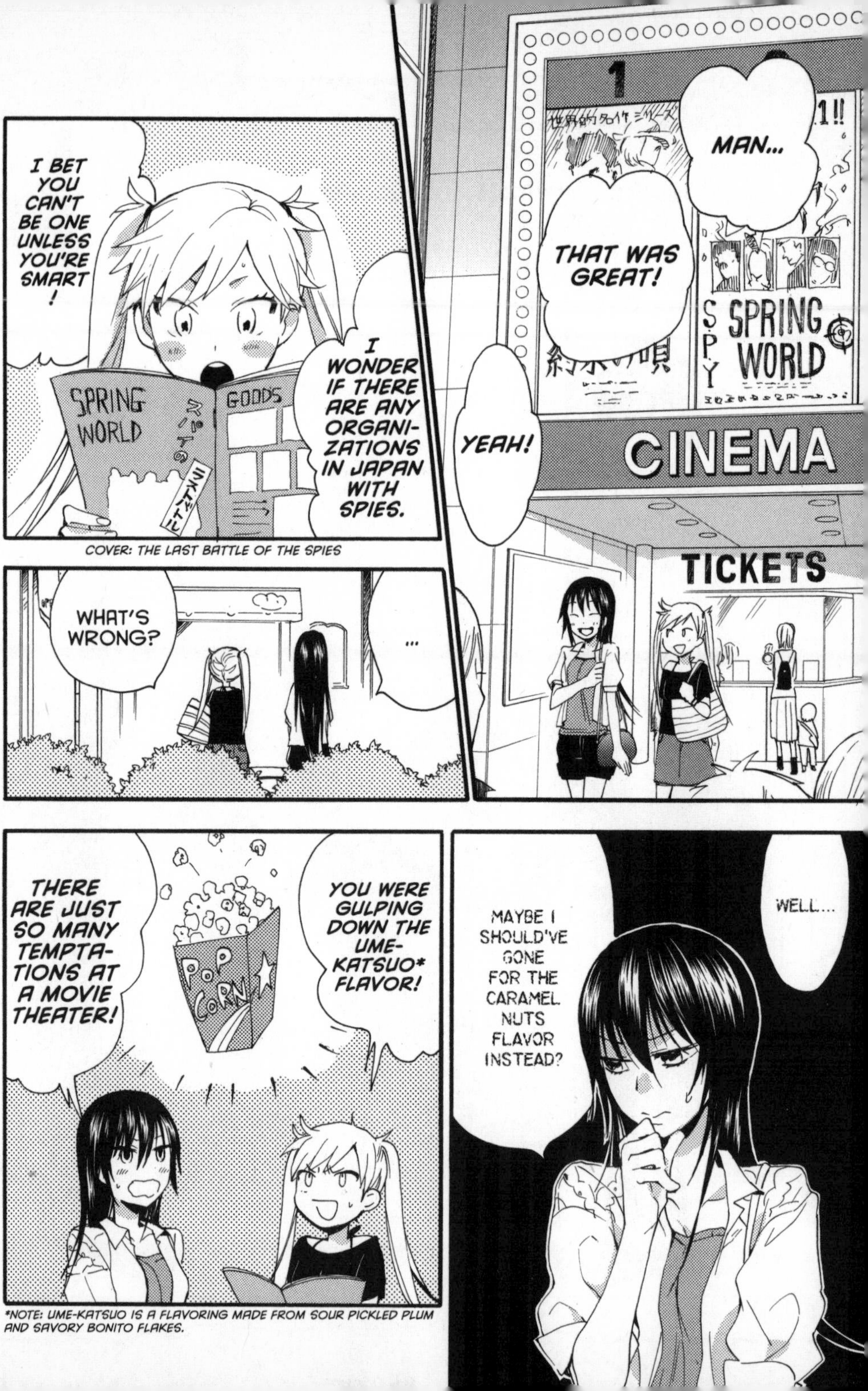
MAN...
THAT WAS GREAT!
YEAH!
SPRING WORLD
SPY
CINEMA
TICKETS
I WONDER IF THERE ARE ANY ORGANIZATIONS IN JAPAN WITH SPIES.
I BET YOU CAN'T BE ONE UNLESS YOU'RE SMART!
SPRING WORLD
GOODS
COVER: THE LAST BATTLE OF THE SPIES
...
WHAT'S WRONG?
WELL...
MAYBE I SHOULD'VE GONE FOR THE CARAMEL NUTS FLAVOR INSTEAD?
YOU WERE GULPING DOWN THE UME-KATSUO* FLAVOR!
POPCORN
THERE ARE JUST SO MANY TEMPTATIONS AT A MOVIE THEATER!

*NOTE: UME-KATSUO IS A FLAVORING MADE FROM SOUR PICKLED PLUM AND SAVORY BONITO FLAKES.

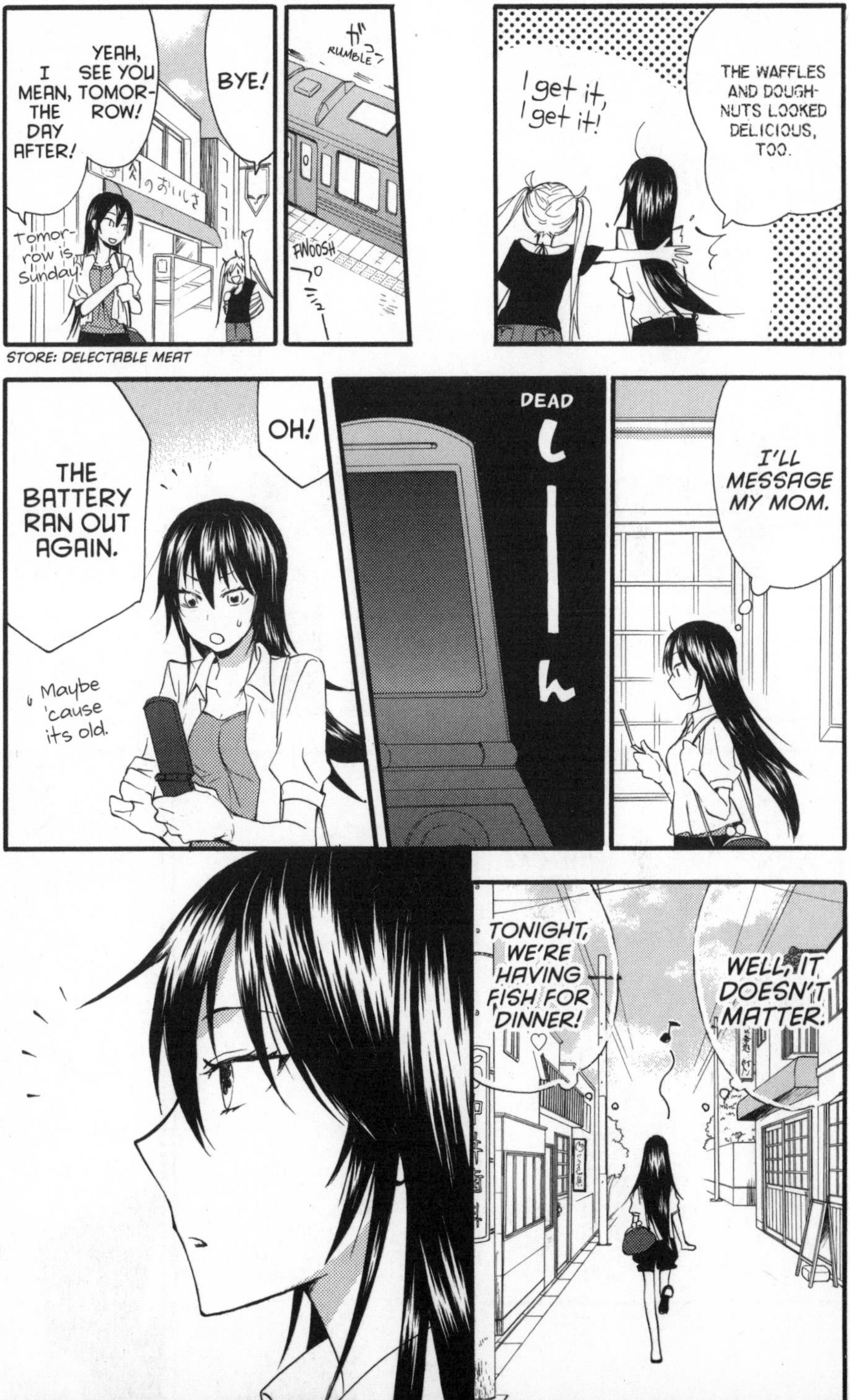
THE WAFFLES AND DOUGHNUTS LOOKED DELICIOUS, TOO.
I get it, I get it!
RUMBLE
FWOOSH
BYE!
YEAH, SEE YOU TOMORROW!
I MEAN, THE DAY AFTER!
Tomorrow is Sunday!
I'LL MESSAGE MY MOM.
DEAD
OH!
THE BATTERY RAN OUT AGAIN.
Maybe 'cause its old.
WELL, IT DOESN'T MATTER.
TONIGHT, WE'RE HAVING FISH FOR DINNER!
STORE: DELECTABLE MEAT

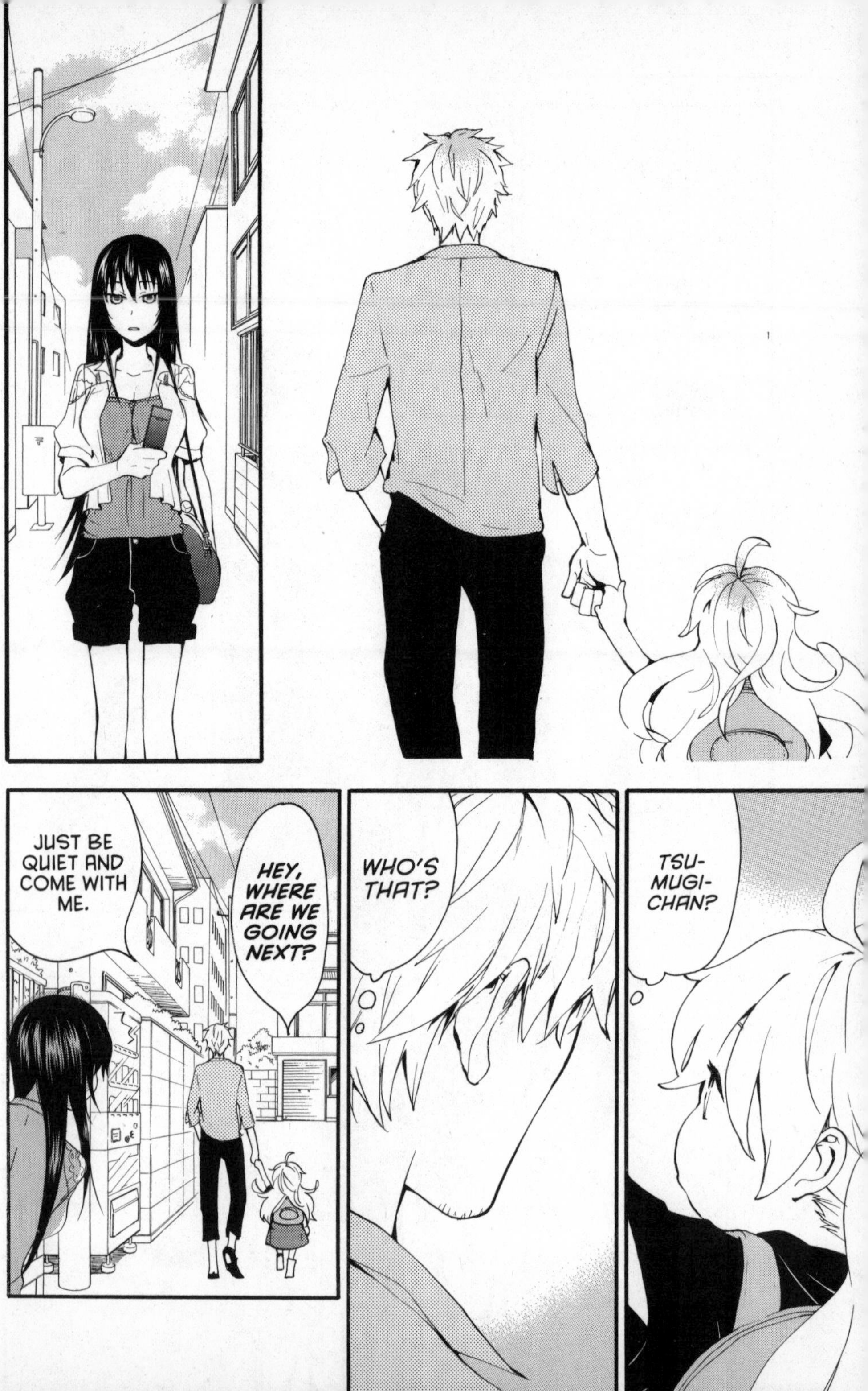
TSU-MUGI-CHAN?
WHO'S THAT?
HEY, WHERE ARE WE GOING NEXT?
JUST BE QUIET AND COME WITH ME.

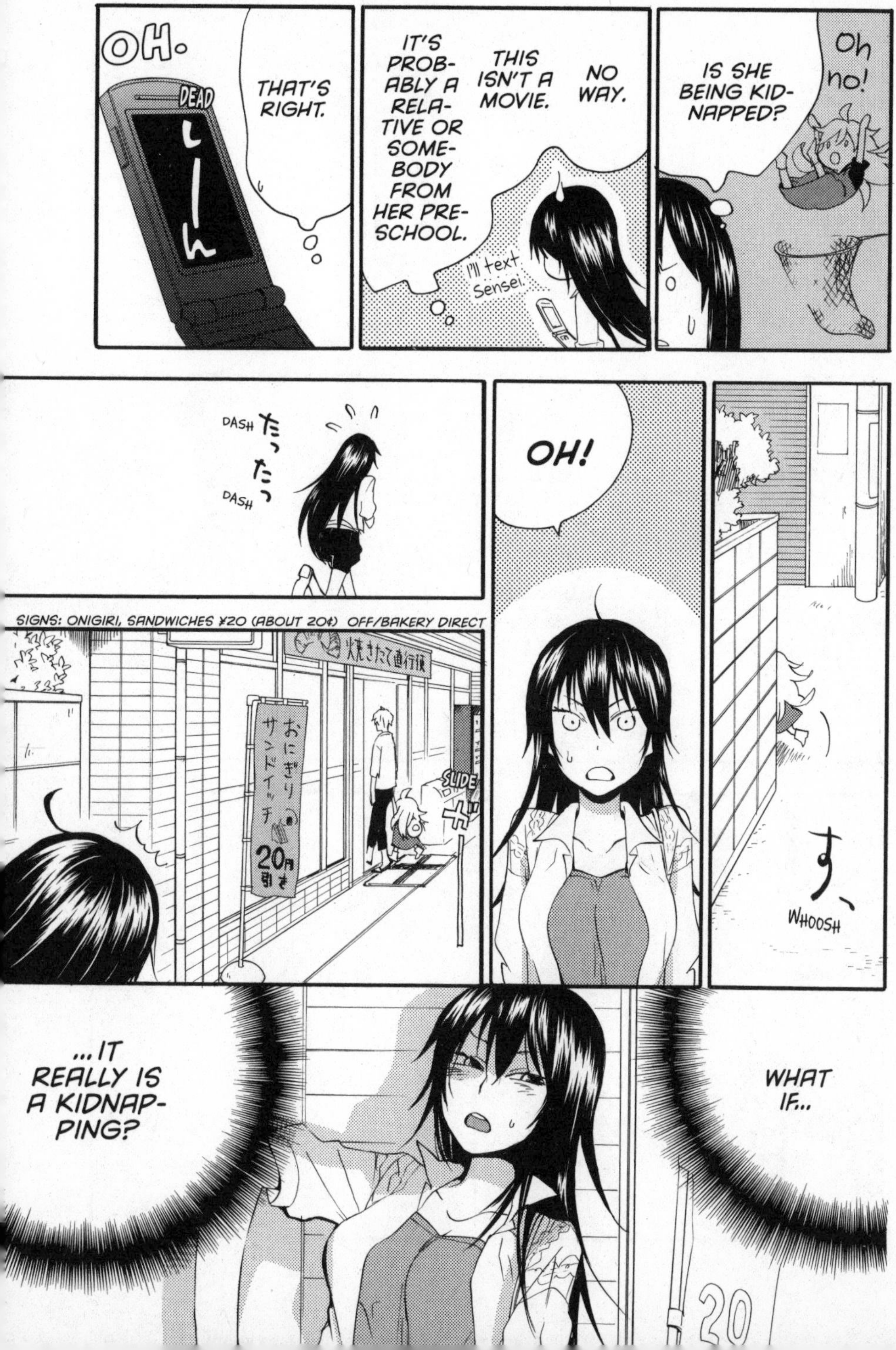
Oh no!
IS SHE BEING KID-NAPPED?
NO WAY.
THIS ISN'T A MOVIE.
IT'S PROB-ABLY A RELA-TIVE OR SOME-BODY FROM HER PRE-SCHOOL.
I'll text Sensei.
THAT'S RIGHT.
OH.
DEAD
しーん
すっ
WHOOSH
OH!
DASH
たったっ
DASH
SIGNS: ONIGIRI, SANDWICHES ¥20 (ABOUT 20¢) OFF/BAKERY DIRECT
焼きたて直行便
おにぎり サンドイッチ 20円引き
SLIDE
WHAT IF...
...IT REALLY IS A KIDNAP-PING?
20

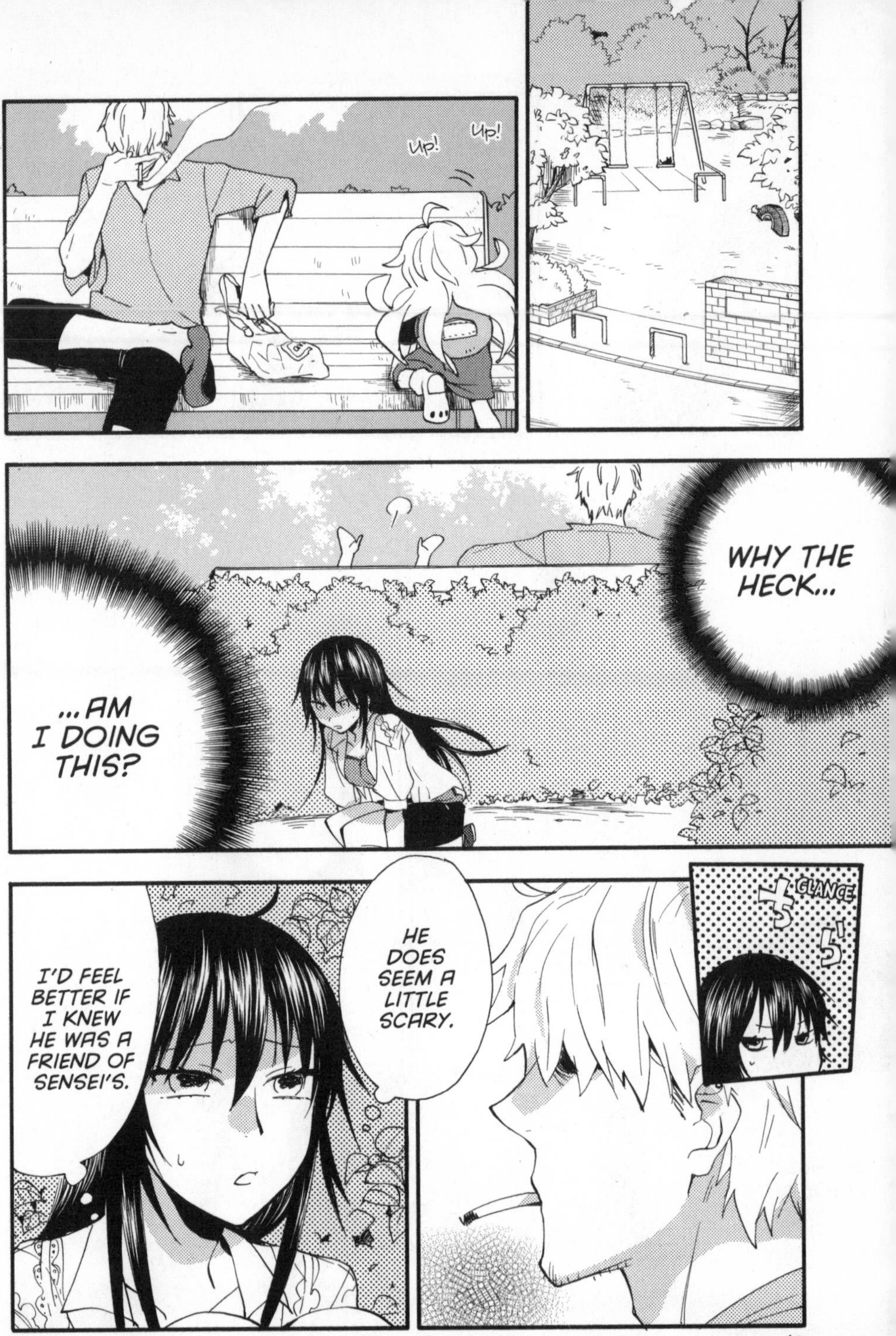
Up!
Up!
WHY THE HECK...
...AM I DOING THIS?
GLANCE
HE DOES SEEM A LITTLE SCARY.
I'D FEEL BETTER IF I KNEW HE WAS A FRIEND OF SENSEI'S.

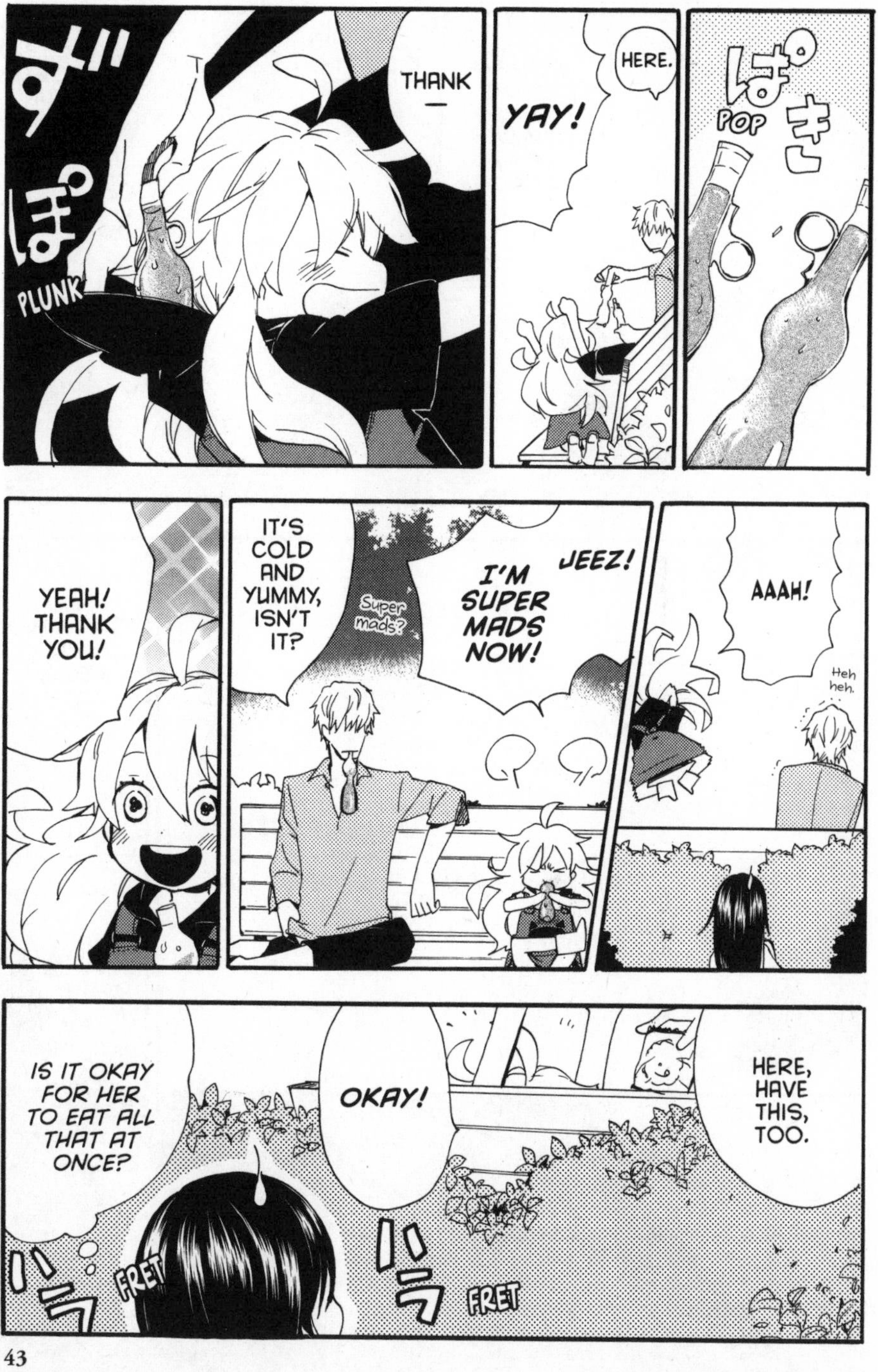
ぱき
POP
HERE.
YAY!
THANK —
ずぽ
PLUNK
AAAH!
Heh heh.
JEEZ!
I'M SUPER MADS NOW!
Super mads?
IT'S COLD AND YUMMY, ISN'T IT?
YEAH! THANK YOU!
HERE, HAVE THIS, TOO.
OKAY!
IS IT OKAY FOR HER TO EAT ALL THAT AT ONCE?
ハラ
FRET
ハラ
FRET

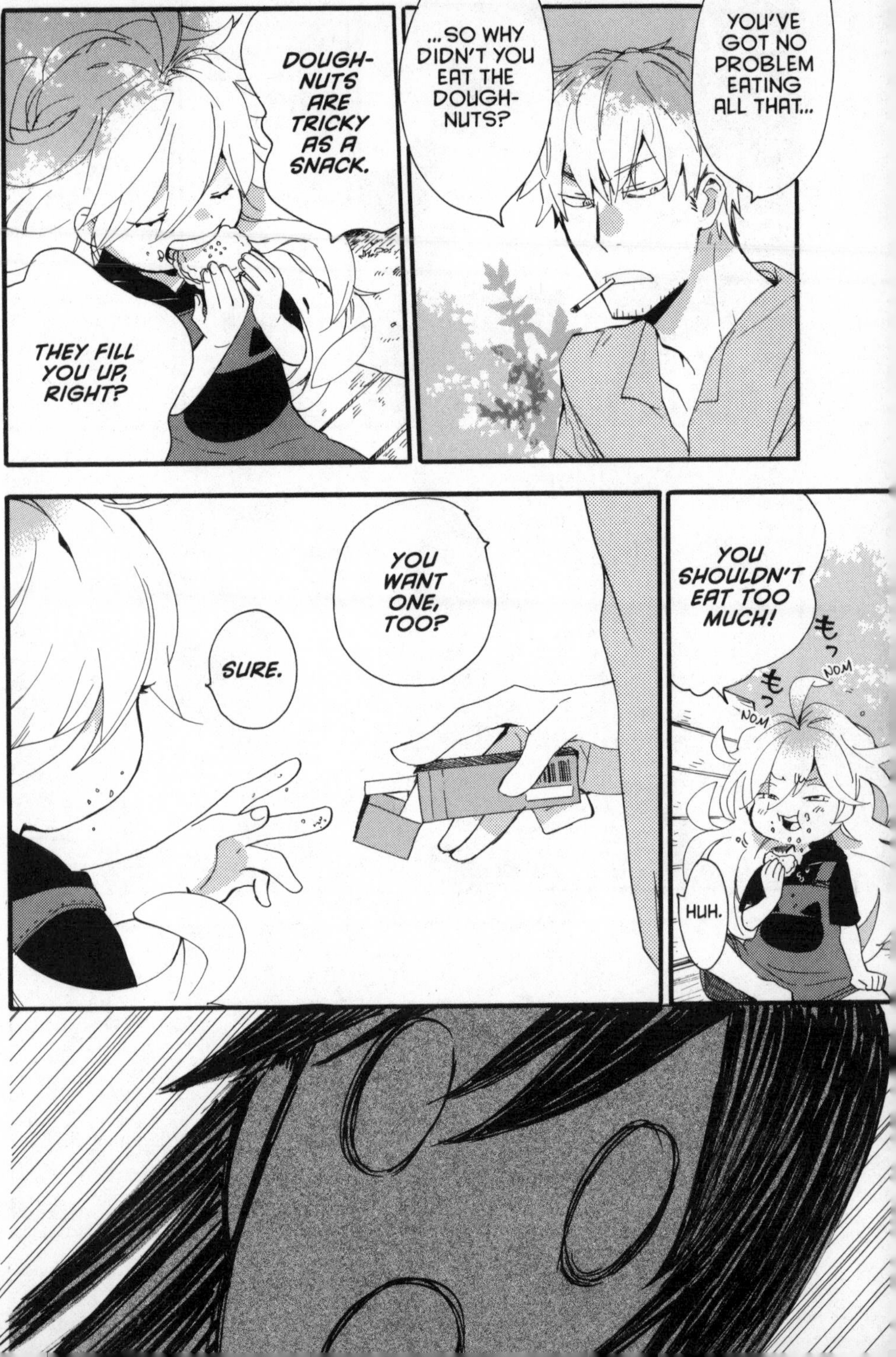
YOU'VE GOT NO PROBLEM EATING ALL THAT...
...SO WHY DIDN'T YOU EAT THE DOUGH-NUTS?
DOUGH-NUTS ARE TRICKY AS A SNACK.
THEY FILL YOU UP, RIGHT?
YOU SHOULDN'T EAT TOO MUCH!
もっ
NOM
もっ
NOM
HUH.
YOU WANT ONE, TOO?
SURE.

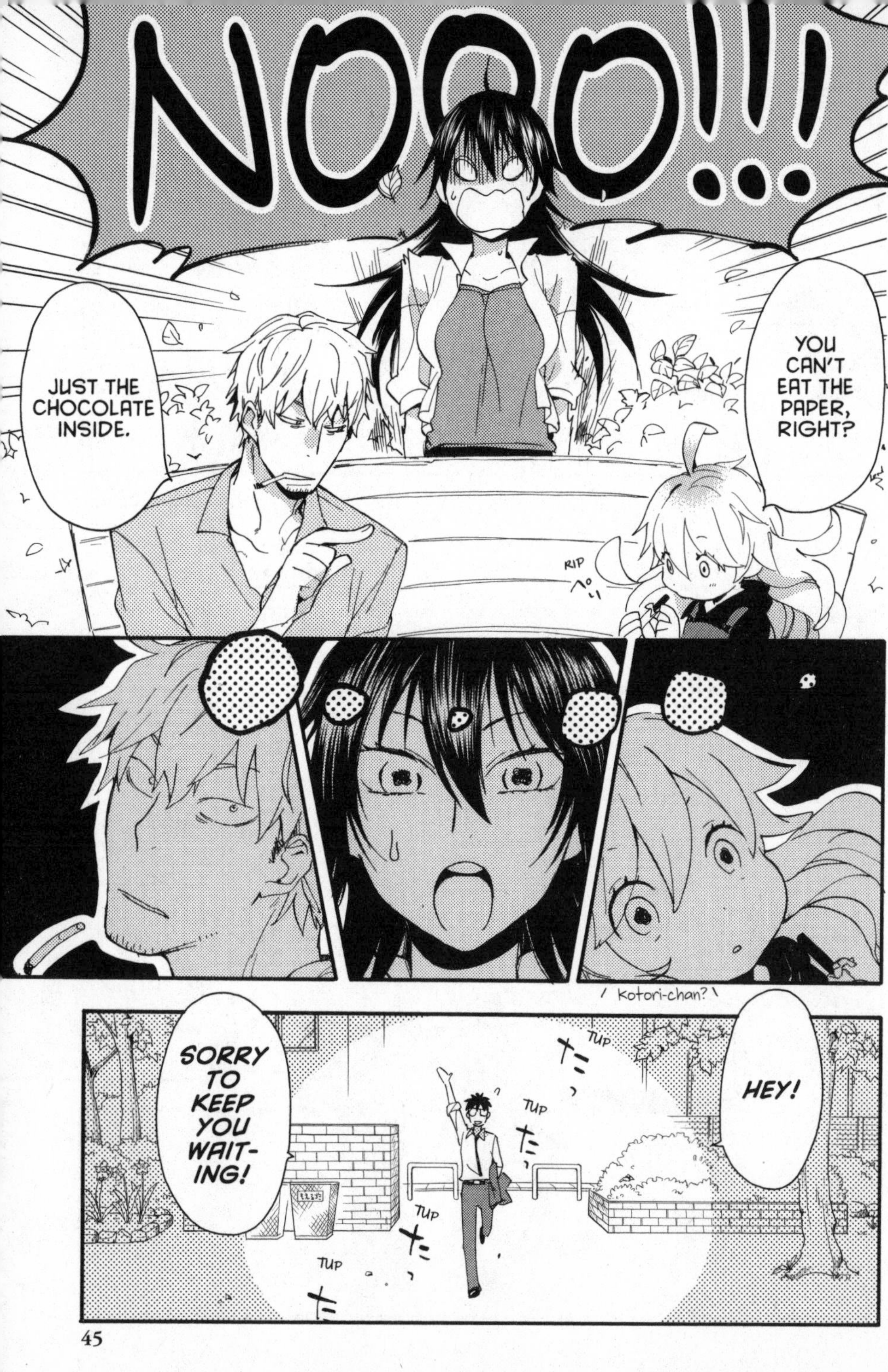
NOOO!!!...
YOU CAN'T EAT THE PAPER, RIGHT?
JUST THE CHOCOLATE INSIDE.
RIP
Kotori-chan?
HEY!
TUP
TUP
SORRY TO KEEP YOU WAIT-ING!
TUP
TUP

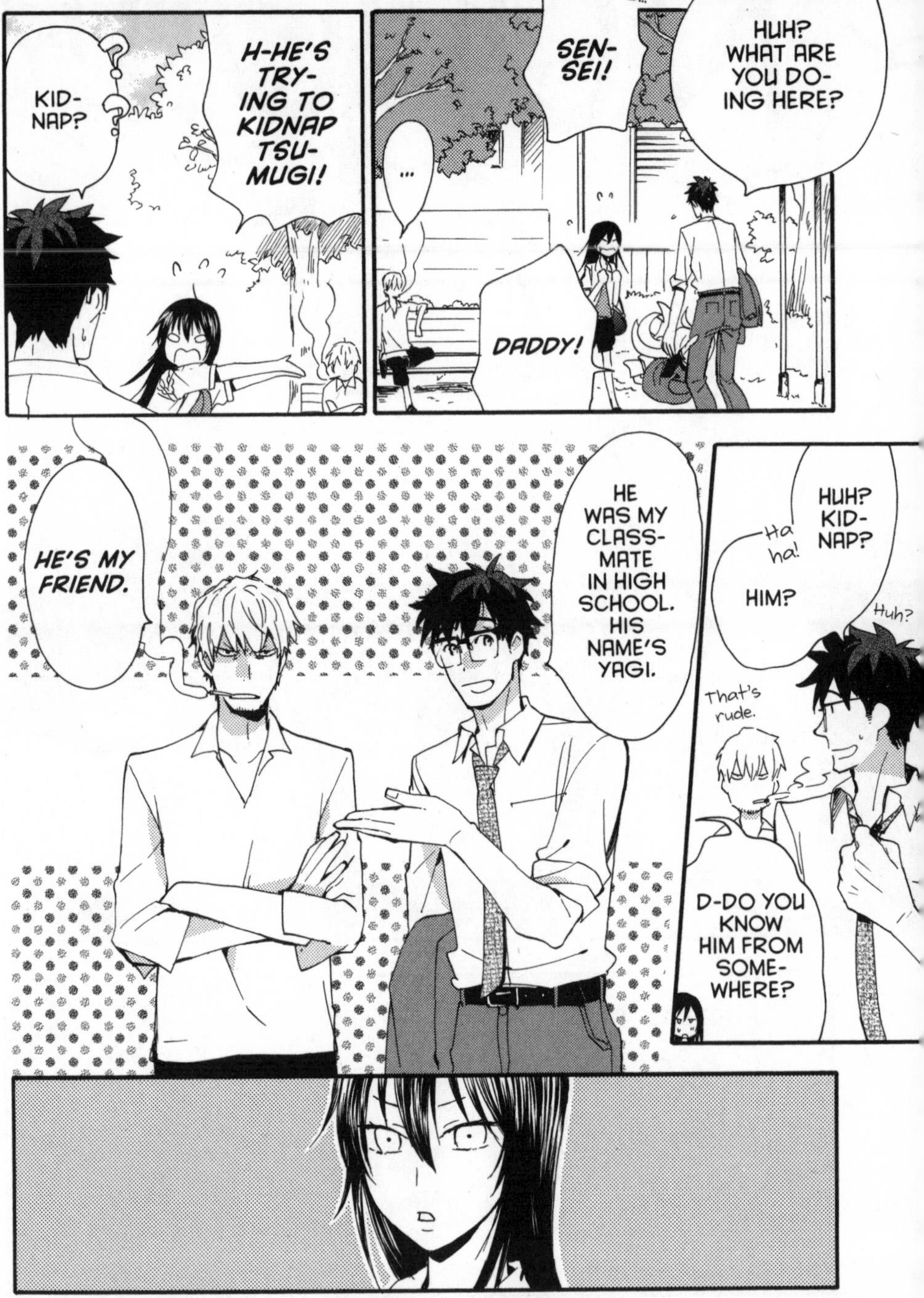
HUH? WHAT ARE YOU DO-ING HERE?
S...
SEN-SEI!
...
DADDY!
H-HE'S TRY-ING TO KIDNAP TSU-MUGI!
KID-NAP?
HUH? KID-NAP?
Huh?
Ha ha!
HIM?
That's rude.
D-DO YOU KNOW HIM FROM SOME-WHERE?
HE WAS MY CLASS-MATE IN HIGH SCHOOL. HIS NAME'S YAGI.
HE'S MY FRIEND.

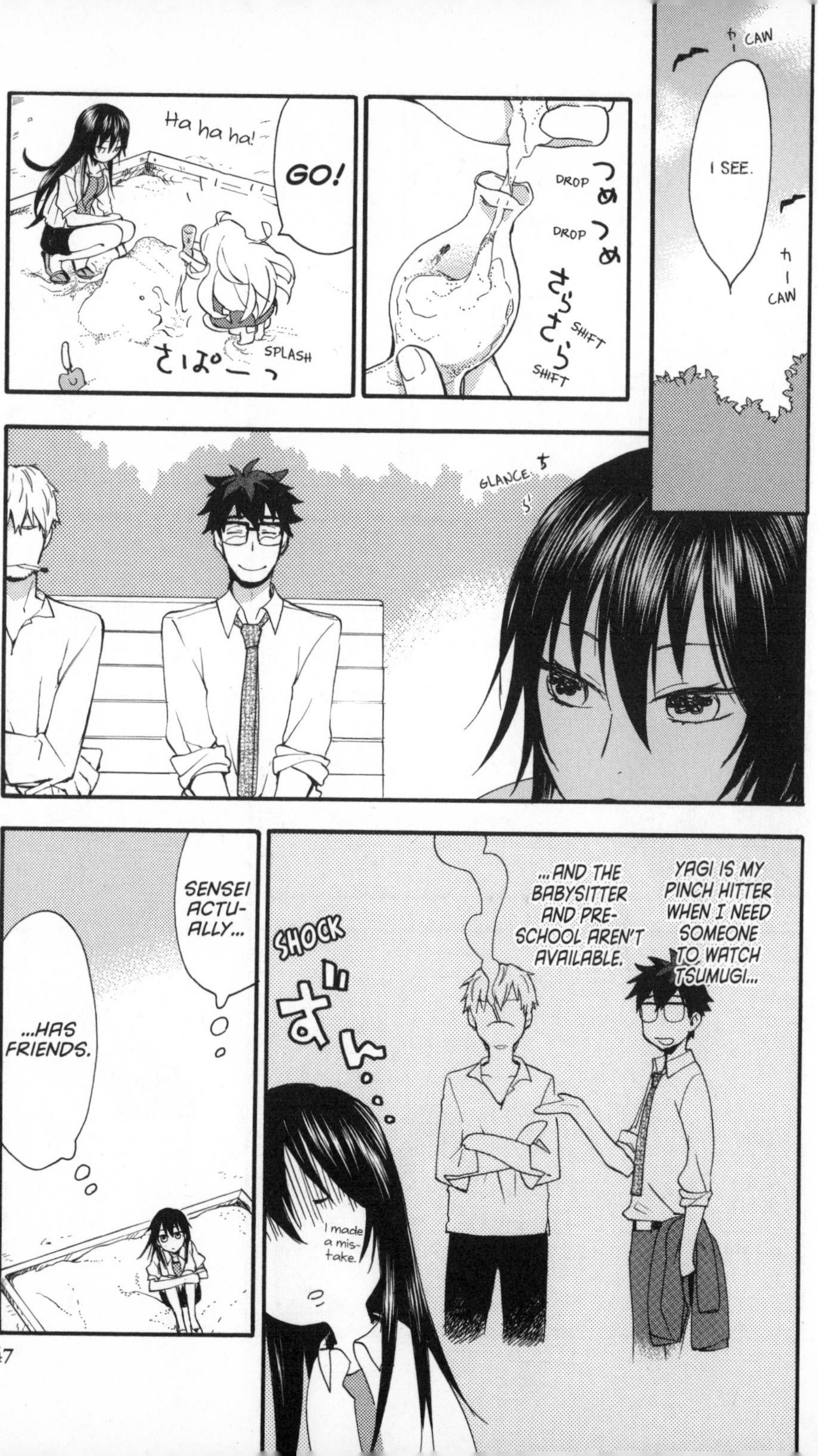
カー CAW
I SEE.
カー CAW
DROP つめ
DROP つめ
さら SHIFT
さら SHIFT
GO!
Ha ha ha!
さぱーっ SPLASH
GLANCE ち
YAGI IS MY PINCH HITTER WHEN I NEED SOMEONE TO WATCH TSUMUGI...
...AND THE BABYSITTER AND PRE-SCHOOL AREN'T AVAILABLE.
SHOCK ずん
I made a mis-take.
SENSEI ACTU-ALLY...
...HAS FRIENDS.

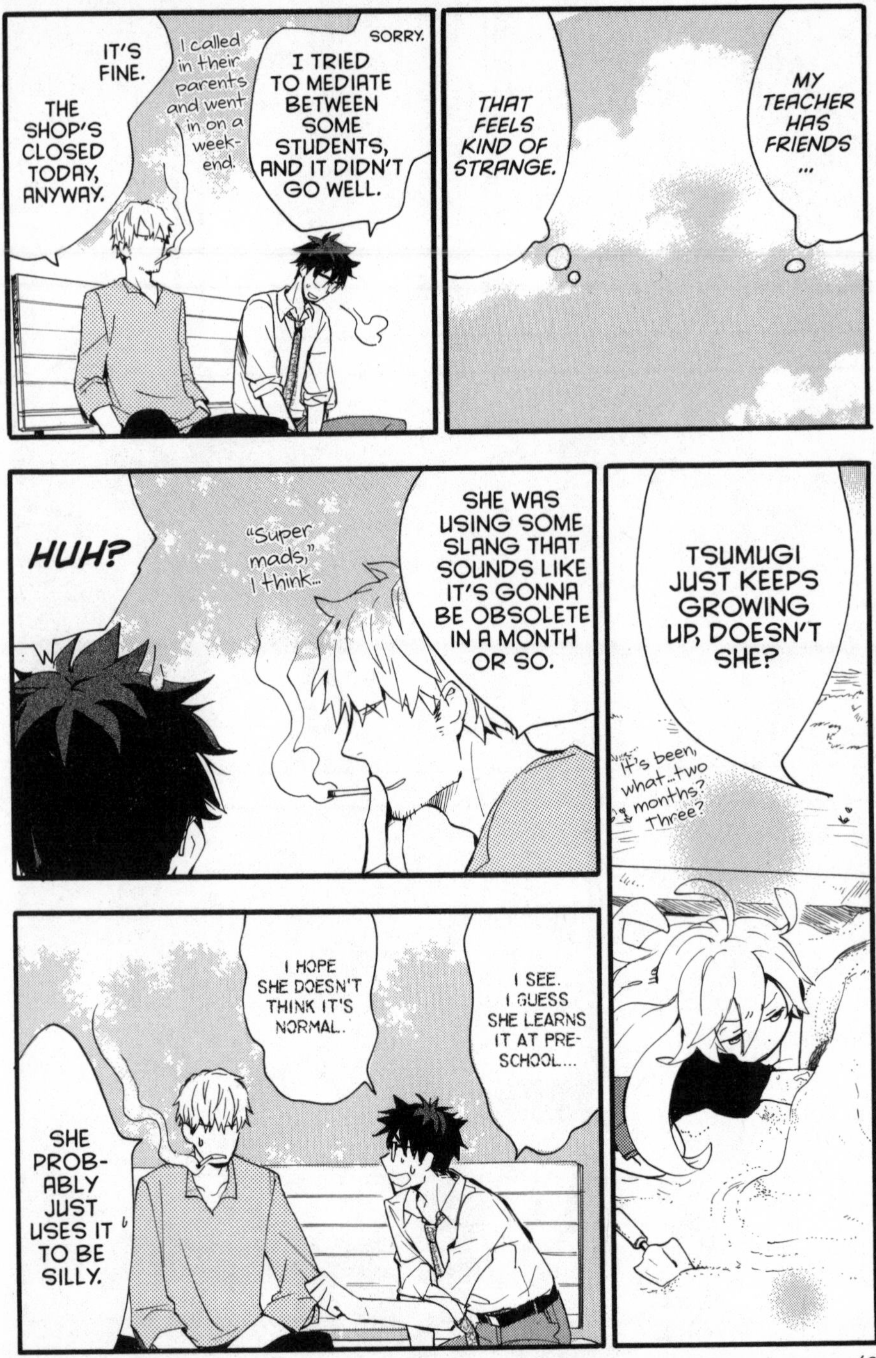
MY TEACHER HAS FRIENDS ...
THAT FEELS KIND OF STRANGE.
SORRY.
I TRIED TO MEDIATE BETWEEN SOME STUDENTS, AND IT DIDN'T GO WELL.
I called in their parents and went in on a week-end.
IT'S FINE.
THE SHOP'S CLOSED TODAY, ANYWAY.
TSUMUGI JUST KEEPS GROWING UP, DOESN'T SHE?
It's been, what...two months? Three?
SHE WAS USING SOME SLANG THAT SOUNDS LIKE IT'S GONNA BE OBSOLETE IN A MONTH OR SO.
"Super mads," I think...
HUH?
I SEE. I GUESS SHE LEARNS IT AT PRE-SCHOOL...
I HOPE SHE DOESN'T THINK IT'S NORMAL.
SHE PROBABLY JUST USES IT TO BE SILLY.

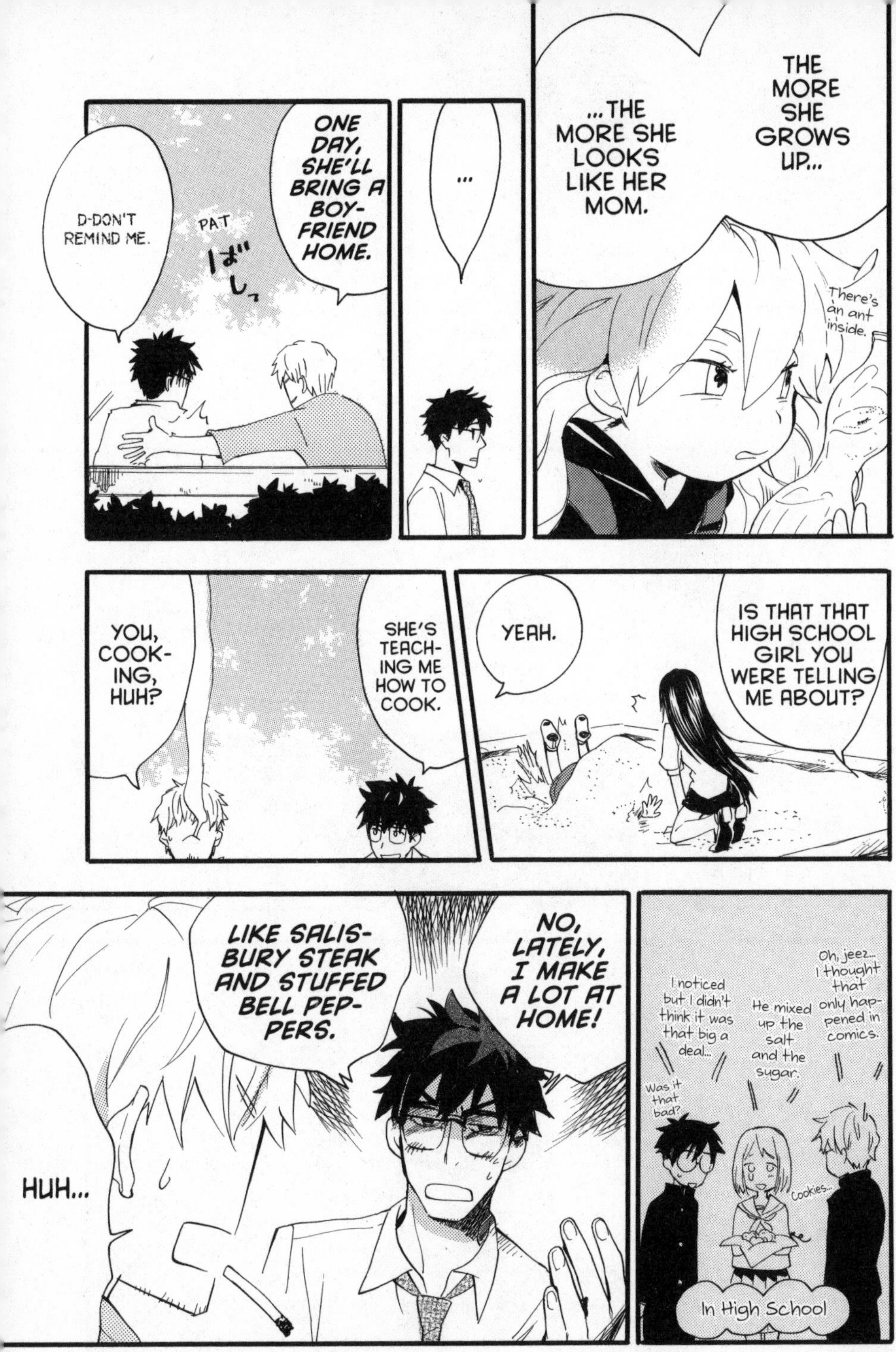
THE MORE SHE GROWS UP...
...THE MORE SHE LOOKS LIKE HER MOM.
There's an ant inside.
...
ONE DAY, SHE'LL BRING A BOY-FRIEND HOME.
PAT
ばしっ
D-DON'T REMIND ME.
IS THAT THAT HIGH SCHOOL GIRL YOU WERE TELLING ME ABOUT?
YEAH.
SHE'S TEACHING ME HOW TO COOK.
YOU, COOKING, HUH?
Oh, jeez... I thought that only happened in comics.
He mixed up the salt and the sugar.
I noticed but I didn't think it was that big a deal...
Was it that bad?
Cookies...
In High School
NO, LATELY, I MAKE A LOT AT HOME!
LIKE SALISBURY STEAK AND STUFFED BELL PEPPERS.
HUH...

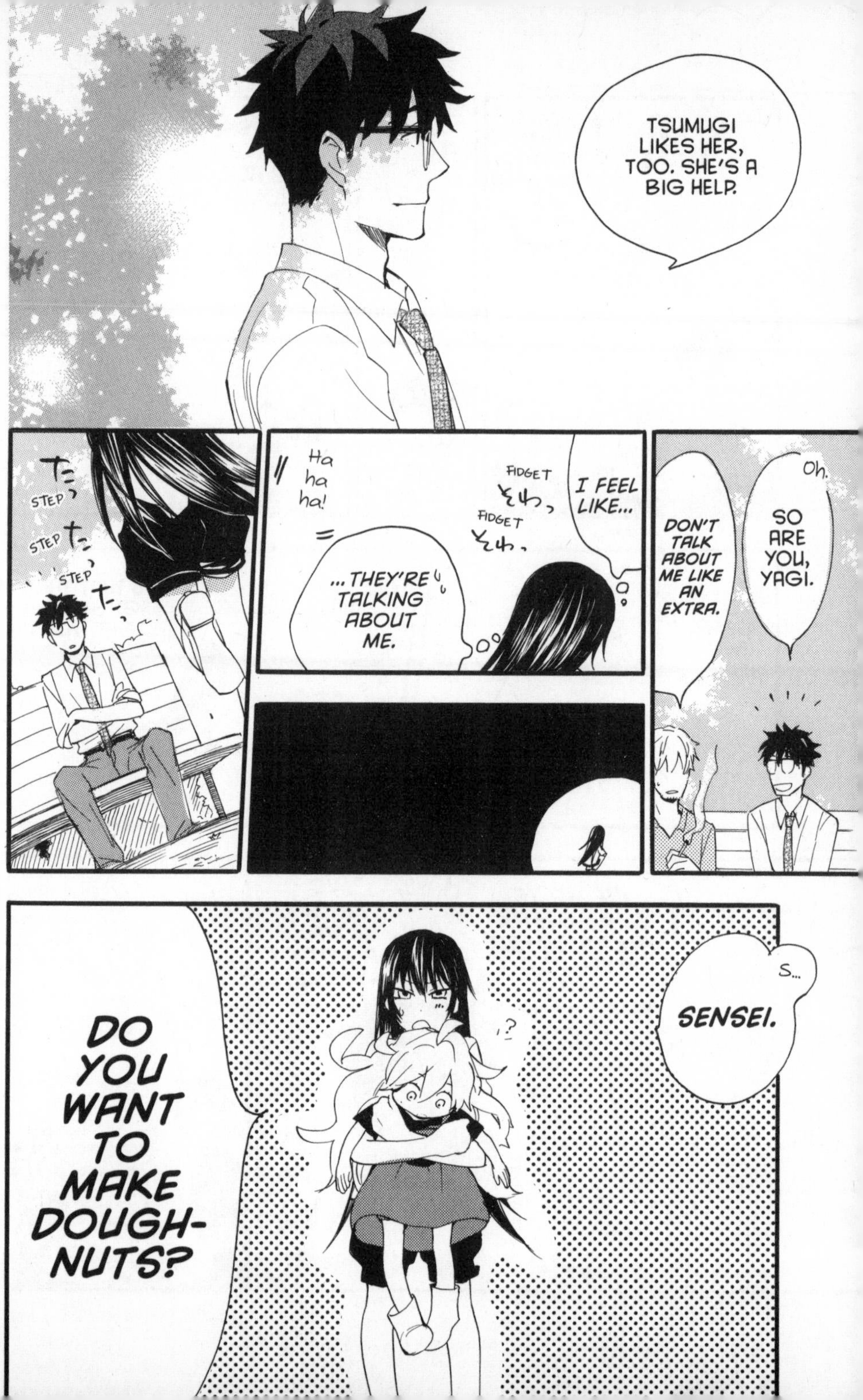
TSUMUGI LIKES HER, TOO. SHE'S A BIG HELP.
Oh.
SO ARE YOU, YAGI.
DON'T TALK ABOUT ME LIKE AN EXTRA.
I FEEL LIKE...
FIDGET そわっ
FIDGET そわっ
...THEY'RE TALKING ABOUT ME.
Ha ha ha!
STEP たっ
STEP たっ
STEP たっ
S...
SENSEI.
!?
DO YOU WANT TO MAKE DOUGH-NUTS?

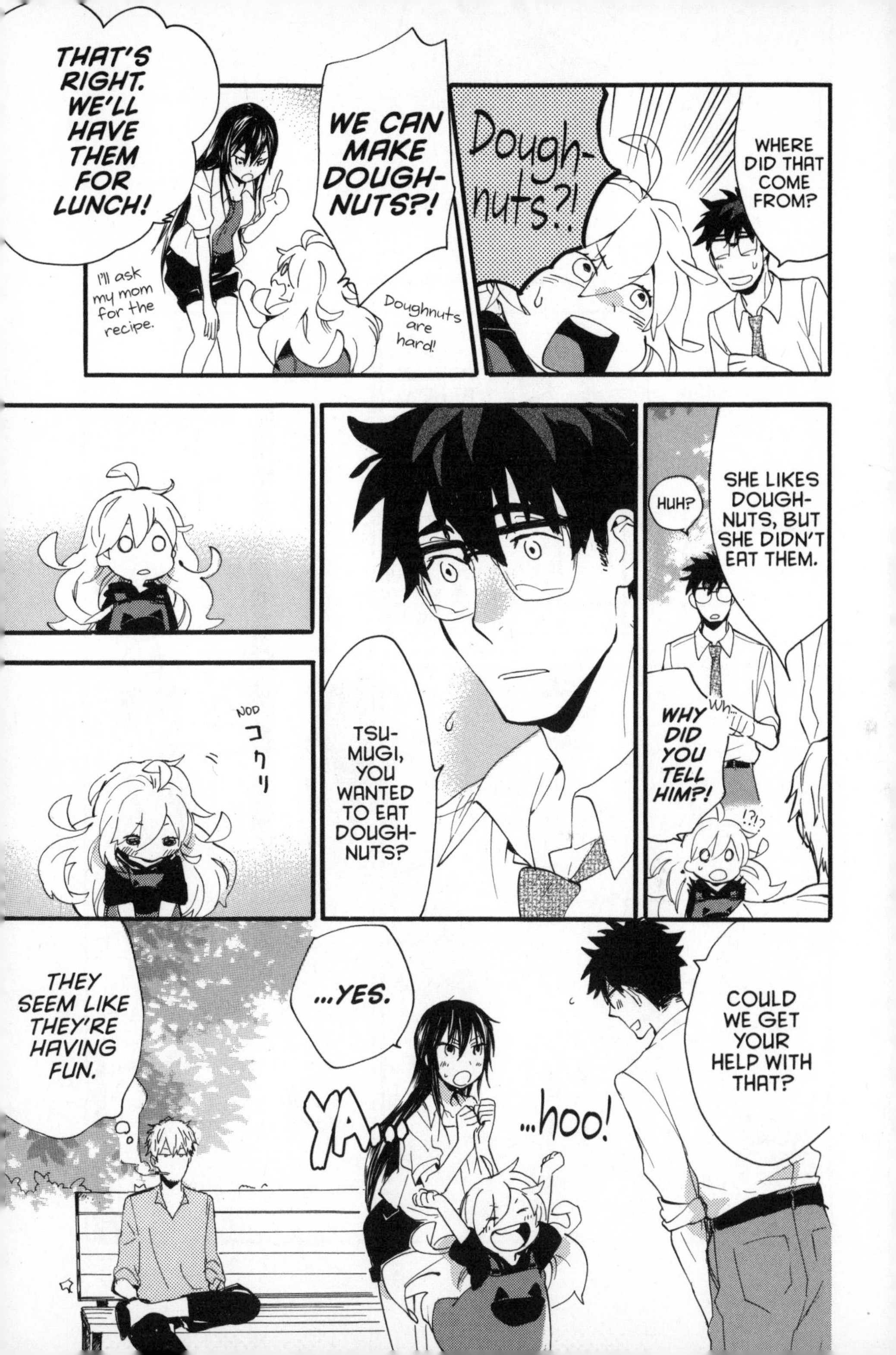

WHERE DID THAT COME FROM?
Dough-nuts?!
WE CAN MAKE DOUGH-NUTS?!
THAT'S RIGHT. WE'LL HAVE THEM FOR LUNCH!
Doughnuts are hard!
I'll ask my mom for the recipe.
SHE LIKES DOUGH-NUTS, BUT SHE DIDN'T EAT THEM.
HUH?
Wh...
WHY DID YOU TELL HIM?!
!?!
TSU-MUGI, YOU WANTED TO EAT DOUGH-NUTS?
NOD
コクリ
COULD WE GET YOUR HELP WITH THAT?
...YES.
YA... ...hoo!
THEY SEEM LIKE THEY'RE HAVING FUN.

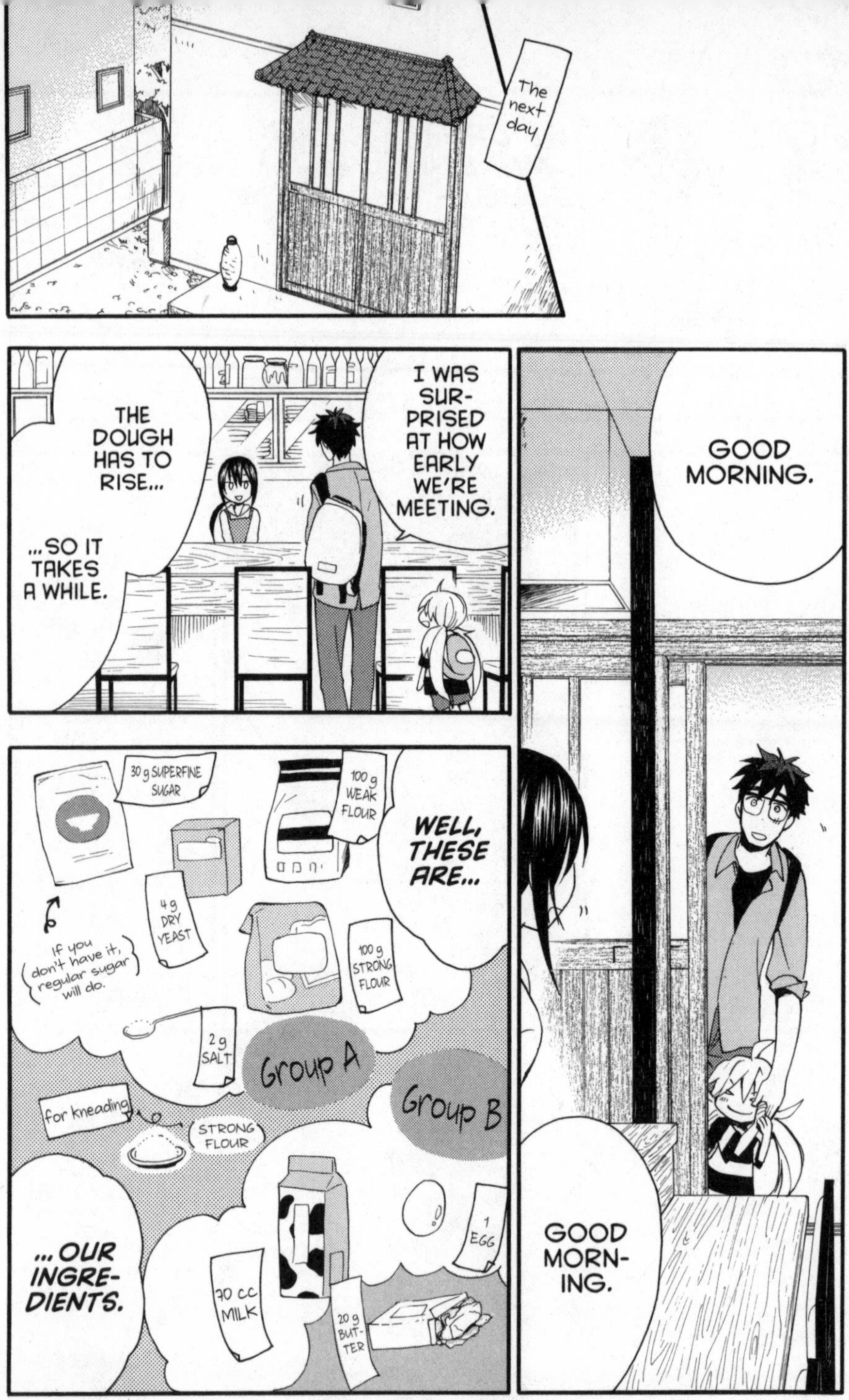
The next day
GOOD MORNING.
GOOD MORN-ING.
I WAS SUR-PRISED AT HOW EARLY WE'RE MEETING.
THE DOUGH HAS TO RISE...
...SO IT TAKES A WHILE.
WELL, THESE ARE...
100 g WEAK FLOUR
30 g SUPERFINE SUGAR
4 g DRY YEAST
100 g STRONG FLOUR
If you don't have it, regular sugar will do.
2 g SALT
Group A
Group B
for kneading
STRONG FLOUR
1 EGG
20 g BUT-TER
70 cc MILK
...OUR INGRE-DIENTS.

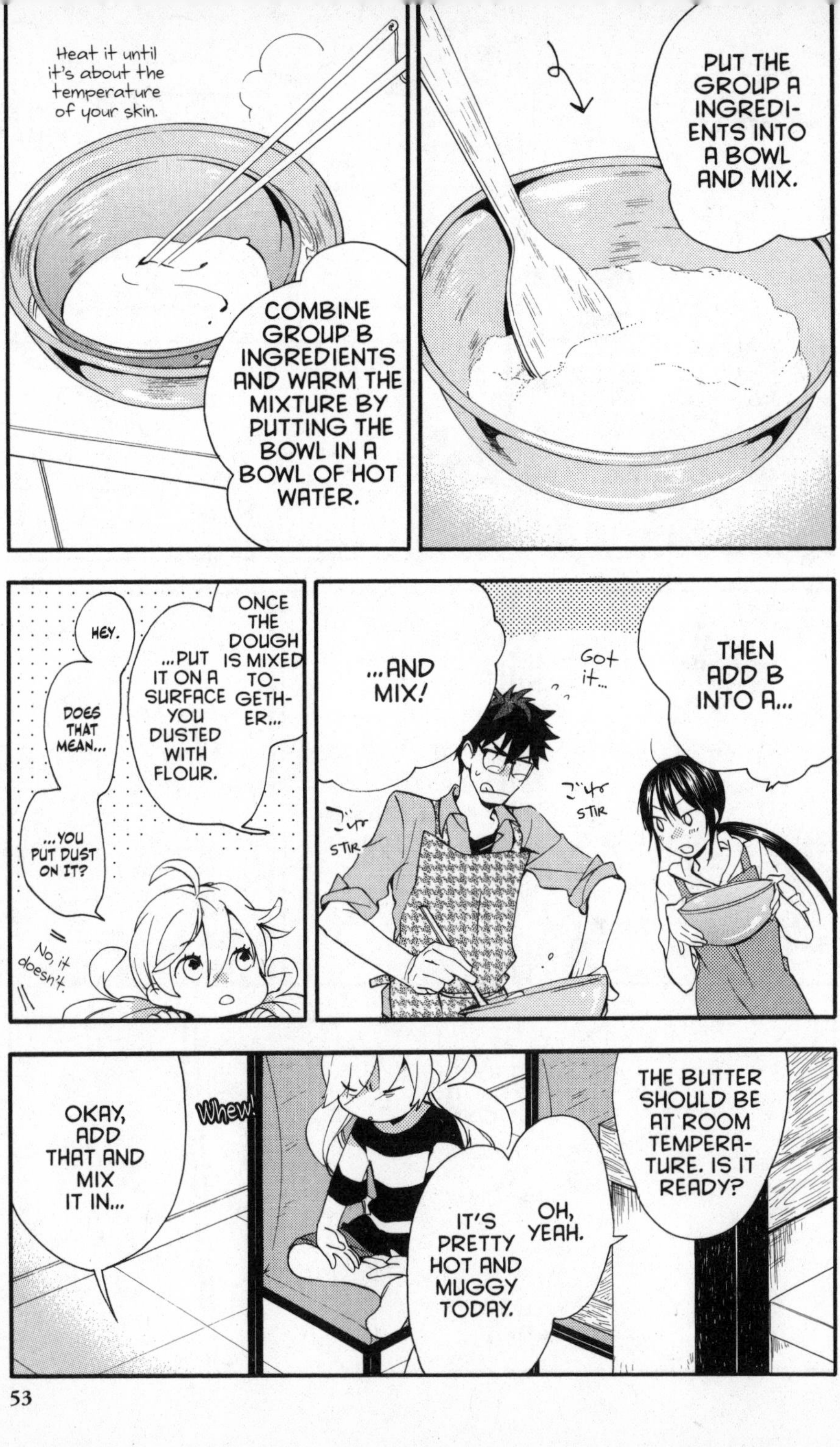
PUT THE GROUP A INGREDIENTS INTO A BOWL AND MIX.
COMBINE GROUP B INGREDIENTS AND WARM THE MIXTURE BY PUTTING THE BOWL IN A BOWL OF HOT WATER.
Heat it until it's about the temperature of your skin.
THEN ADD B INTO A...
Got it...
...AND MIX!
STIR
STIR
ONCE THE DOUGH IS MIXED TOGETHER...
...PUT IT ON A SURFACE YOU DUSTED WITH FLOUR.
HEY.
DOES THAT MEAN...
...YOU PUT DUST ON IT?
No, it doesn't.
THE BUTTER SHOULD BE AT ROOM TEMPERATURE. IS IT READY?
OH, YEAH.
IT'S PRETTY HOT AND MUGGY TODAY.
Whew!
OKAY, ADD THAT AND MIX IT IN...

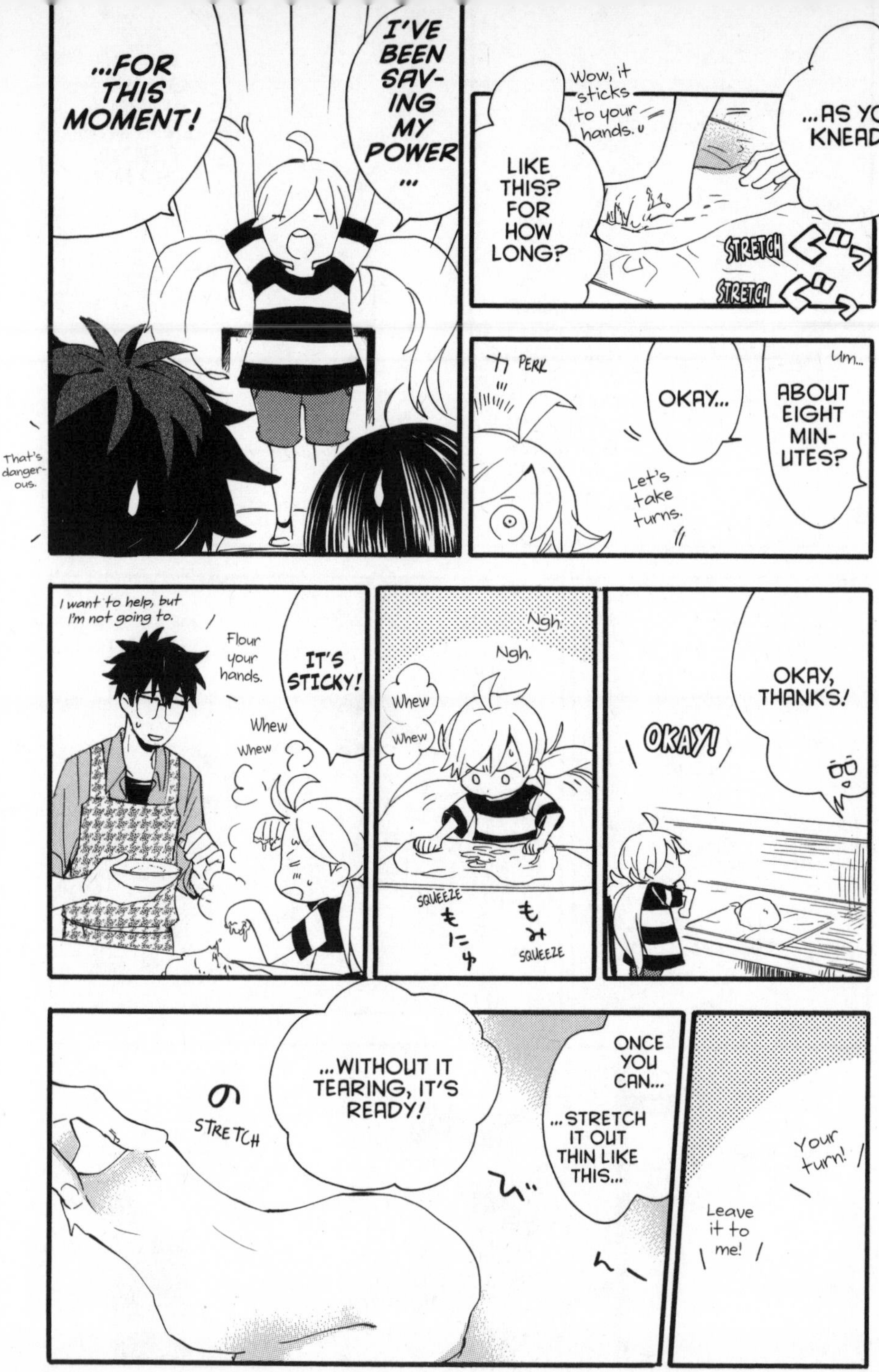
...AS YOU KNEAD!
Wow, it sticks to your hands.
LIKE THIS? FOR HOW LONG?
STRETCH
STRETCH
Um...
ABOUT EIGHT MIN-UTES?
OKAY...
PERK
Let's take turns.
I'VE BEEN SAV-ING MY POWER...
...FOR THIS MOMENT!
That's danger-ous.
OKAY, THANKS!
OKAY!
Ngh.
Ngh.
Whew
Whew
SQUEEZE
SQUEEZE
IT'S STICKY!
Flour your hands.
Whew
Whew
I want to help, but I'm not going to.
Your turn!
Leave it to me!
ONCE YOU CAN...
...STRETCH IT OUT THIN LIKE THIS...
...WITHOUT IT TEARING, IT'S READY!
STRETCH

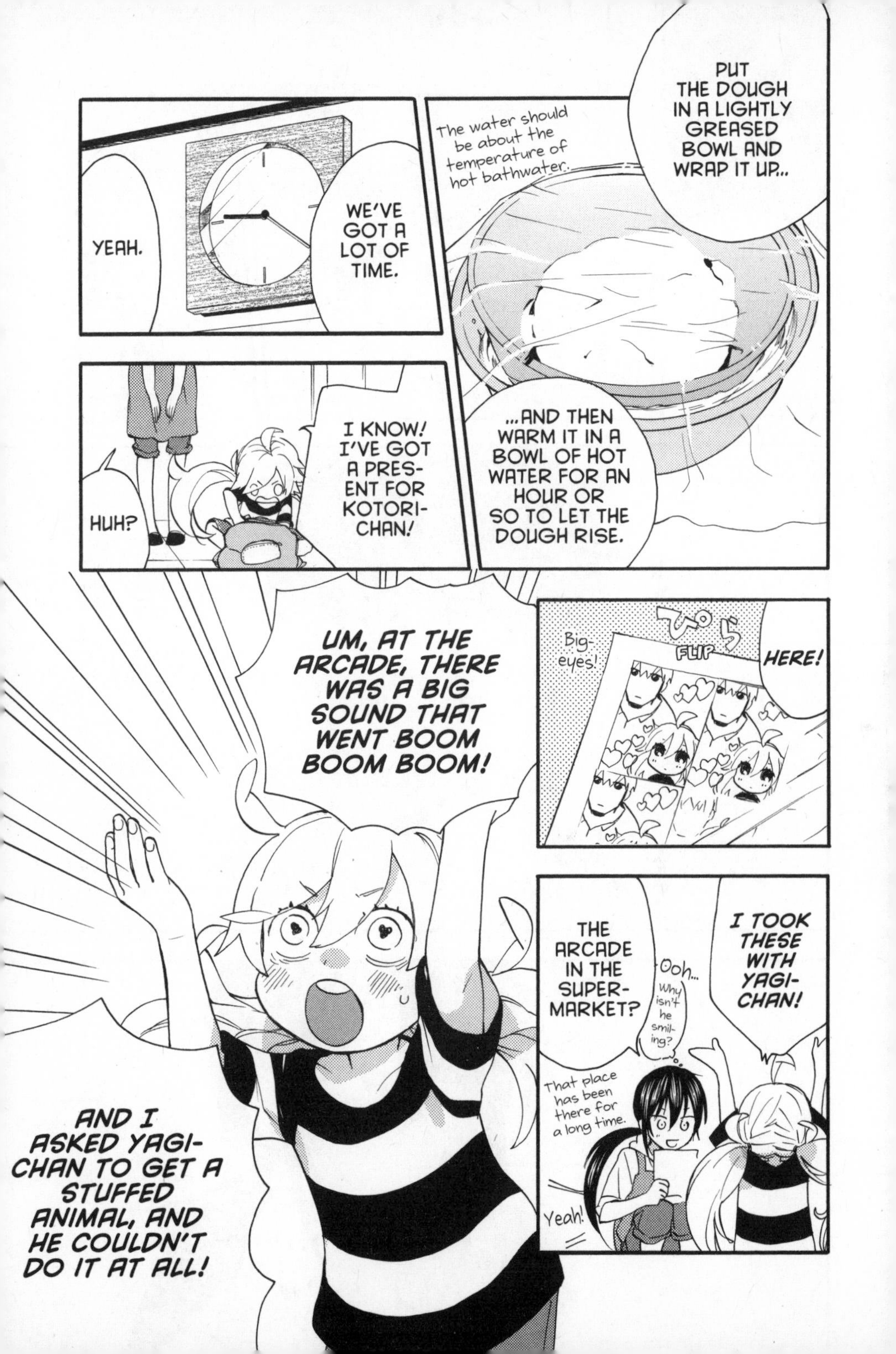
PUT THE DOUGH IN A LIGHTLY GREASED BOWL AND WRAP IT UP...
The water should be about the temperature of hot bathwater.
...AND THEN WARM IT IN A BOWL OF HOT WATER FOR AN HOUR OR SO TO LET THE DOUGH RISE.
WE'VE GOT A LOT OF TIME.
YEAH.
I KNOW! I'VE GOT A PRESENT FOR KOTORI-CHAN!
HUH?
HERE!
ぴら
FLIP
Big-eyes!
I TOOK THESE WITH YAGI-CHAN!
Ooh...
Why isn't he smiling?
THE ARCADE IN THE SUPER-MARKET?
That place has been there for a long time.
Yeah!
UM, AT THE ARCADE, THERE WAS A BIG SOUND THAT WENT BOOM BOOM BOOM!
AND I ASKED YAGI-CHAN TO GET A STUFFED ANIMAL, AND HE COULDN'T DO IT AT ALL!

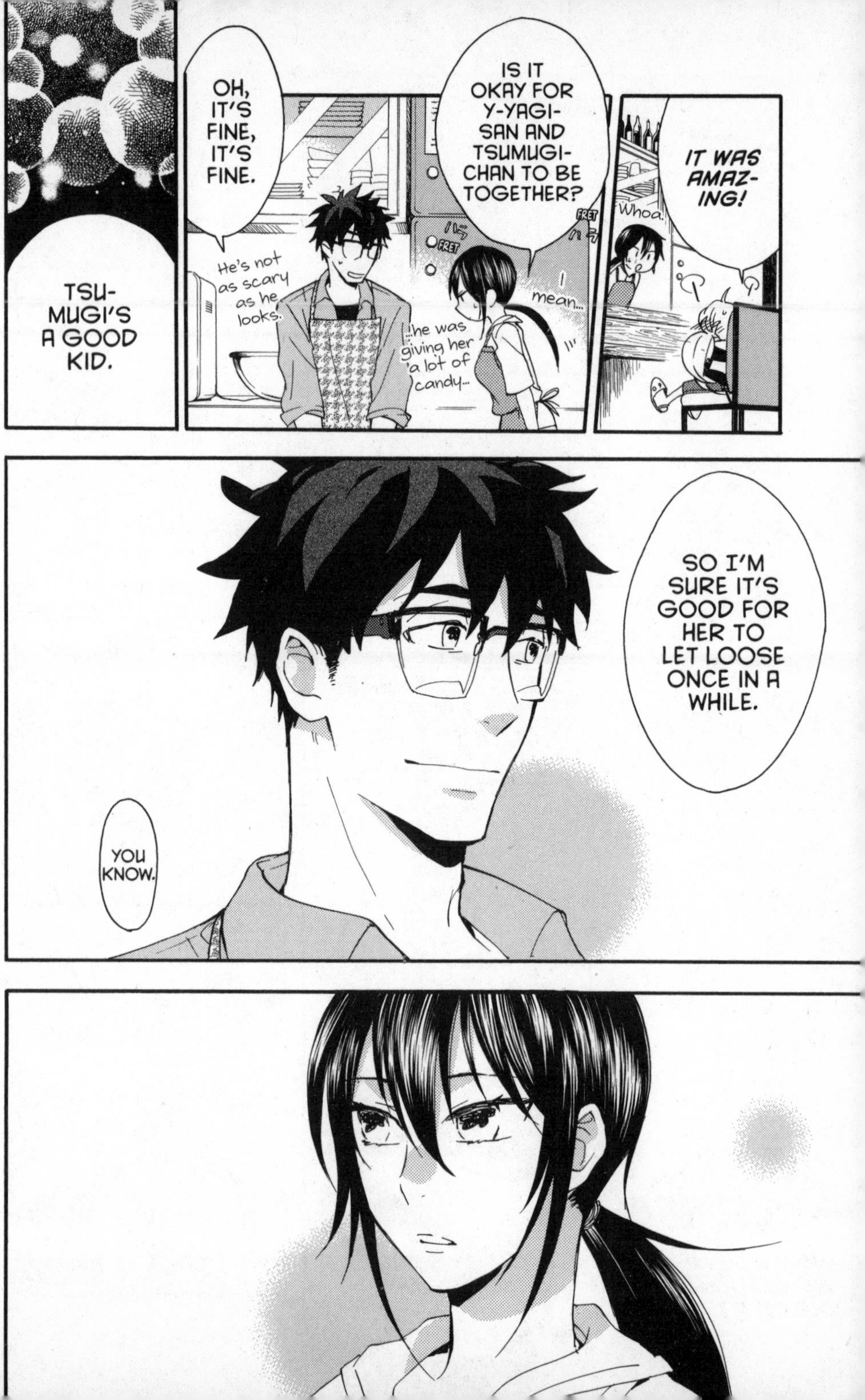
Whoa.
IT WAS AMAZING!
IS IT OKAY FOR Y-YAGI-SAN AND TSUMUGI-CHAN TO BE TOGETHER?
FRET
FRET
I mean...
OH, IT'S FINE, IT'S FINE.
He's not as scary as he looks.
...he was giving her a lot of candy...
TSUMUGI'S A GOOD KID.
SO I'M SURE IT'S GOOD FOR HER TO LET LOOSE ONCE IN A WHILE.
YOU KNOW.

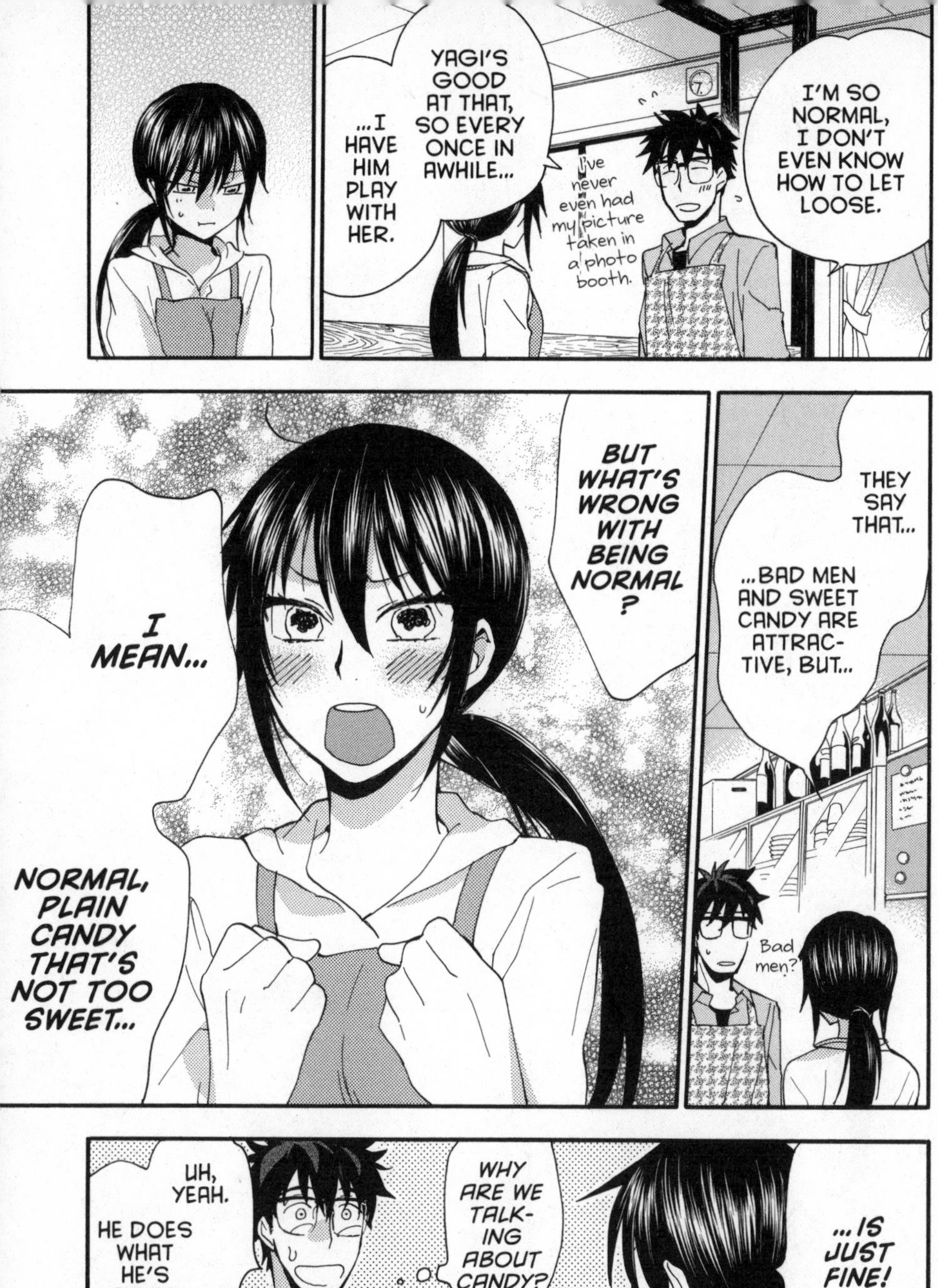
I'M SO NORMAL, I DON'T EVEN KNOW HOW TO LET LOOSE.
I've never even had my picture taken in a photo booth.
YAGI'S GOOD AT THAT, SO EVERY ONCE IN AWHILE...
...I HAVE HIM PLAY WITH HER.
THEY SAY THAT...
...BAD MEN AND SWEET CANDY ARE ATTRACTIVE, BUT...
Bad men?
BUT WHAT'S WRONG WITH BEING NORMAL?
I MEAN...
NORMAL, PLAIN CANDY THAT'S NOT TOO SWEET...
...IS JUST FINE!
WHY ARE WE TALKING ABOUT CANDY?
UH, YEAH.
HE DOES WHAT HE'S GOOD AT, AND SO DO I...

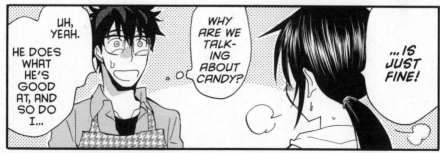

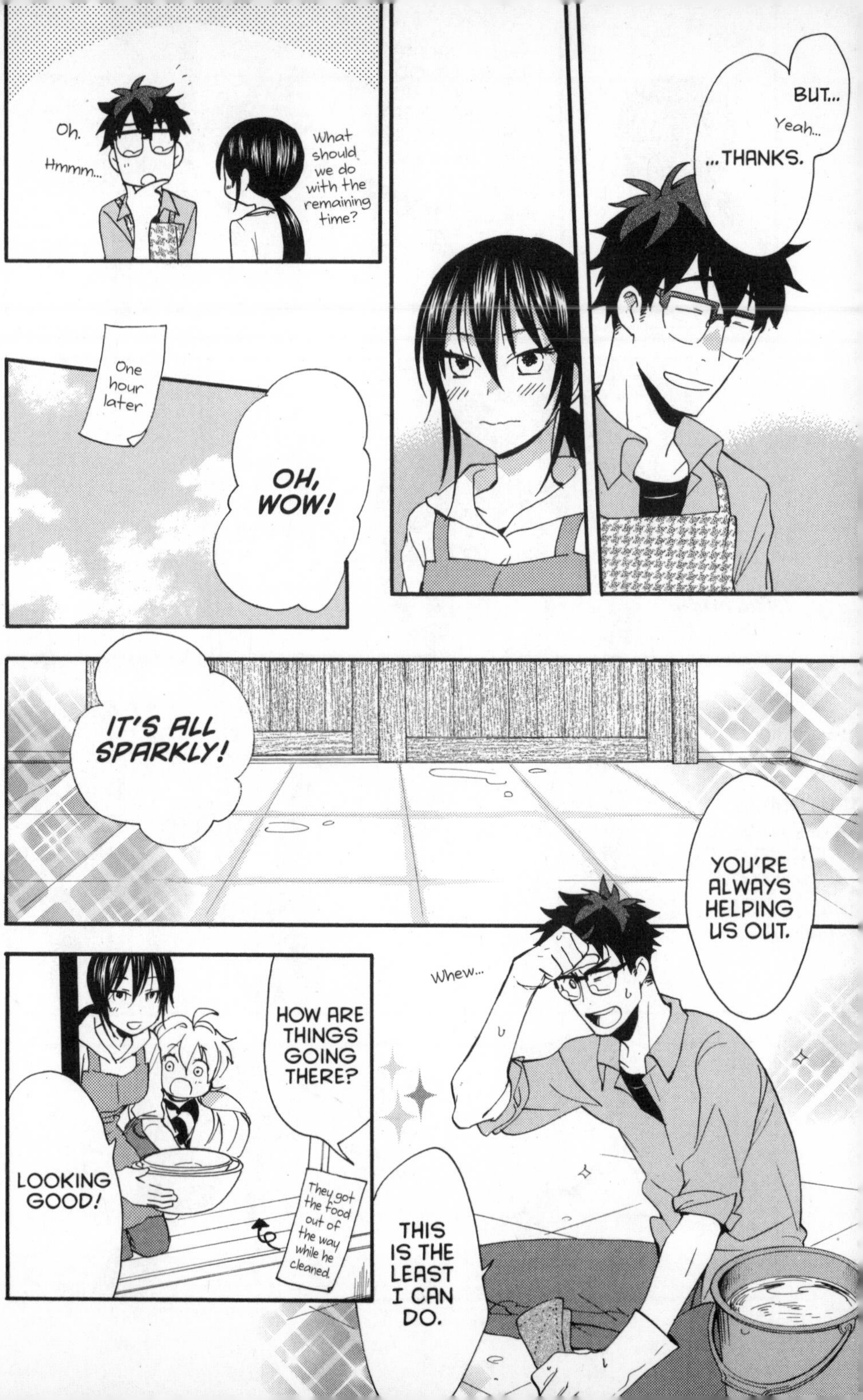
BUT...
Yeah...
...THANKS.
What should we do with the remaining time?
Oh.
Hmmm...
One hour later
OH, WOW!
IT'S ALL SPARKLY!
YOU'RE ALWAYS HELPING US OUT.
Whew...
THIS IS THE LEAST I CAN DO.
HOW ARE THINGS GOING THERE?
LOOKING GOOD!
They got the food out of the way while he cleaned.

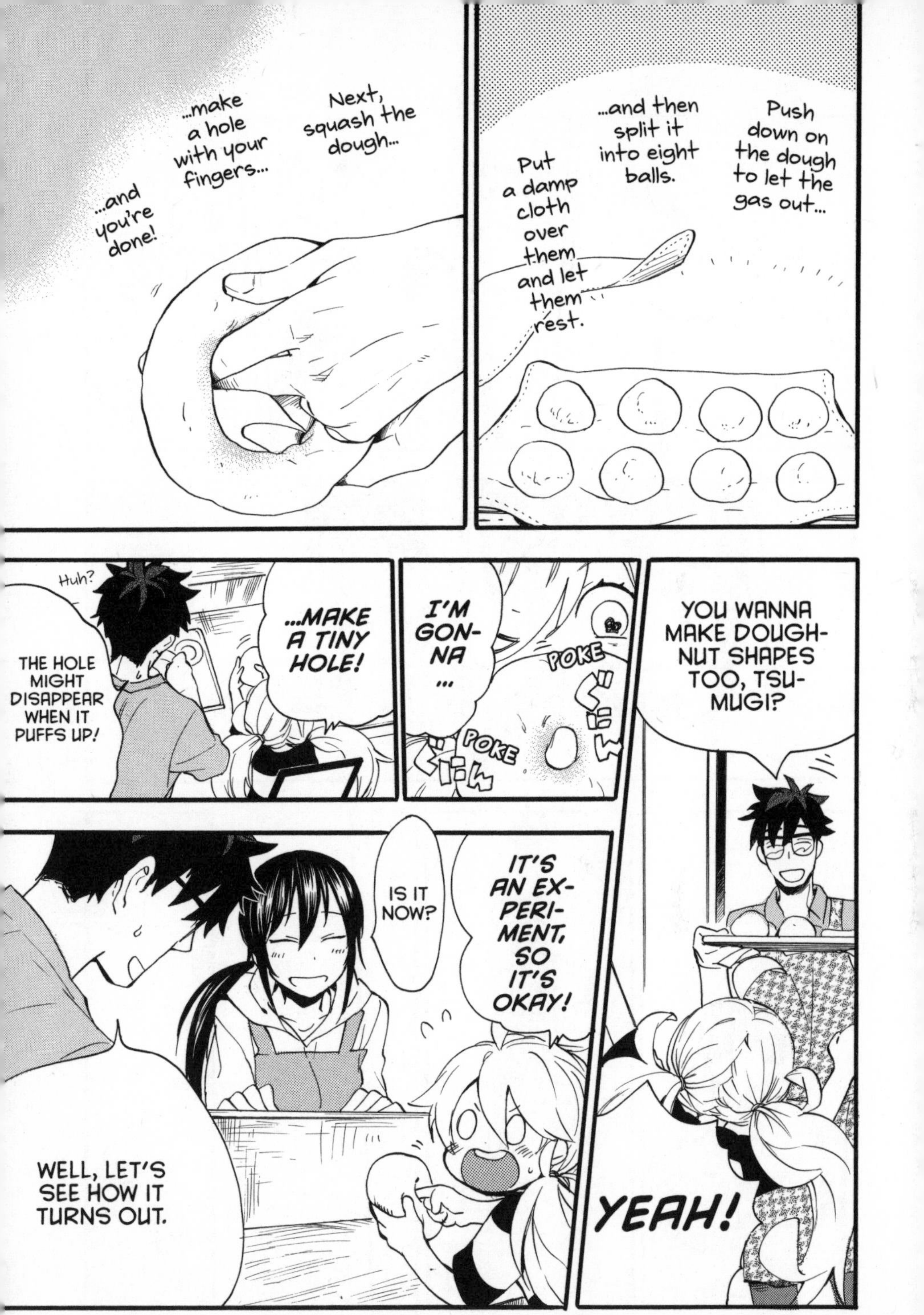
Push down on the dough to let the gas out...
...and then split it into eight balls.
Put a damp cloth over them and let them rest.
Next, squash the dough...
...make a hole with your fingers...
...and you're done!
YOU WANNA MAKE DOUGH-NUT SHAPES TOO, TSU-MUGI?
YEAH!
I'M GON-NA...
POKE
POKE
...MAKE A TINY HOLE!
Huh?
THE HOLE MIGHT DISAPPEAR WHEN IT PUFFS UP!
IT'S AN EX-PERI-MENT, SO IT'S OKAY!
IS IT NOW?
WELL, LET'S SEE HOW IT TURNS OUT.

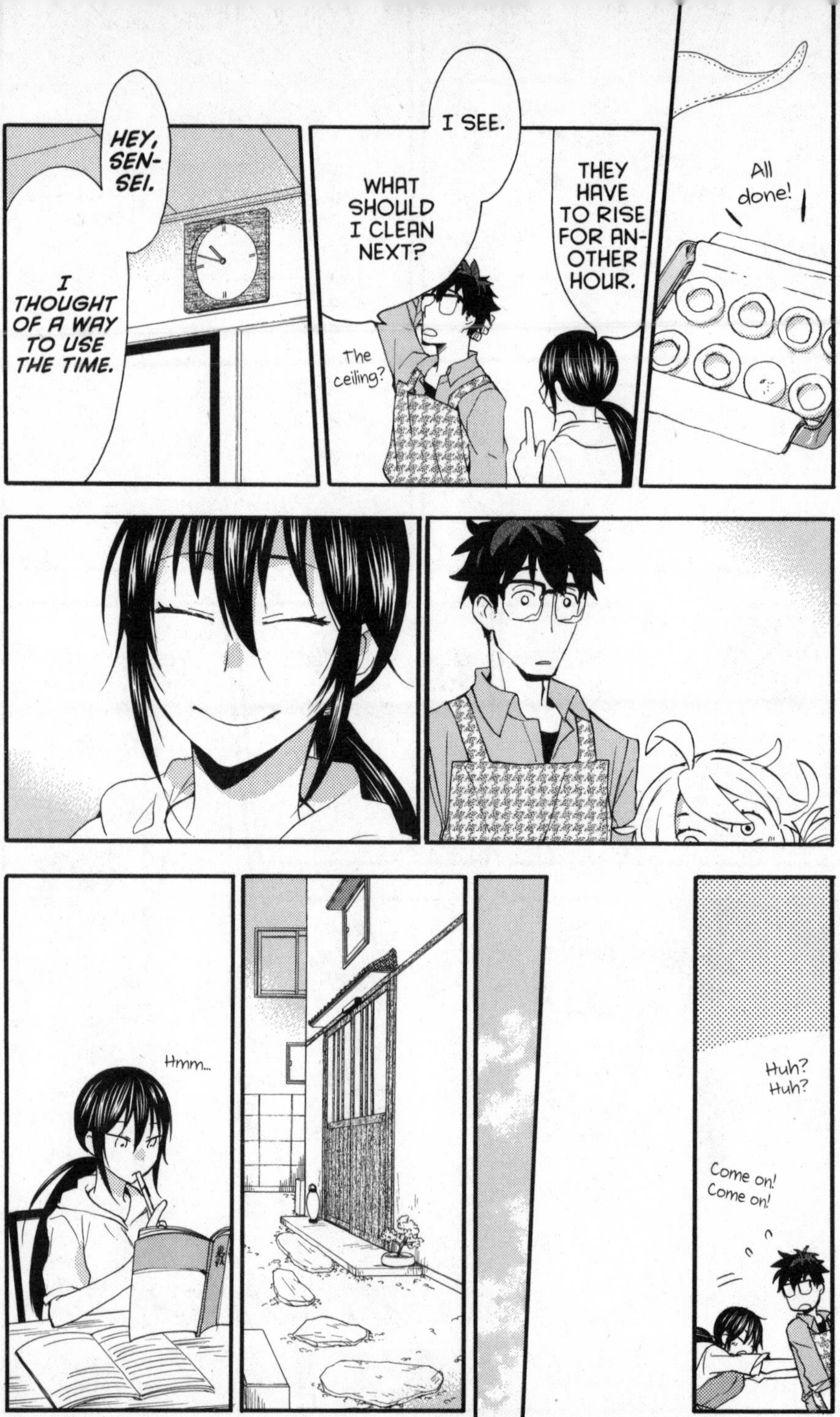
All done!
THEY HAVE TO RISE FOR AN-OTHER HOUR.
I SEE.
WHAT SHOULD I CLEAN NEXT?
The ceiling?
HEY, SEN-SEI.
I THOUGHT OF A WAY TO USE THE TIME.
Huh? Huh?
Come on! Come on!
Hmm...

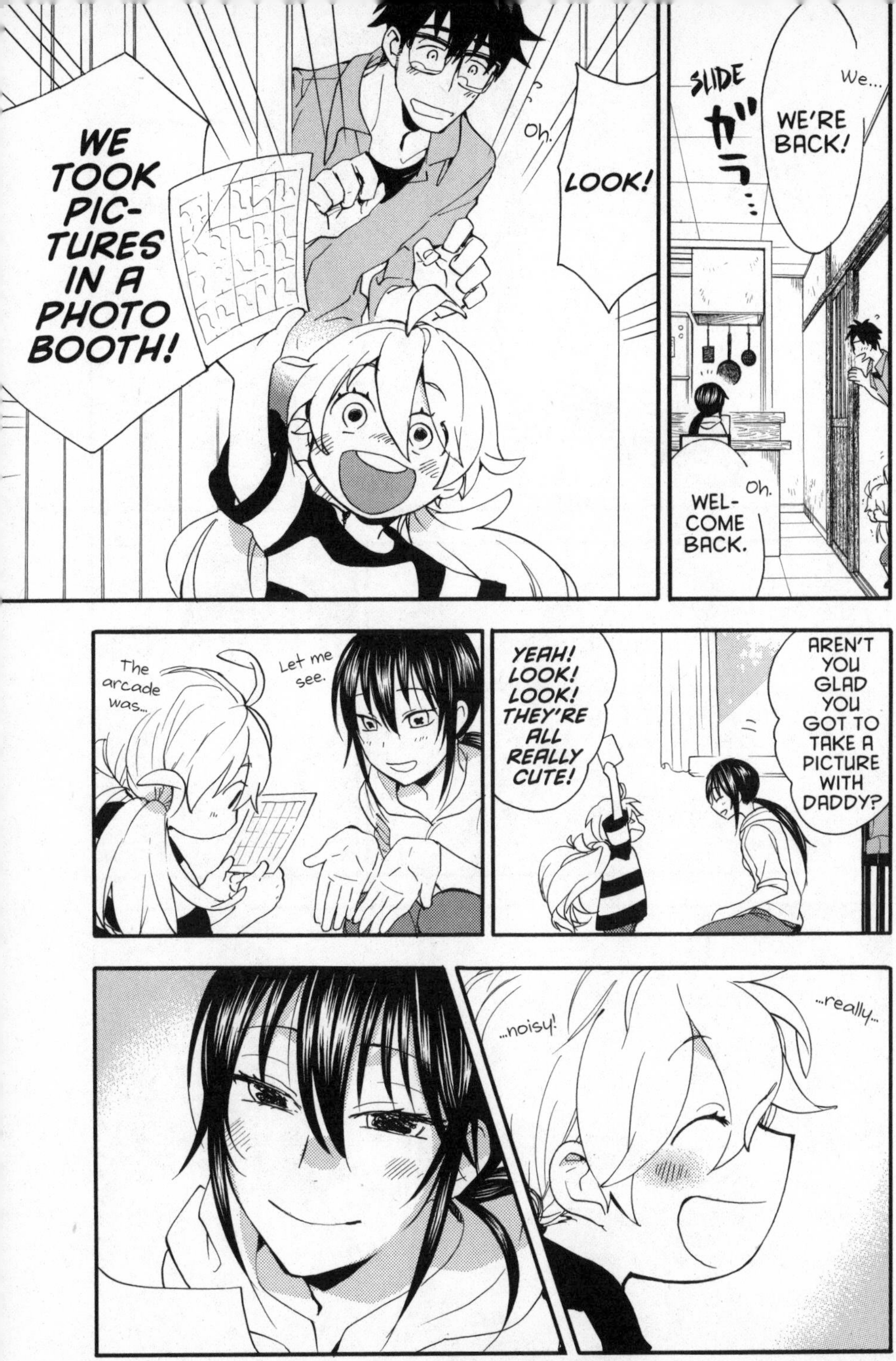
SLIDE
ガラ…
We…
WE'RE BACK!
Oh.
WEL-
COME
BACK.
Oh.
LOOK!
WE TOOK PIC-TURES IN A PHOTO BOOTH!
AREN'T YOU GLAD YOU GOT TO TAKE A PICTURE WITH DADDY?
YEAH! LOOK! LOOK! THEY'RE ALL REALLY CUTE!
Let me see.
The arcade was…
…really…
…noisy!

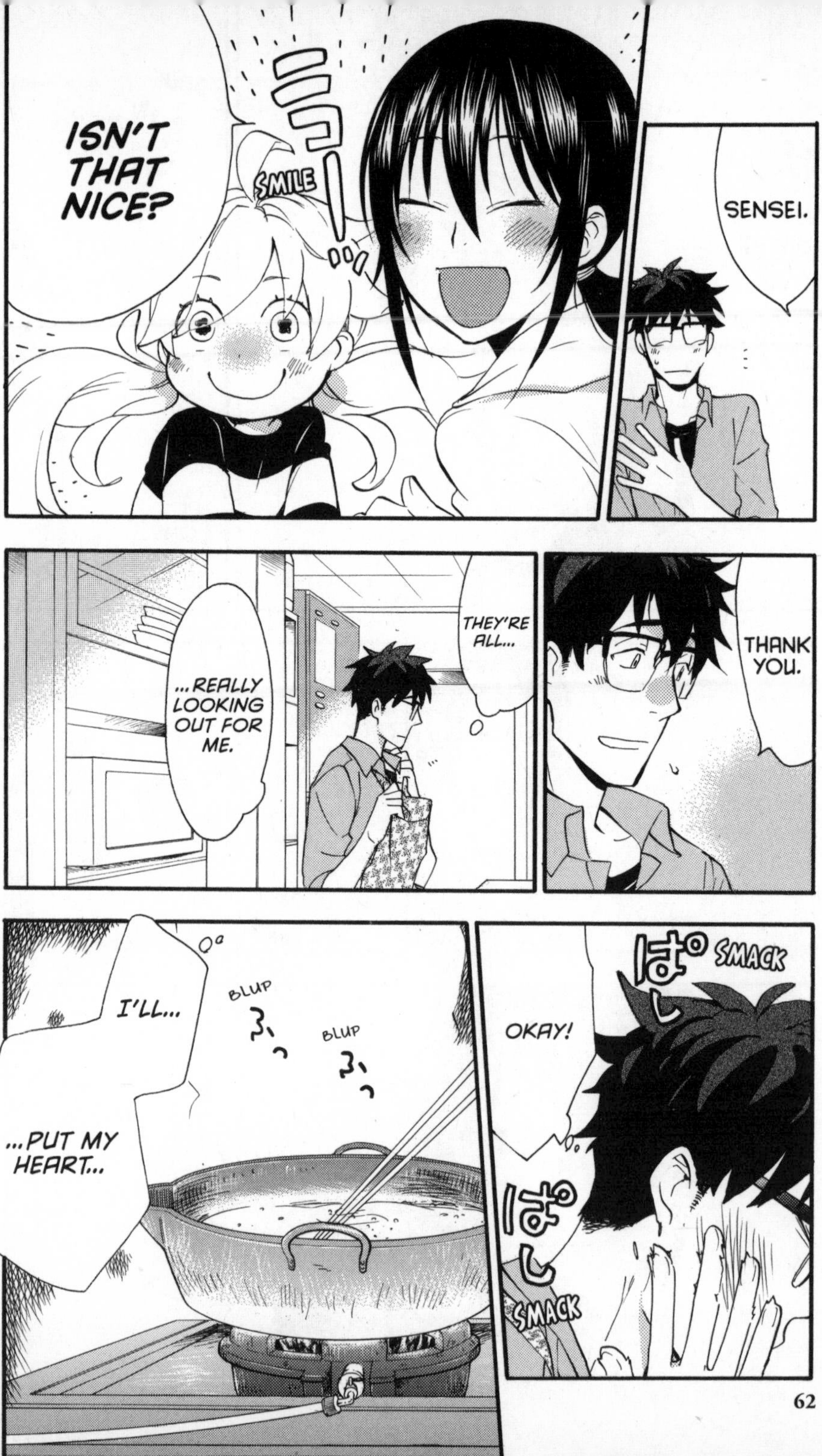
SENSEI.
ISN'T THAT NICE?
SMILE
THANK YOU.
THEY'RE ALL...
...REALLY LOOKING OUT FOR ME.
ぱし
SMACK
OKAY!
ぱし
SMACK
I'LL...
BLUP
ふっ
BLUP
ふっ
...PUT MY HEART...

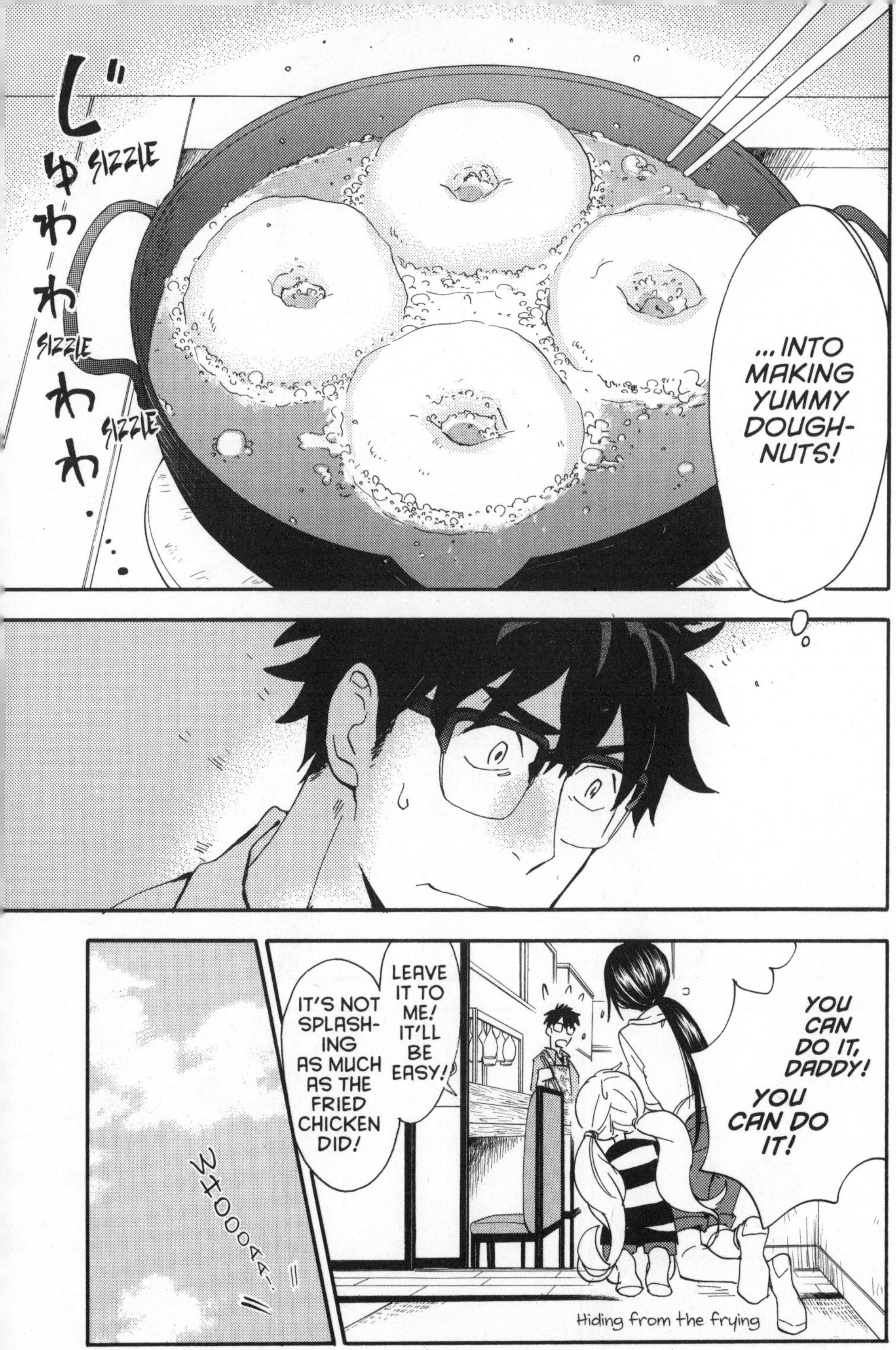
じゅわわわ
SIZZLE
SIZZLE
SIZZLE
...INTO MAKING YUMMY DOUGH-NUTS!
YOU CAN DO IT, DADDY!
YOU CAN DO IT!
LEAVE IT TO ME! IT'LL BE EASY!
IT'S NOT SPLASHING AS MUCH AS THE FRIED CHICKEN DID!
Hiding from the frying
WHOOOAA-!!

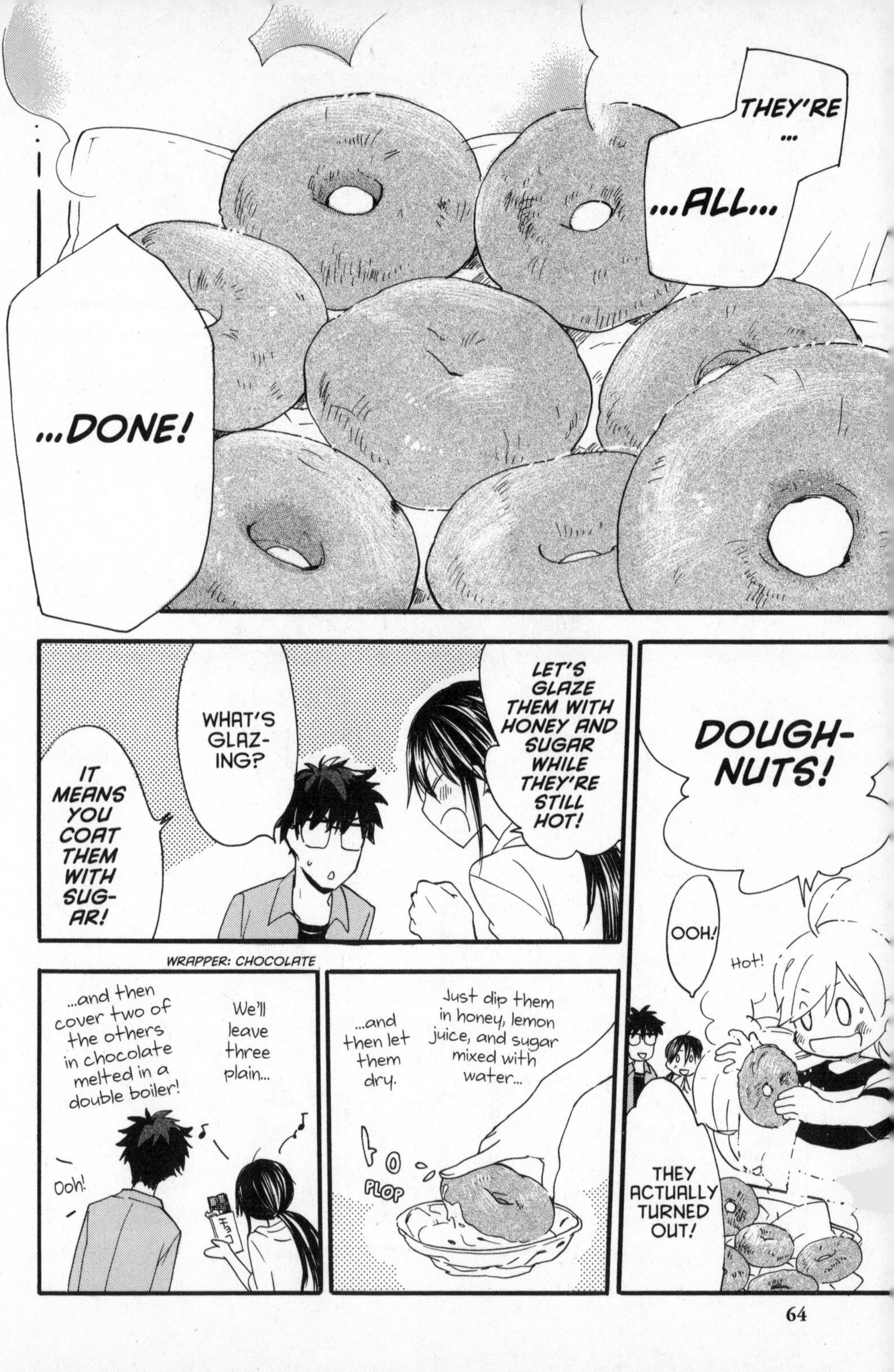
THEY'RE ...
...ALL...
...DONE!
DOUGH-NUTS!
OOH!
Hot!
THEY ACTUALLY TURNED OUT!
LET'S GLAZE THEM WITH HONEY AND SUGAR WHILE THEY'RE STILL HOT!
WHAT'S GLAZ-ING?
IT MEANS YOU COAT THEM WITH SUG-AR!
Just dip them in honey, lemon juice, and sugar mixed with water...
...and then let them dry.
PLOP
We'll leave three plain...
...and then cover two of the others in chocolate melted in a double boiler!
Ooh!
WRAPPER: CHOCOLATE

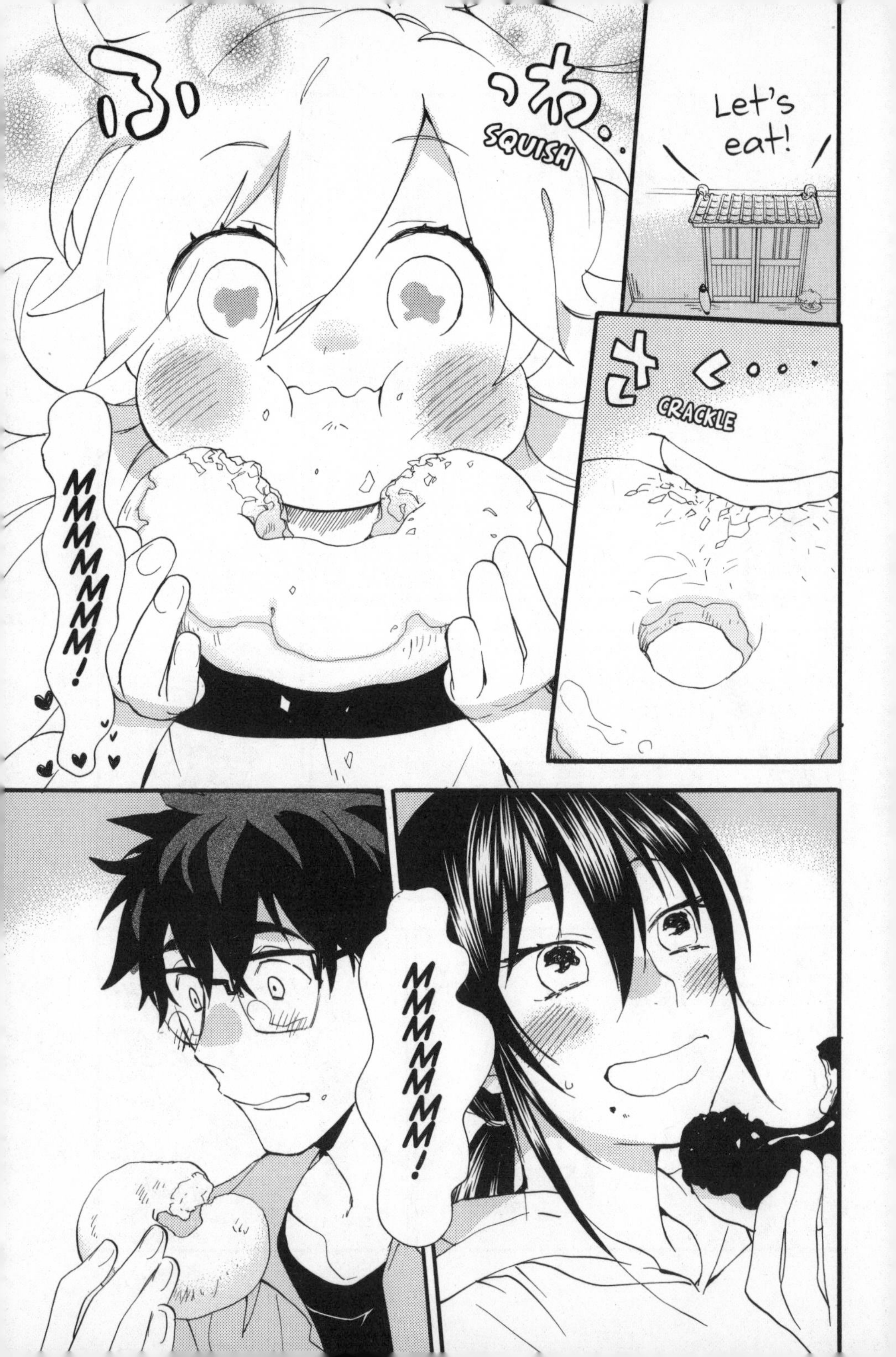

Let's eat!
さく・・・
CRACKLE
ふわっ。。
SQUISH
MMMMMMMM!
MMMMMMM!

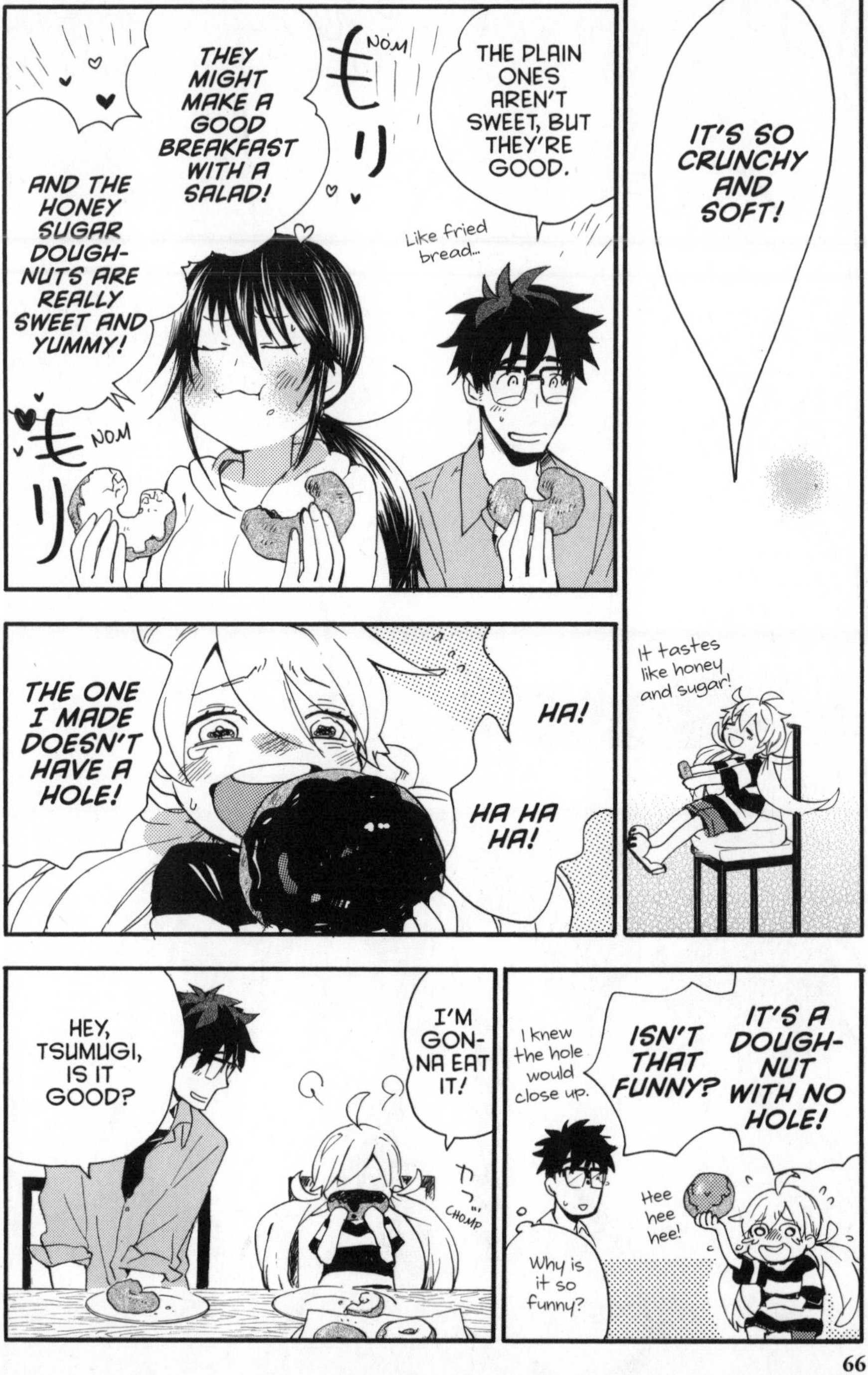
IT'S SO CRUNCHY AND SOFT!
It tastes like honey and sugar!
THE PLAIN ONES AREN'T SWEET, BUT THEY'RE GOOD.
Like fried bread...
モリ NOM
THEY MIGHT MAKE A GOOD BREAKFAST WITH A SALAD!
AND THE HONEY SUGAR DOUGHNUTS ARE REALLY SWEET AND YUMMY!
モリ NOM
HA!
HA HA HA!
THE ONE I MADE DOESN'T HAVE A HOLE!
IT'S A DOUGHNUT WITH NO HOLE!
ISN'T THAT FUNNY?
I knew the hole would close up.
Hee hee hee!
Why is it so funny?
I'M GONNA EAT IT!
カプ CHOMP
HEY, TSUMUGI, IS IT GOOD?

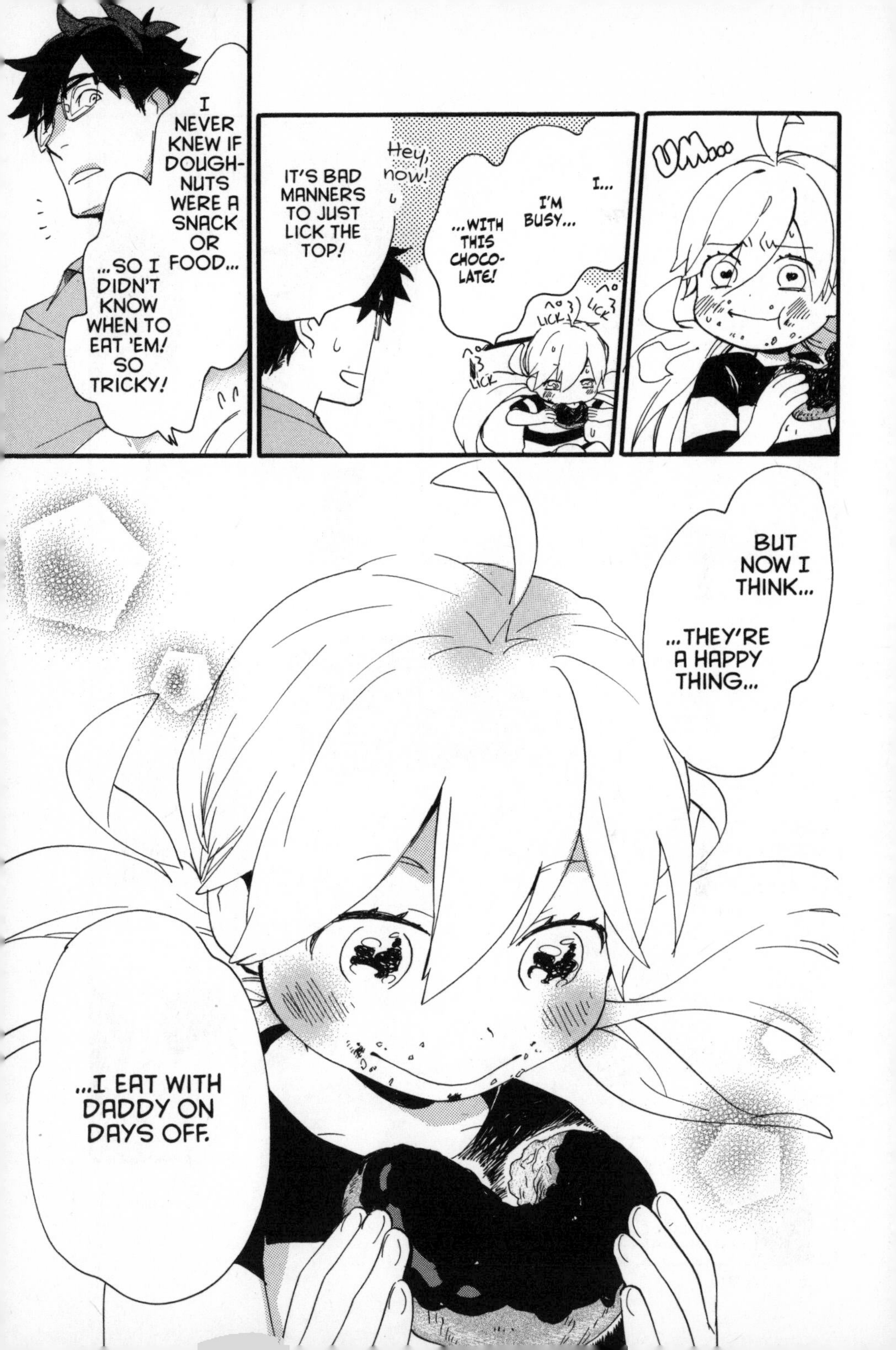
UM...
I...
I'M BUSY...
...WITH THIS CHOCOLATE!
LICK
LICK
LICK
Hey, now!
IT'S BAD MANNERS TO JUST LICK THE TOP!
I NEVER KNEW IF DOUGHNUTS WERE A SNACK OR FOOD...
...SO I DIDN'T KNOW WHEN TO EAT 'EM! SO TRICKY!
BUT NOW I THINK...
...THEY'RE A HAPPY THING...
...I EAT WITH DADDY ON DAYS OFF.

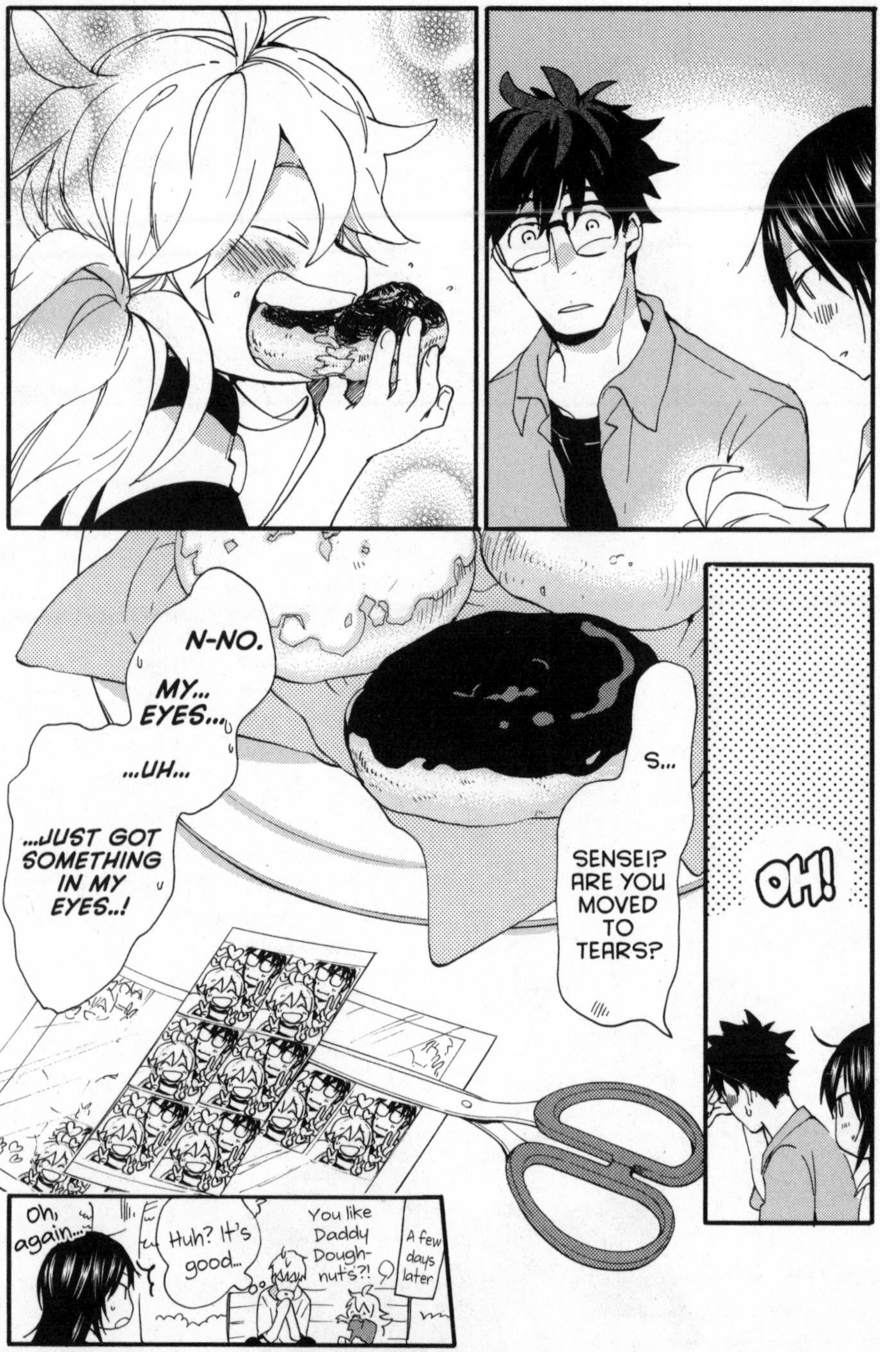
OH!
S...
SENSEI? ARE YOU MOVED TO TEARS?
N-NO.
MY... EYES...
...UH...
...JUST GOT SOMETHING IN MY EYES...!
A few days later
You like Daddy Dough-nuts?!
Huh? It's good...
Oh, again...

Chapter 7 - END

YEAST DOUGHNUTS

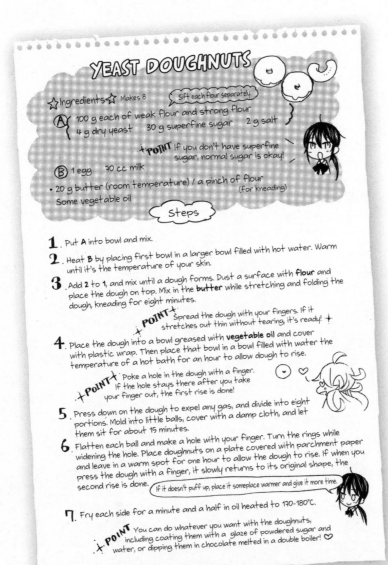

☆Ingredients☆ Makes 8

(Sift each flour separately.)

Ⓐ 100 g each of weak flour and strong flour
4 g dry yeast 30 g superfine sugar 2 g salt

POINT If you don't have superfine sugar, normal sugar is okay!

Ⓑ 1 egg 70 cc milk

- 20 g butter (room temperature) / a pinch of flour (for kneading)

Some vegetable oil

Steps

1. Put **A** into bowl and mix.
2. Heat **B** by placing first bowl in a larger bowl filled with hot water. Warm until it's the temperature of your skin.
3. Add **2** to **1**, and mix until a dough forms. Dust a surface with **flour** and place the dough on top. Mix in the **butter** while stretching and folding the dough, kneading for eight minutes.

   POINT Spread the dough with your fingers. If it stretches out thin without tearing, it's ready!

4. Place the dough into a bowl greased with **vegetable oil** and cover with plastic wrap. Then place that bowl in a bowl filled with water the temperature of a hot bath for an hour to allow dough to rise.

   POINT Poke a hole in the dough with a finger. If the hole stays there after you take your finger out, the first rise is done!

5. Press down on the dough to expel any gas, and divide into eight portions. Mold into little balls, cover with a damp cloth, and let them sit for about 15 minutes.
6. Flatten each ball and make a hole with your finger. Turn the rings while widening the hole. Place doughnuts on a plate covered with parchment paper and leave in a warm spot for one hour to allow the dough to rise. If when you press the dough with a finger, it slowly returns to its original shape, the second rise is done.

   (If it doesn't puff up, place it someplace warmer and give it more time.)

7. Fry each side for a minute and a half in oil heated to 170-180°C.

   POINT You can do whatever you want with the doughnuts, including coating them with a glaze of powdered sugar and water, or dipping them in chocolate melted in a double boiler! ♡

Sweetness & Lightning | Recipe — 7

CONVERSION NOTES:
100 G SIFTED FLOUR = ABOUT 1 CUP, 4 G DRY YEAST = .14 OZ, 30 G SUGAR = ABOUT 2 TBSP, 2 G SALT = ABOUT 3/4 TSP, 70 CC MILK = ABOUT 1/3 CUP, 20 G BUTTER = 4 TSP, 170-180°C = ABOUT 350°F

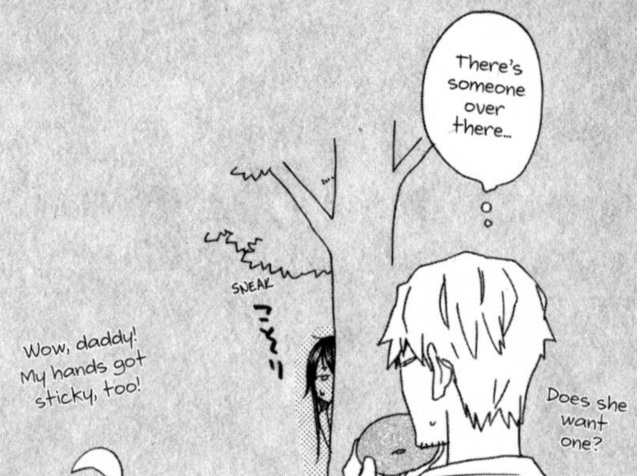
There's someone over there...
...
SNEAK
Does she want one?
Wow, daddy! My hands got sticky, too!

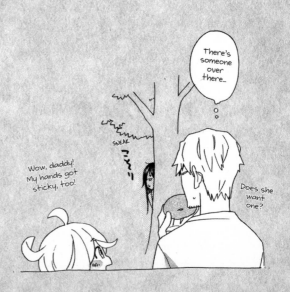

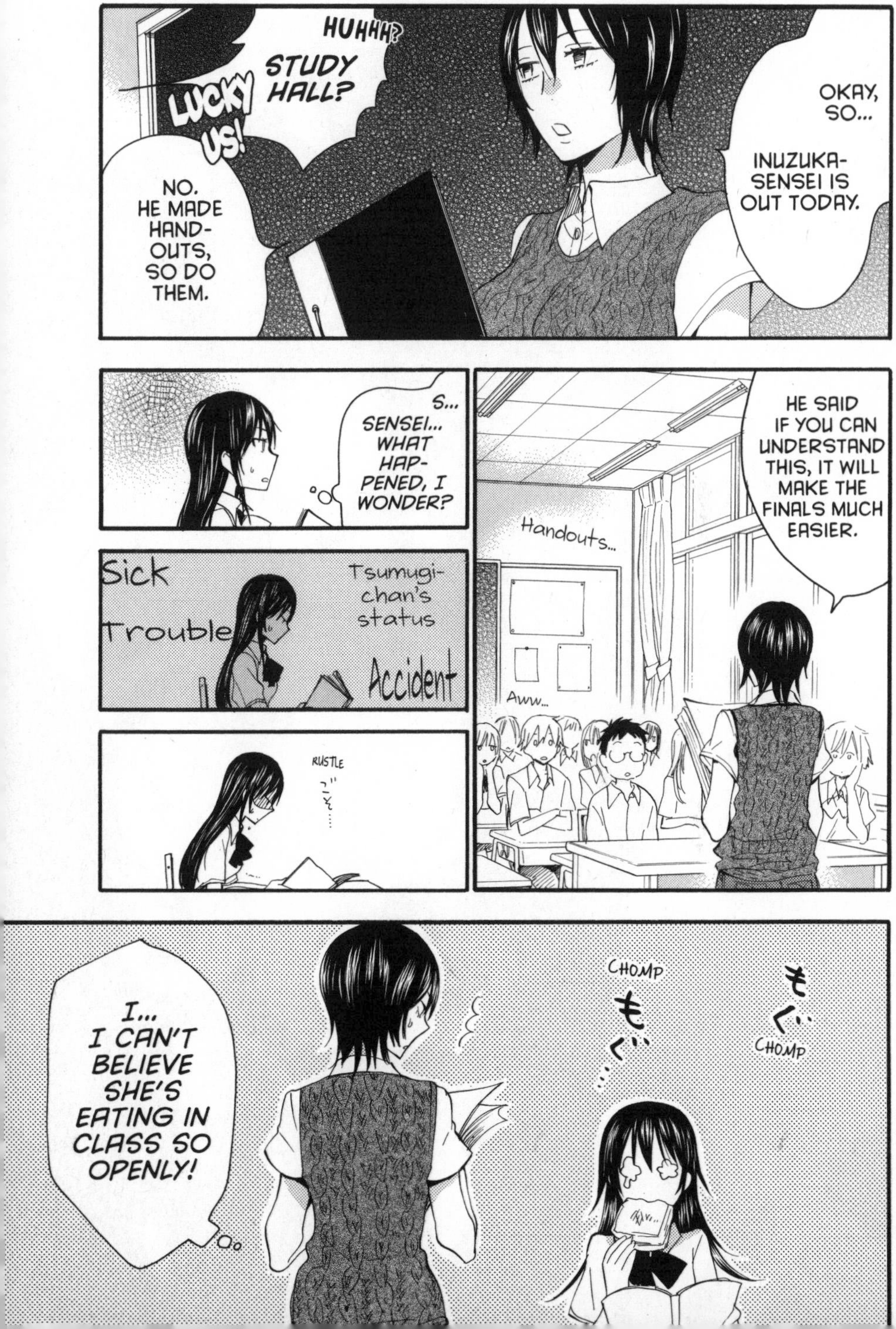
OKAY, SO...
INUZUKA-SENSEI IS OUT TODAY.
HUHHH?
STUDY HALL?
LUCKY US!
NO. HE MADE HAND-OUTS, SO DO THEM.
HE SAID IF YOU CAN UNDERSTAND THIS, IT WILL MAKE THE FINALS MUCH EASIER.
Handouts...
Aww...
S... SENSEI... WHAT HAP-PENED, I WONDER?
Tsumugi-chan's status
Sick
Trouble
Accident
RUSTLE
もぐ
CHOMP
もぐ
CHOMP
I... I CAN'T BELIEVE SHE'S EATING IN CLASS SO OPENLY!

Chapter 8 Squid and Taro Stew That's Still Yummy The Next Day

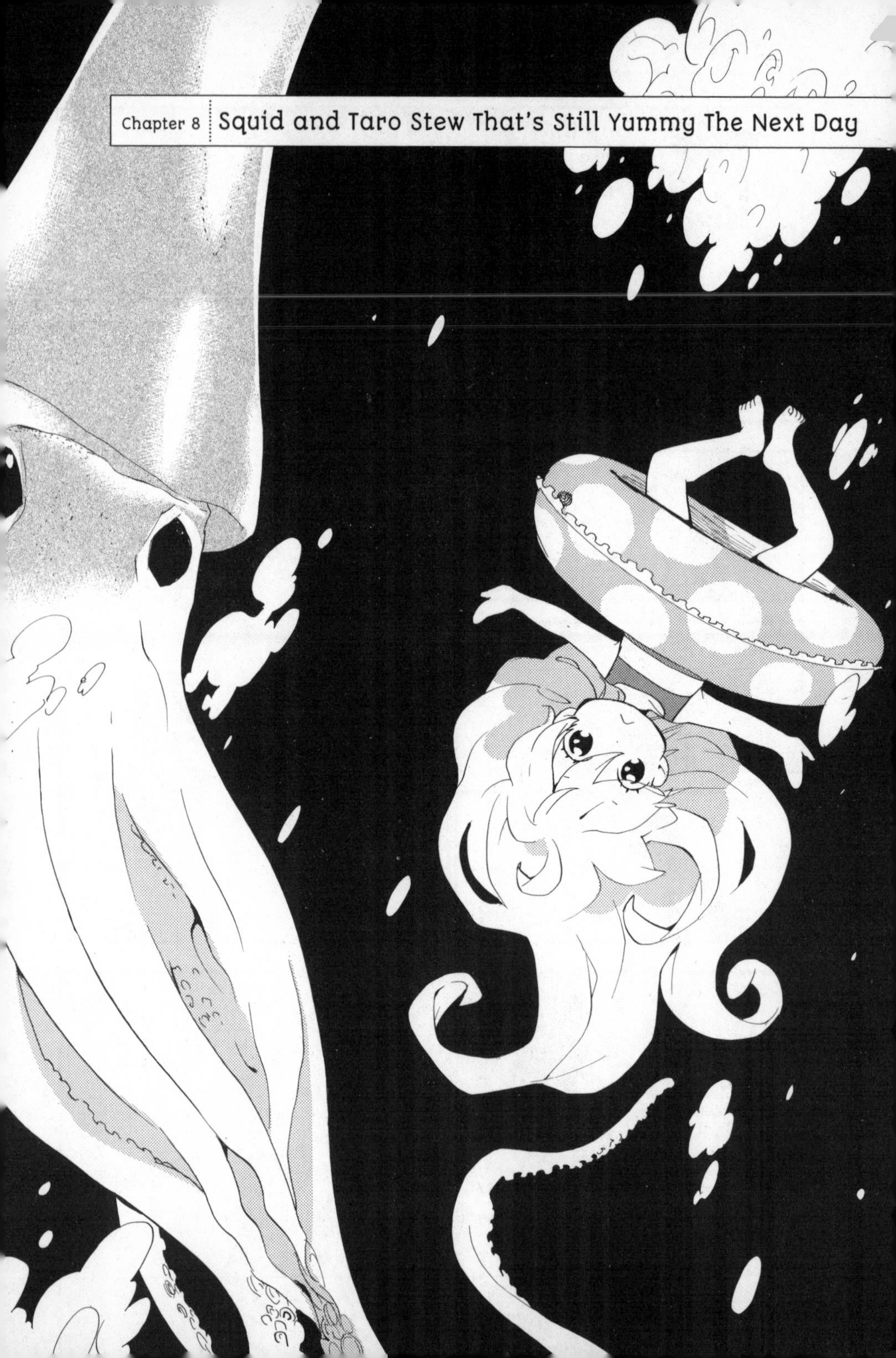

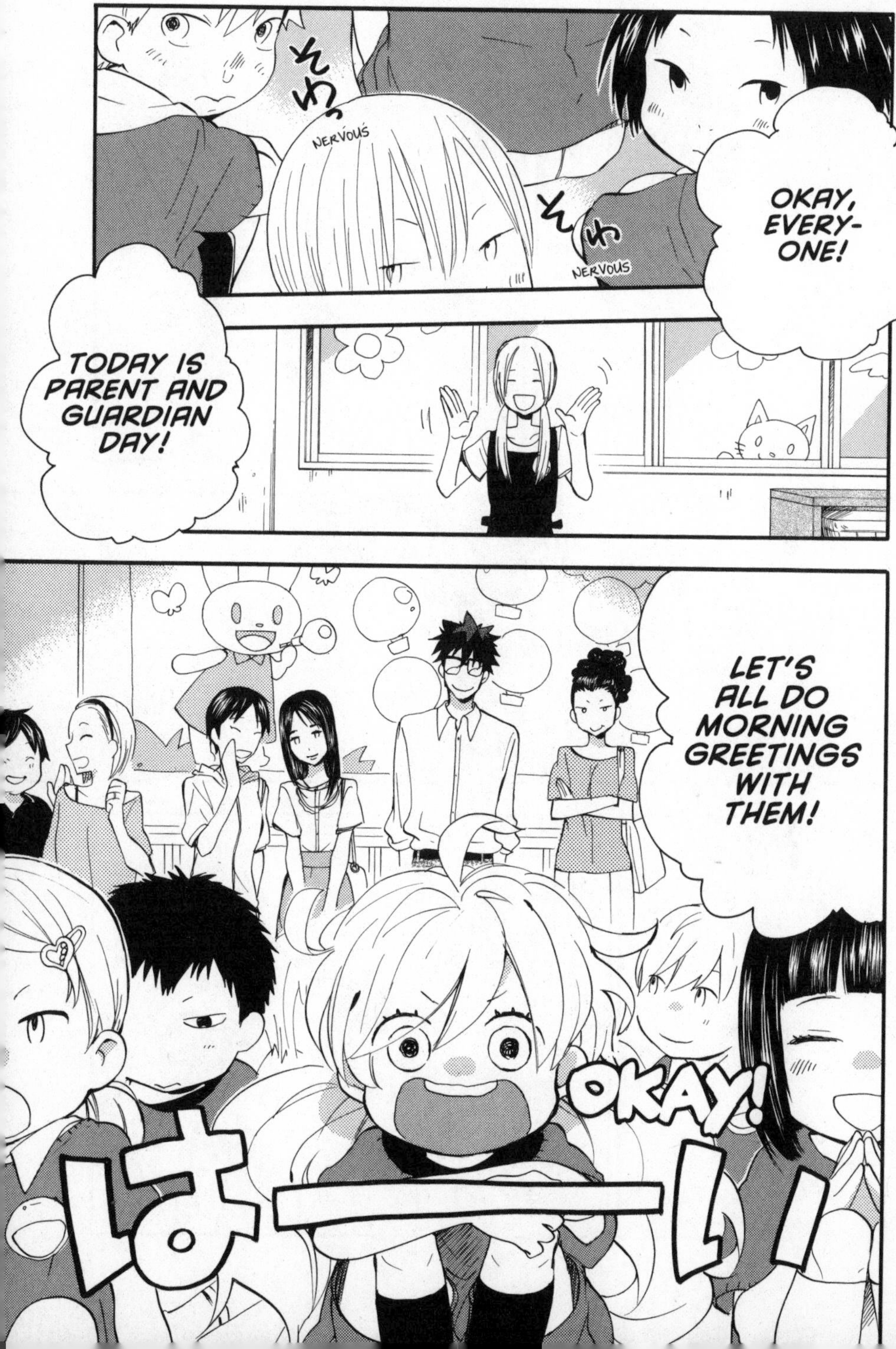
そわ
NERVOUS
そわっ
NERVOUS
OKAY, EVERYONE!
TODAY IS PARENT AND GUARDIAN DAY!
LET'S ALL DO MORNING GREETINGS WITH THEM!
OKAY!
はーい!

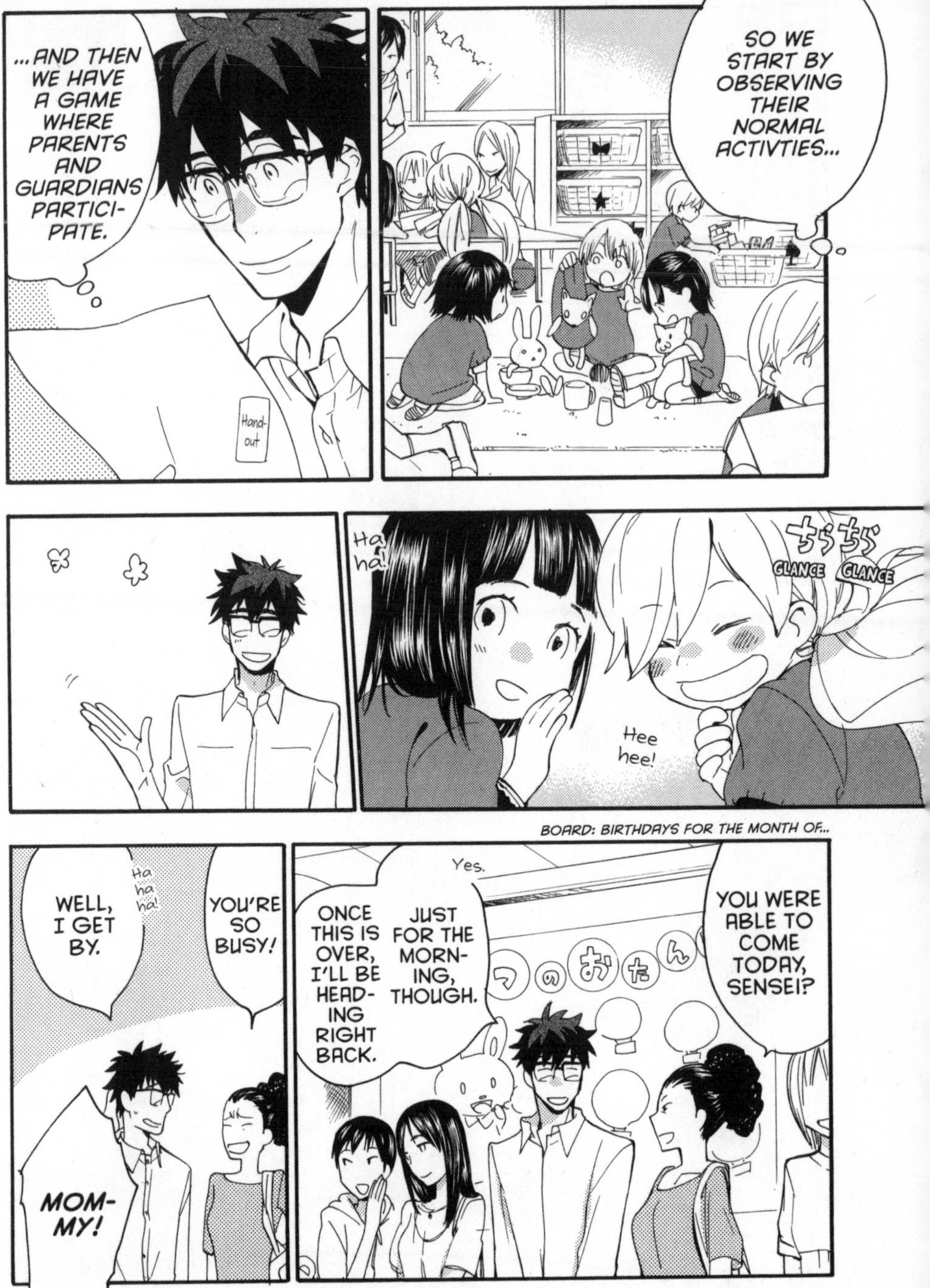
SO WE START BY OBSERVING THEIR NORMAL ACTIVTIES...
...AND THEN WE HAVE A GAME WHERE PARENTS AND GUARDIANS PARTICI-PATE.
Hand-out
ちらちら
GLANCE GLANCE
Ha ha!
Hee hee!
BOARD: BIRTHDAYS FOR THE MONTH OF...
YOU WERE ABLE TO COME TODAY, SENSEI?
Yes.
JUST FOR THE MORN-ING, THOUGH.
ONCE THIS IS OVER, I'LL BE HEAD-ING RIGHT BACK.
つのおたん
YOU'RE SO BUSY!
Ha ha ha!
WELL, I GET BY.
MOM-MY!

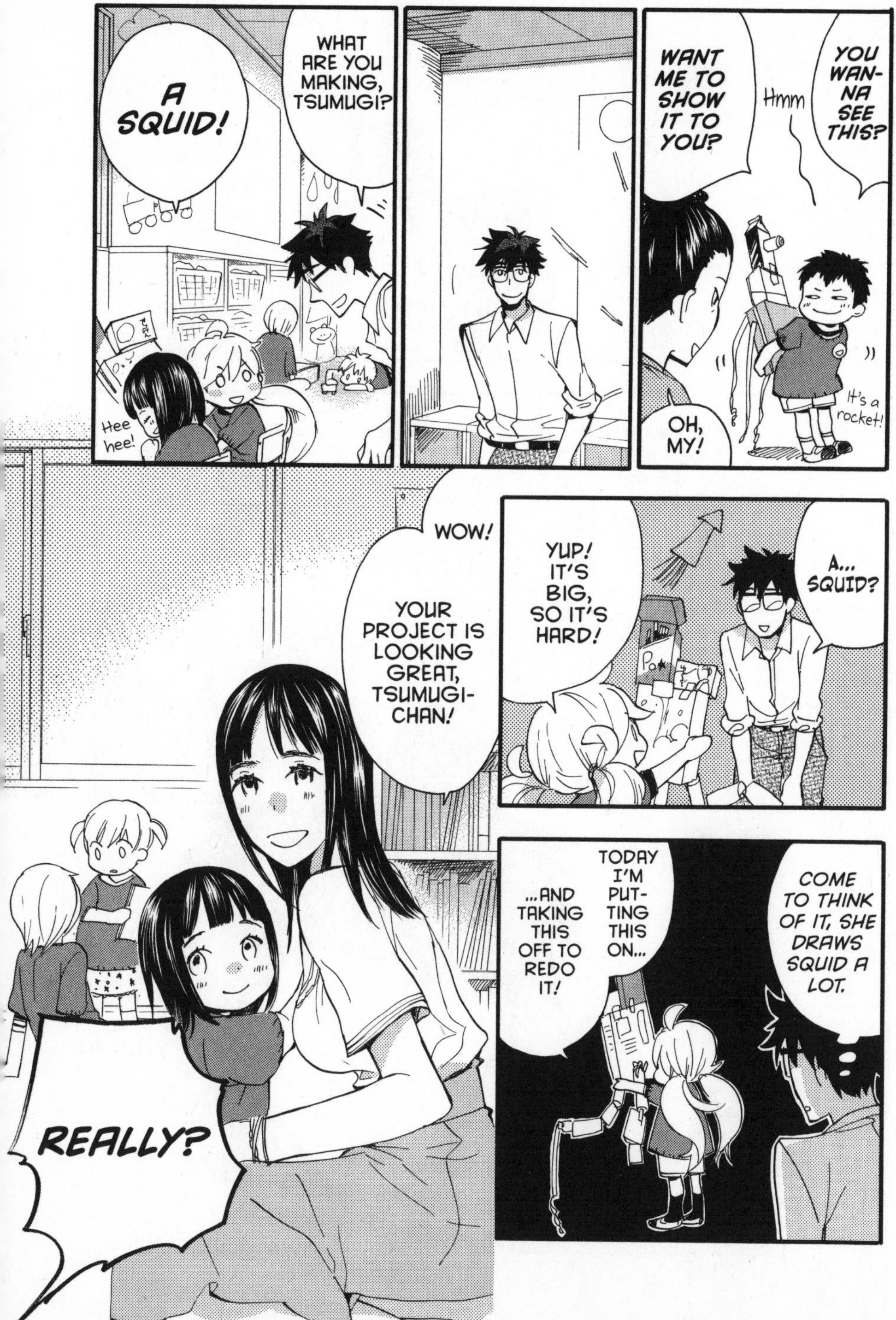
YOU WAN-NA SEE THIS?
Hmm
WANT ME TO SHOW IT TO YOU?
OH, MY!
It's a rocket!
WHAT ARE YOU MAKING, TSUMUGI?
A SQUID!
Hee hee!
A... SQUID?
YUP! IT'S BIG, SO IT'S HARD!
COME TO THINK OF IT, SHE DRAWS SQUID A LOT.
TODAY I'M PUT-TING THIS ON...
...AND TAKING THIS OFF TO REDO IT!
WOW!
YOUR PROJECT IS LOOKING GREAT, TSUMUGI-CHAN!
REALLY?

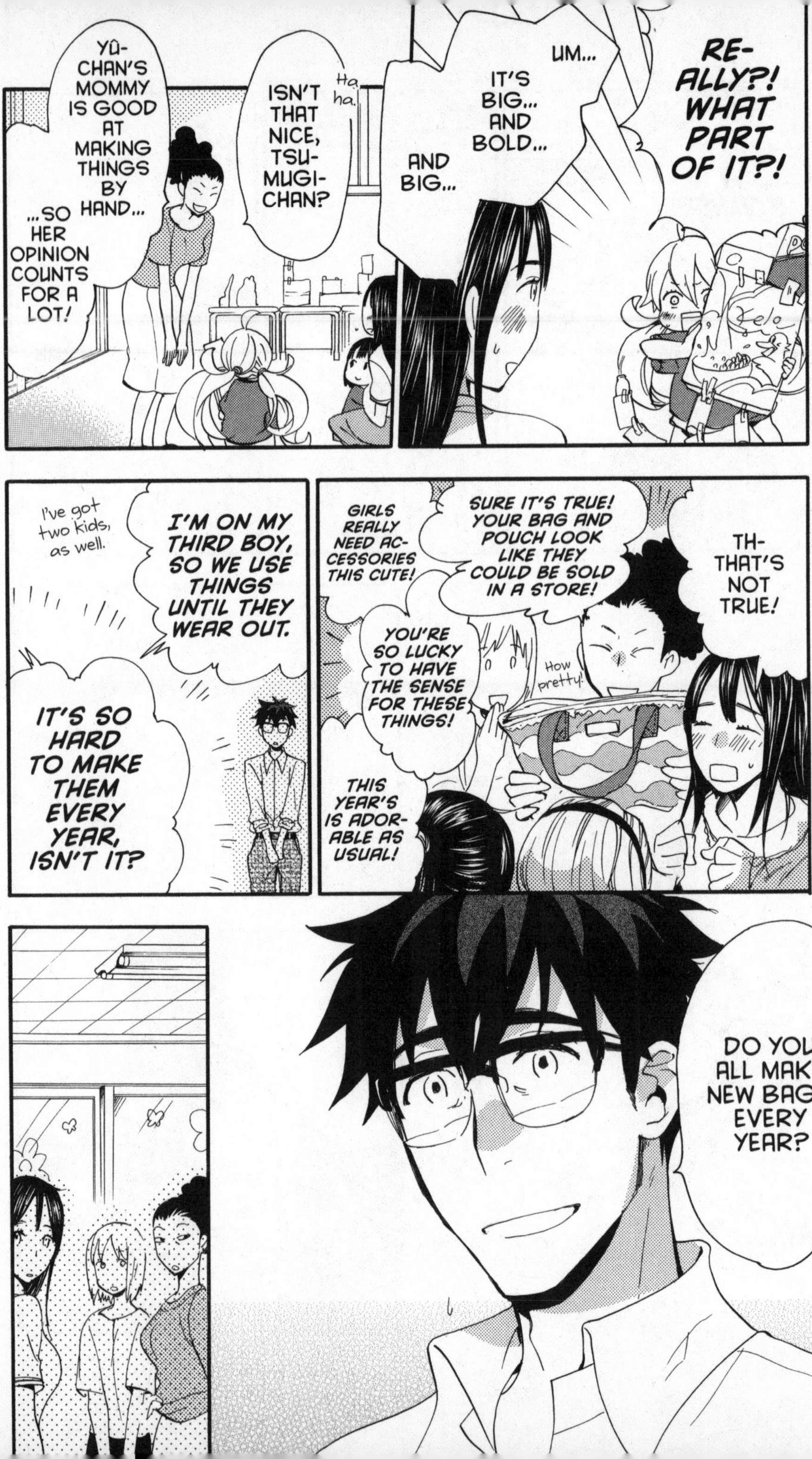
RE-ALLY?! WHAT PART OF IT?!
UM...
IT'S BIG... AND BOLD...
AND BIG...
Ha ha.
ISN'T THAT NICE, TSU-MUGI-CHAN?
YÛ-CHAN'S MOMMY IS GOOD AT MAKING THINGS BY HAND...
...SO HER OPINION COUNTS FOR A LOT!
TH-THAT'S NOT TRUE!
SURE IT'S TRUE! YOUR BAG AND POUCH LOOK LIKE THEY COULD BE SOLD IN A STORE!
GIRLS REALLY NEED AC-CESSORIES THIS CUTE!
How pretty!
YOU'RE SO LUCKY TO HAVE THE SENSE FOR THESE THINGS!
THIS YEAR'S IS ADOR-ABLE AS USUAL!
I'M ON MY THIRD BOY, SO WE USE THINGS UNTIL THEY WEAR OUT.
I've got two kids, as well.
IT'S SO HARD TO MAKE THEM EVERY YEAR, ISN'T IT?
DO YOU ALL MAKE NEW BAGS EVERY YEAR?

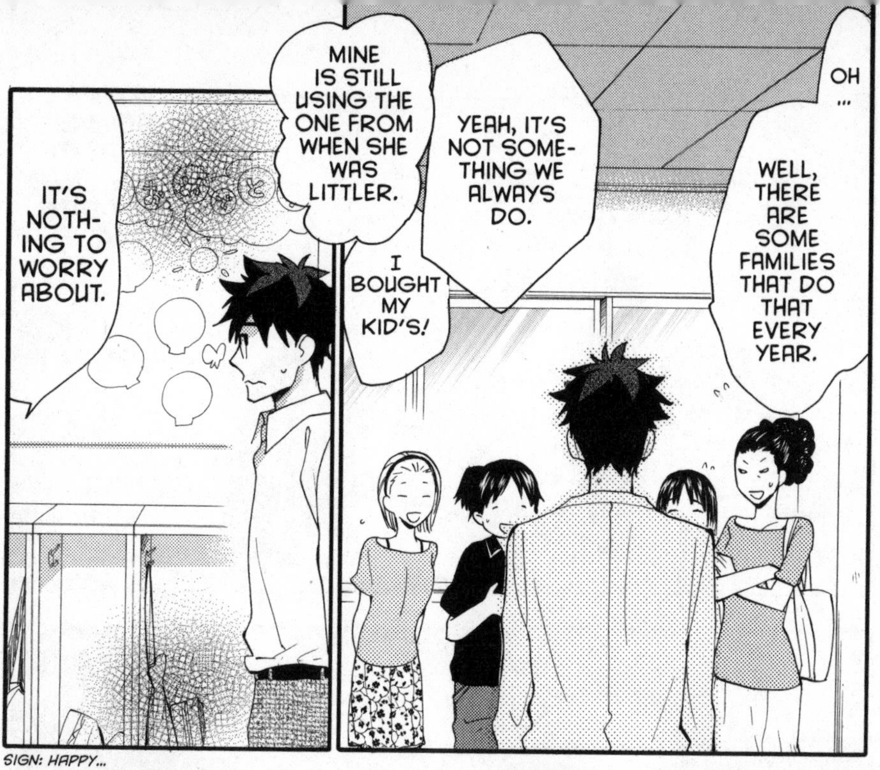
OH ...
WELL, THERE ARE SOME FAMILIES THAT DO THAT EVERY YEAR.
YEAH, IT'S NOT SOMETHING WE ALWAYS DO.
MINE IS STILL USING THE ONE FROM WHEN SHE WAS LITTLER.
I BOUGHT MY KID'S!
IT'S NOTHING TO WORRY ABOUT.
SIGN: HAPPY...

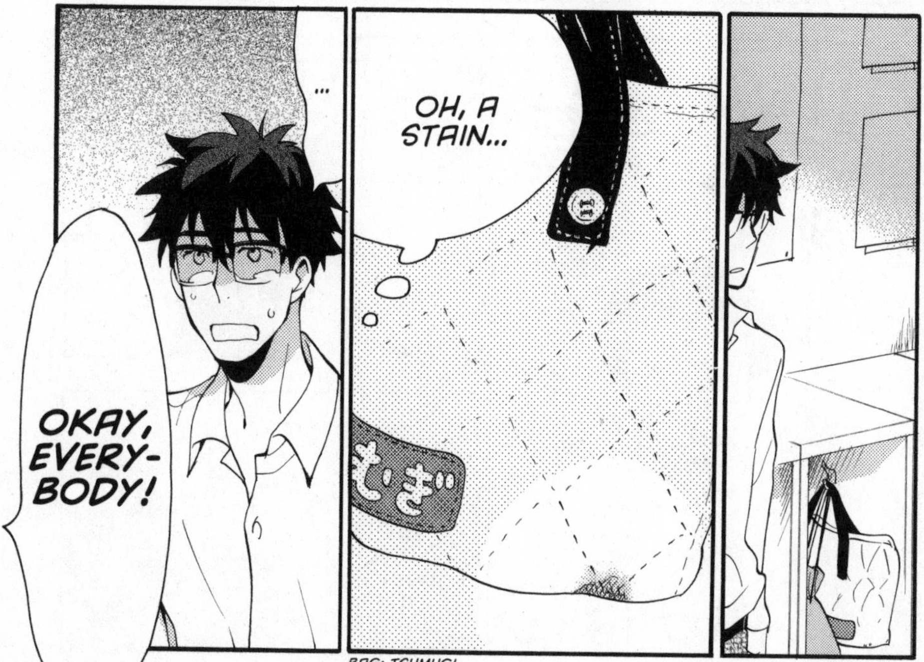
OH, A STAIN...
...
OKAY, EVERYBODY!
BAG: TSUMUGI

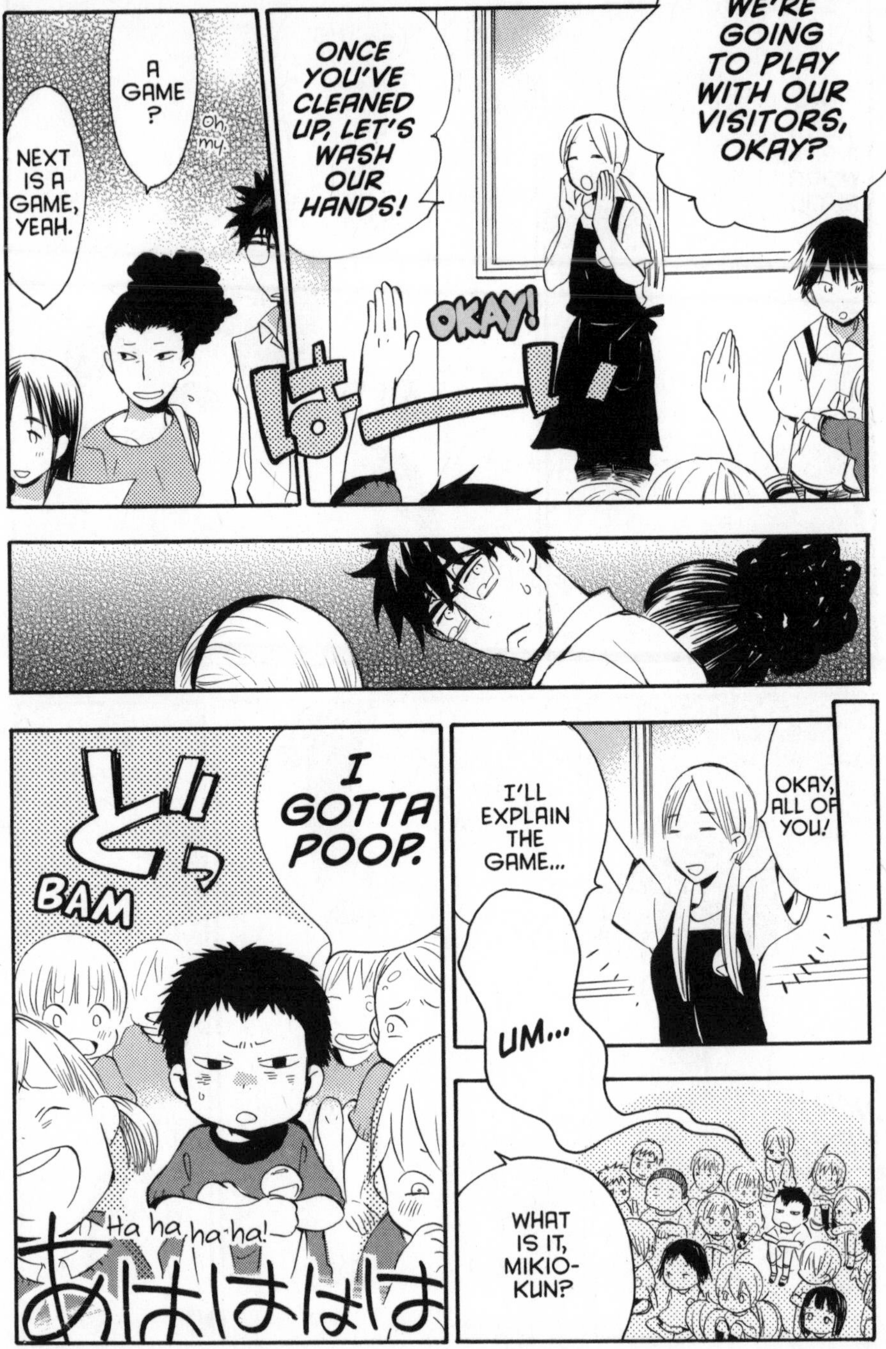
WE'RE GOING TO PLAY WITH OUR VISITORS, OKAY?
ONCE YOU'VE CLEANED UP, LET'S WASH OUR HANDS!
OKAY!
はーーい
A GAME?
Oh, my.
NEXT IS A GAME, YEAH.
OKAY, ALL OF YOU!
I'LL EXPLAIN THE GAME...
UM...
WHAT IS IT, MIKIO-KUN?
I GOTTA POOP.
どっ
BAM
Ha ha ha ha!
あははははは

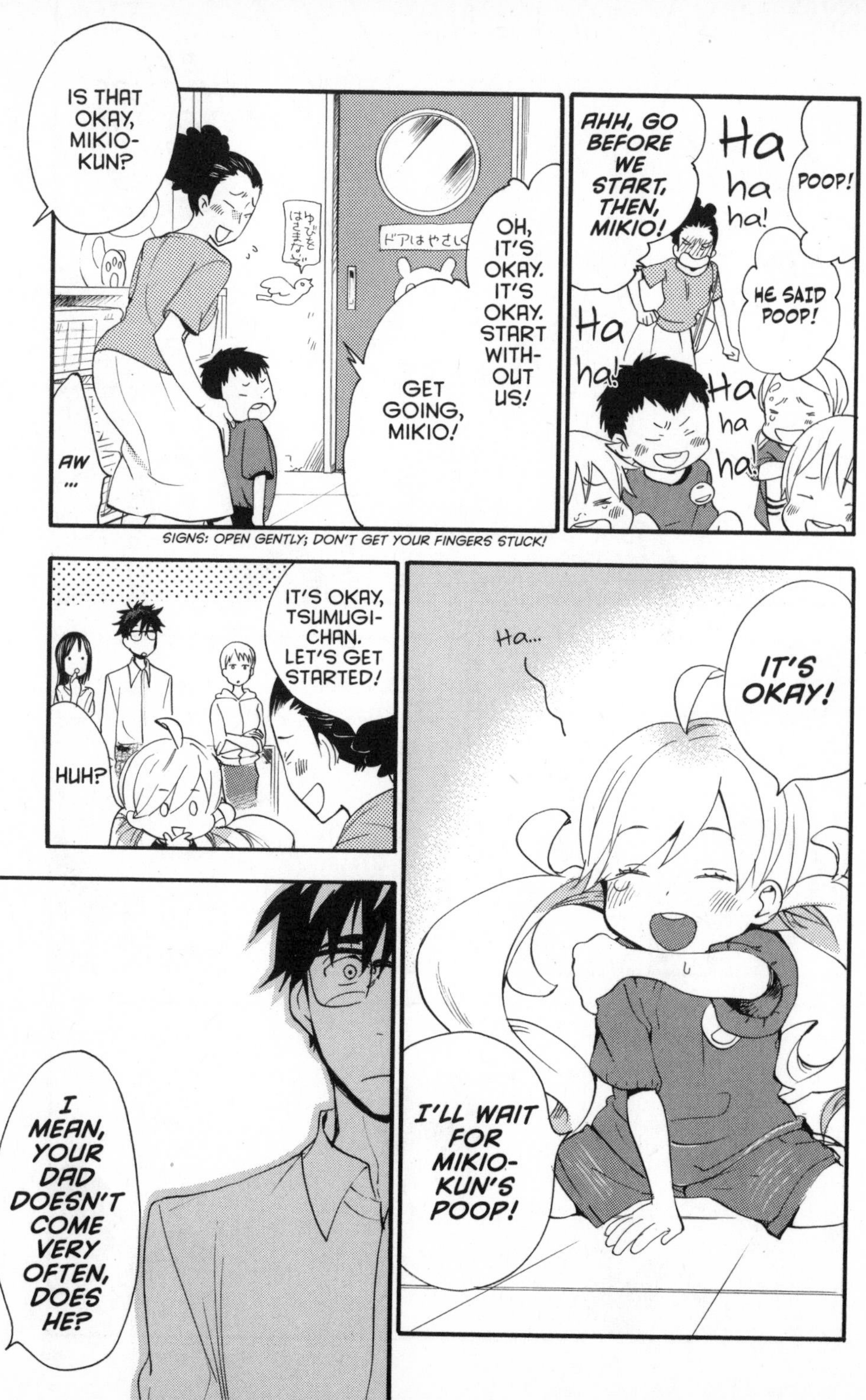
AHH, GO BEFORE WE START, THEN, MIKIO!
Ha ha ha!
POOP!
HE SAID POOP!
Ha ha!
Ha ha ha!
IS THAT OKAY, MIKIO-KUN?
ドアはやさしく
OH, IT'S OKAY. IT'S OKAY. START WITH-OUT US!
GET GOING, MIKIO!
AW ...
Ha...
IT'S OKAY!
I'LL WAIT FOR MIKIO-KUN'S POOP!
IT'S OKAY, TSUMUGI-CHAN. LET'S GET STARTED!
HUH?
I MEAN, YOUR DAD DOESN'T COME VERY OFTEN, DOES HE?
SIGNS: OPEN GENTLY; DON'T GET YOUR FINGERS STUCK!

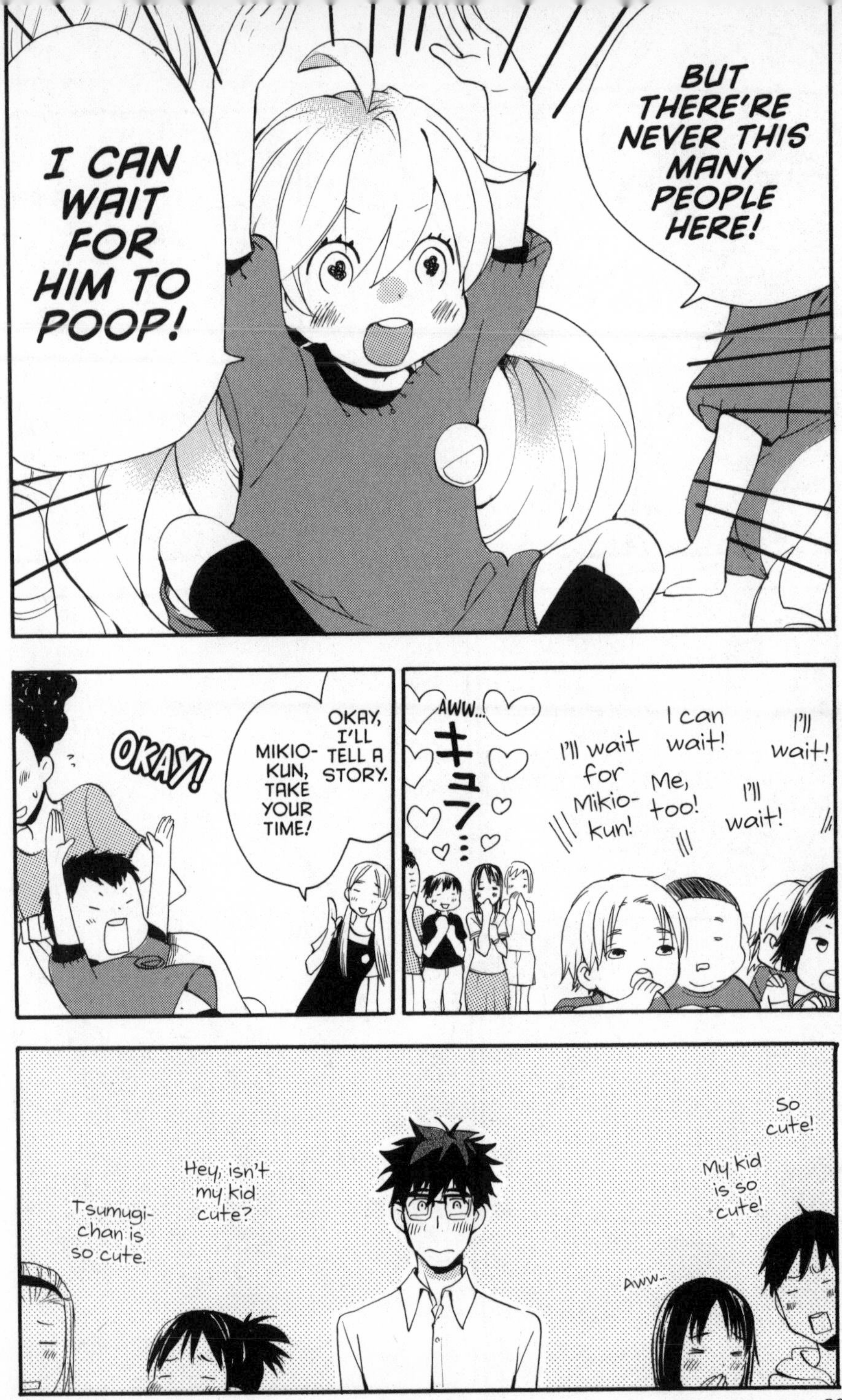

BUT THERE'RE NEVER THIS MANY PEOPLE HERE!
I CAN WAIT FOR HIM TO POOP!
AWW...
キュン
I can wait!
I'll wait!
I'll wait for Mikio-kun!
Me, too!
I'll wait!
OKAY, I'LL TELL A STORY.
MIKIO-KUN, TAKE YOUR TIME!
OKAY!
So cute!
My kid is so cute!
Aww...
Hey, isn't my kid cute?
Tsumugi-chan is so cute.

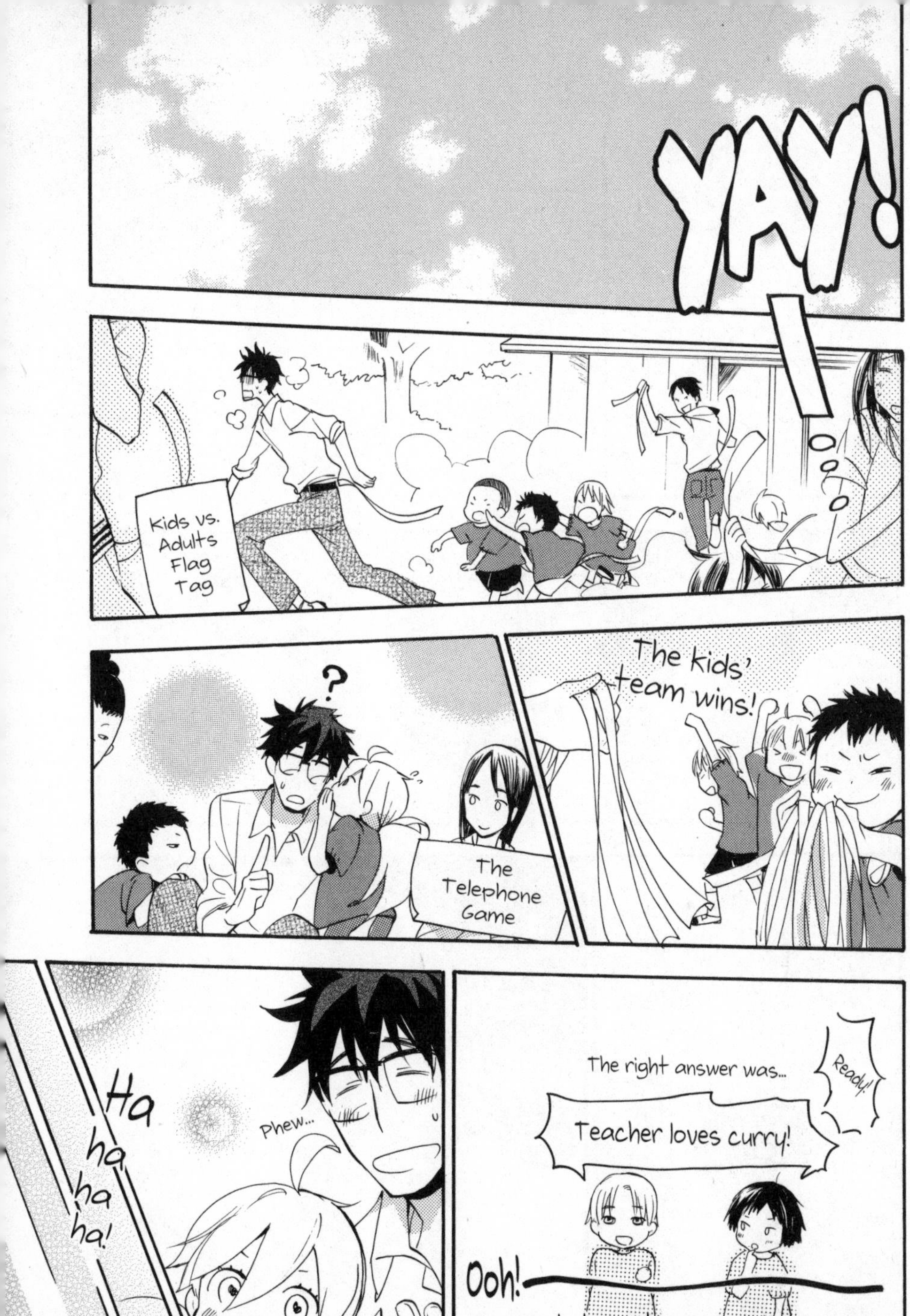
YAY!
Kids vs. Adults Flag Tag
The kids' team wins!
?
The Telephone Game
Ready!
The right answer was...
Teacher loves curry!
Ooh! You got it right!
Phew...
Ha ha ha ha!

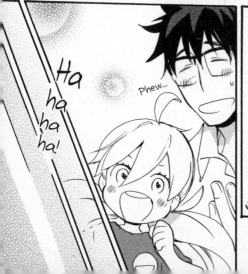

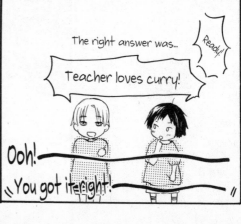

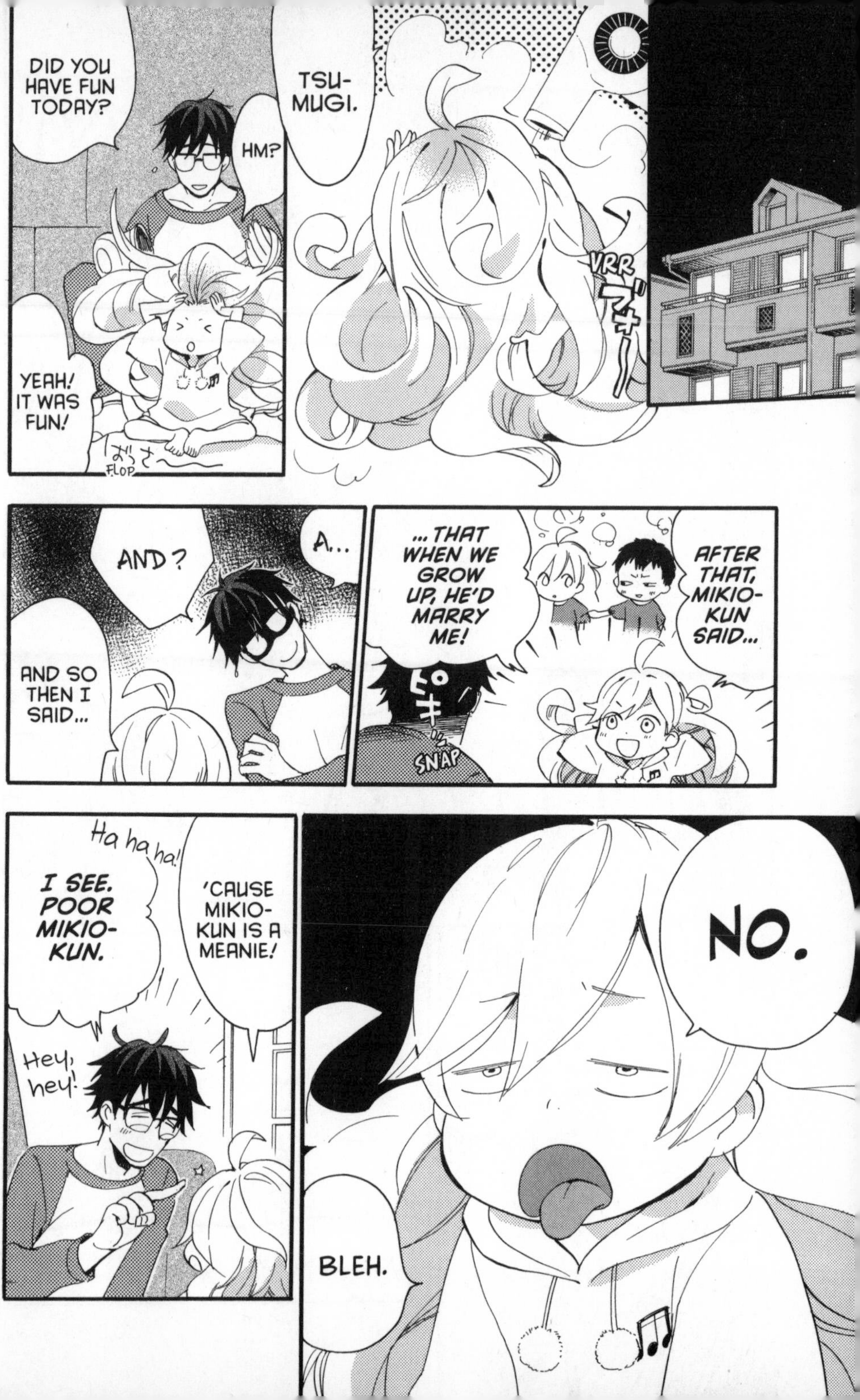
VRR
TSU-MUGI.
HM?
DID YOU HAVE FUN TODAY?
YEAH! IT WAS FUN!
FLOP
AFTER THAT, MIKIO-KUN SAID...
...THAT WHEN WE GROW UP, HE'D MARRY ME!
SNAP
A...
AND?
AND SO THEN I SAID...
NO.
BLEH.
'CAUSE MIKIO-KUN IS A MEANIE!
Ha ha ha!
I SEE. POOR MIKIO-KUN.
Hey, hey!

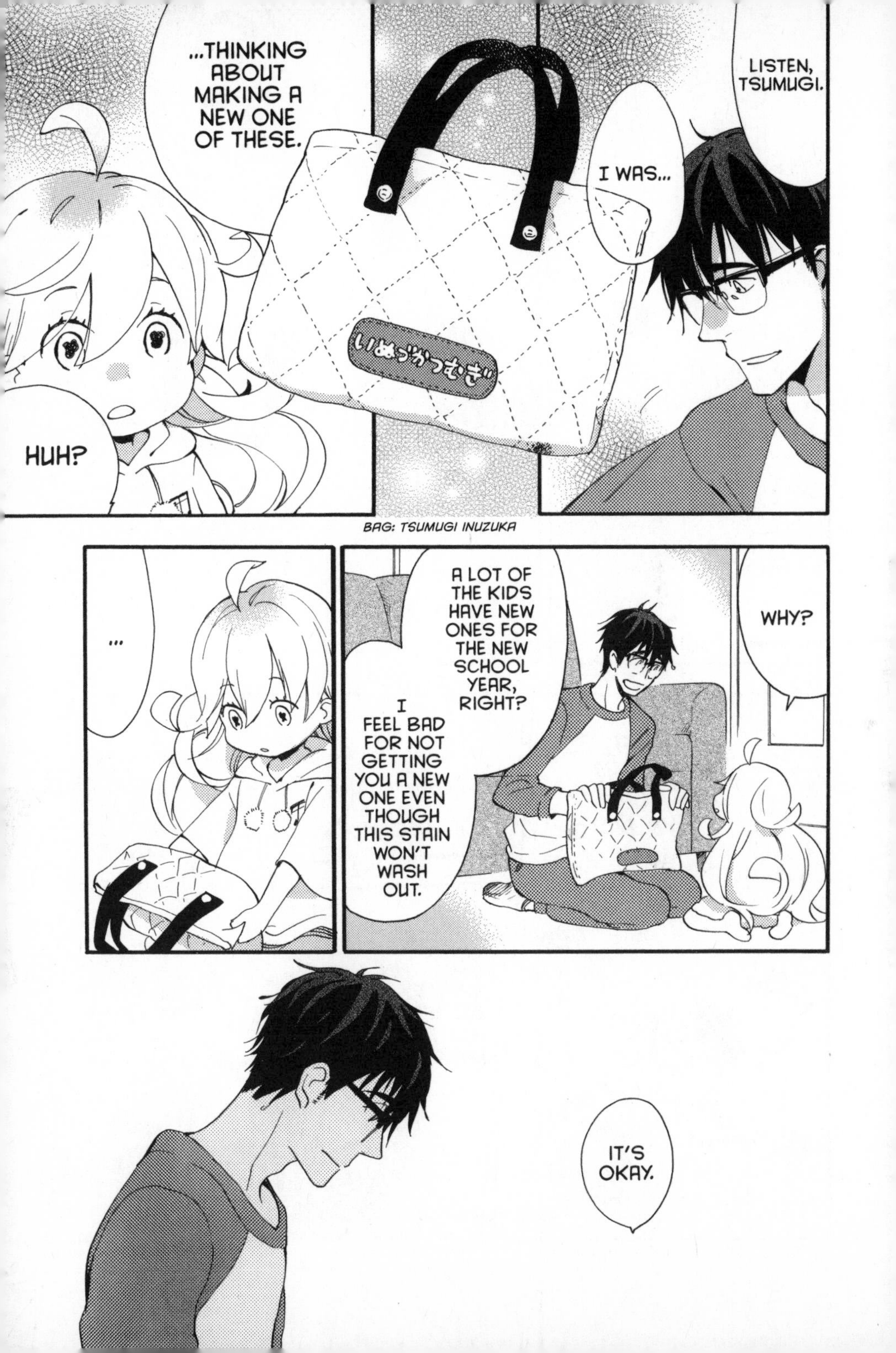
LISTEN, TSUMUGI.
I WAS...
...THINKING ABOUT MAKING A NEW ONE OF THESE.
いぬづかつむぎ
HUH?
BAG: TSUMUGI INUZUKA
WHY?
A LOT OF THE KIDS HAVE NEW ONES FOR THE NEW SCHOOL YEAR, RIGHT?
I FEEL BAD FOR NOT GETTING YOU A NEW ONE EVEN THOUGH THIS STAIN WON'T WASH OUT.
...
IT'S OKAY.

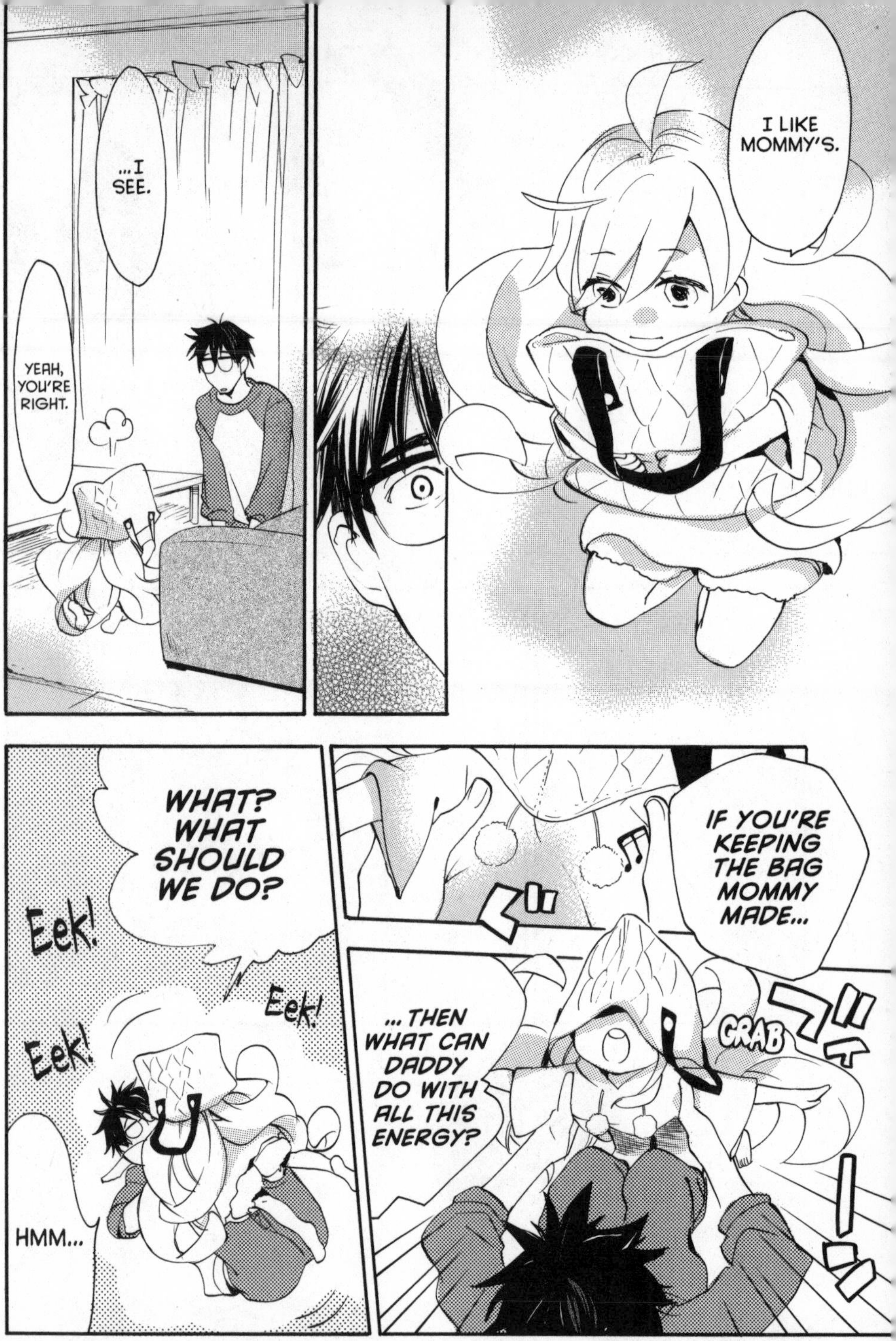
I LIKE MOMMY'S.
...I SEE.
YEAH, YOU'RE RIGHT.
IF YOU'RE KEEPING THE BAG MOMMY MADE...
...THEN WHAT CAN DADDY DO WITH ALL THIS ENERGY?
GRAB
WHAT? WHAT SHOULD WE DO?
Eek!
Eek!
Eek!
HMM...

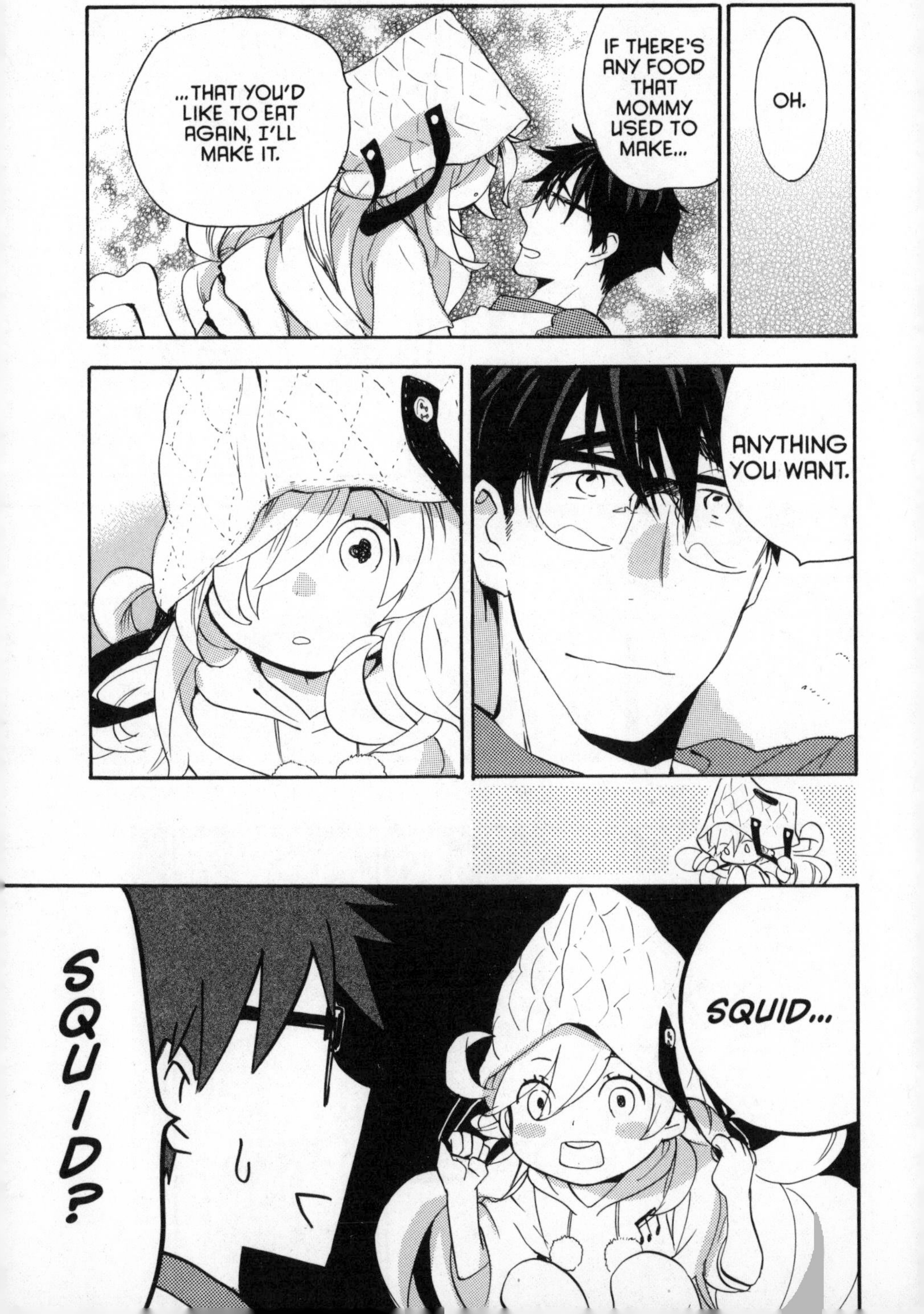
OH.
IF THERE'S ANY FOOD THAT MOMMY USED TO MAKE...
...THAT YOU'D LIKE TO EAT AGAIN, I'LL MAKE IT.
ANYTHING YOU WANT.
SQUID...
SQUID?

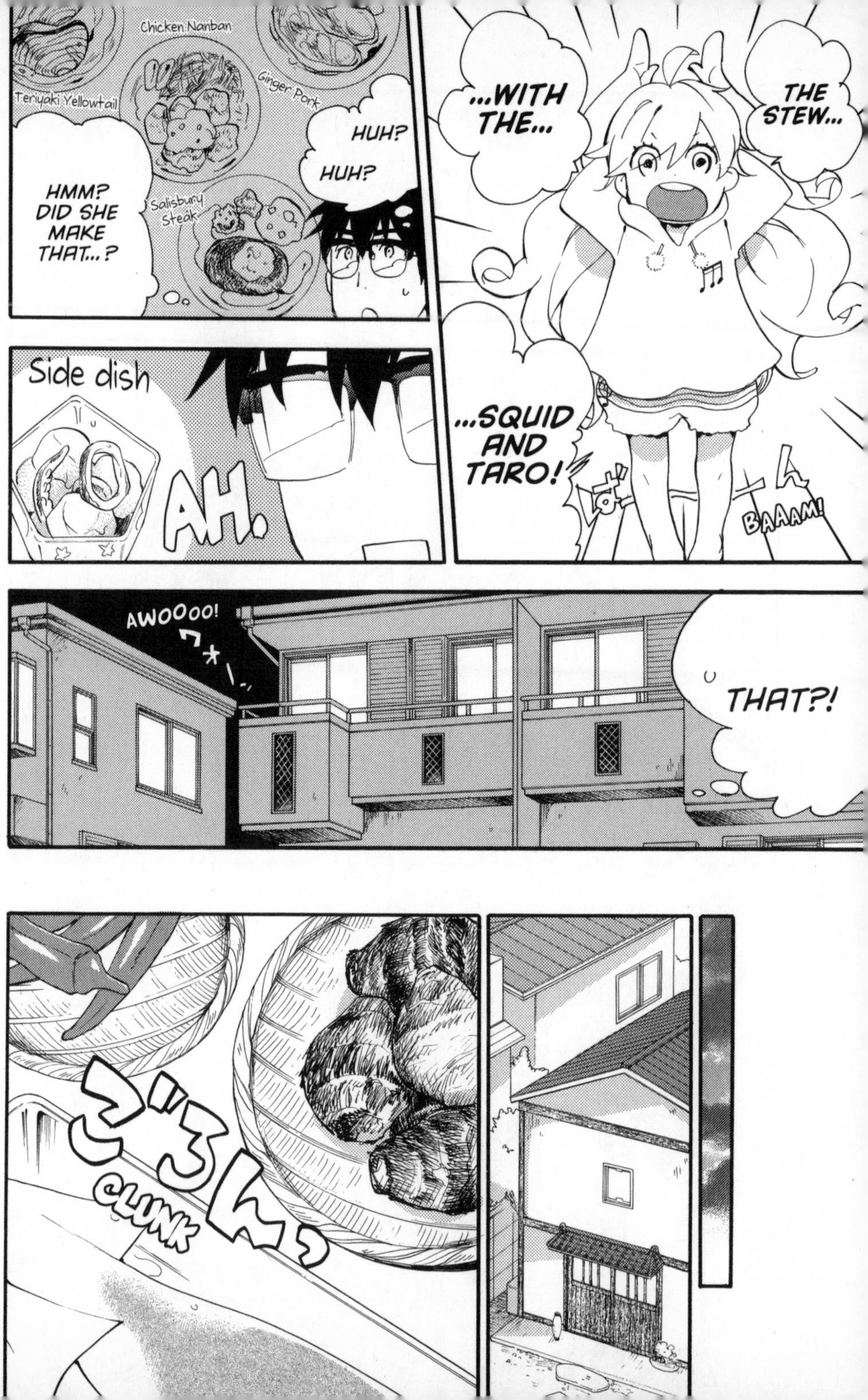
THE STEW...
...WITH THE...
...SQUID AND TARO!
BAAAM!
HUH?
HUH?
Chicken Nanban
Ginger Pork
Teriyaki Yellowtail
HMM? DID SHE MAKE THAT...?
Salisbury Steak
Side dish
AH.
THAT?!
AWOOOO!
ワオー
ごろん
CLUNK

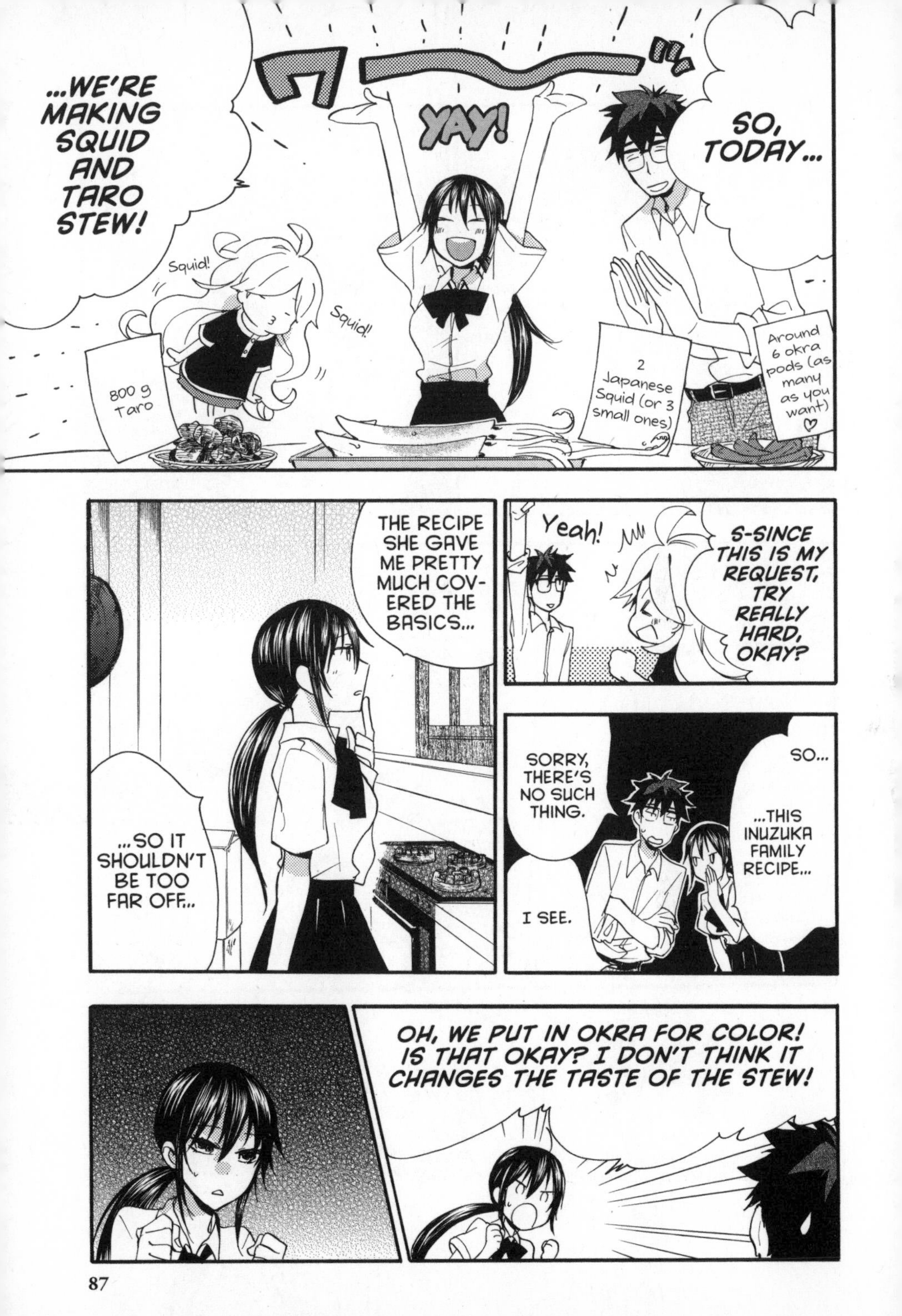
SO, TODAY...
YAY!
...WE'RE MAKING SQUID AND TARO STEW!
Around 6 okra pods (as many as you want) ♡
2 Japanese Squid (or 3 small ones)
Squid!
Squid!
800 g Taro
S-SINCE THIS IS MY REQUEST, TRY REALLY HARD, OKAY?
Yeah!
SO...
...THIS INUZUKA FAMILY RECIPE...
SORRY, THERE'S NO SUCH THING.
I SEE.
THE RECIPE SHE GAVE ME PRETTY MUCH COVERED THE BASICS...
...SO IT SHOULDN'T BE TOO FAR OFF...
OH, WE PUT IN OKRA FOR COLOR! IS THAT OKAY? I DON'T THINK IT CHANGES THE TASTE OF THE STEW!

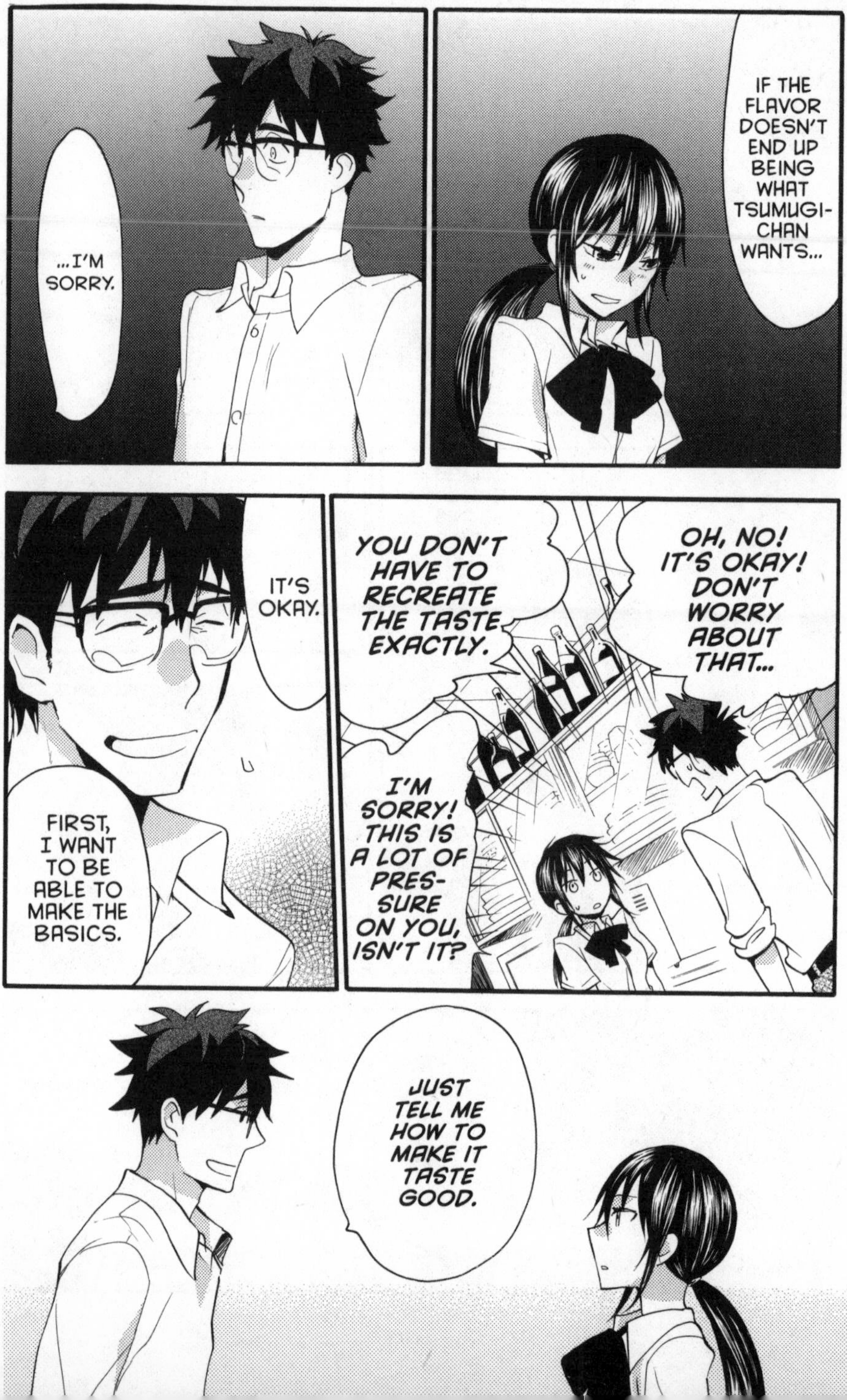
IF THE FLAVOR DOESN'T END UP BEING WHAT TSUMUGI-CHAN WANTS...
...I'M SORRY.
OH, NO! IT'S OKAY! DON'T WORRY ABOUT THAT...
YOU DON'T HAVE TO RECREATE THE TASTE EXACTLY.
I'M SORRY! THIS IS A LOT OF PRES-SURE ON YOU, ISN'T IT?
IT'S OKAY.
FIRST, I WANT TO BE ABLE TO MAKE THE BASICS.
JUST TELL ME HOW TO MAKE IT TASTE GOOD.

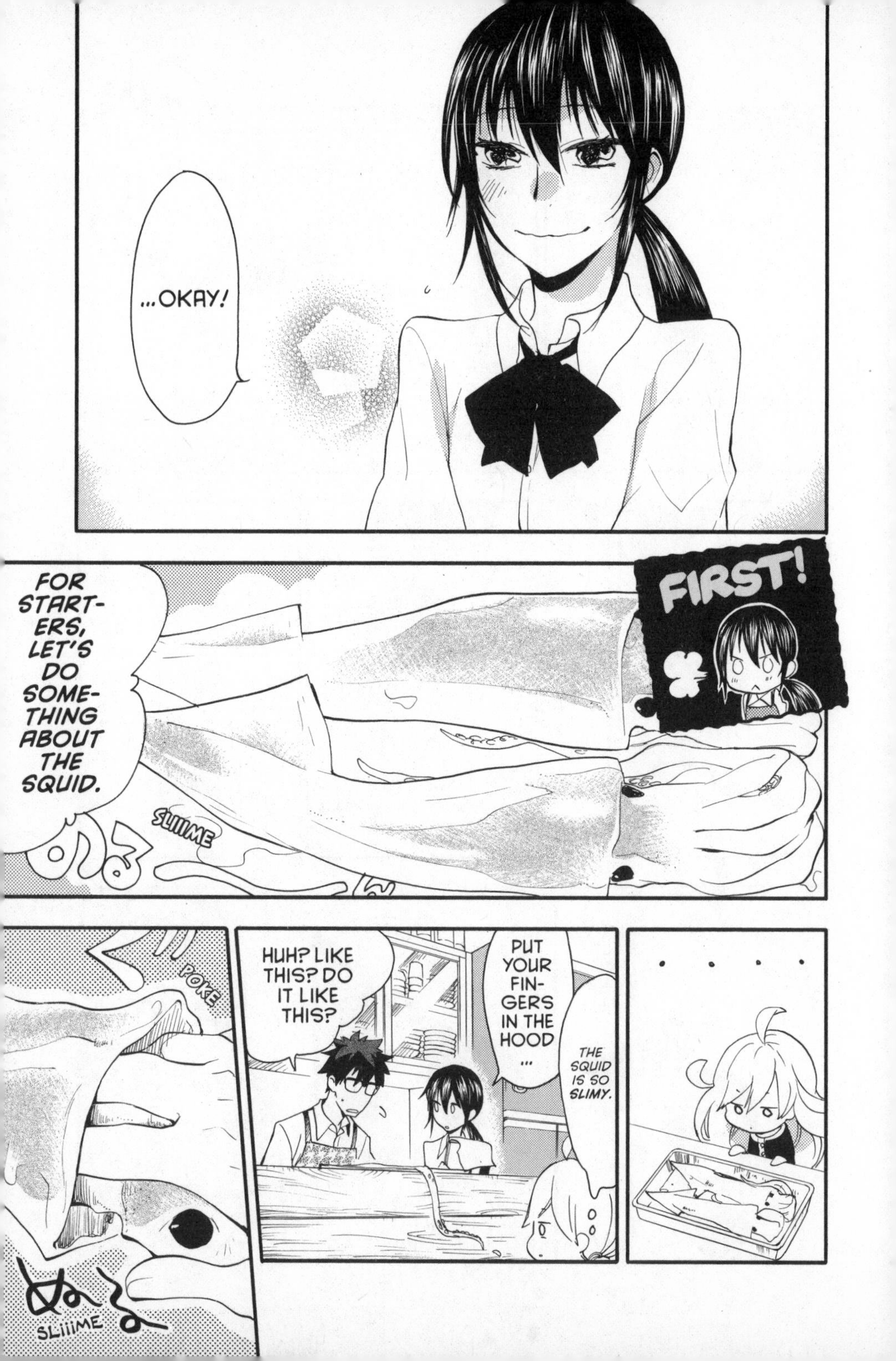
...OKAY!
FIRST!
FOR STARTERS, LET'S DO SOMETHING ABOUT THE SQUID.
SLIIIME
. . . .
PUT YOUR FINGERS IN THE HOOD...
HUH? LIKE THIS? DO IT LIKE THIS?
THE SQUID IS SO SLIMY.
POKE
SLIIIME

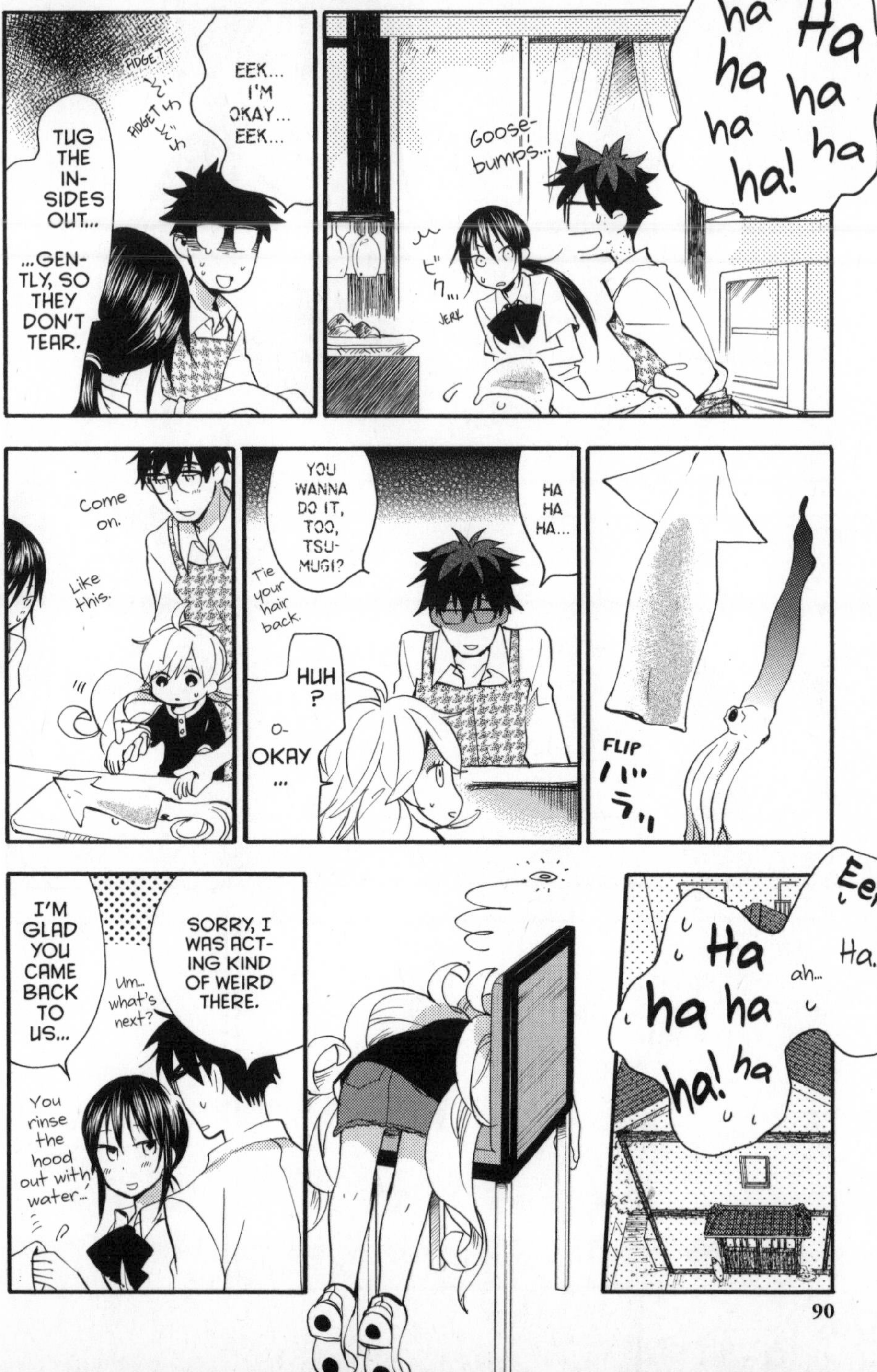
ha Ha ha ha ha ha ha ha!
Goose-bumps...
JERK
EEK... I'M OKAY... EEK...
FIDGET FIDGET
TUG THE INSIDES OUT...
...GENTLY, SO THEY DON'T TEAR.
FLIP
HA HA HA...
YOU WANNA DO IT, TOO, TSUMUGI?
Tie your hair back.
HUH?
O-OKAY...
Come on.
Like this.
Eek!
Ha ha ha ha ha!
Ha...
ah...
SORRY, I WAS ACTING KIND OF WEIRD THERE.
I'M GLAD YOU CAME BACK TO US...
Um... what's next?
You rinse the hood out with water...

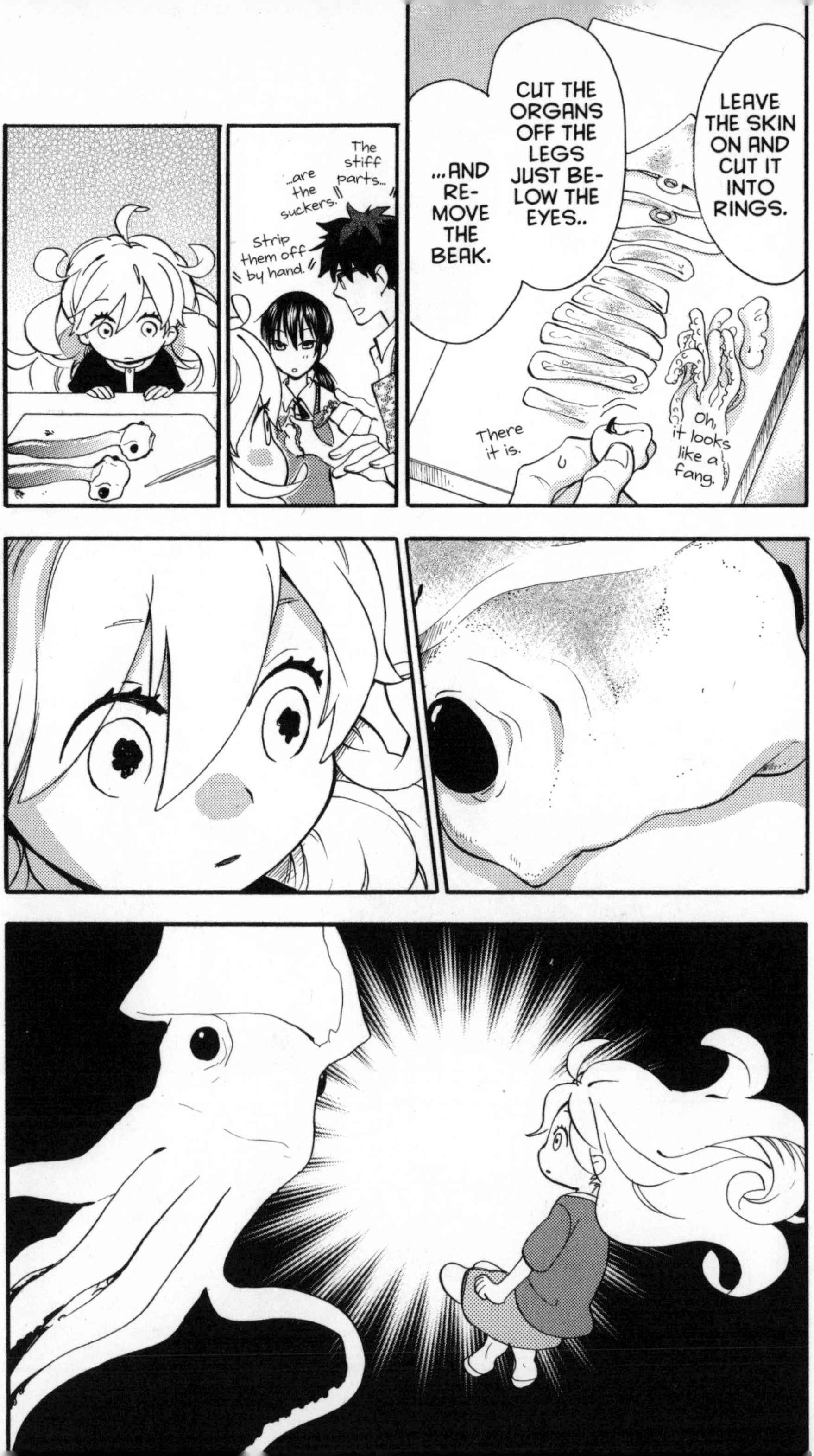
LEAVE THE SKIN ON AND CUT IT INTO RINGS.
CUT THE ORGANS OFF THE LEGS JUST BE-LOW THE EYES..
...AND RE-MOVE THE BEAK.
Oh, it looks like a fang.
There it is.
The stiff parts...
...are the suckers.
Strip them off by hand.

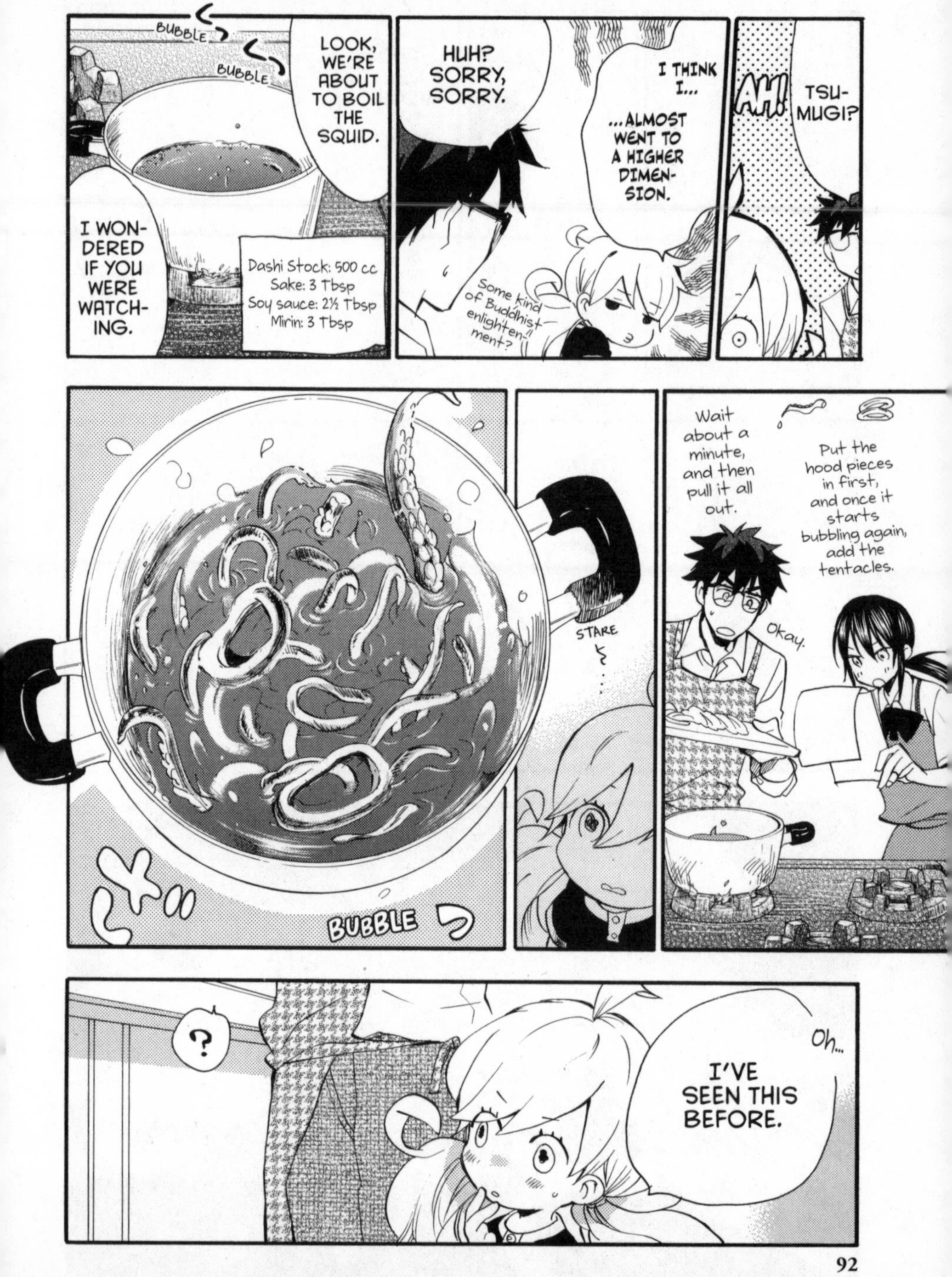
TSU-MUGI?
AH!
I THINK I...
...ALMOST WENT TO A HIGHER DIMEN-SION.
HUH? SORRY, SORRY.
Some kind of Buddhist enlighten-ment?
LOOK, WE'RE ABOUT TO BOIL THE SQUID.
BUBBLE
BUBBLE
I WON-DERED IF YOU WERE WATCH-ING.
Dashi Stock: 500 cc
Sake: 3 Tbsp
Soy sauce: 2½ Tbsp
Mirin: 3 Tbsp
Put the hood pieces in first, and once it starts bubbling again, add the tentacles.
Wait about a minute, and then pull it all out.
Okay.
STARE
BUBBLE
Oh...
I'VE SEEN THIS BEFORE.
?

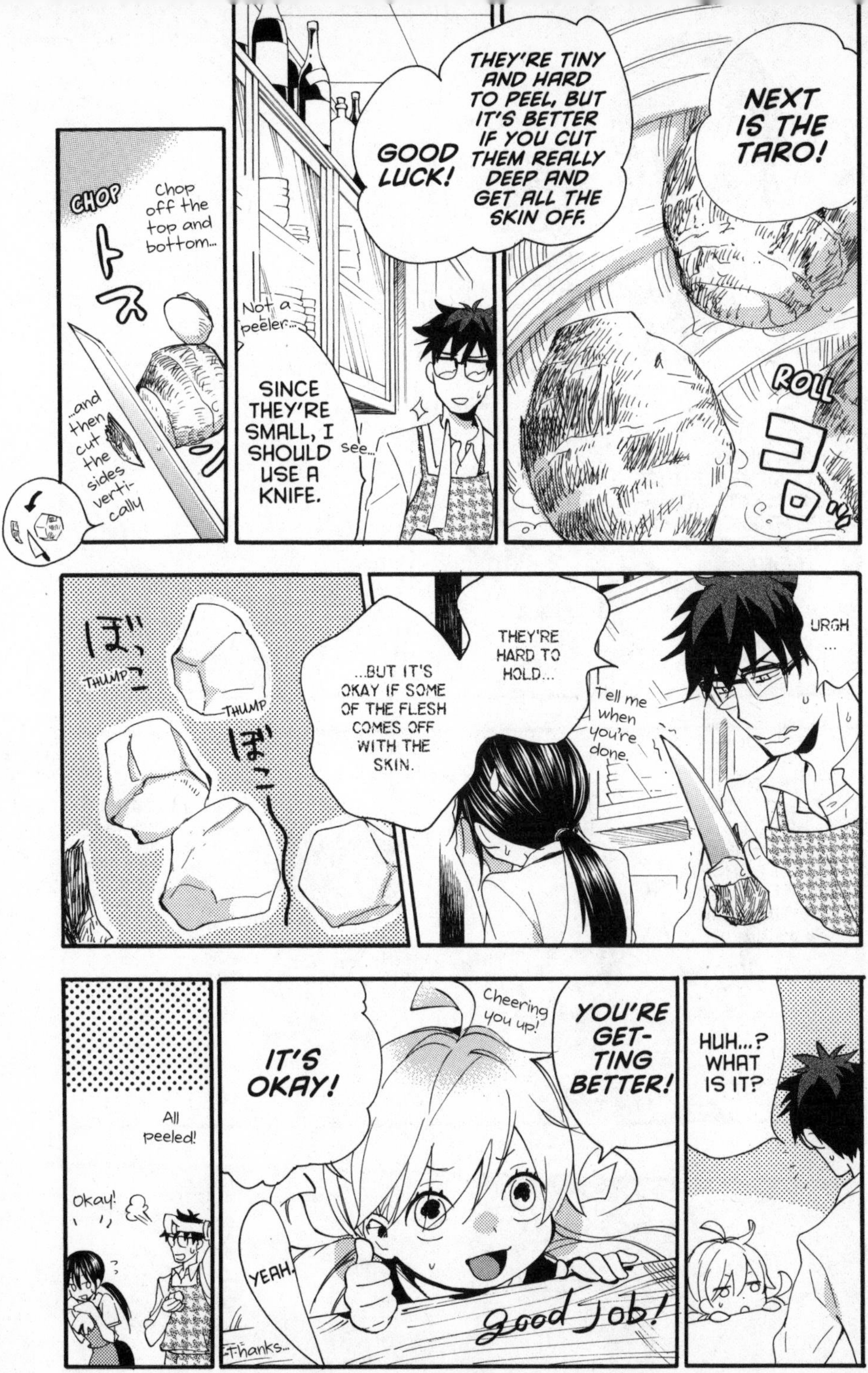
NEXT IS THE TARO!
ROLL
THEY'RE TINY AND HARD TO PEEL, BUT IT'S BETTER IF YOU CUT THEM REALLY DEEP AND GET ALL THE SKIN OFF.
GOOD LUCK!
Not a peeler...
SINCE THEY'RE SMALL, I SHOULD USE A KNIFE.
see...
CHOP
Chop off the top and bottom...
...and then cut the sides verti-cally
URGH ...
THEY'RE HARD TO HOLD...
Tell me when you're done.
...BUT IT'S OKAY IF SOME OF THE FLESH COMES OFF WITH THE SKIN.
THUMP
THUMP
HUH...? WHAT IS IT?
YOU'RE GET-TING BETTER!
Cheering you up!
IT'S OKAY!
YEAH.
Good Job!
T-Thanks...
All peeled!
Okay!

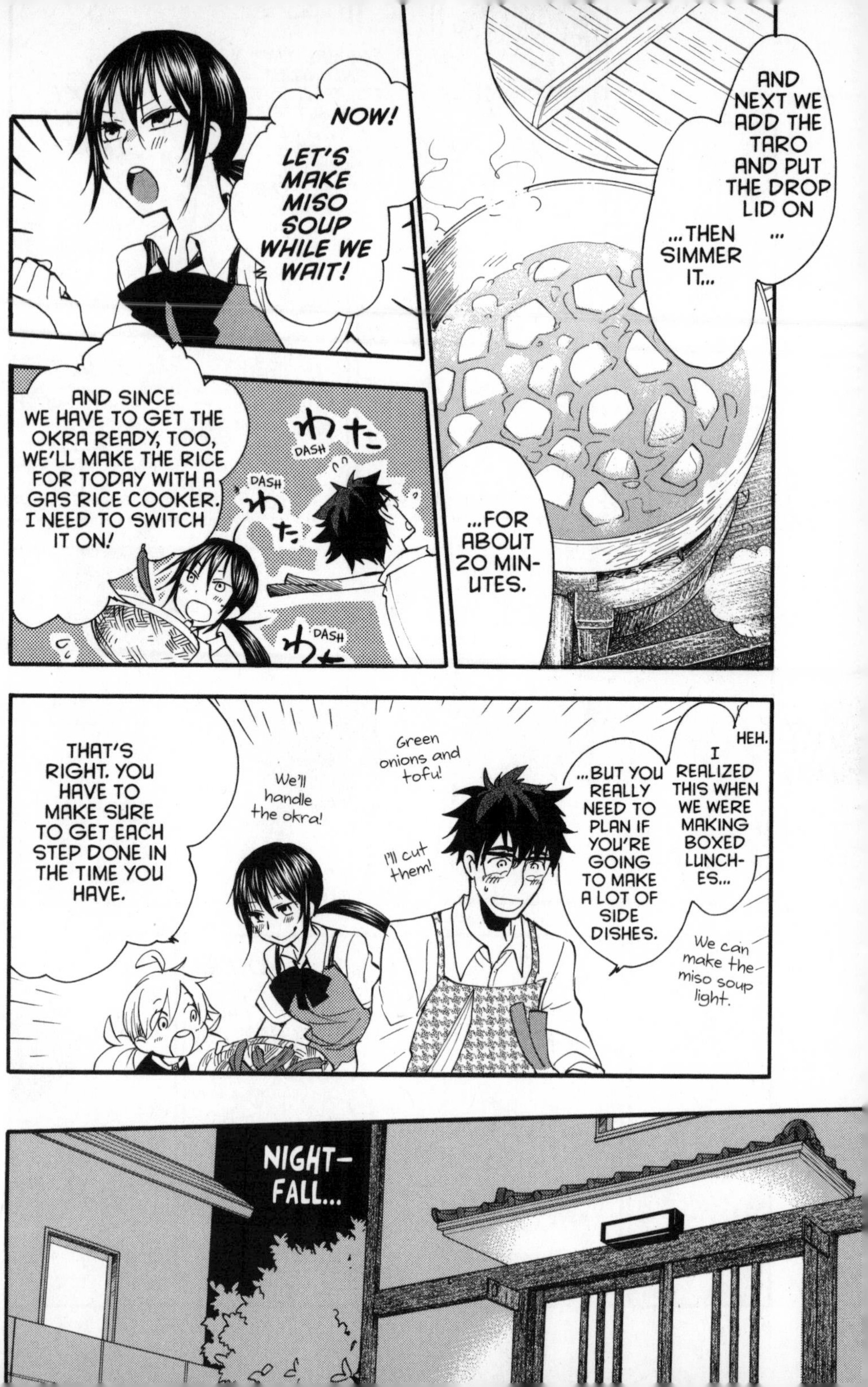
AND NEXT WE ADD THE TARO AND PUT THE DROP LID ON ...
...THEN SIMMER IT...
...FOR ABOUT 20 MINUTES.
NOW!
LET'S MAKE MISO SOUP WHILE WE WAIT!
AND SINCE WE HAVE TO GET THE OKRA READY, TOO, WE'LL MAKE THE RICE FOR TODAY WITH A GAS RICE COOKER. I NEED TO SWITCH IT ON!
わた DASH
わた DASH
わた DASH
HEH.
I REALIZED THIS WHEN WE WERE MAKING BOXED LUNCH-ES...
...BUT YOU REALLY NEED TO PLAN IF YOU'RE GOING TO MAKE A LOT OF SIDE DISHES.
We can make the miso soup light.
Green onions and tofu!
I'll cut them!
We'll handle the okra!
THAT'S RIGHT. YOU HAVE TO MAKE SURE TO GET EACH STEP DONE IN THE TIME YOU HAVE.
NIGHT-FALL...

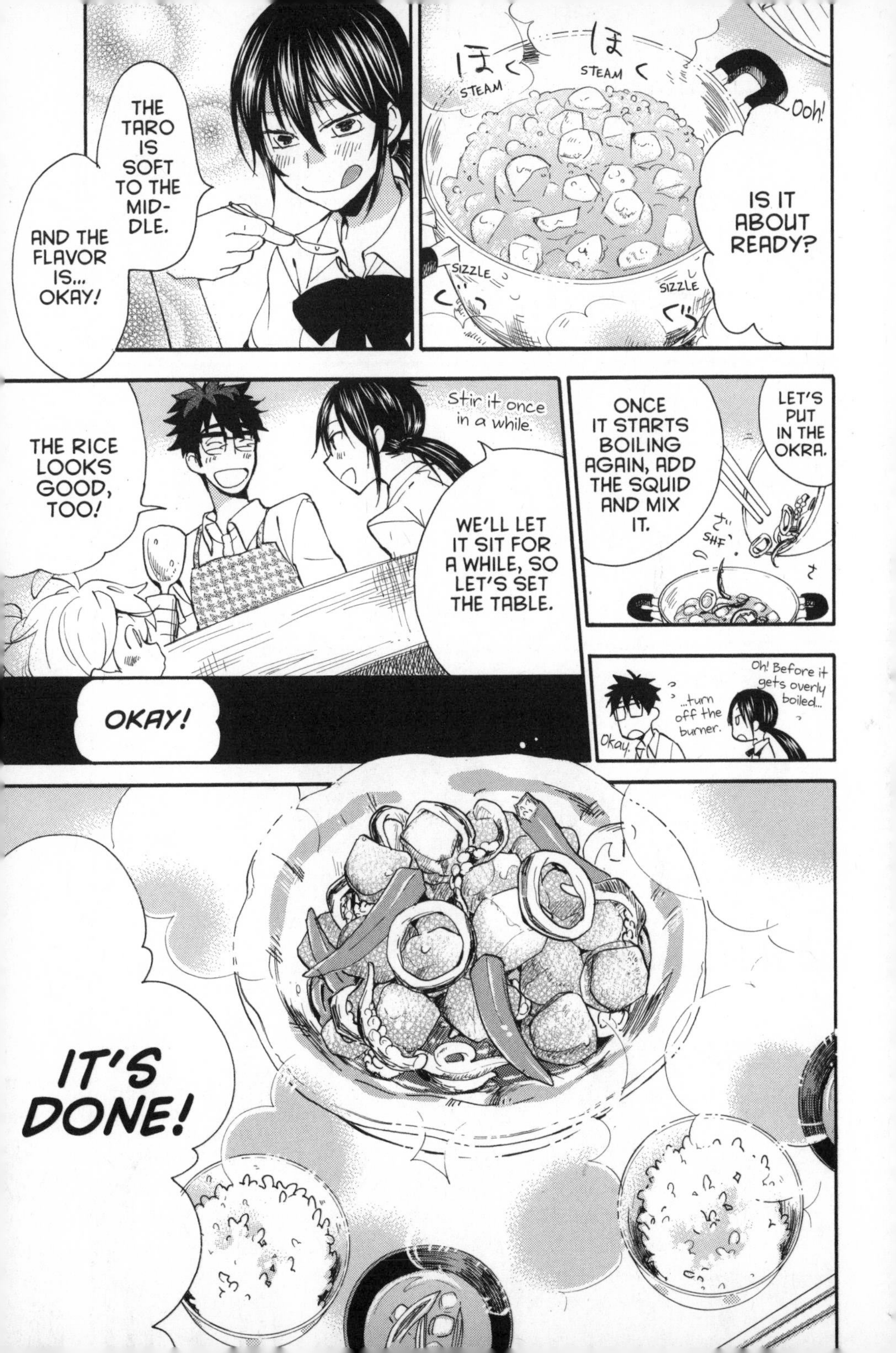
ほく
STEAM
ほく
STEAM
Ooh!
IS IT ABOUT READY?
ぐつ
SIZZLE
SIZZLE
THE TARO IS SOFT TO THE MIDDLE.
AND THE FLAVOR IS... OKAY!
LET'S PUT IN THE OKRA.
ONCE IT STARTS BOILING AGAIN, ADD THE SQUID AND MIX IT.
SHF
Oh! Before it gets overly boiled...
...turn off the burner.
Okay.
Stir it once in a while.
WE'LL LET IT SIT FOR A WHILE, SO LET'S SET THE TABLE.
THE RICE LOOKS GOOD, TOO!
OKAY!
IT'S DONE!

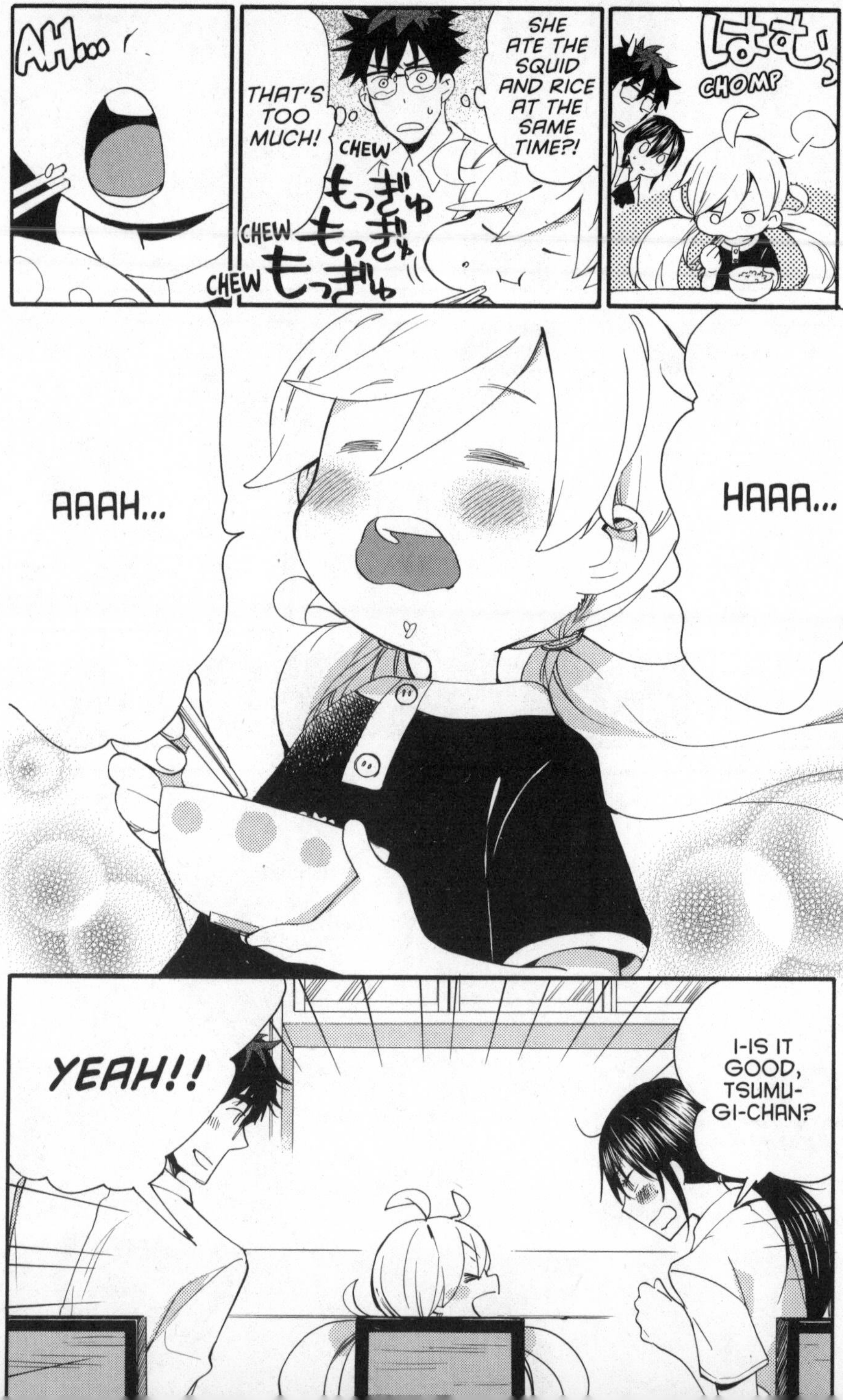
はむっ
CHOMP
SHE ATE THE SQUID AND RICE AT THE SAME TIME?!
THAT'S TOO MUCH!
CHEW もっぎゅ
CHEW もっぎゅ
CHEW もっぎゅ
AH...
HAAA...
AAAH...
I-IS IT GOOD, TSUMUGI-CHAN?
YEAH!!

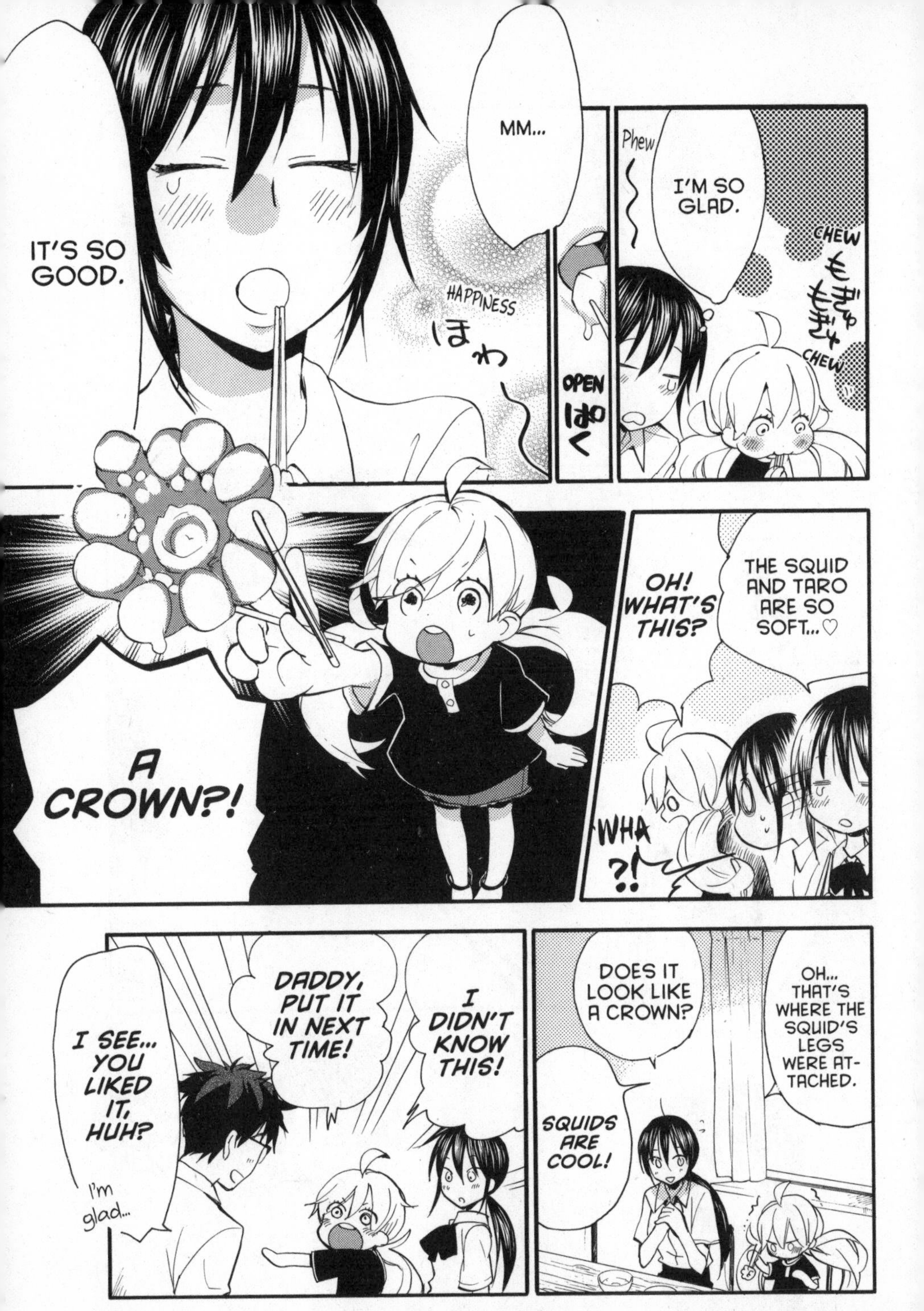
Phew ~
I'M SO GLAD.
CHEW もぎゅ もぎゅ CHEW
OPEN ぱく
MM...
HAPPINESS ほわ
IT'S SO GOOD.
THE SQUID AND TARO ARE SO SOFT...♡
OH! WHAT'S THIS?
WHA ?!
A CROWN?!
OH... THAT'S WHERE THE SQUID'S LEGS WERE AT-TACHED.
DOES IT LOOK LIKE A CROWN?
SQUIDS ARE COOL!
I DIDN'T KNOW THIS!
DADDY, PUT IT IN NEXT TIME!
I SEE... YOU LIKED IT, HUH?
I'm glad...

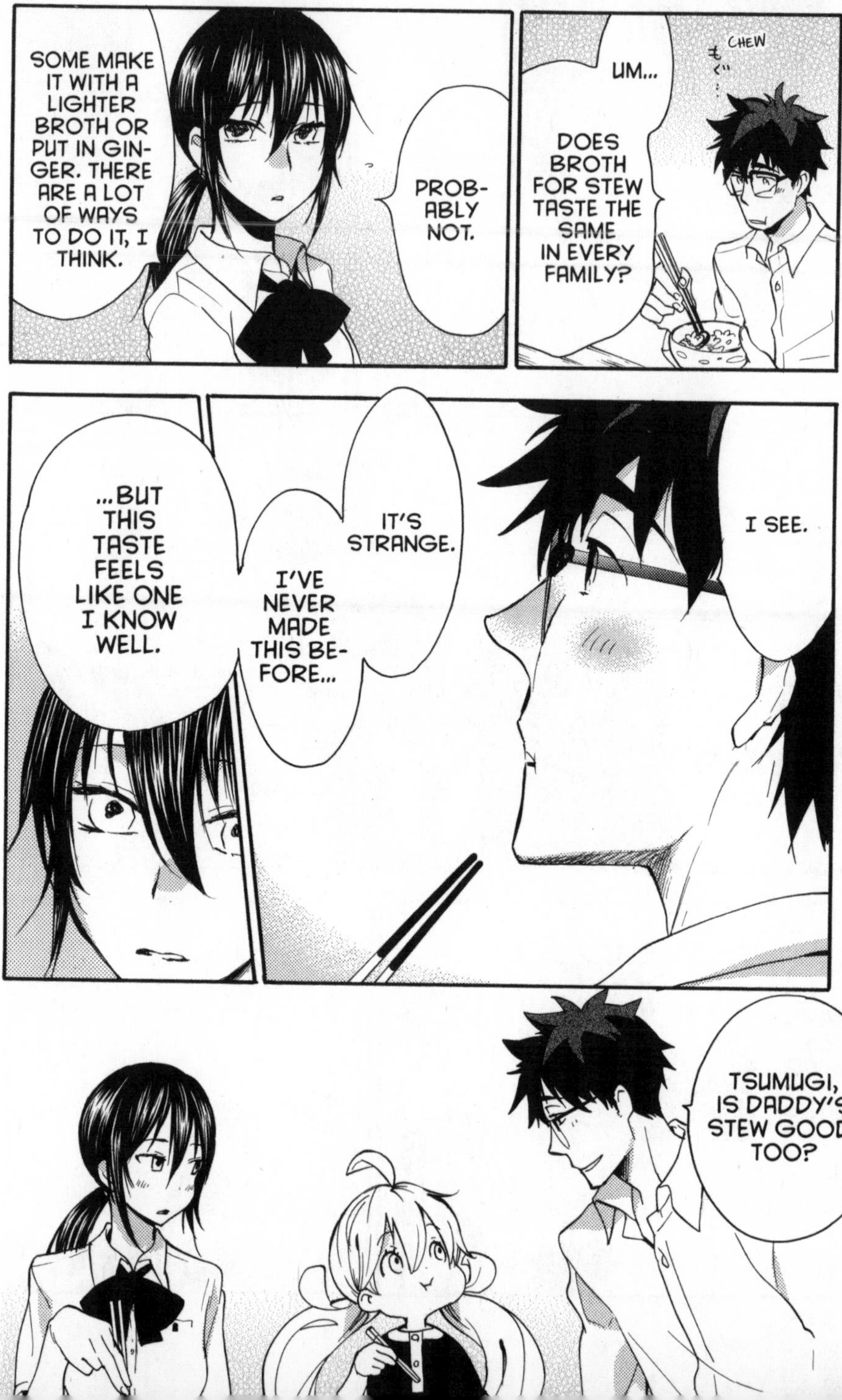
CHEW
もぐ…
UM...
DOES BROTH FOR STEW TASTE THE SAME IN EVERY FAMILY?
PROB-ABLY NOT.
SOME MAKE IT WITH A LIGHTER BROTH OR PUT IN GIN-GER. THERE ARE A LOT OF WAYS TO DO IT, I THINK.
I SEE.
IT'S STRANGE.
I'VE NEVER MADE THIS BE-FORE...
...BUT THIS TASTE FEELS LIKE ONE I KNOW WELL.
TSUMUGI, IS DADDY'S STEW GOOD, TOO?

YEAH!

I LIKE THE TASTE!

I'LL MAKE IT AGAIN, OKAY?

I'M GLAD.

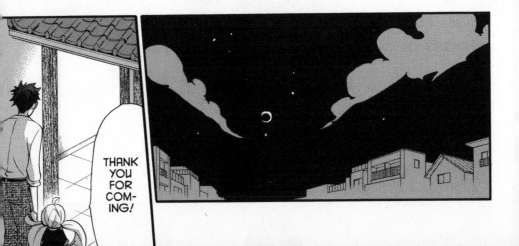

THANK YOU FOR COMING!

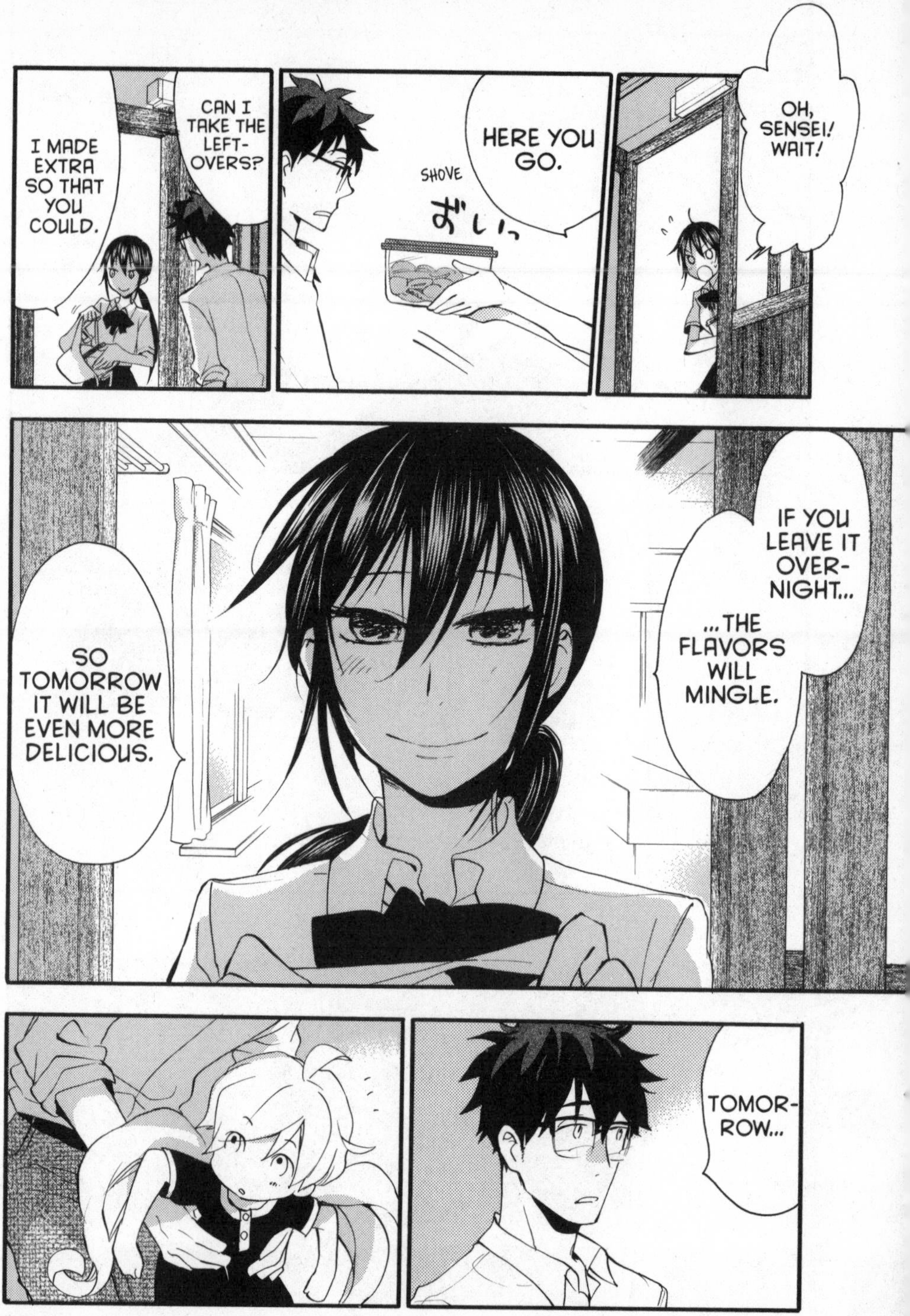

OH, SENSEI! WAIT!
HERE YOU GO.
SHOVE
ずいっ
CAN I TAKE THE LEFT-OVERS?
I MADE EXTRA SO THAT YOU COULD.
IF YOU LEAVE IT OVER-NIGHT...
...THE FLAVORS WILL MINGLE.
SO TOMORROW IT WILL BE EVEN MORE DELICIOUS.
TOMOR-ROW...

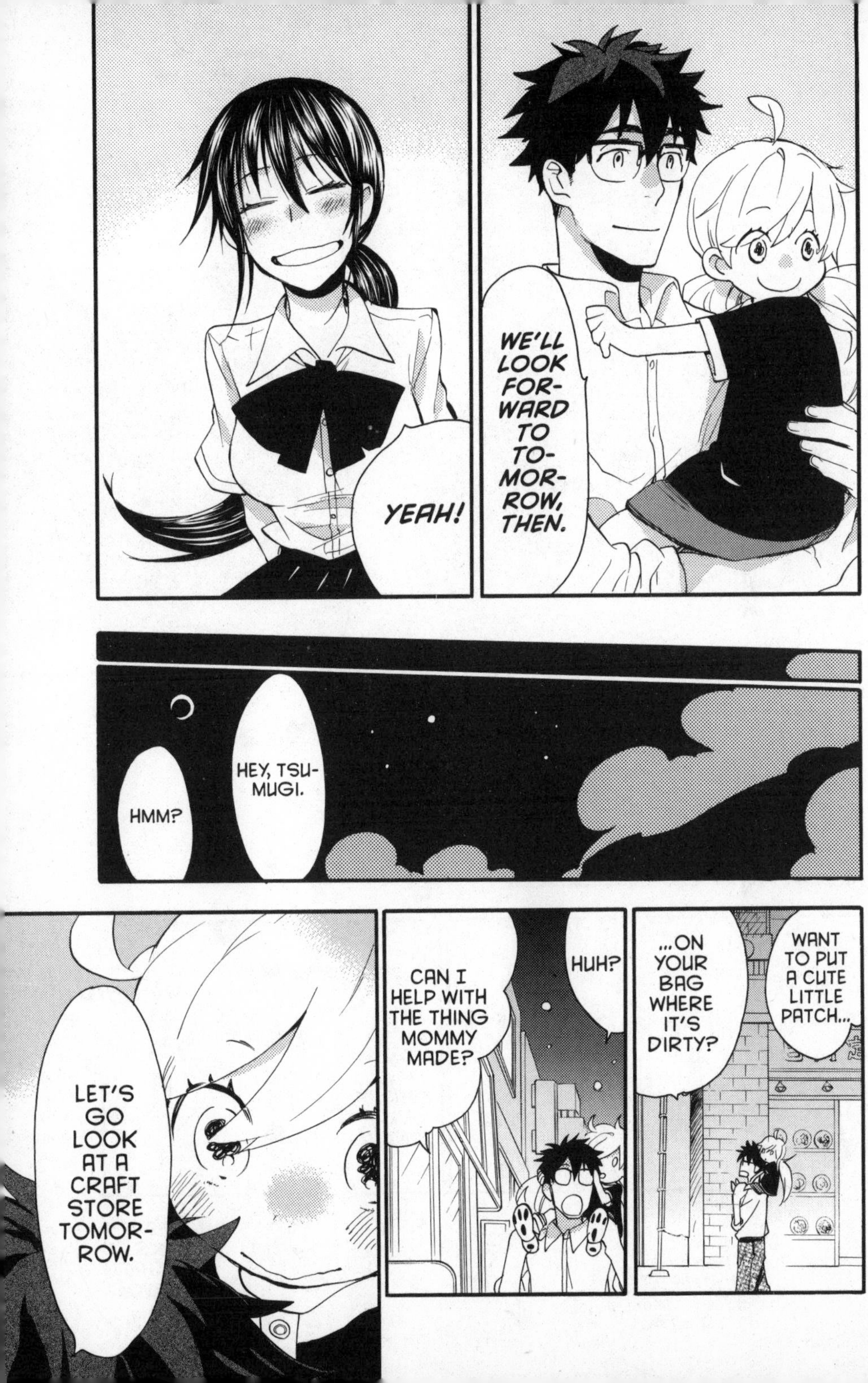
WE'LL LOOK FORWARD TO TOMORROW, THEN.
YEAH!
HEY, TSUMUGI.
HMM?
WANT TO PUT A CUTE LITTLE PATCH...
...ON YOUR BAG WHERE IT'S DIRTY?
HUH?
CAN I HELP WITH THE THING MOMMY MADE?
LET'S GO LOOK AT A CRAFT STORE TOMORROW.

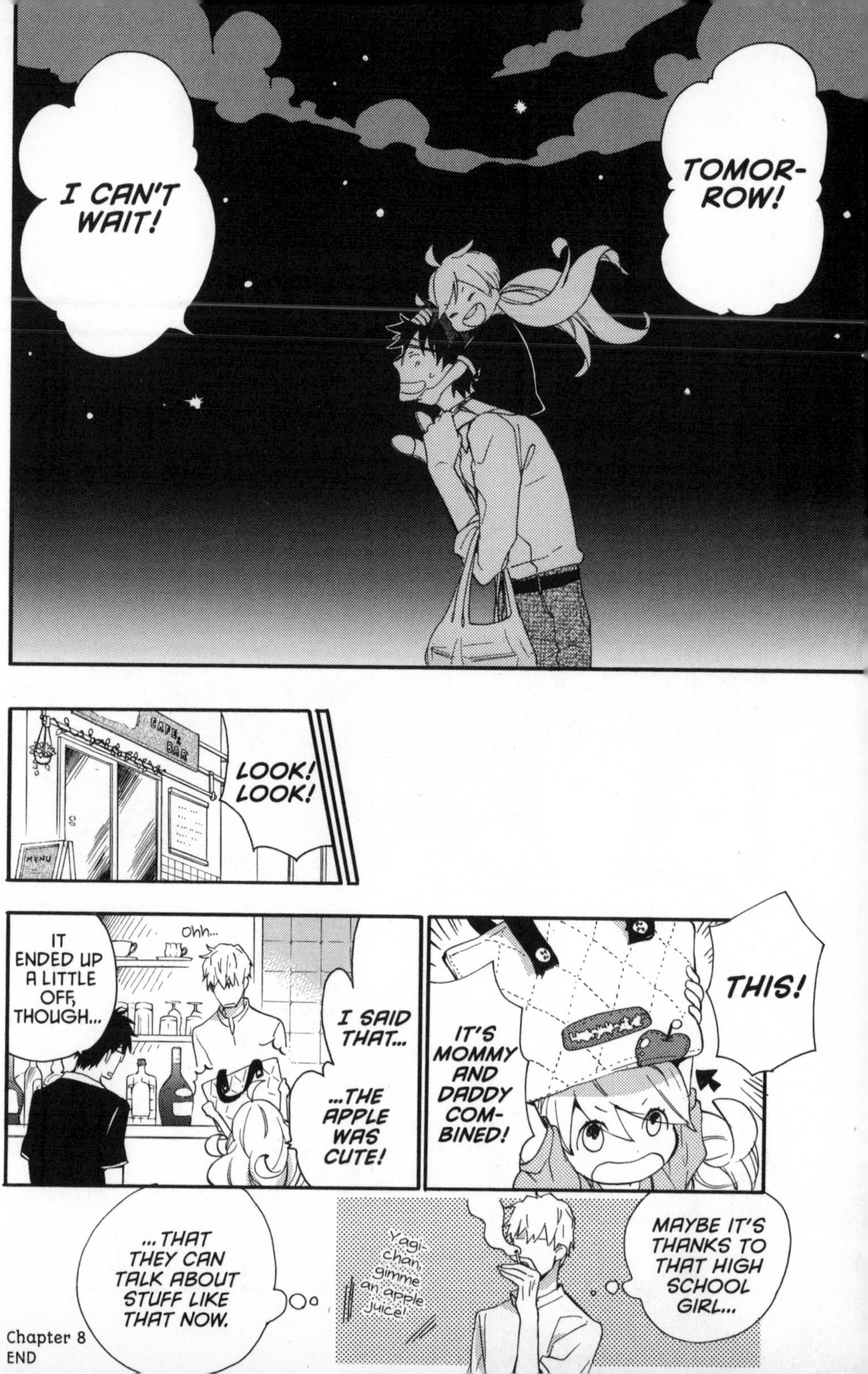
TOMOR-ROW!
I CAN'T WAIT!
CAFE & BAR
MENU
LOOK! LOOK!
THIS!
IT'S MOMMY AND DADDY COMBINED!
I SAID THAT...
...THE APPLE WAS CUTE!
Ohh...
IT ENDED UP A LITTLE OFF, THOUGH...
MAYBE IT'S THANKS TO THAT HIGH SCHOOL GIRL...
Yagi-chan, gimme an apple juice!
...THAT THEY CAN TALK ABOUT STUFF LIKE THAT NOW.

Chapter 8
END

SQUID AND TARO STEW

☆ Ingredients ☆ ☆ Serves 3-4

800 g taro   some okra

2 (3 if small) Japanese squid

(A) 500 cc dashi stock   3 Tbsp each sake and mirin   2 1/2 Tbsp soy sauce

S T E P S °°° °°

1. Wash the **taro** carefully and scrape off any mud or roots. Wipe any water off, leave them in a strainer, and once dry, peel (cutting deeply into the taro).

Taro, ✦ **POINT** ✦ Taro is slippery when wet. It will be easier to peel if you let it dry first!

2. Put your fingers into the hood of the **squid** and pull out the legs and organs. Take out the cartilage and rinse the inside of the hood. Then cut it into rings, leaving the skin on. Separate the legs and organs below the eyes and remove the beak. Use a knife to remove the suckers from the legs and cut into bite-sized pieces.

3. Put **A** into a pot and boil. Then add the hood from **Step 2**. Once the broth starts to boil again, add the tentacles of the squid and let it cook for a minute. Then remove the squid from the pot.

4. Add the **taro** to the pot from **Step 3** and cover it with a drop lid. Once the stew starts to boil again, turn the heat to low and cook for 15-20 minutes.

5. Once the taro is soft, season to taste. Put in the **okra**, and when it starts to boil again, add the squid from **Step 3** and stir. Turn off the heat before everything gets overly boiled.

✦ **POINT** ✦ After this, let it sit and stir it once in a while to allow the taste to soak in.

Squid ♥

I see!

CONVERSION NOTES:
800 G TARO = 1.75 LBS, 500 CC BROTH = ABOUT 2 1/4 CUPS

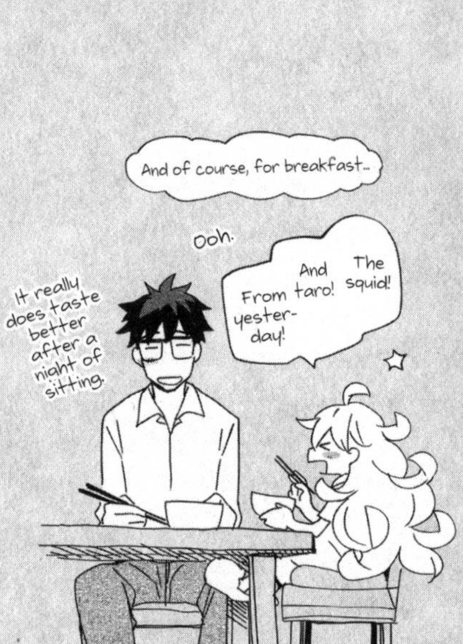
And of course, for breakfast...
Ooh.
The squid! And taro! From yesterday!
It really does taste better after a night of sitting.

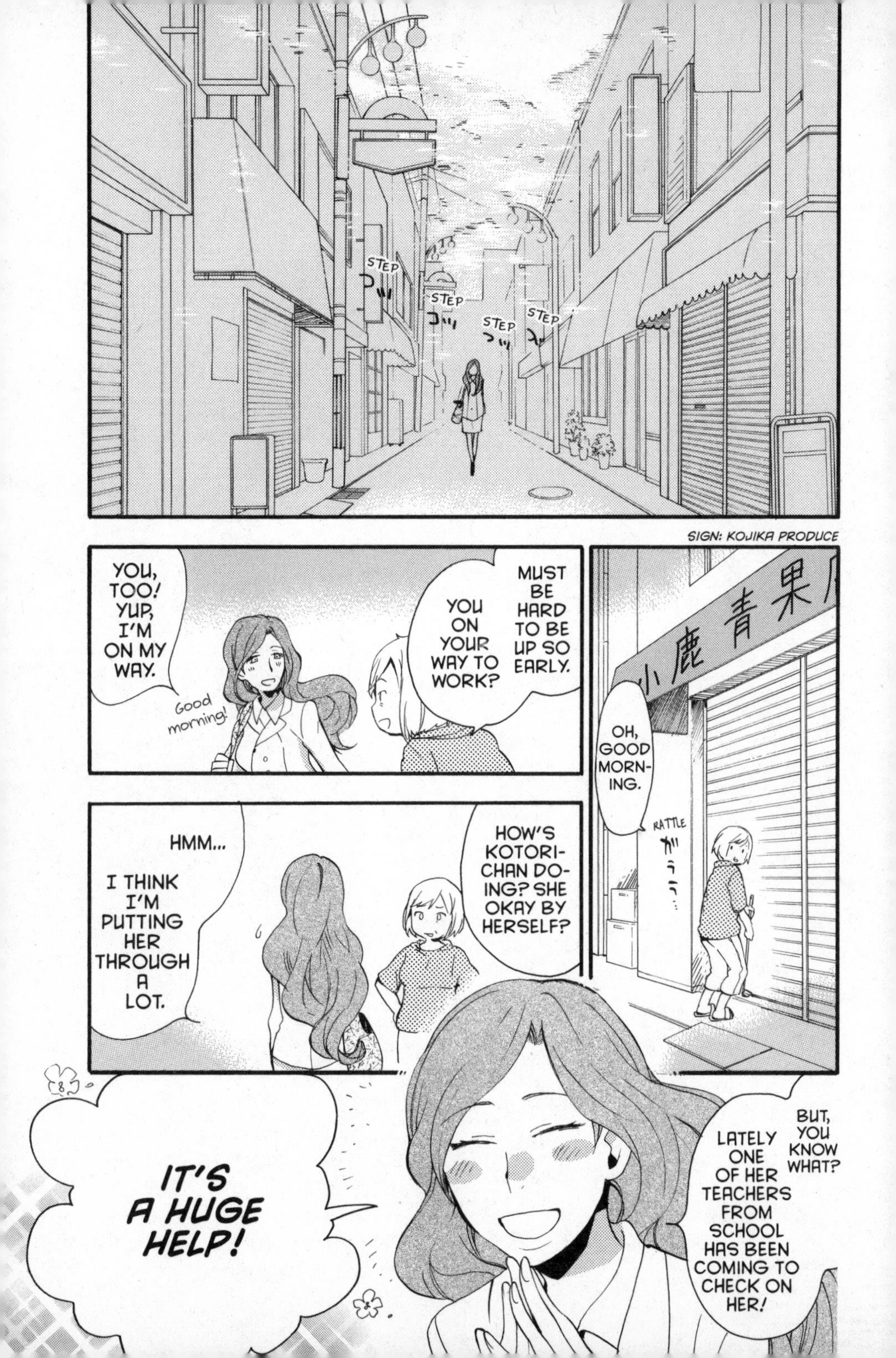
STEP
STEP
STEP
STEP
SIGN: KOJIKA PRODUCE
小鹿青果
OH, GOOD MORNING.
RATTLE
MUST BE HARD TO BE UP SO EARLY.
YOU ON YOUR WAY TO WORK?
YOU, TOO! YUP, I'M ON MY WAY.
Good morning!
HOW'S KOTORI-CHAN DOING? SHE OKAY BY HERSELF?
HMM...
I THINK I'M PUTTING HER THROUGH A LOT.
BUT, YOU KNOW WHAT?
LATELY ONE OF HER TEACHERS FROM SCHOOL HAS BEEN COMING TO CHECK ON HER!
IT'S A HUGE HELP!

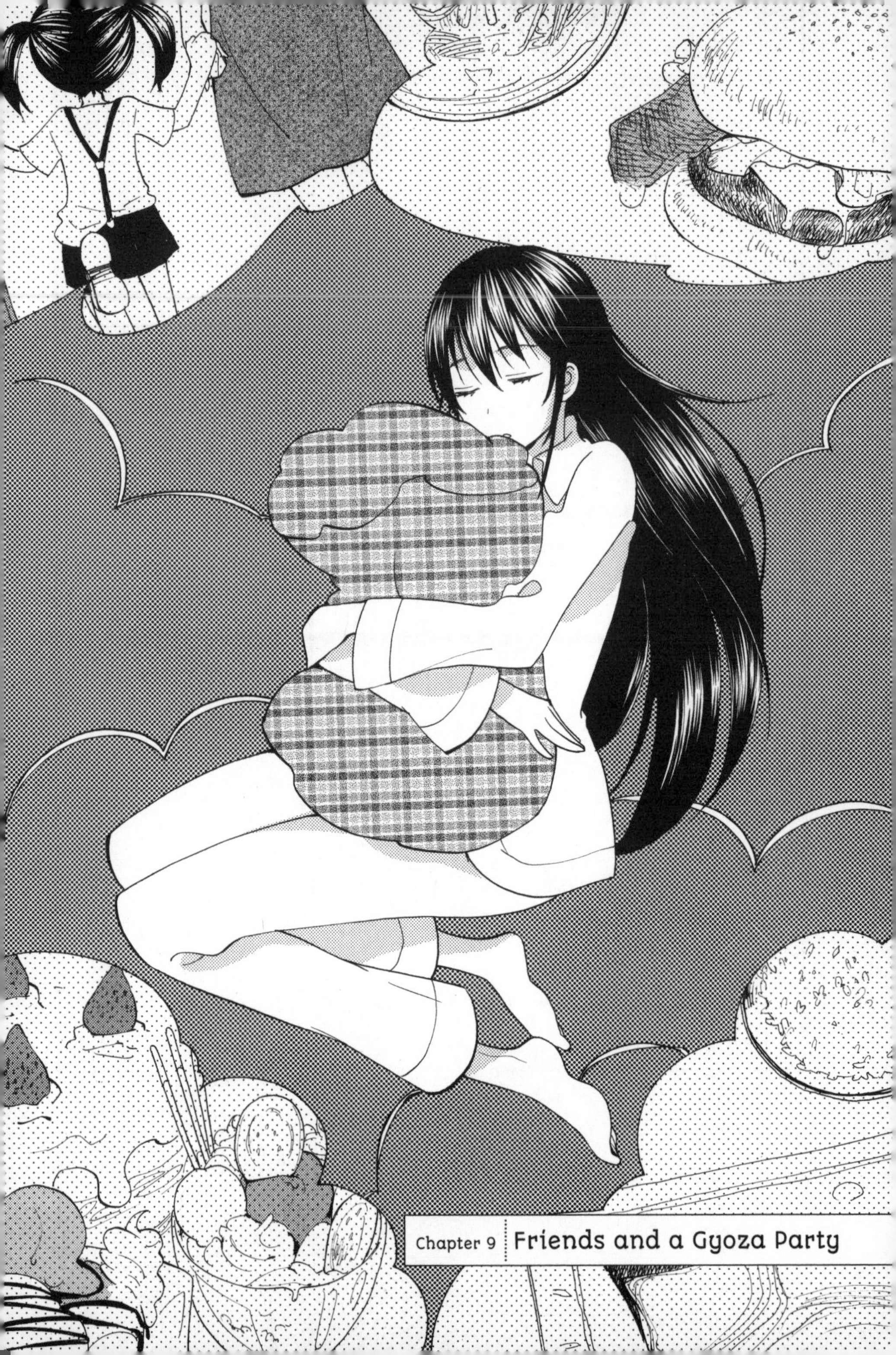
Chapter 9 | Friends and a Gyoza Party

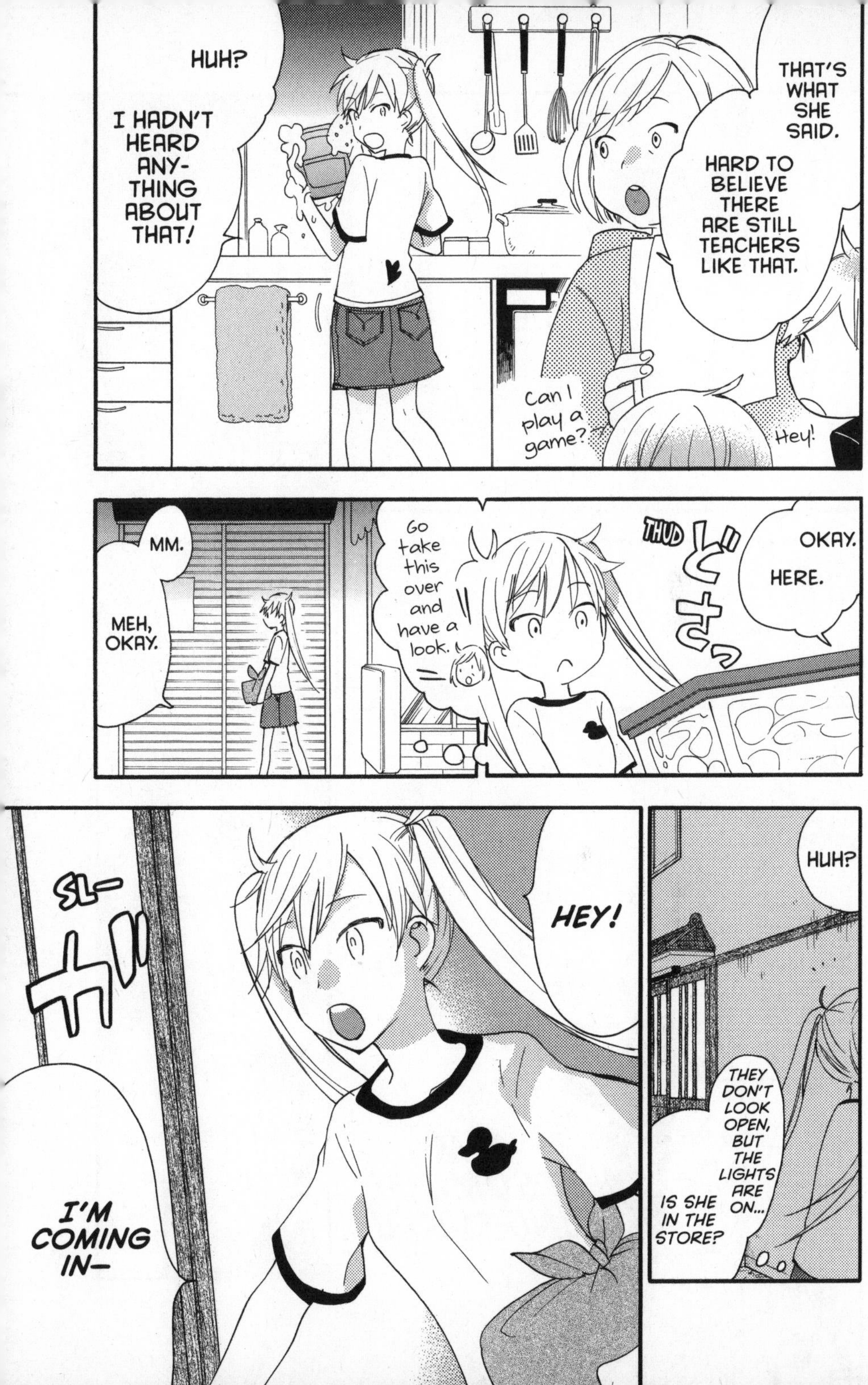
THAT'S WHAT SHE SAID.
HARD TO BELIEVE THERE ARE STILL TEACHERS LIKE THAT.
Hey!
Can I play a game?
HUH?
I HADN'T HEARD ANY-THING ABOUT THAT!
OKAY.
HERE.
THUD どさっ
Go take this over and have a look.
MM.
MEH, OKAY.
HUH?
THEY DON'T LOOK OPEN, BUT THE LIGHTS ARE ON...
IS SHE IN THE STORE?
HEY!
SL– ガ
I'M COMING IN–

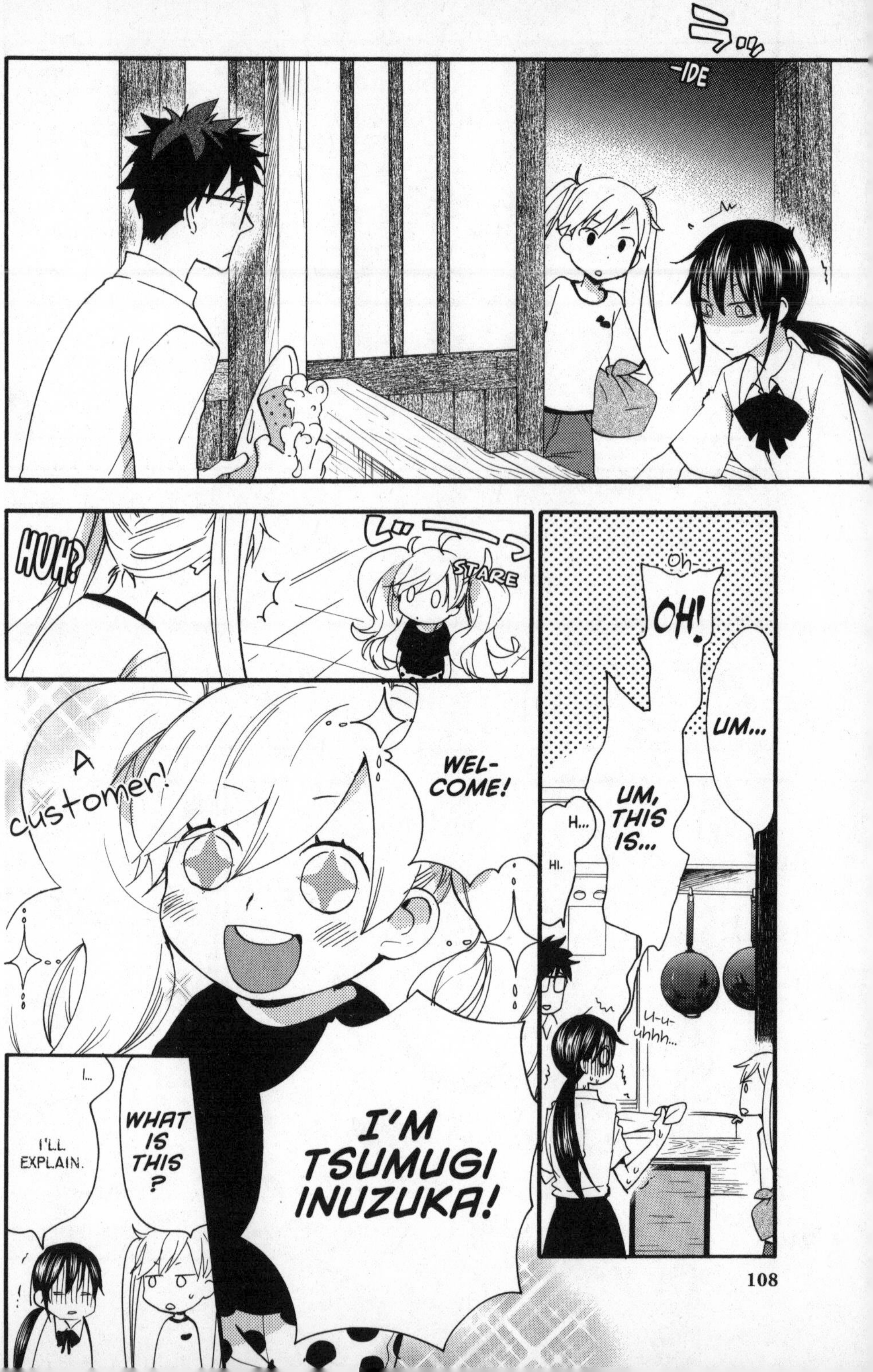
ラッ
-IDE
Oh-
OH!
UM...
UM, THIS IS...
H...
HI.
U-u-uhhh...
STARE
HUH?
WEL-COME!
A customer!
I'M TSUMUGI INUZUKA!
WHAT IS THIS?
I... I'LL EXPLAIN.

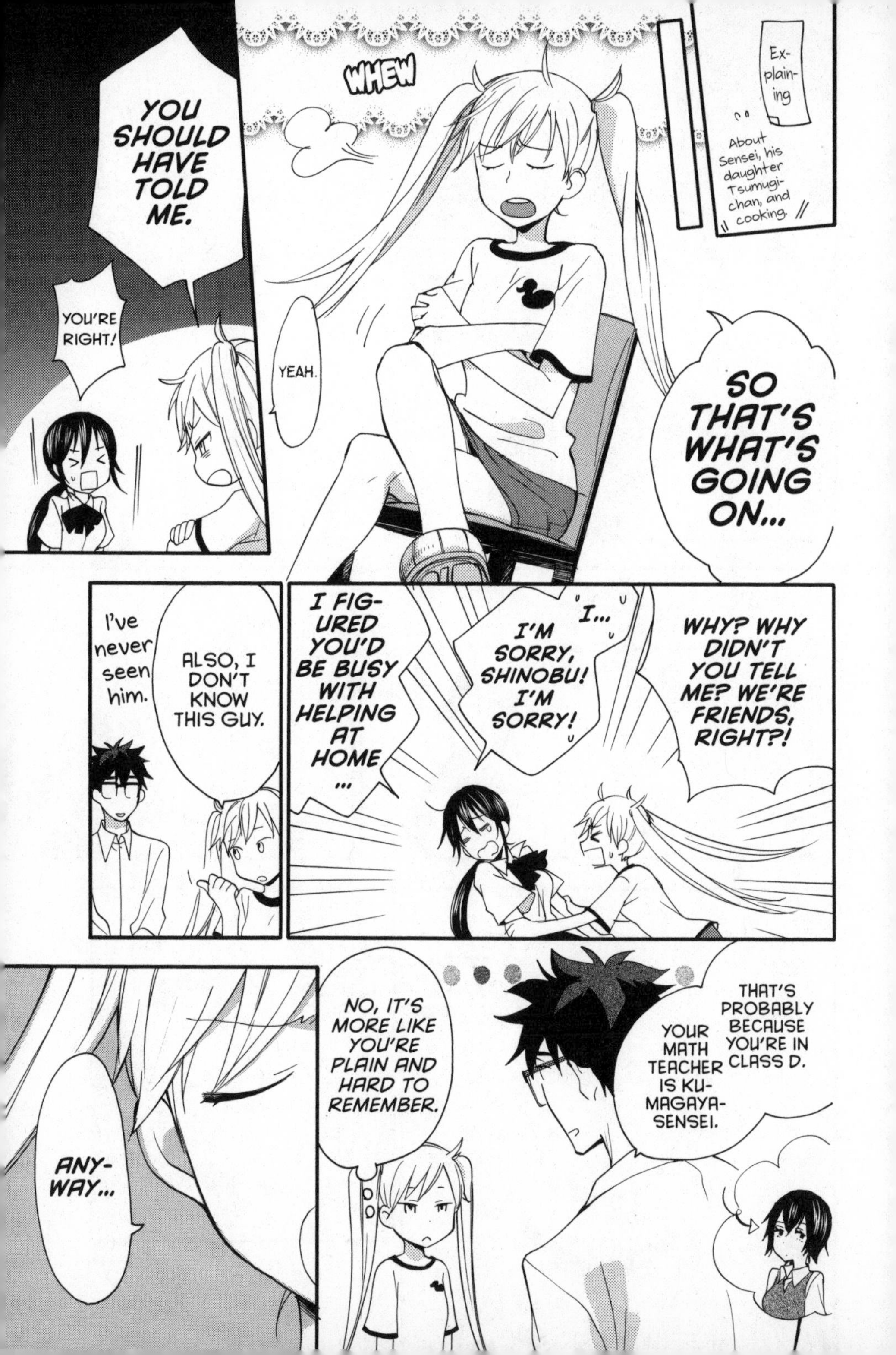

WHEW
Explaining
About Sensei, his daughter Tsumugi-chan, and cooking.
SO THAT'S WHAT'S GOING ON...
YEAH.
YOU SHOULD HAVE TOLD ME.
YOU'RE RIGHT!
WHY? WHY DIDN'T YOU TELL ME? WE'RE FRIENDS, RIGHT?!
I...
I'M SORRY, SHINOBU! I'M SORRY!
I FIGURED YOU'D BE BUSY WITH HELPING AT HOME...
ALSO, I DON'T KNOW THIS GUY.
I've never seen him.
THAT'S PROBABLY BECAUSE YOU'RE IN CLASS D.
YOUR MATH TEACHER IS KUMAGAYA-SENSEI.
NO, IT'S MORE LIKE YOU'RE PLAIN AND HARD TO REMEMBER.
ANYWAY...

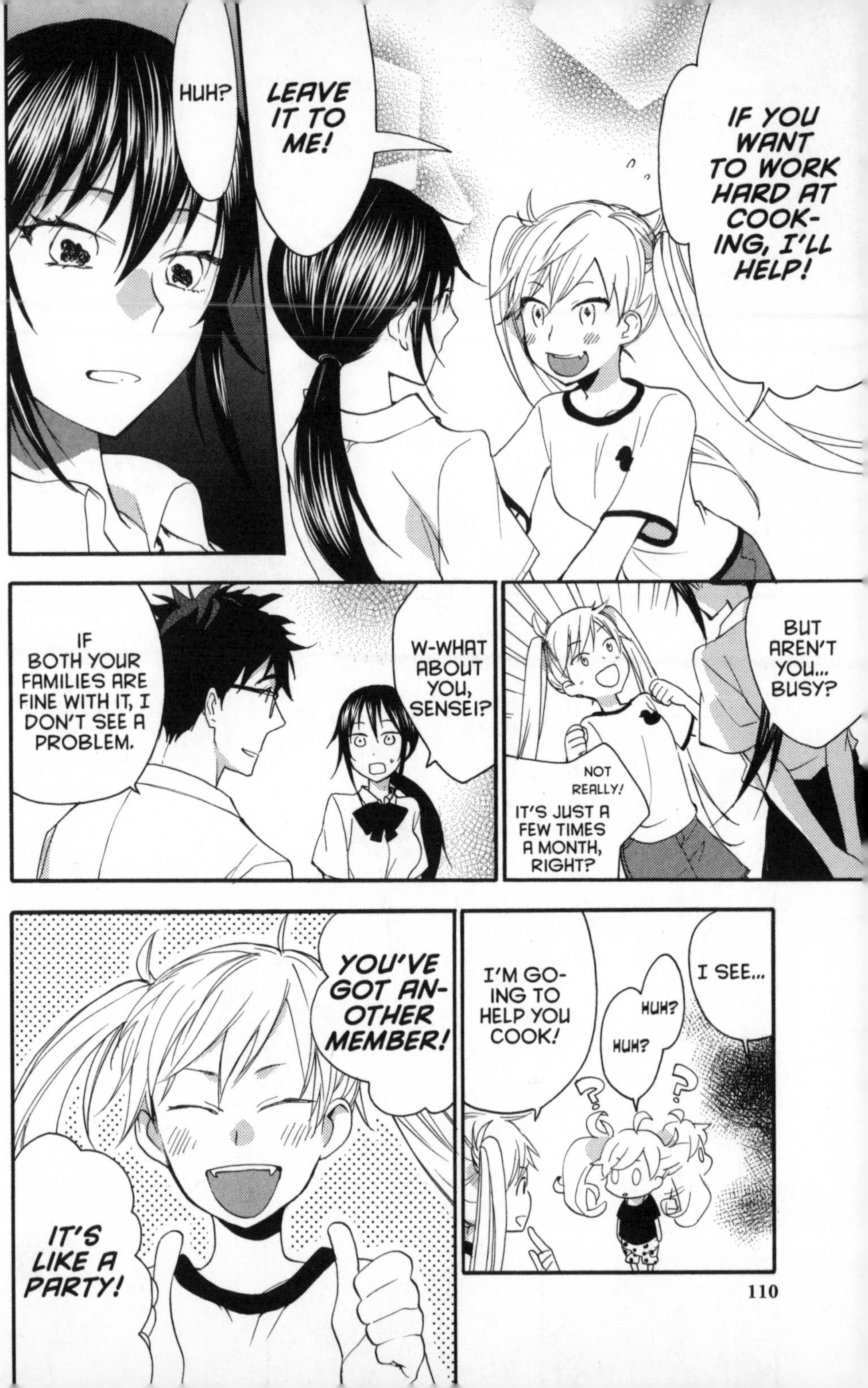
IF YOU WANT TO WORK HARD AT COOK-ING, I'LL HELP!
LEAVE IT TO ME!
HUH?
BUT AREN'T YOU... BUSY?
NOT REALLY!
IT'S JUST A FEW TIMES A MONTH, RIGHT?
W-WHAT ABOUT YOU, SENSEI?
IF BOTH YOUR FAMILIES ARE FINE WITH IT, I DON'T SEE A PROBLEM.
I SEE...
HUH?
HUH?
I'M GO-ING TO HELP YOU COOK!
YOU'VE GOT AN-OTHER MEMBER!
IT'S LIKE A PARTY!

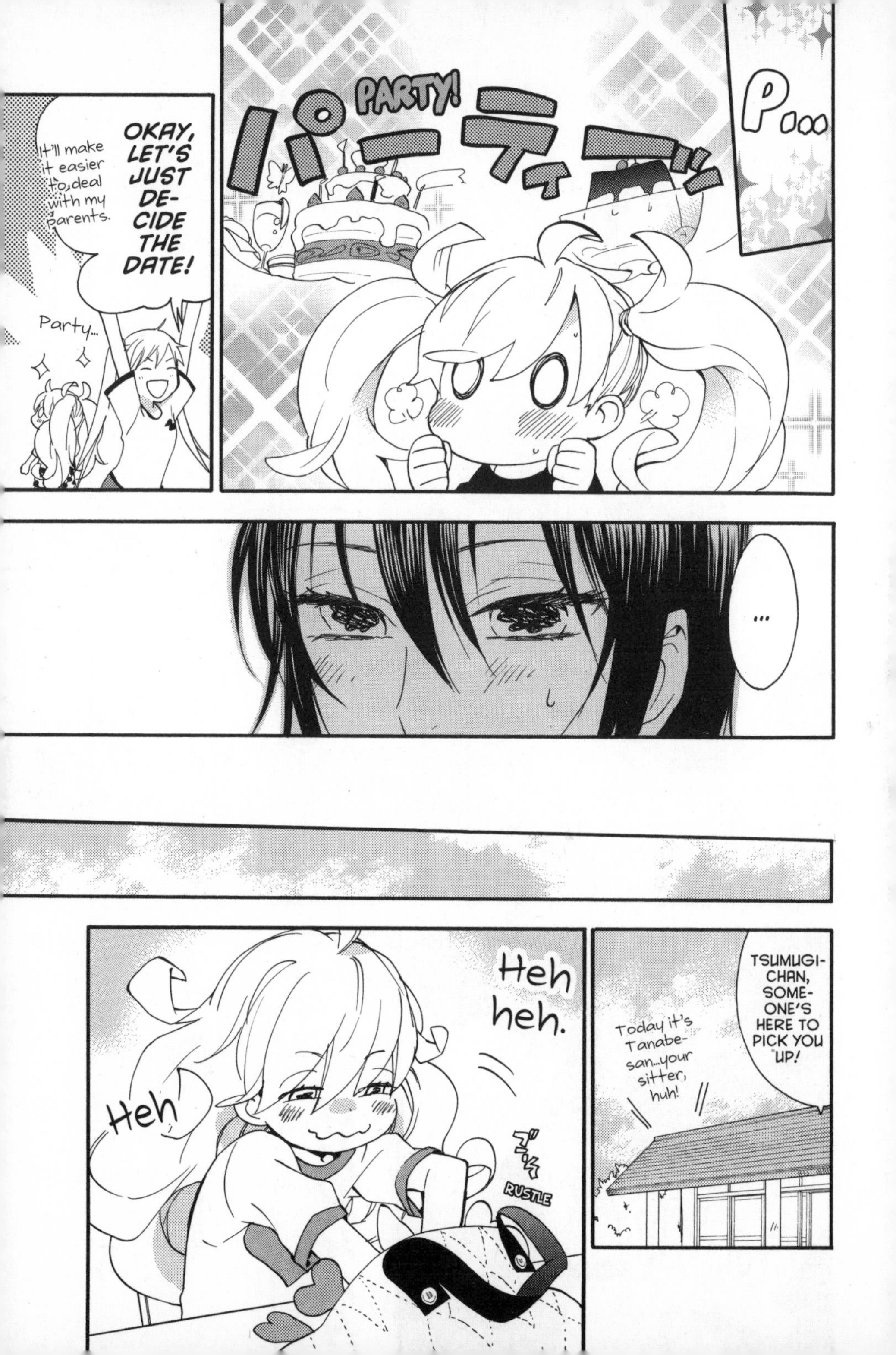
P...
PARTY!
パーティーッ
OKAY, LET'S JUST DE-CIDE THE DATE!
It'll make it easier to deal with my parents.
Party...
...
TSUMUGI-CHAN, SOME-ONE'S HERE TO PICK YOU UP!
Today it's Tanabe-san...your sitter, huh!
Heh heh.
Heh
RUSTLE

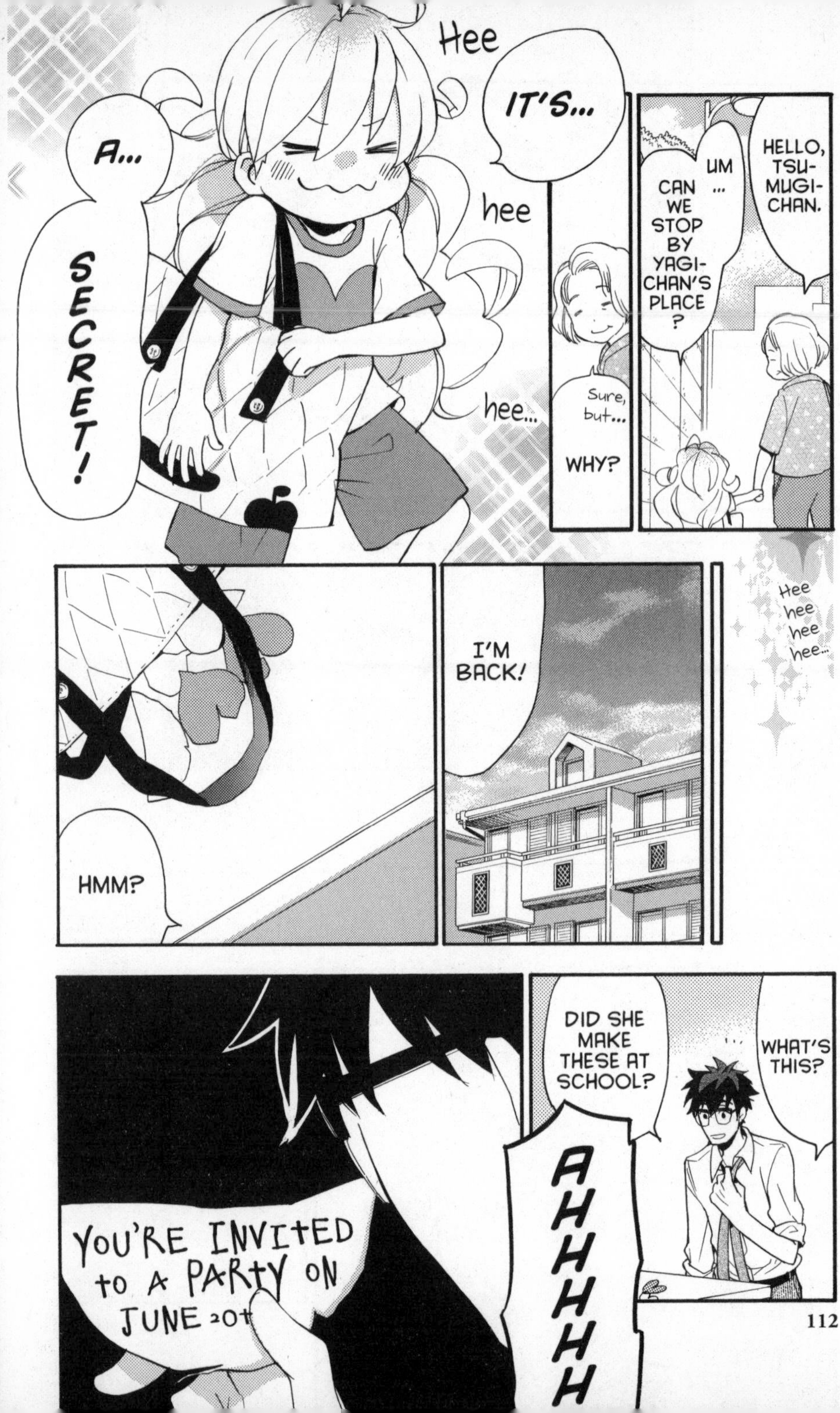
HELLO, TSUMUGI-CHAN.
UM... CAN WE STOP BY YAGI-CHAN'S PLACE?
Sure, but...
WHY?
Hee
IT'S...
hee
hee...
A...
SECRET!
Hee hee hee hee...
I'M BACK!
HMM?
WHAT'S THIS?
...
DID SHE MAKE THESE AT SCHOOL?
AHHHHHH
YOU'RE INVITED to A PARTY ON JUNE 20th

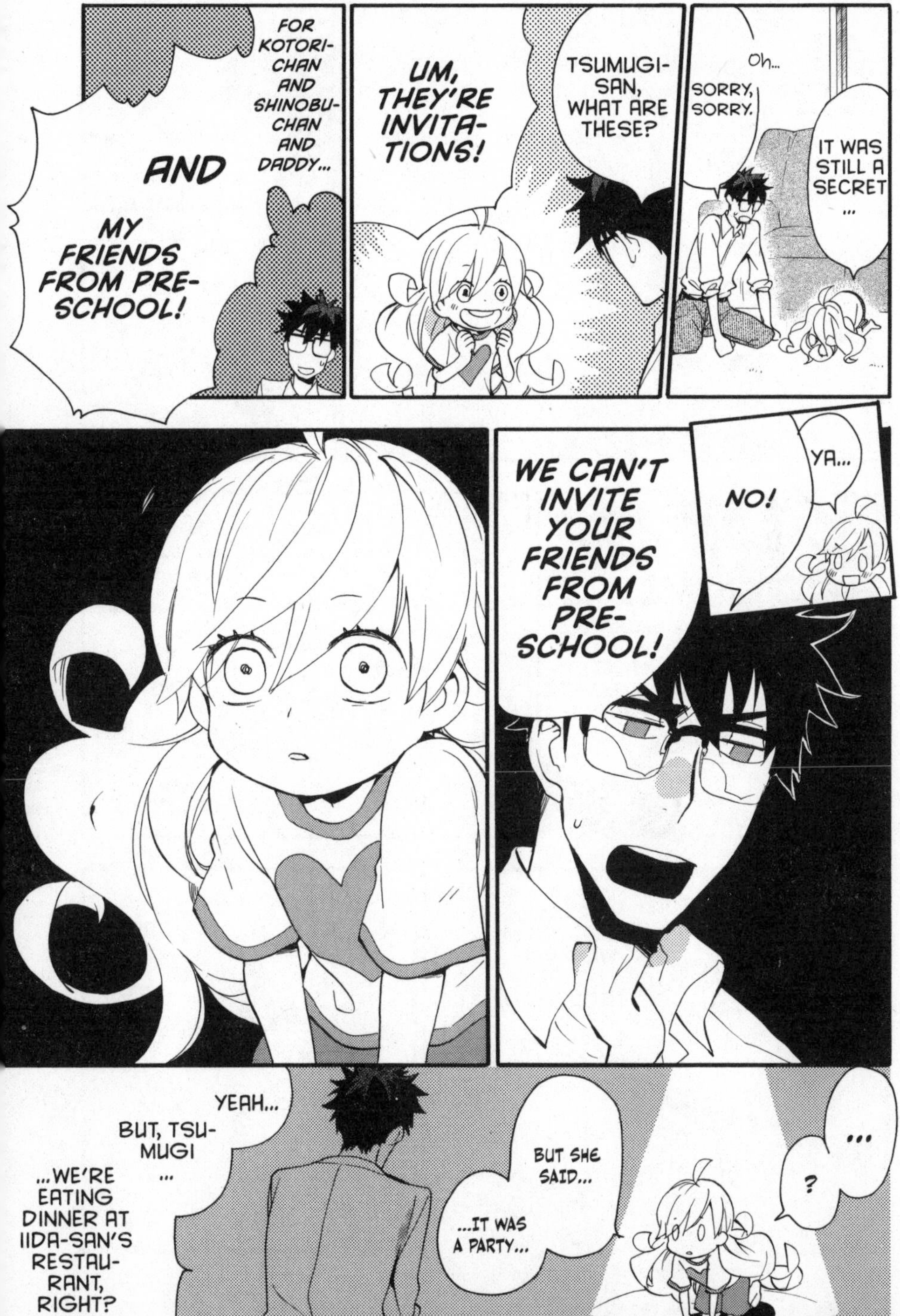
Oh... SORRY, SORRY.
IT WAS STILL A SECRET ...
TSUMUGI-SAN, WHAT ARE THESE?
UM, THEY'RE INVITATIONS!
FOR KOTORI-CHAN AND SHINOBU-CHAN AND DADDY...
AND MY FRIENDS FROM PRE-SCHOOL!
YA...
NO!
WE CAN'T INVITE YOUR FRIENDS FROM PRE-SCHOOL!
...
?
BUT SHE SAID...
...IT WAS A PARTY...
YEAH...
BUT, TSUMUGI ...
...WE'RE EATING DINNER AT IIDA-SAN'S RESTAURANT, RIGHT?

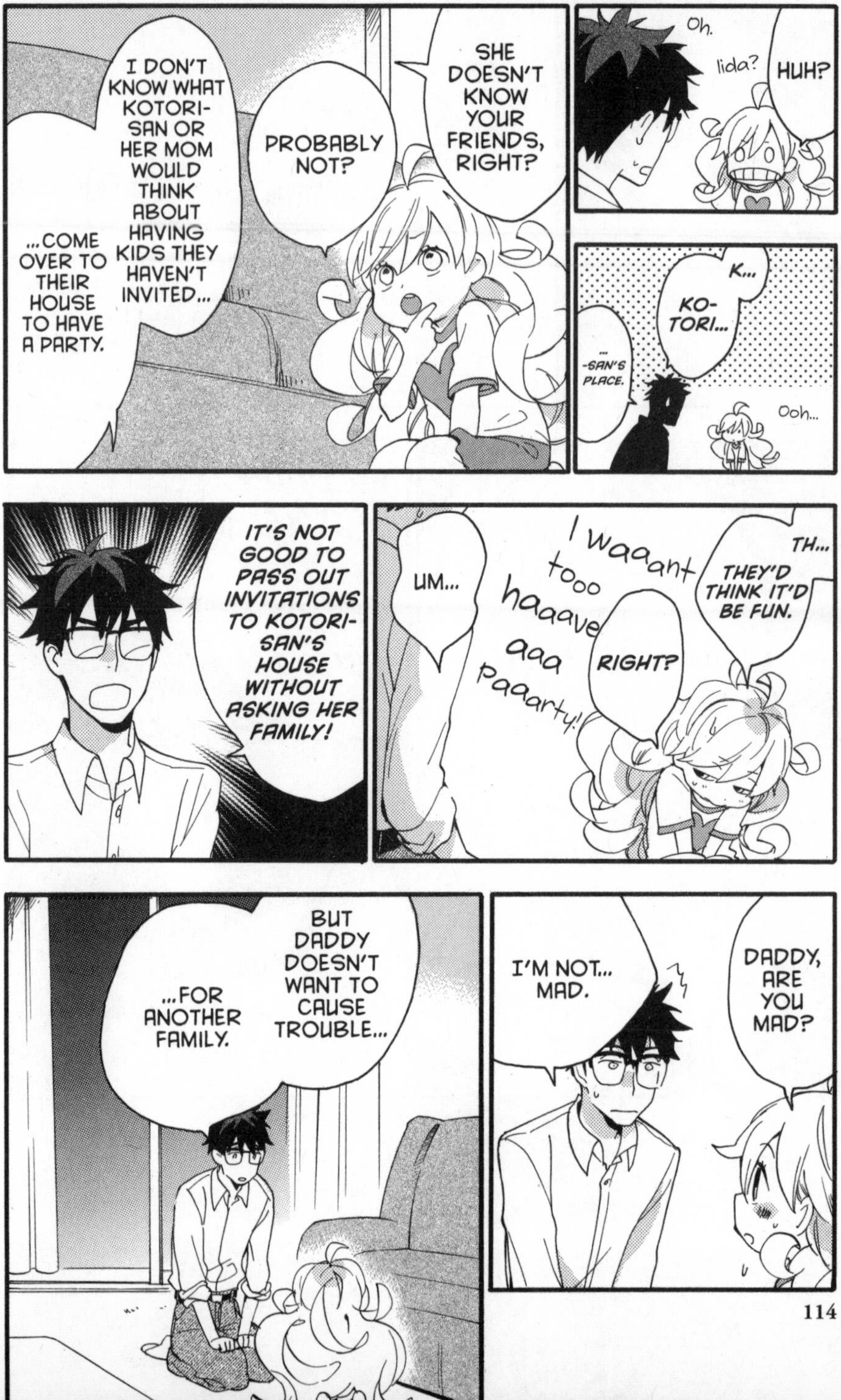
HUH?
Iida?
Oh.
K... KO-TORI...
...-SAN'S PLACE.
Ooh...
SHE DOESN'T KNOW YOUR FRIENDS, RIGHT?
PROBABLY NOT?
I DON'T KNOW WHAT KOTORI-SAN OR HER MOM WOULD THINK ABOUT HAVING KIDS THEY HAVEN'T INVITED...
...COME OVER TO THEIR HOUSE TO HAVE A PARTY.
TH... THEY'D THINK IT'D BE FUN.
RIGHT?
I waaaant tooo haaave aaa paaarty!
UM...
IT'S NOT GOOD TO PASS OUT INVITATIONS TO KOTORI-SAN'S HOUSE WITHOUT ASKING HER FAMILY!
DADDY, ARE YOU MAD?
I'M NOT... MAD.
BUT DADDY DOESN'T WANT TO CAUSE TROUBLE...
...FOR ANOTHER FAMILY.

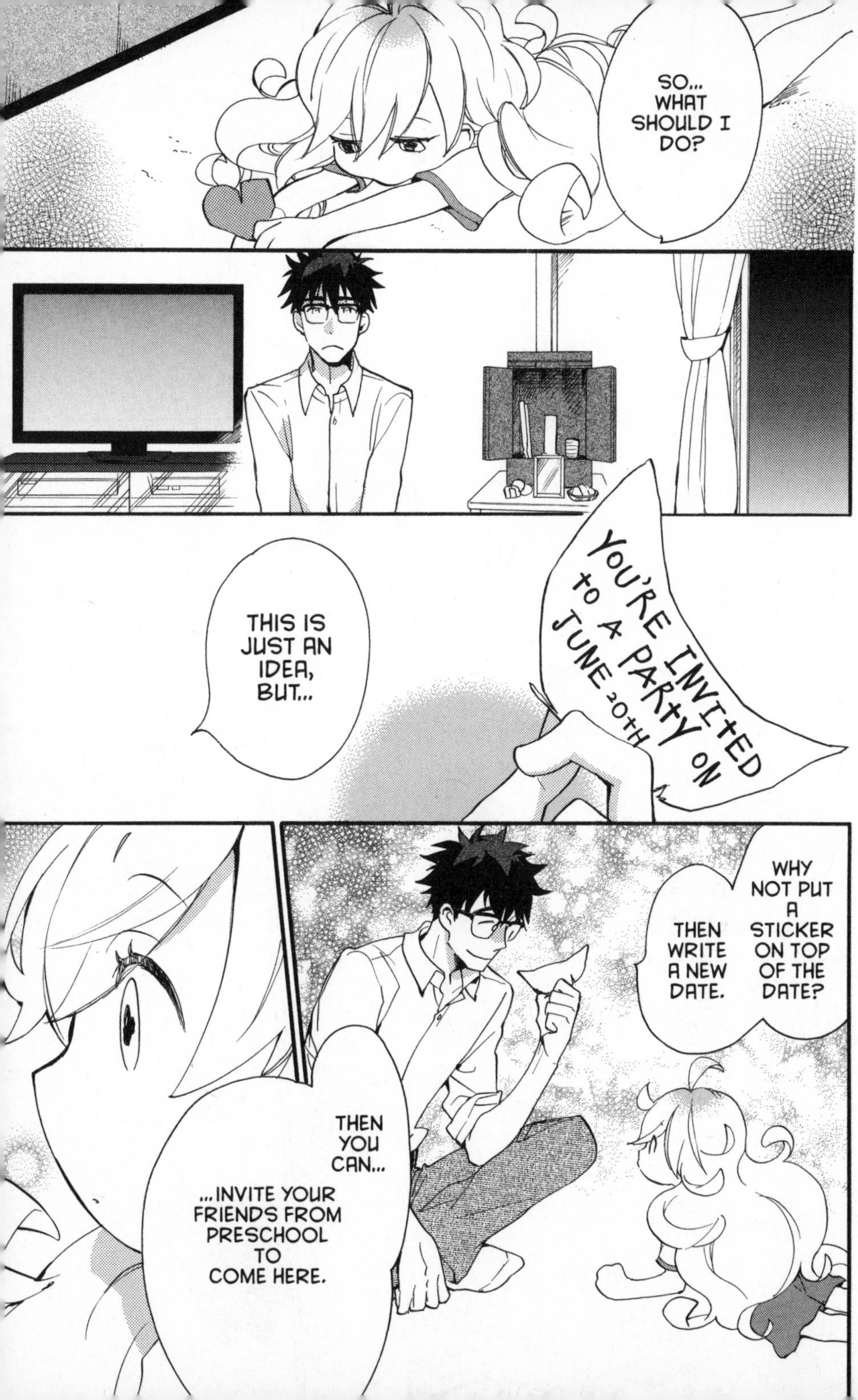
SO... WHAT SHOULD I DO?
YOU'RE INVITED to A PARTY ON JUNE 20TH
THIS IS JUST AN IDEA, BUT...
WHY NOT PUT A STICKER ON TOP OF THE DATE?
THEN WRITE A NEW DATE.
THEN YOU CAN...
...INVITE YOUR FRIENDS FROM PRESCHOOL TO COME HERE.

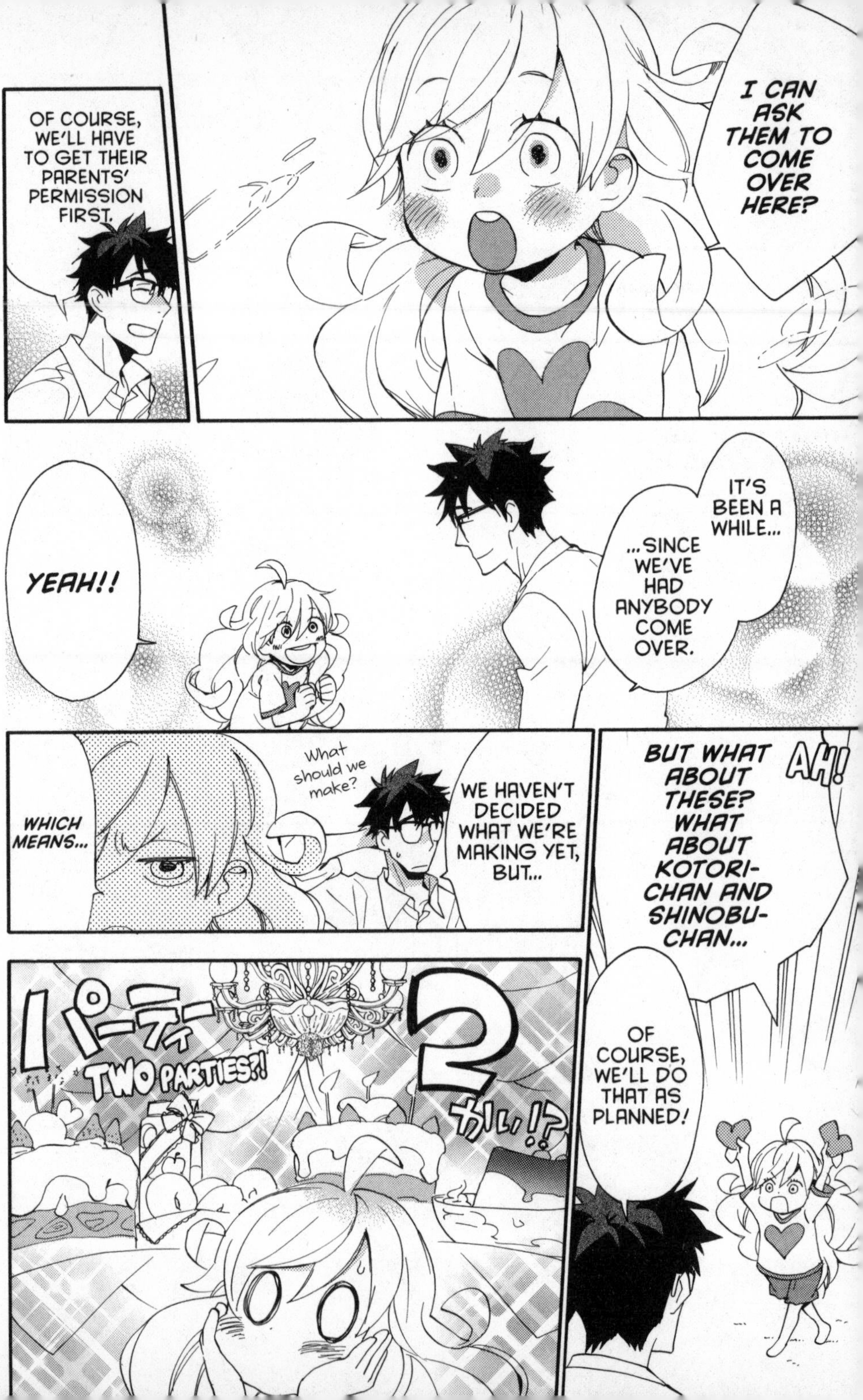
I CAN ASK THEM TO COME OVER HERE?
OF COURSE, WE'LL HAVE TO GET THEIR PARENTS' PERMISSION FIRST.
IT'S BEEN A WHILE...
...SINCE WE'VE HAD ANYBODY COME OVER.
YEAH!!
AH!
BUT WHAT ABOUT THESE? WHAT ABOUT KOTORI-CHAN AND SHINOBU-CHAN...
OF COURSE, WE'LL DO THAT AS PLANNED!
WE HAVEN'T DECIDED WHAT WE'RE MAKING YET, BUT...
What should we make?
WHICH MEANS...
パーティ2かい!?
TWO PARTIES?!

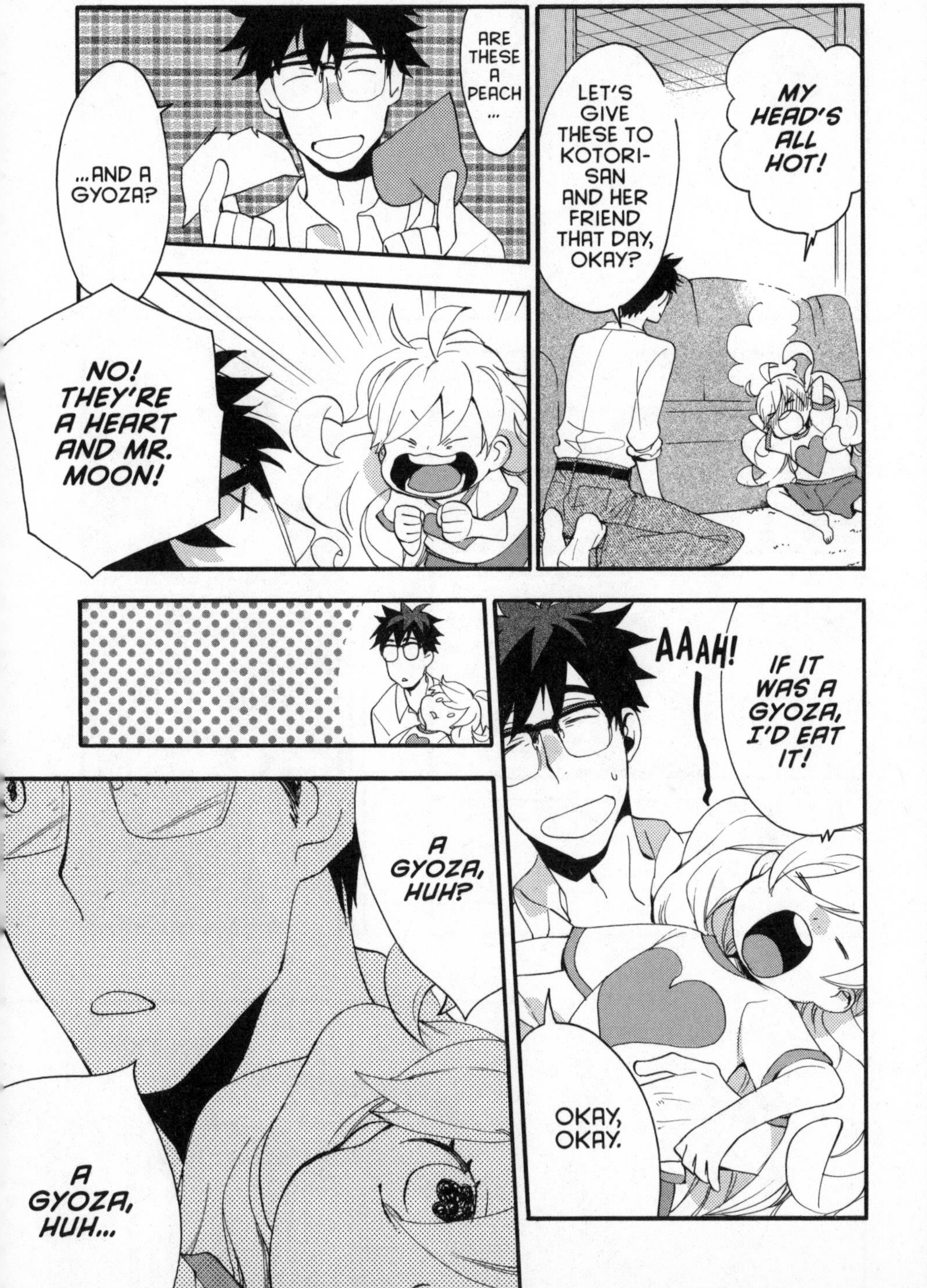
MY HEAD'S ALL HOT!
LET'S GIVE THESE TO KOTORI-SAN AND HER FRIEND THAT DAY, OKAY?
ARE THESE A PEACH ...
...AND A GYOZA?
NO! THEY'RE A HEART AND MR. MOON!
IF IT WAS A GYOZA, I'D EAT IT!
AAAH!
OKAY, OKAY.
A GYOZA, HUH?
A GYOZA, HUH...

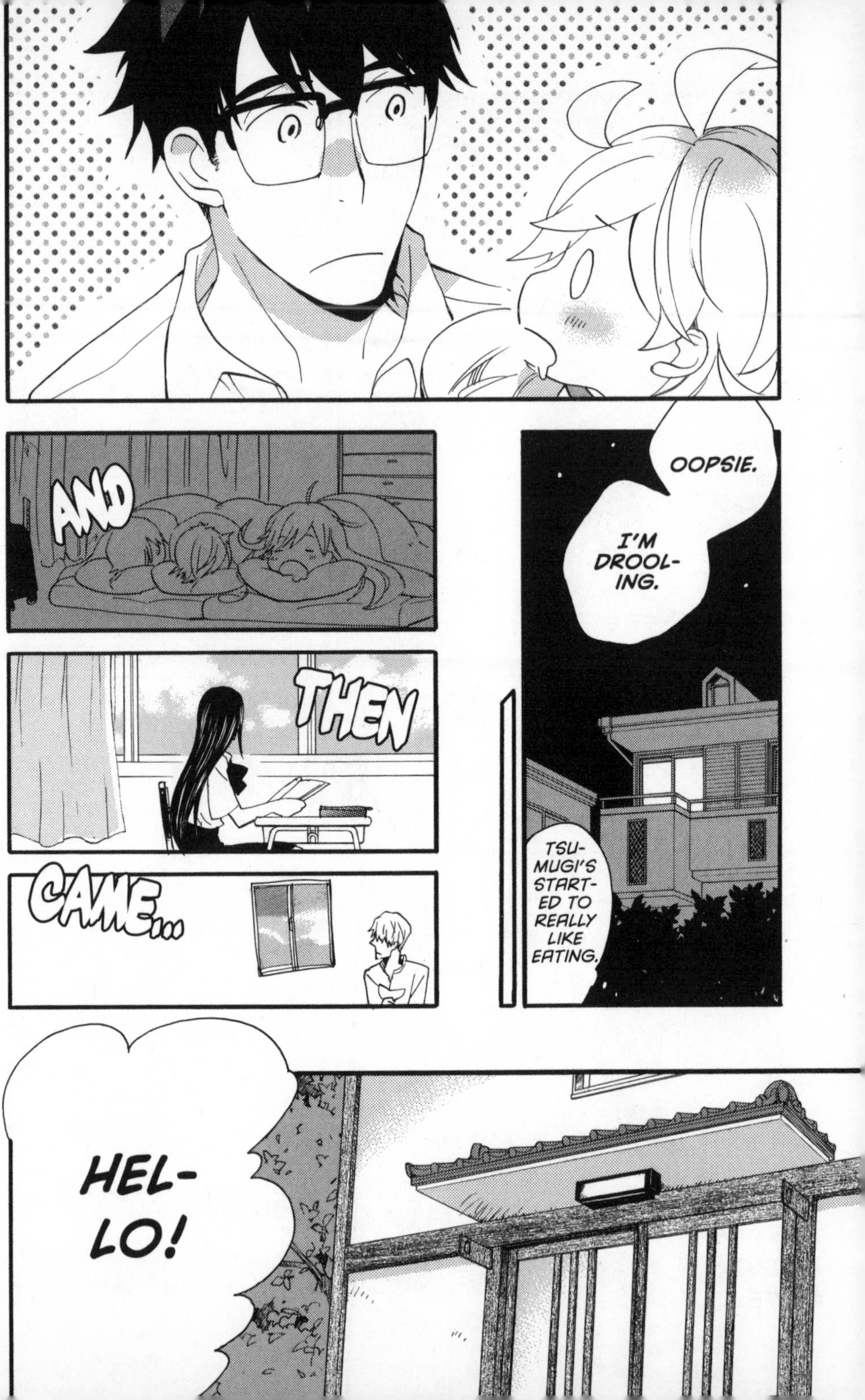
OOPSIE.
I'M DROOL-ING.
TSU-MUGI'S START-ED TO REALLY LIKE EATING.
AND
THEN
CAME...
HEL-LO!

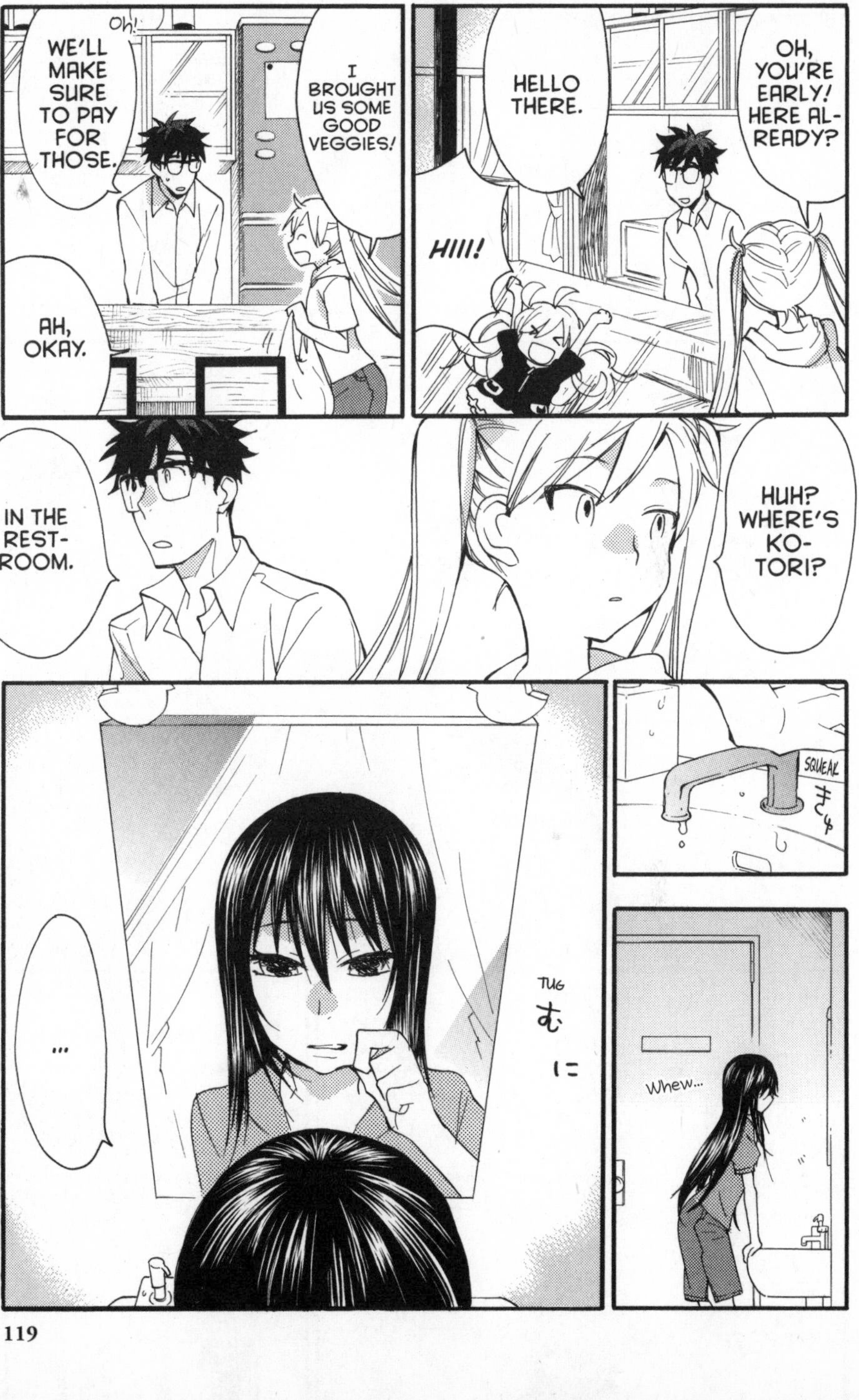
OH, YOU'RE EARLY! HERE AL-READY?
HELLO THERE.
HIII!
I BROUGHT US SOME GOOD VEGGIES!
Oh!
WE'LL MAKE SURE TO PAY FOR THOSE.
AH, OKAY.
HUH? WHERE'S KO-TORI?
IN THE REST-ROOM.
SQUEAK
きゅ
Whew...
TUG
むに
...

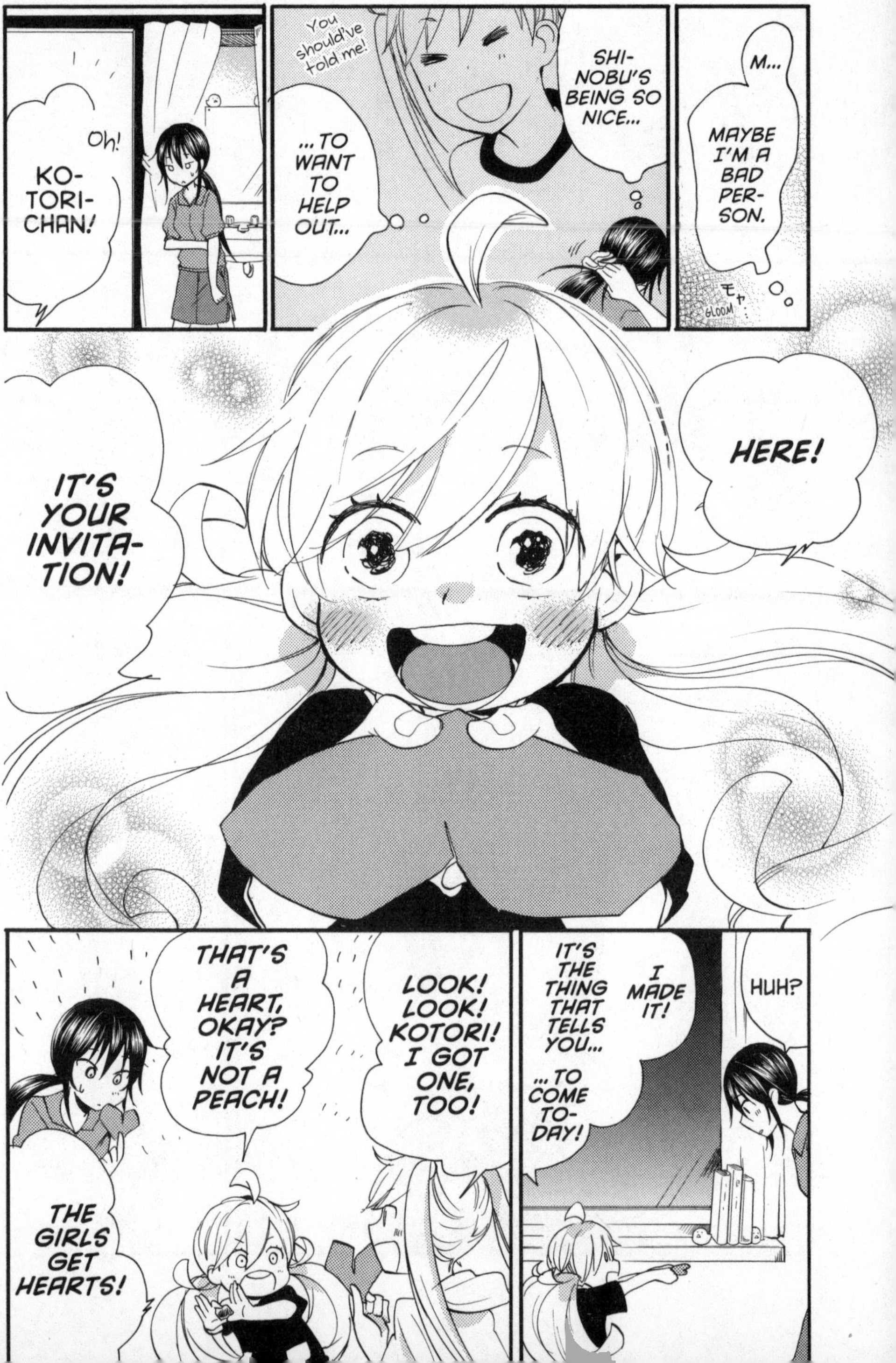
M... MAYBE I'M A BAD PERSON.
モヤ GLOOM
SHINOBU'S BEING SO NICE...
...TO WANT TO HELP OUT...
You should've told me!
Oh! KOTORI-CHAN!
HERE!
IT'S YOUR INVITATION!
HUH?
I MADE IT!
IT'S THE THING THAT TELLS YOU...
...TO COME TODAY!
LOOK! LOOK! KOTORI! I GOT ONE, TOO!
THAT'S A HEART, OKAY? IT'S NOT A PEACH!
THE GIRLS GET HEARTS!

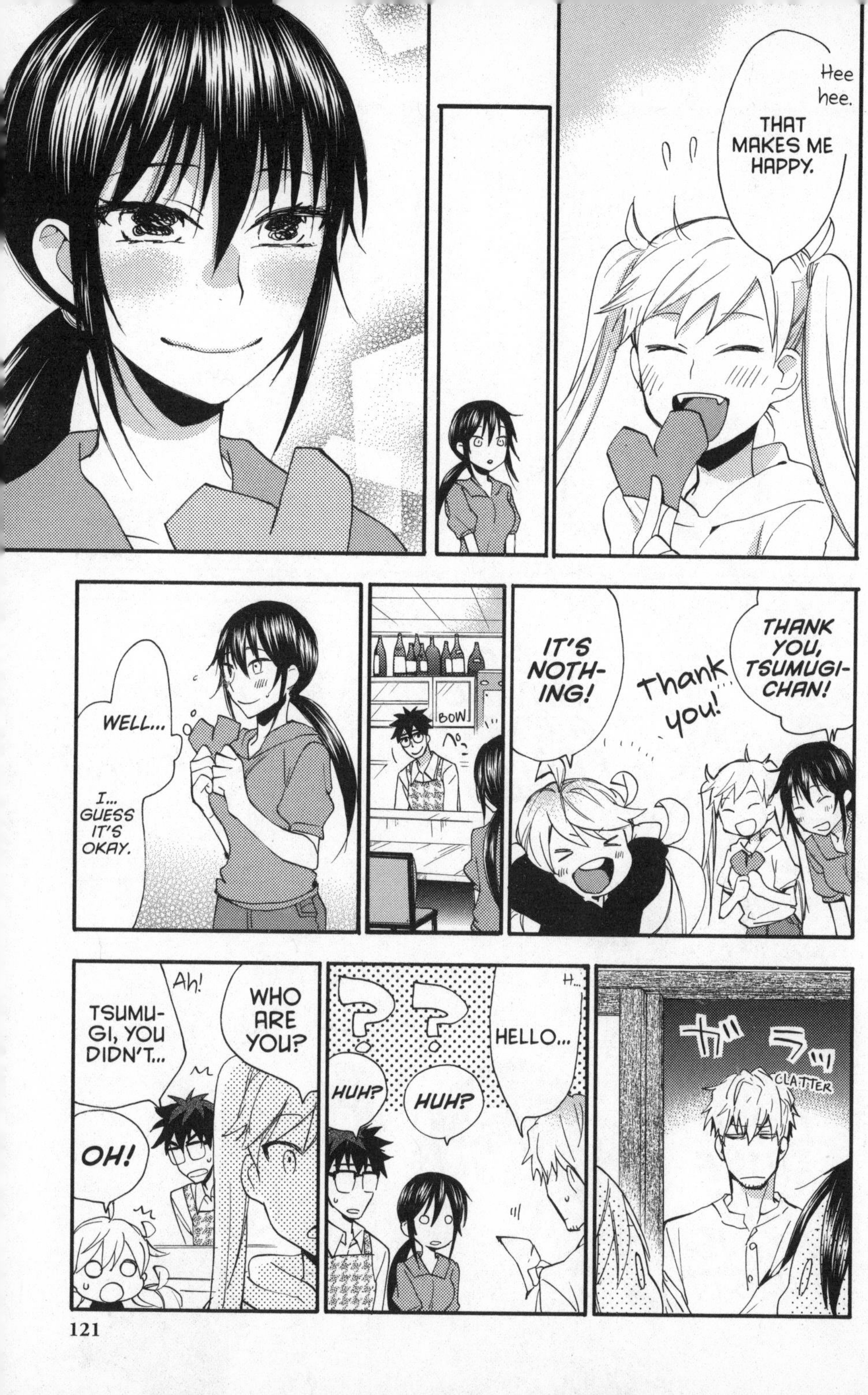
Hee hee.
THAT MAKES ME HAPPY.
THANK YOU, TSUMUGI-CHAN!
Thank you!
IT'S NOTHING!
BOW
WELL...
I... GUESS IT'S OKAY.
ガラッ
CLATTER
H...
HELLO...
HUH?
HUH?
WHO ARE YOU?
Ah!
TSUMUGI, YOU DIDN'T...
OH!

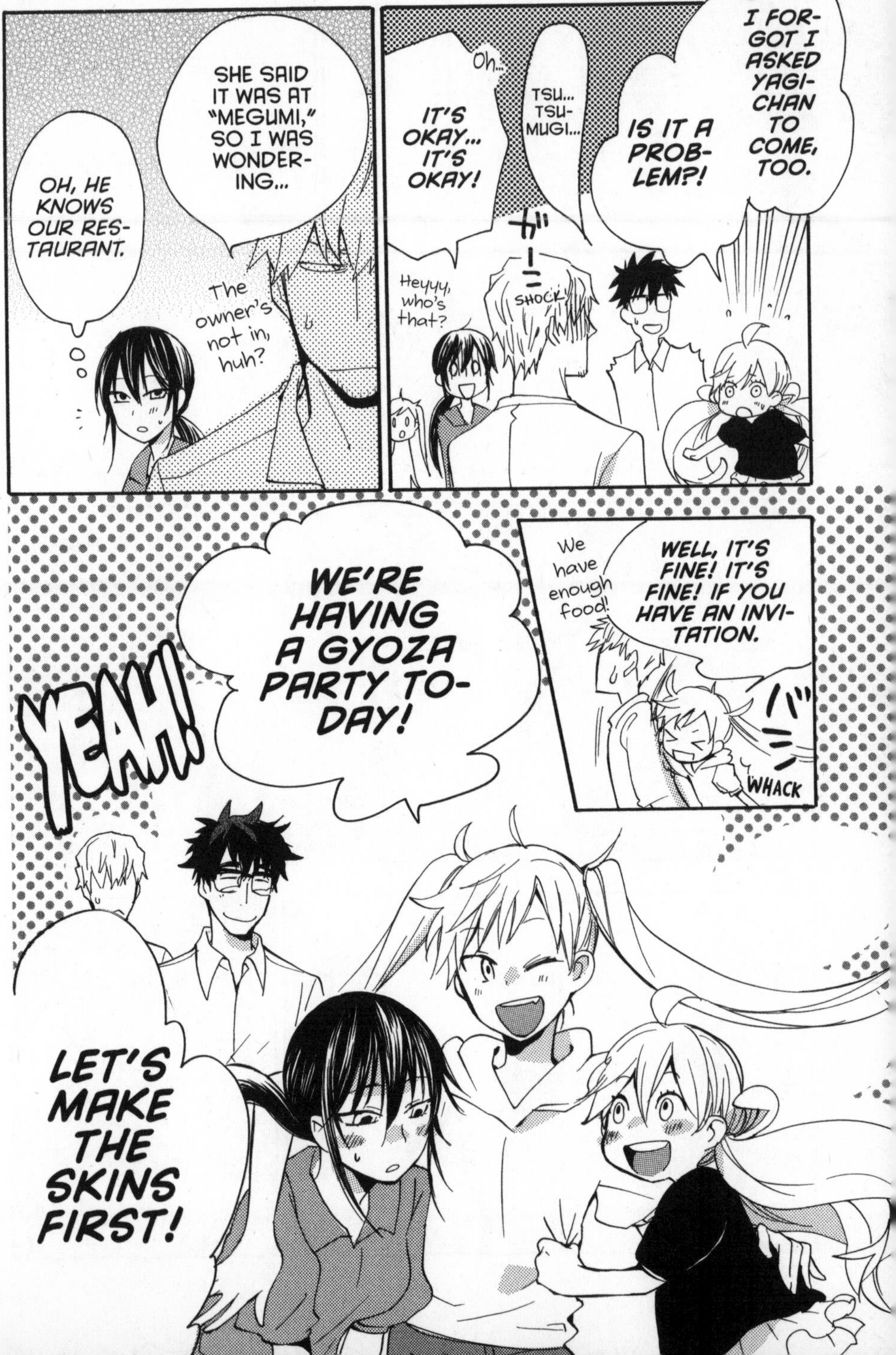
I FORGOT I ASKED YAGI-CHAN TO COME, TOO.
IS IT A PROBLEM?!
Oh...
TSU... TSU-MUGI...
IT'S OKAY... IT'S OKAY!
SHOCK
Heyyy, who's that?
SHE SAID IT WAS AT "MEGUMI," SO I WAS WONDERING...
The owner's not in, huh?
OH, HE KNOWS OUR RESTAURANT.
WELL, IT'S FINE! IT'S FINE! IF YOU HAVE AN INVITATION.
We have enough food!
WHACK
WE'RE HAVING A GYOZA PARTY TODAY!
YEAH!
LET'S MAKE THE SKINS FIRST!

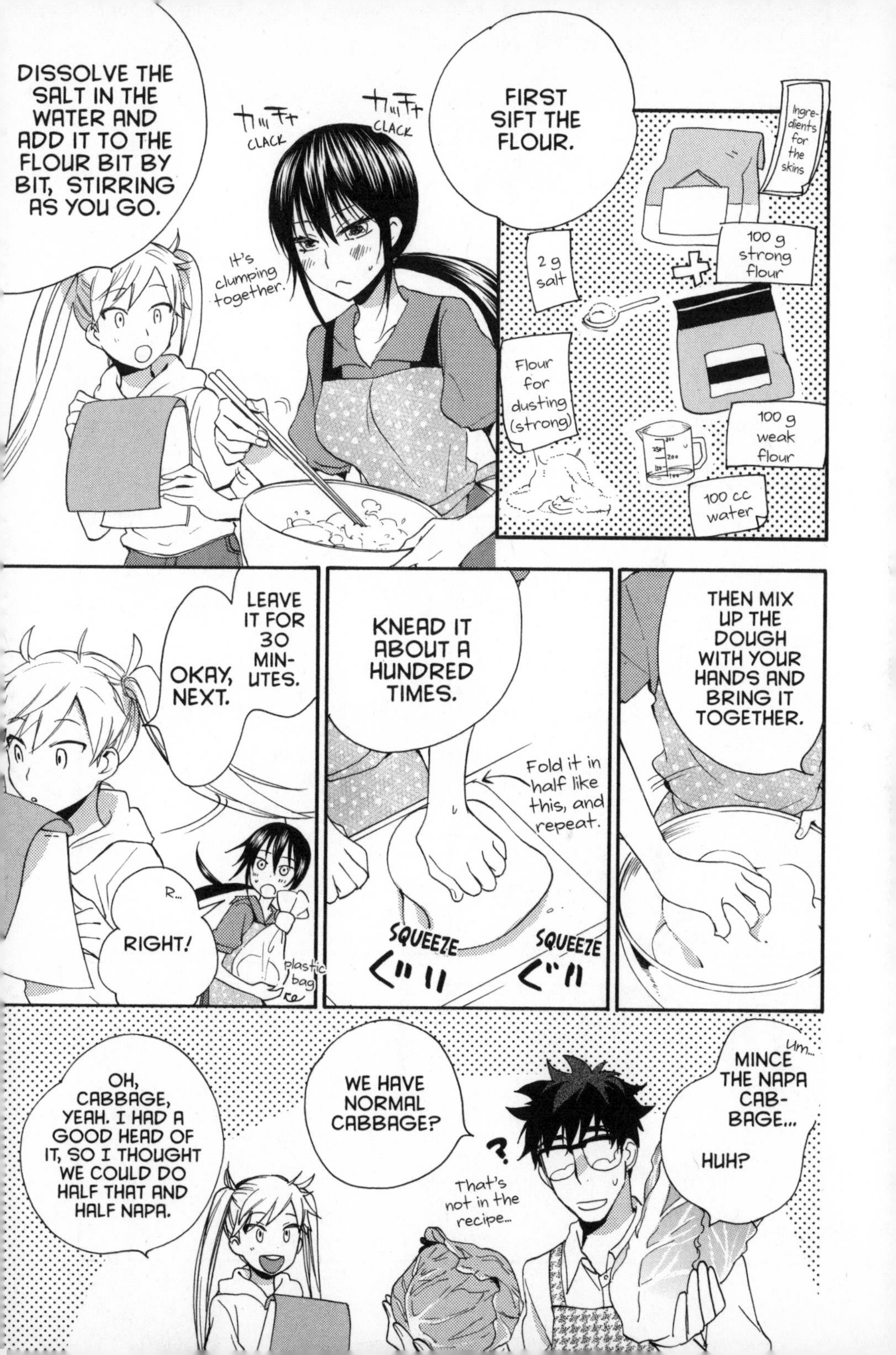
FIRST SIFT THE FLOUR.
Ingredients for the skins
100 g strong flour
2 g salt
Flour for dusting (strong)
100 g weak flour
100 cc water
CLACK
CLACK
DISSOLVE THE SALT IN THE WATER AND ADD IT TO THE FLOUR BIT BY BIT, STIRRING AS YOU GO.
It's clumping together.
THEN MIX UP THE DOUGH WITH YOUR HANDS AND BRING IT TOGETHER.
KNEAD IT ABOUT A HUNDRED TIMES.
Fold it in half like this, and repeat.
SQUEEZE
SQUEEZE
LEAVE IT FOR 30 MINUTES.
OKAY, NEXT.
R...
RIGHT!
plastic bag
Um...
MINCE THE NAPA CABBAGE...
HUH?
That's not in the recipe...
WE HAVE NORMAL CABBAGE?
OH, CABBAGE, YEAH. I HAD A GOOD HEAD OF IT, SO I THOUGHT WE COULD DO HALF THAT AND HALF NAPA.

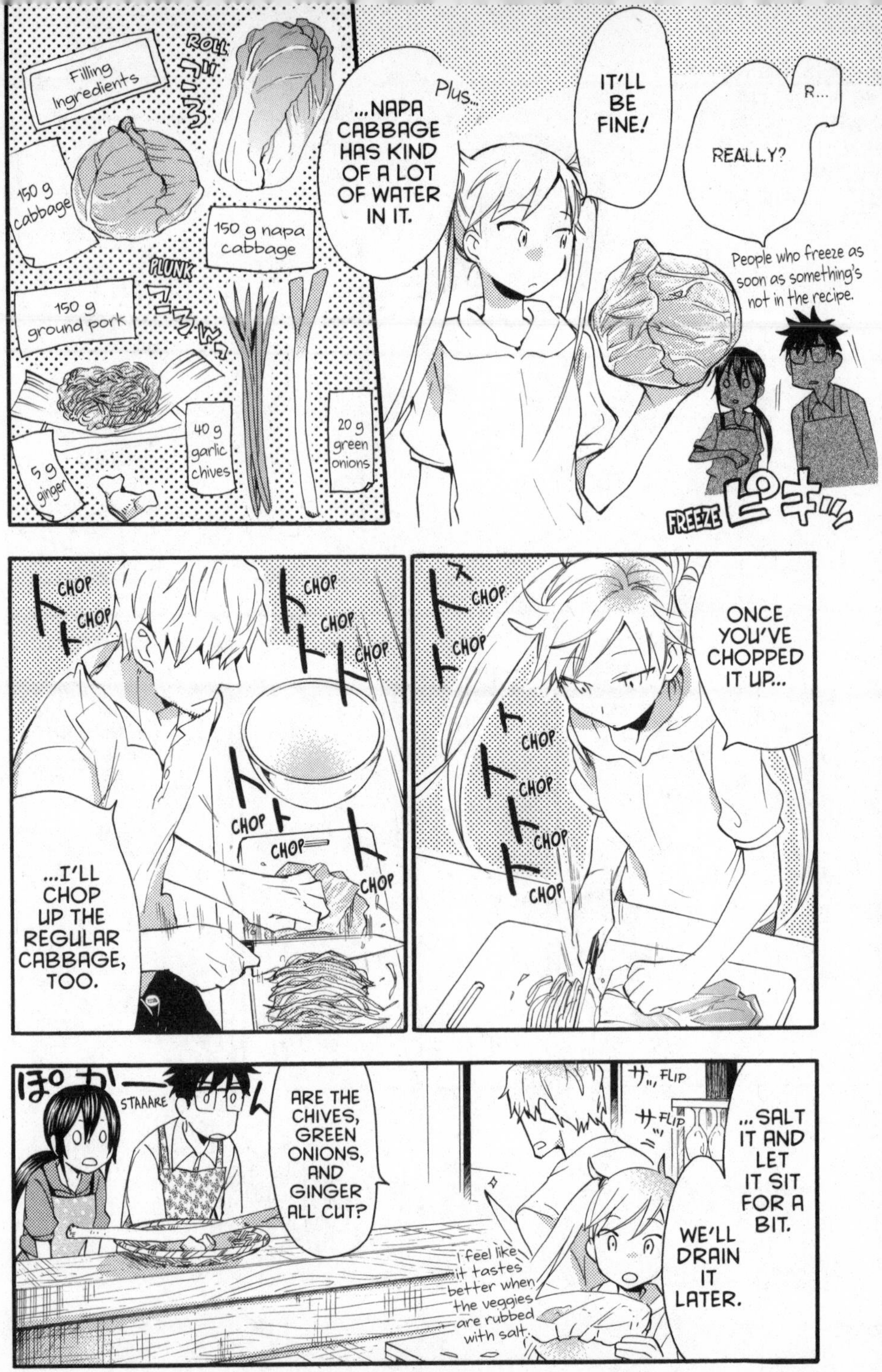
R... REALLY?
IT'LL BE FINE!
Plus...
...NAPA CABBAGE HAS KIND OF A LOT OF WATER IN IT.
People who freeze as soon as something's not in the recipe.
FREEZE
ROLL
Filling Ingredients
150 g cabbage
150 g napa cabbage
PLUNK
150 g ground pork
40 g garlic chives
20 g green onions
5 g ginger
CHOP CHOP
ONCE YOU'VE CHOPPED IT UP...
CHOP CHOP CHOP CHOP
CHOP CHOP CHOP
CHOP CHOP CHOP
CHOP CHOP CHOP
...I'LL CHOP UP THE REGULAR CABBAGE, TOO.
FLIP
FLIP
...SALT IT AND LET IT SIT FOR A BIT.
WE'LL DRAIN IT LATER.
I feel like it tastes better when the veggies are rubbed with salt.
ARE THE CHIVES, GREEN ONIONS, AND GINGER ALL CUT?
STAAARE

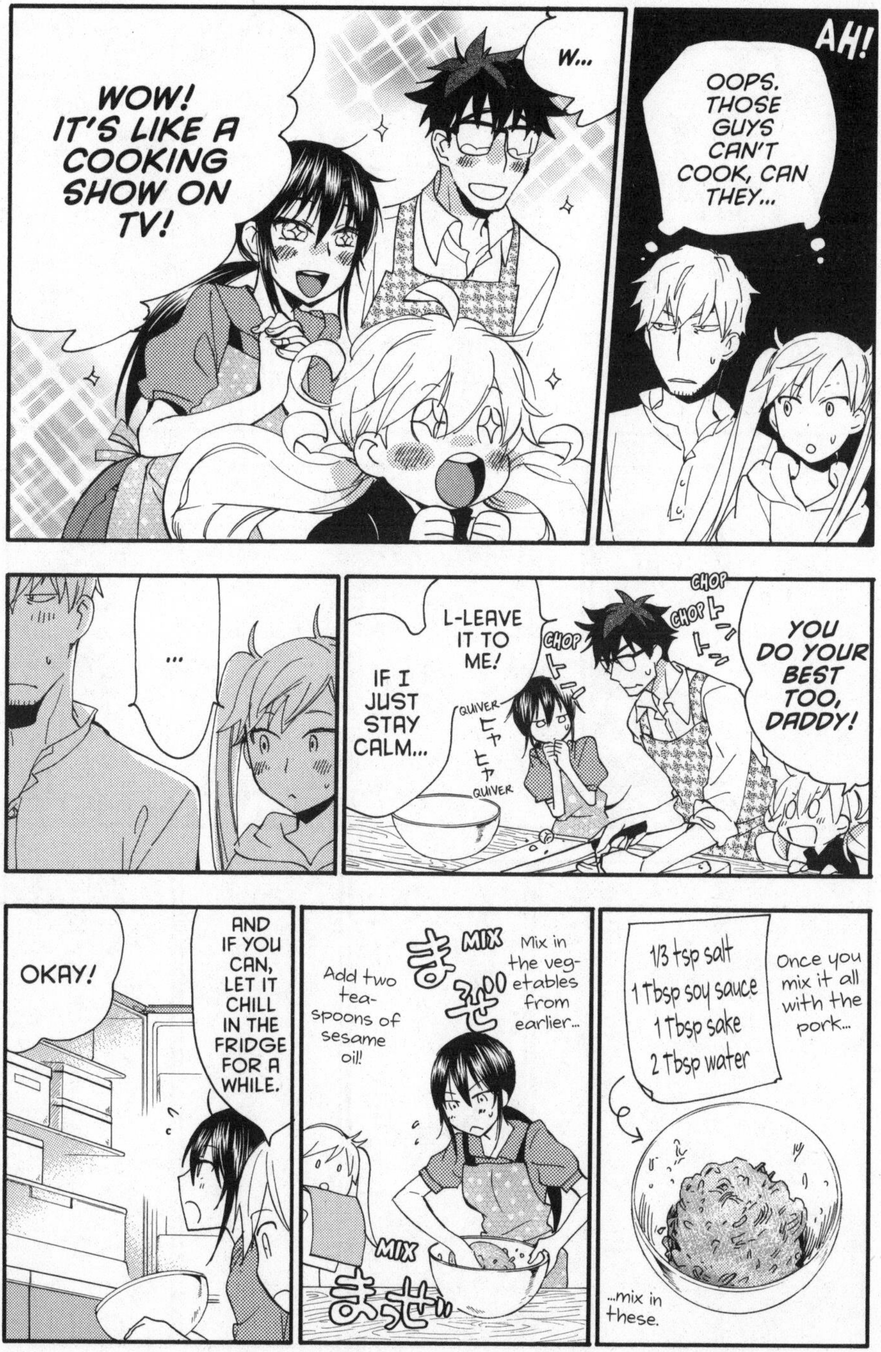
AH!
OOPS. THOSE GUYS CAN'T COOK, CAN THEY...
W...
WOW! IT'S LIKE A COOKING SHOW ON TV!
YOU DO YOUR BEST TOO, DADDY!
CHOP
CHOP
CHOP
L-LEAVE IT TO ME!
IF I JUST STAY CALM...
QUIVER
ヒャ
ヒャ
QUIVER
...
Once you mix it all with the pork...
1/3 tsp salt
1 Tbsp soy sauce
1 Tbsp sake
2 Tbsp water
...mix in these.
Mix in the vegetables from earlier...
MIX
まぜ
Add two teaspoons of sesame oil!
MIX
まぜ
AND IF YOU CAN, LET IT CHILL IN THE FRIDGE FOR A WHILE.
OKAY!

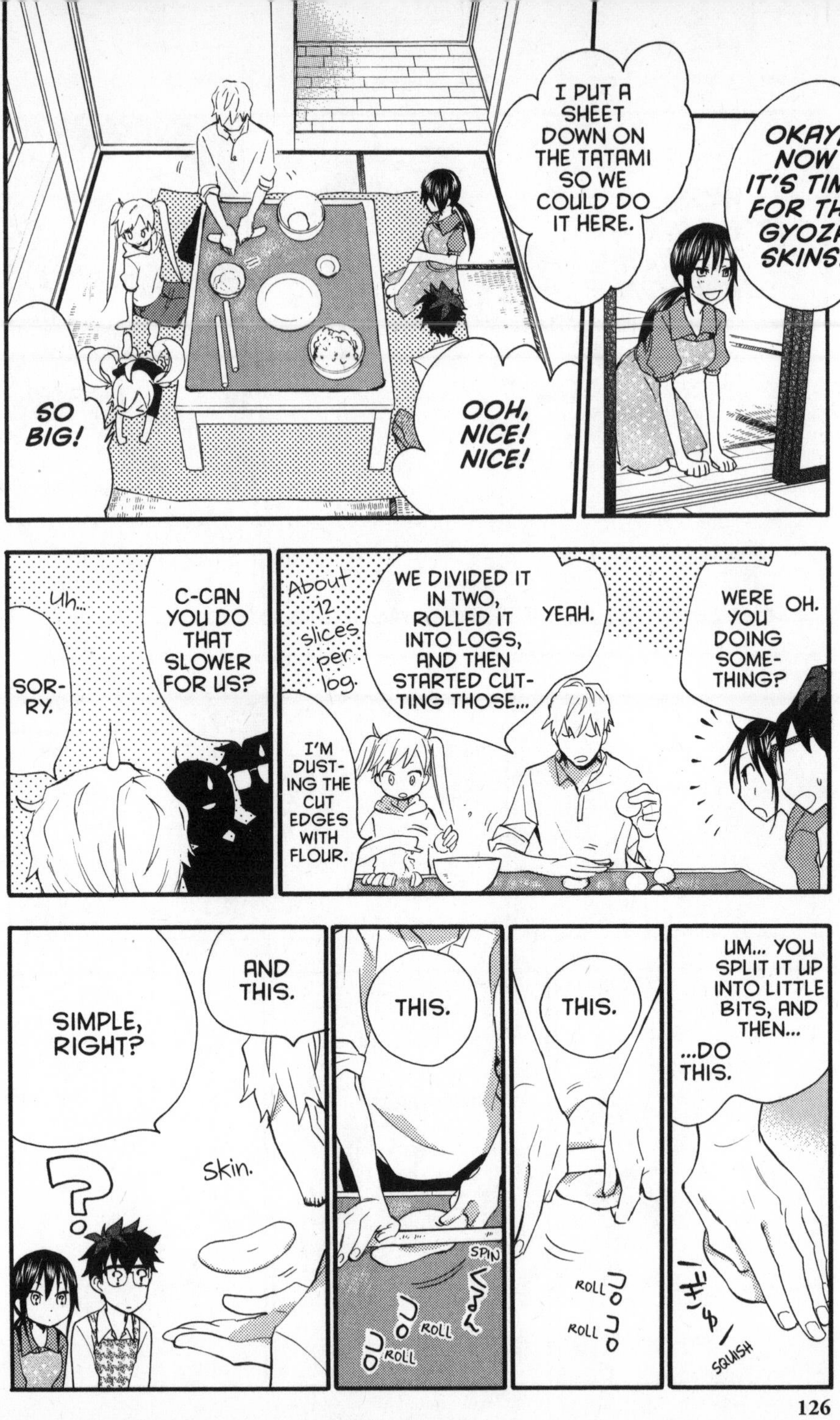
OKAY, NOW IT'S TIME FOR THE GYOZA SKINS!
I PUT A SHEET DOWN ON THE TATAMI SO WE COULD DO IT HERE.
OOH, NICE! NICE!
SO BIG!
OH.
WERE YOU DOING SOME-THING?
YEAH.
WE DIVIDED IT IN TWO, ROLLED IT INTO LOGS, AND THEN STARTED CUT-TING THOSE...
About 12 slices per log.
I'M DUST-ING THE CUT EDGES WITH FLOUR.
C-CAN YOU DO THAT SLOWER FOR US?
Uh...
SOR-RY.
UM... YOU SPLIT IT UP INTO LITTLE BITS, AND THEN...
...DO THIS.
SQUISH
THIS.
ROLL
ROLL
THIS.
SPIN
ROLL
ROLL
AND THIS.
SIMPLE, RIGHT?
Skin.
?

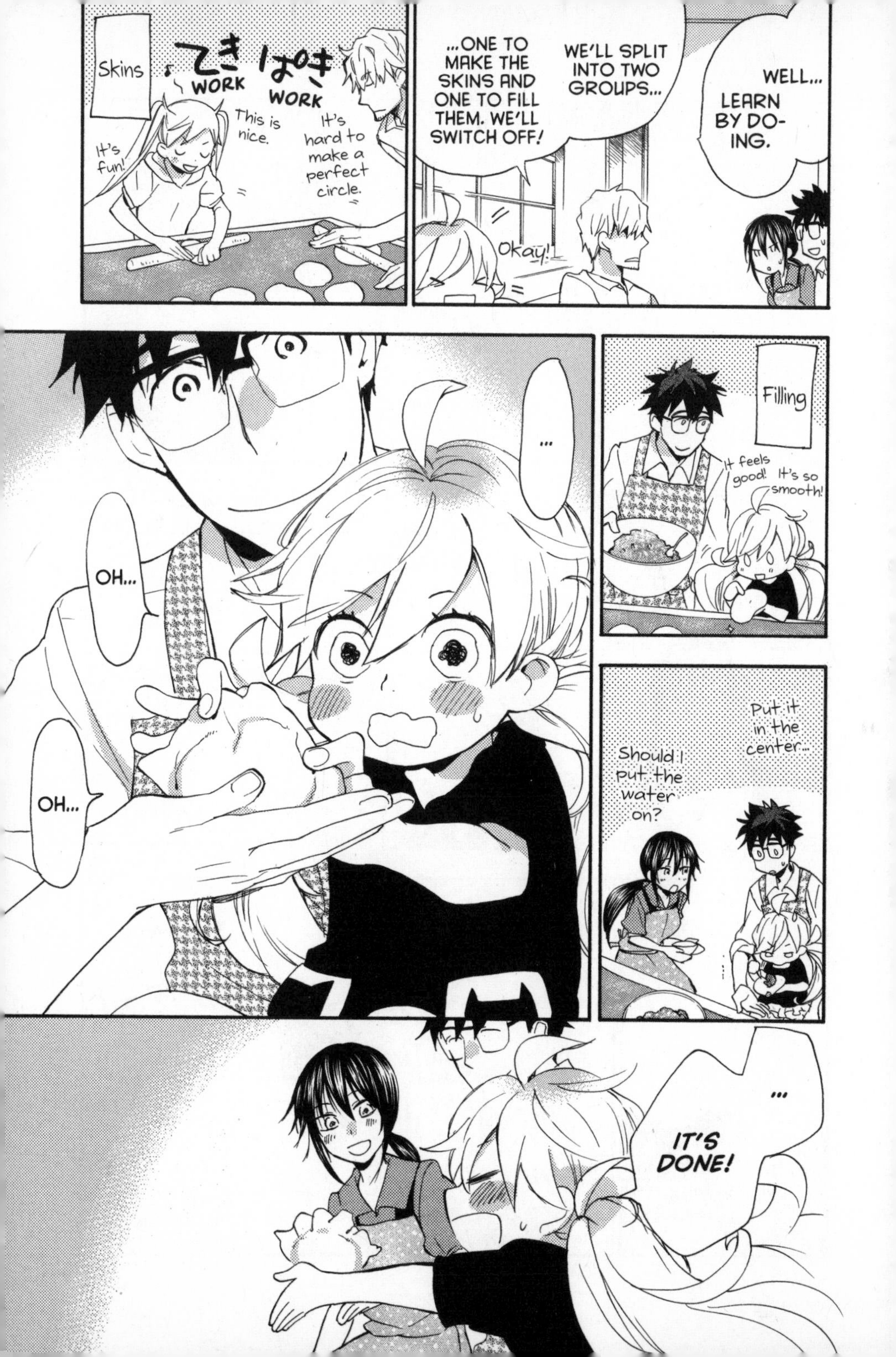
WELL... LEARN BY DO-ING.
WE'LL SPLIT INTO TWO GROUPS...
...ONE TO MAKE THE SKINS AND ONE TO FILL THEM. WE'LL SWITCH OFF!
Okay!
てきぱき
WORK WORK
It's hard to make a perfect circle.
This is nice.
Skins
It's fun!
Filling
It's so smooth!
It feels good!
Put it in the center...
Should I put the water on?
...
OH...
OH...
... IT'S DONE!

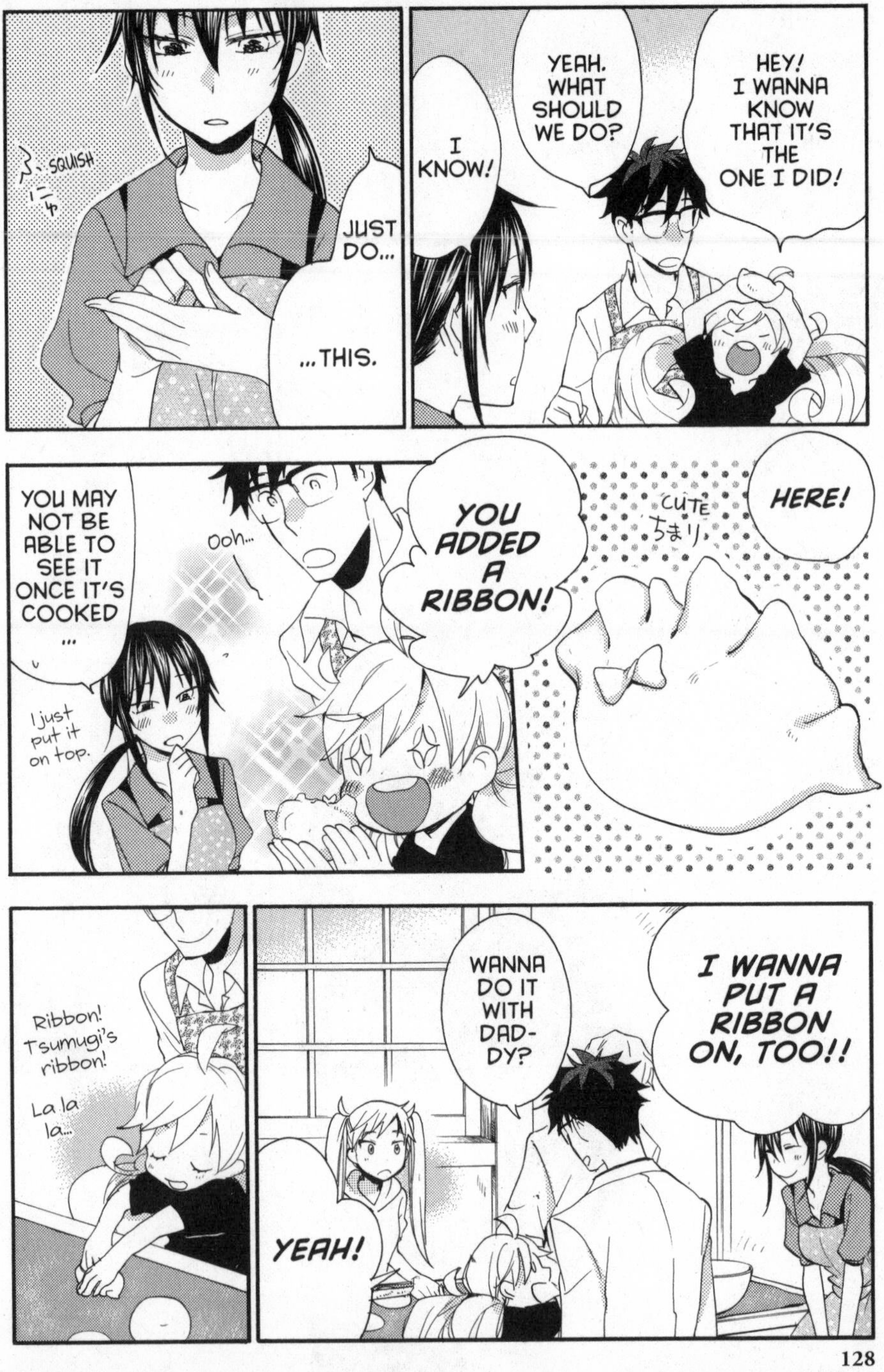
HEY! I WANNA KNOW THAT IT'S THE ONE I DID!
YEAH. WHAT SHOULD WE DO?
I KNOW!
SQUISH
JUST DO...
...THIS.
HERE!
CUTE
YOU ADDED A RIBBON!
Ooh...
YOU MAY NOT BE ABLE TO SEE IT ONCE IT'S COOKED...
I just put it on top.
I WANNA PUT A RIBBON ON, TOO!!
WANNA DO IT WITH DAD-DY?
YEAH!
Ribbon! Tsumugi's ribbon!
La la la...

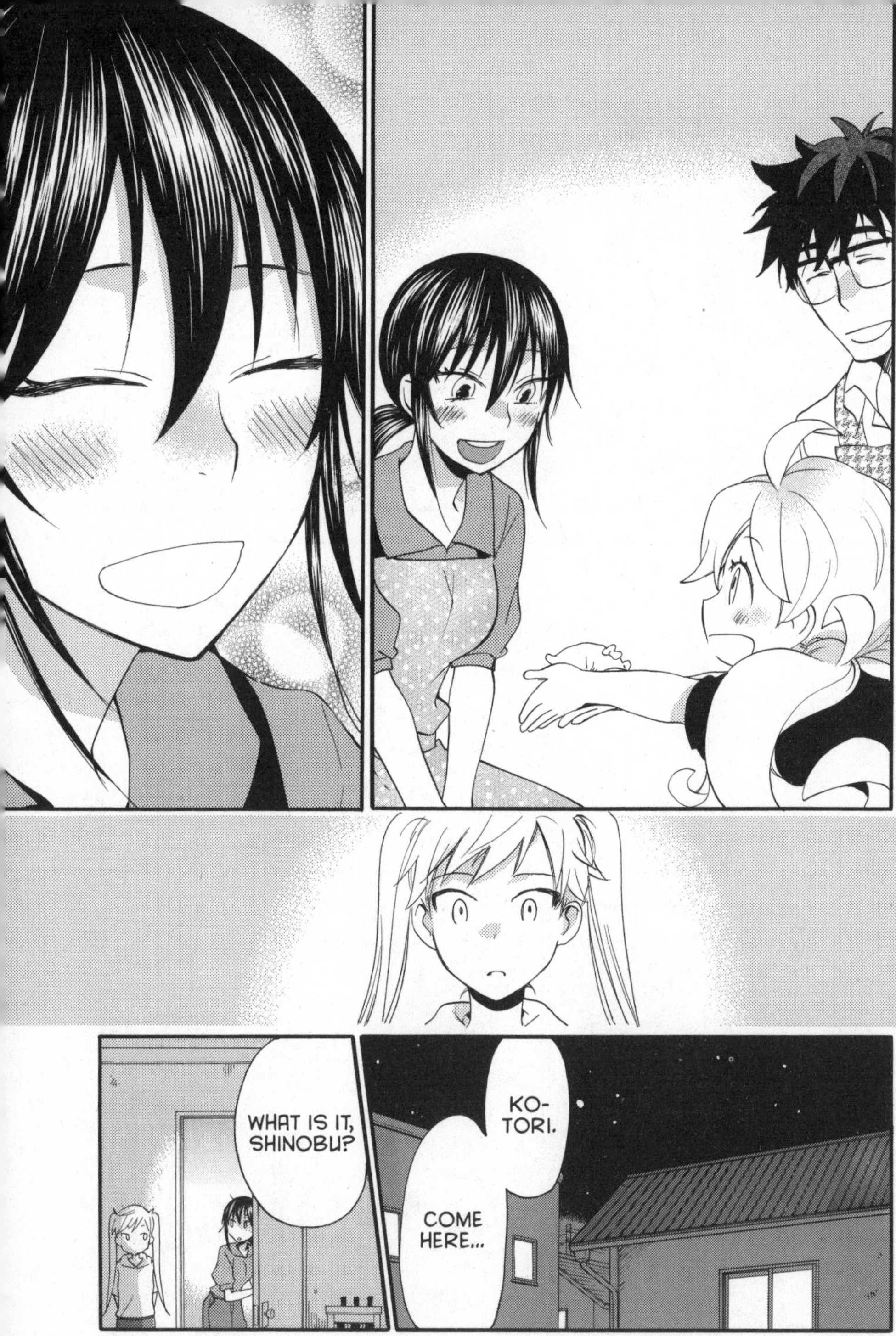
KO-TORI.
COME HERE...
WHAT IS IT, SHINOBU?

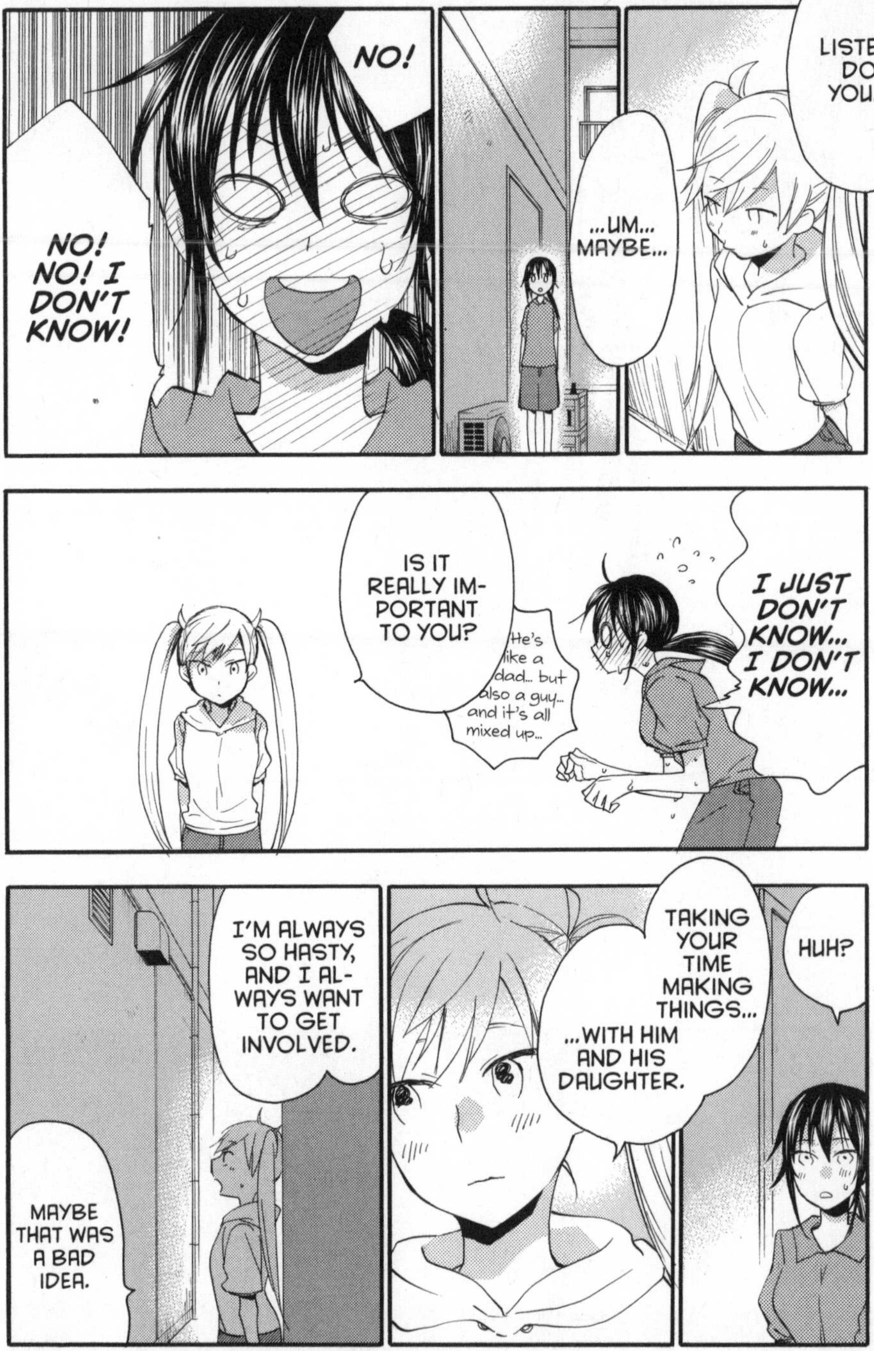
LISTEN, DO YOU...
...UM... MAYBE...
NO!
NO! NO! I DON'T KNOW!
I JUST DON'T KNOW... I DON'T KNOW...
He's like a dad... but also a guy... and it's all mixed up...
IS IT REALLY IM-PORTANT TO YOU?
HUH?
TAKING YOUR TIME MAKING THINGS...
...WITH HIM AND HIS DAUGHTER.
I'M ALWAYS SO HASTY, AND I AL-WAYS WANT TO GET INVOLVED.
MAYBE THAT WAS A BAD IDEA.

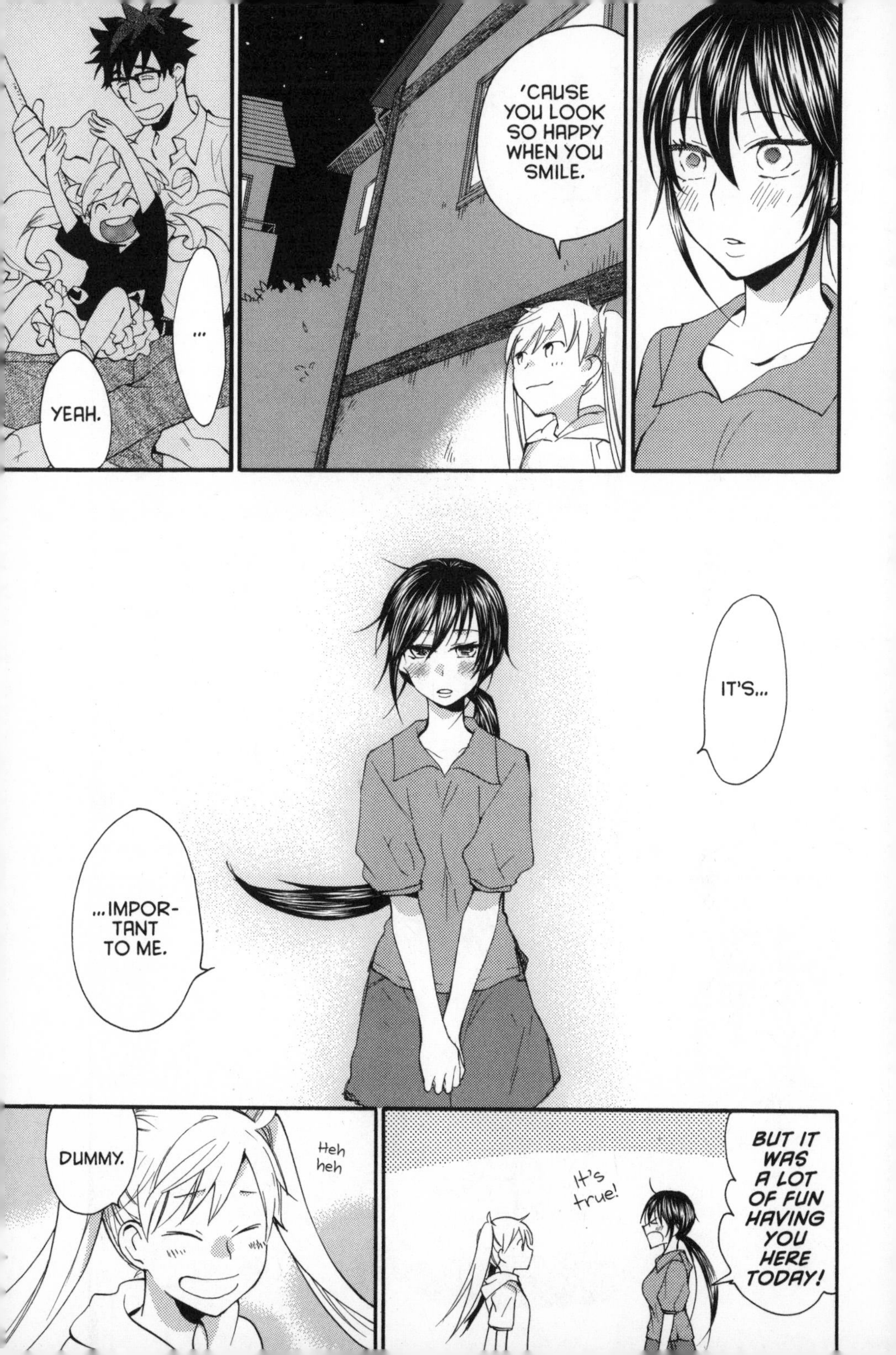
'CAUSE YOU LOOK SO HAPPY WHEN YOU SMILE.
...
YEAH.
IT'S...
...IMPOR-TANT TO ME.
BUT IT WAS A LOT OF FUN HAVING YOU HERE TODAY!
It's true!
Heh heh
DUMMY.

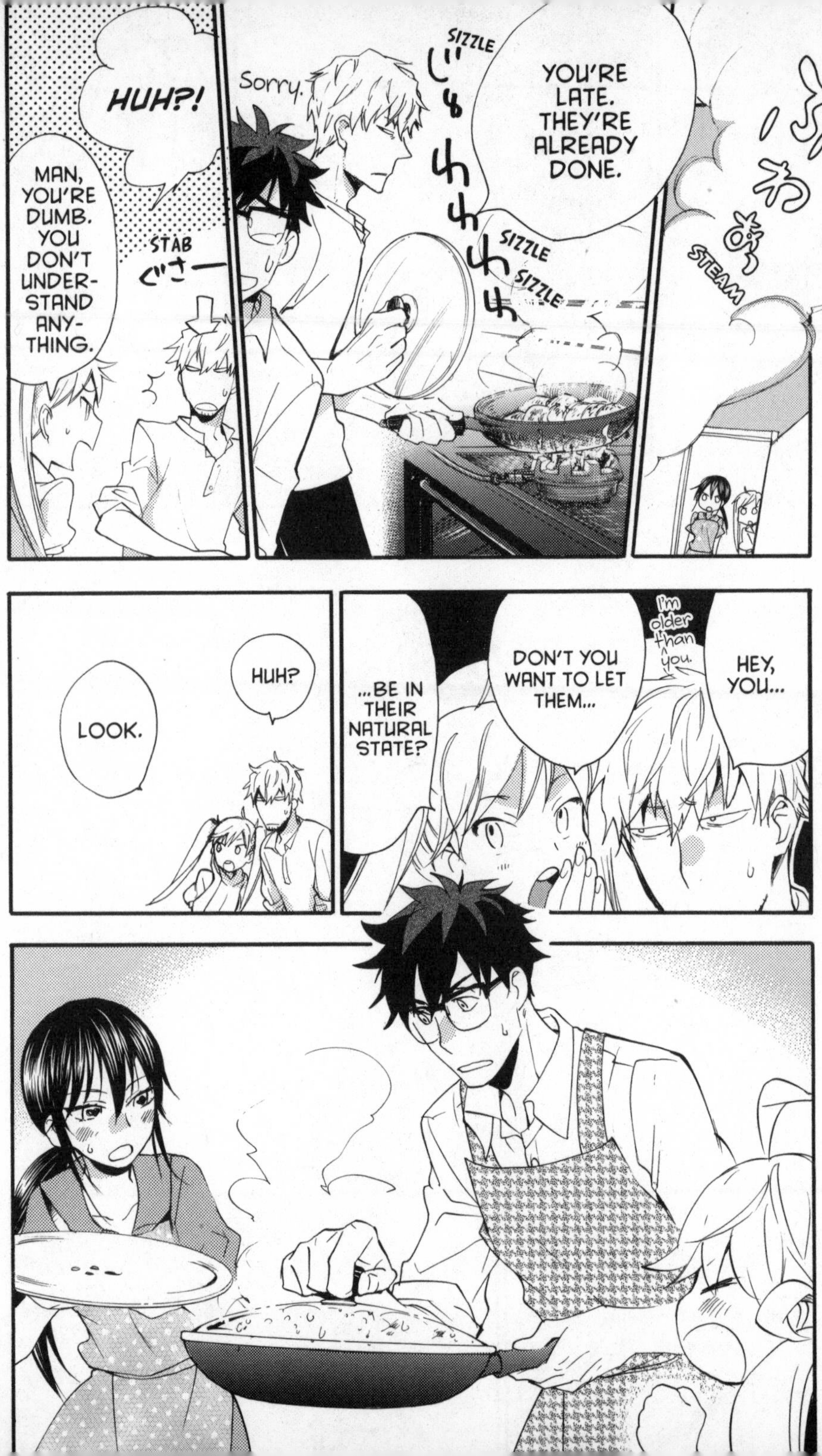
ふわぁ
STEAM
SIZZLE
じゅわわわわ
SIZZLE
SIZZLE
YOU'RE LATE. THEY'RE ALREADY DONE.
Sorry.
HUH?!
MAN, YOU'RE DUMB. YOU DON'T UNDER-STAND ANY-THING.
STAB
ぐさー
HEY, YOU...
I'm older than you.
DON'T YOU WANT TO LET THEM...
...BE IN THEIR NATURAL STATE?
HUH?
LOOK.

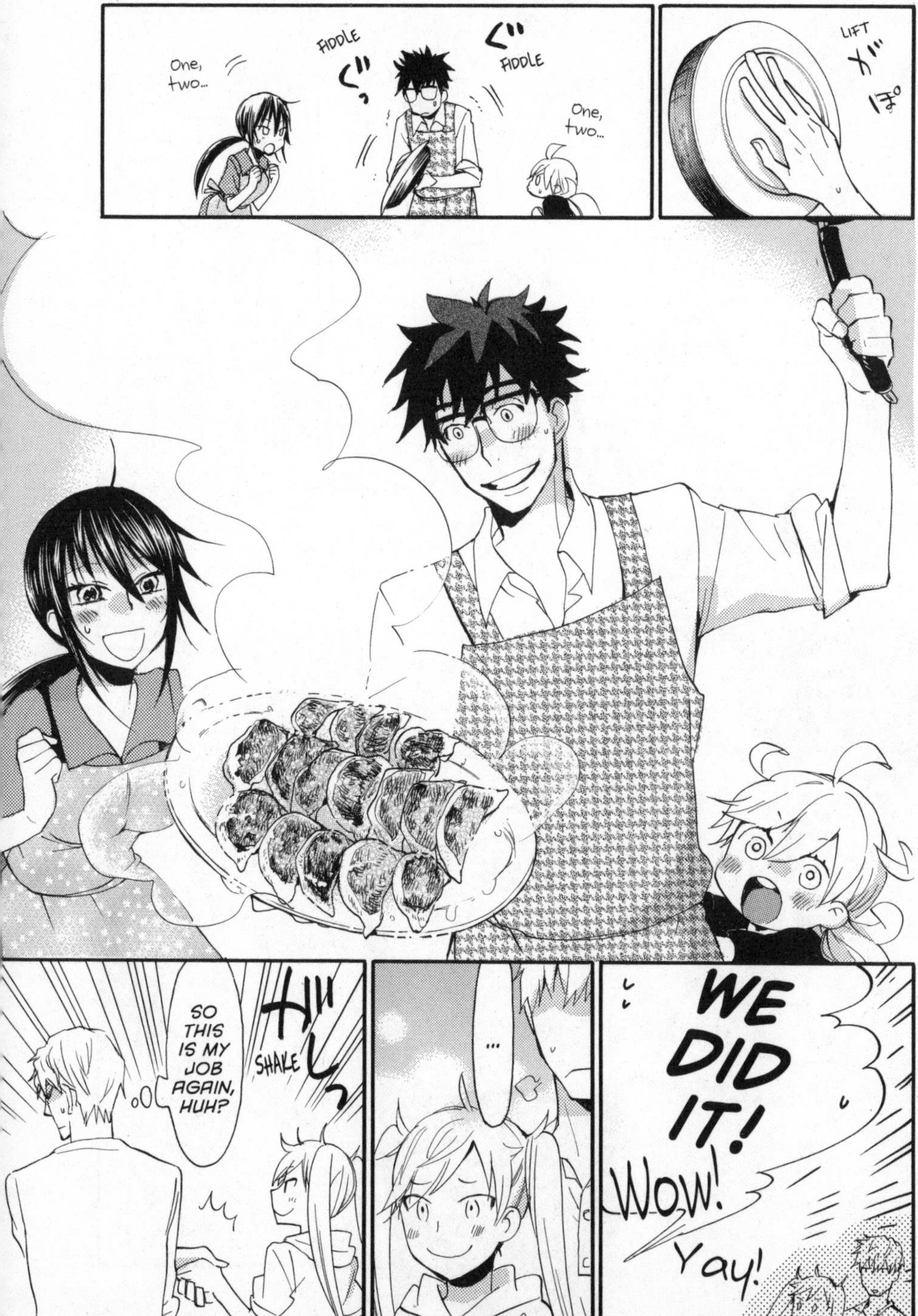
LIFT
ガぽ
ぐ
FIDDLE
One, two...
FIDDLE
ぐ
One, two...
WE DID IT!
WOW!
Yay!
...
SHAKE
SO THIS IS MY JOB AGAIN, HUH?

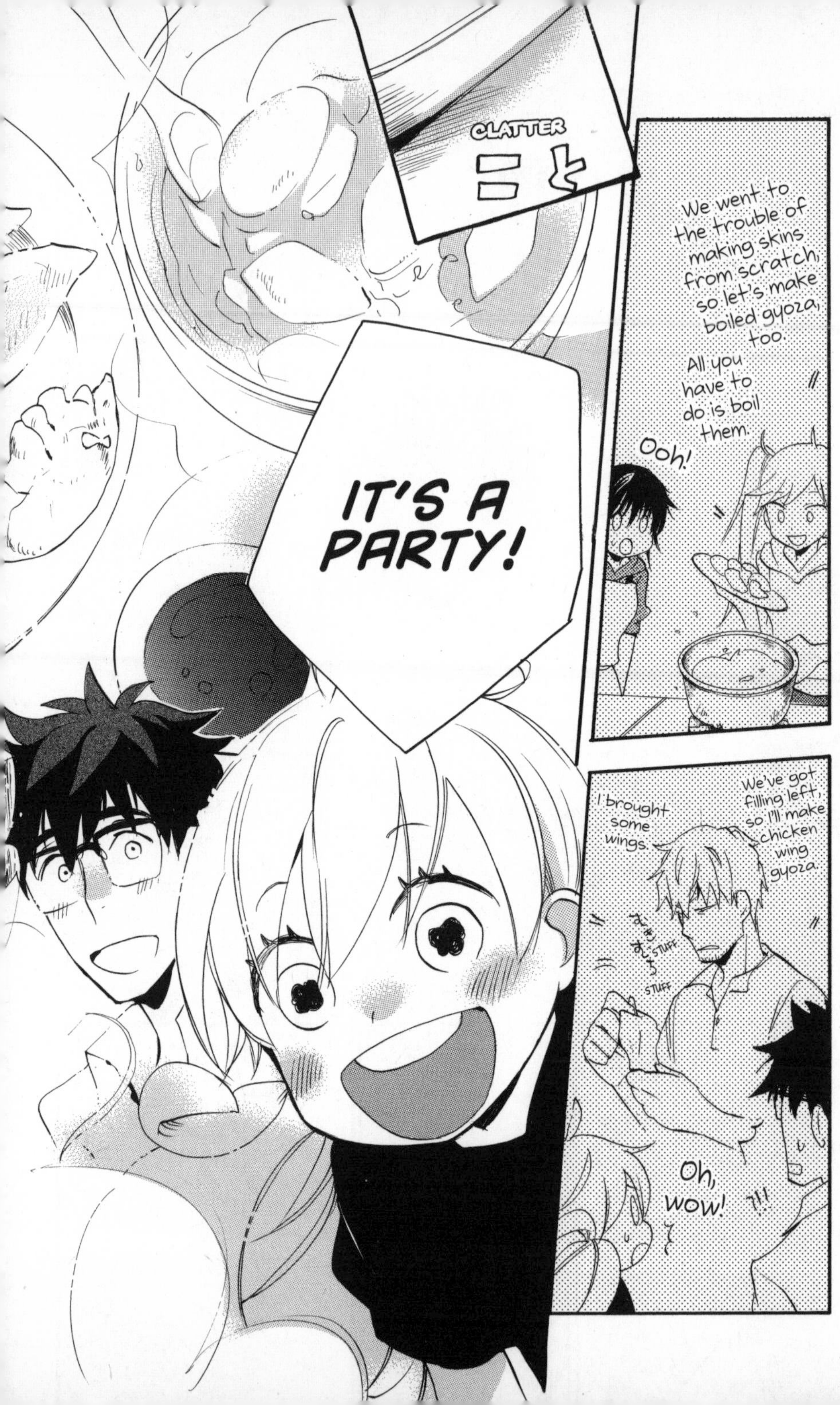
We went to the trouble of making skins from scratch, so let's make boiled gyoza, too.
All you have to do is boil them.
Ooh!
We've got filling left, so I'll make chicken wing gyoza.
I brought some wings.
STUFF
STUFF
Oh, wow!
?!!
CLATTER
IT'S A PARTY!

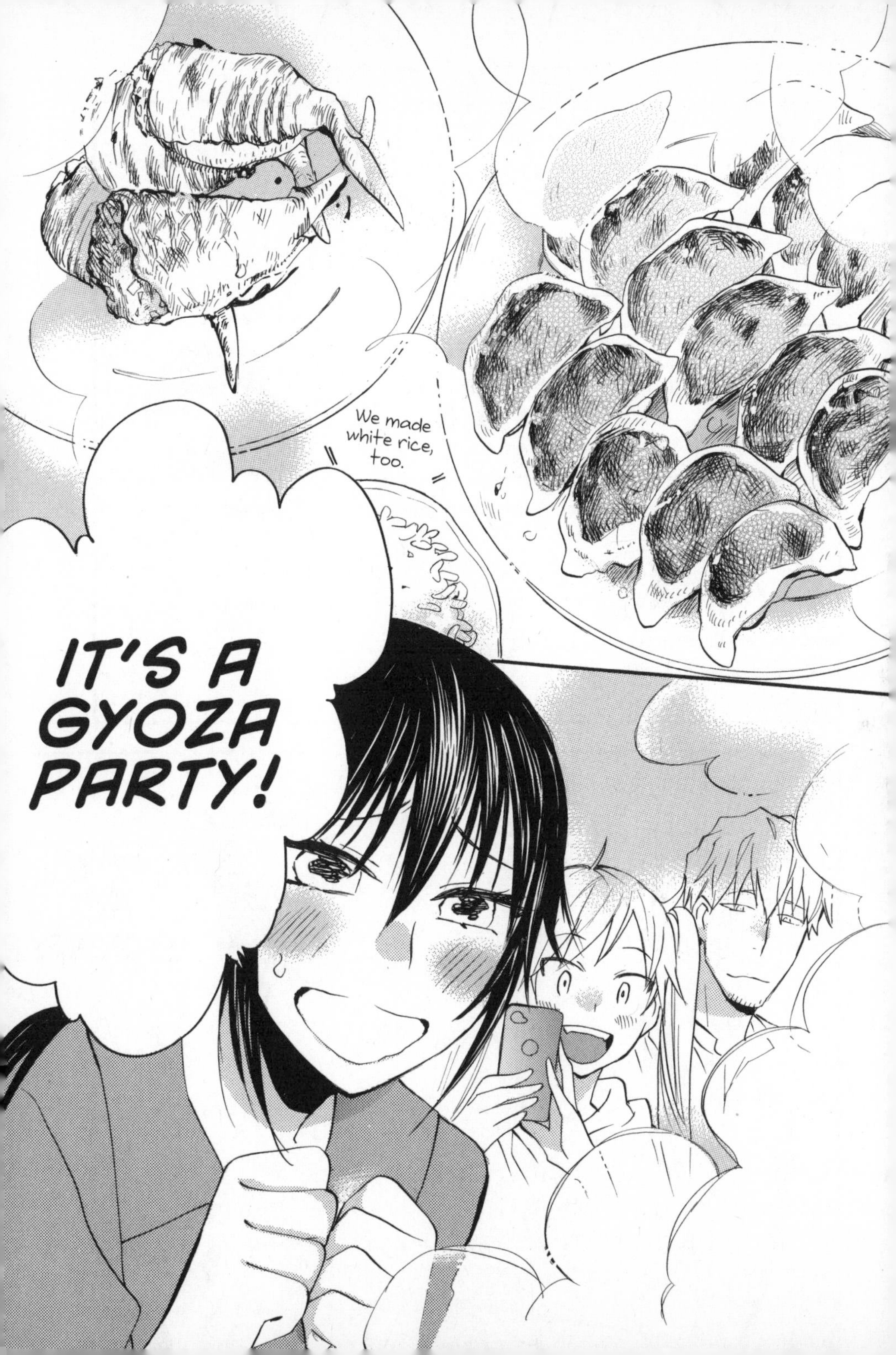
We made white rice, too.
IT'S A GYOZA PARTY!

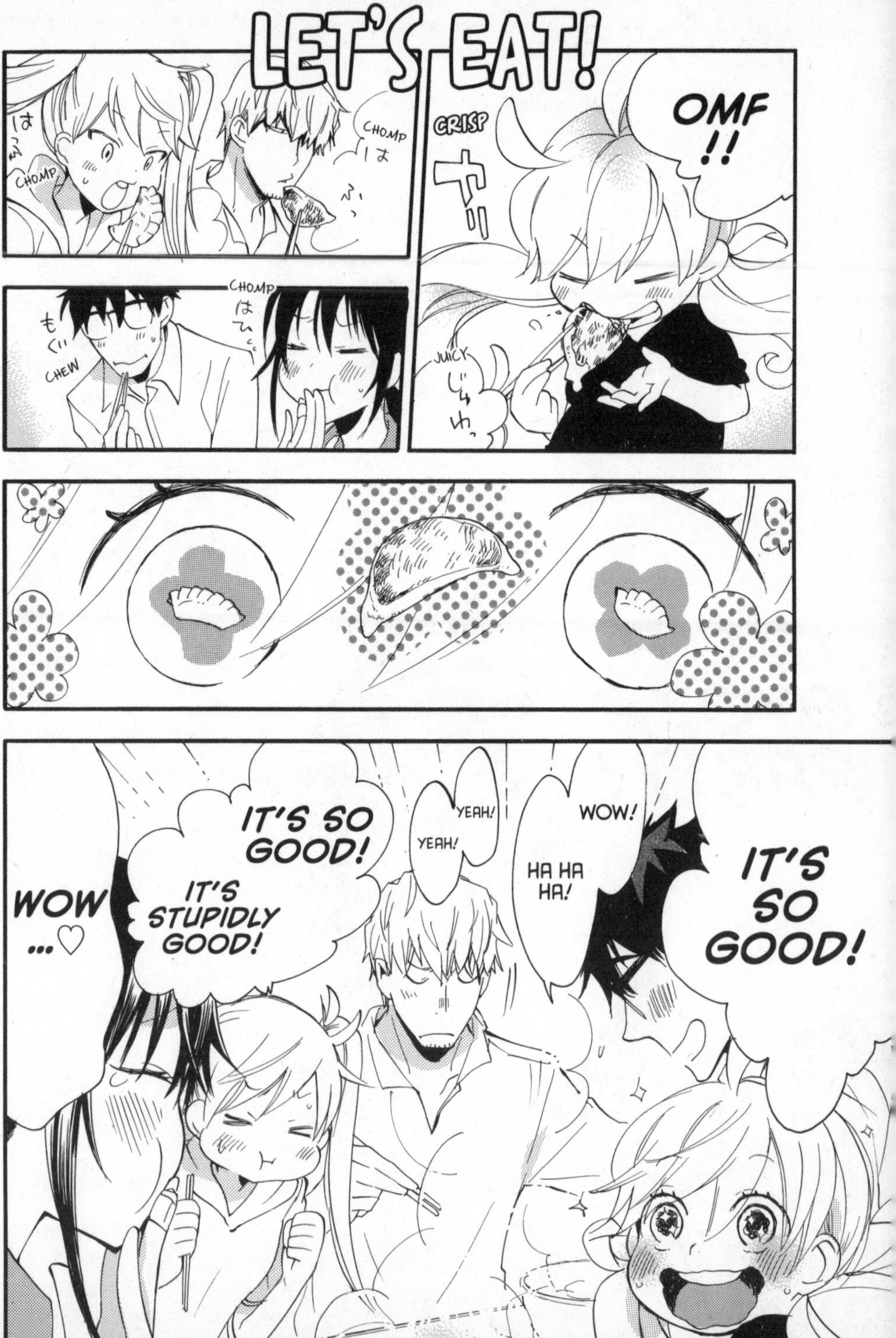
LET'S EAT!
CRISP
OMF !!
JUICY
CHOMP
CHOMP
CHOMP
CHEW
IT'S SO GOOD!
WOW!
HA HA HA!
YEAH!
YEAH!
IT'S SO GOOD!
IT'S STUPIDLY GOOD!
WOW ...♡

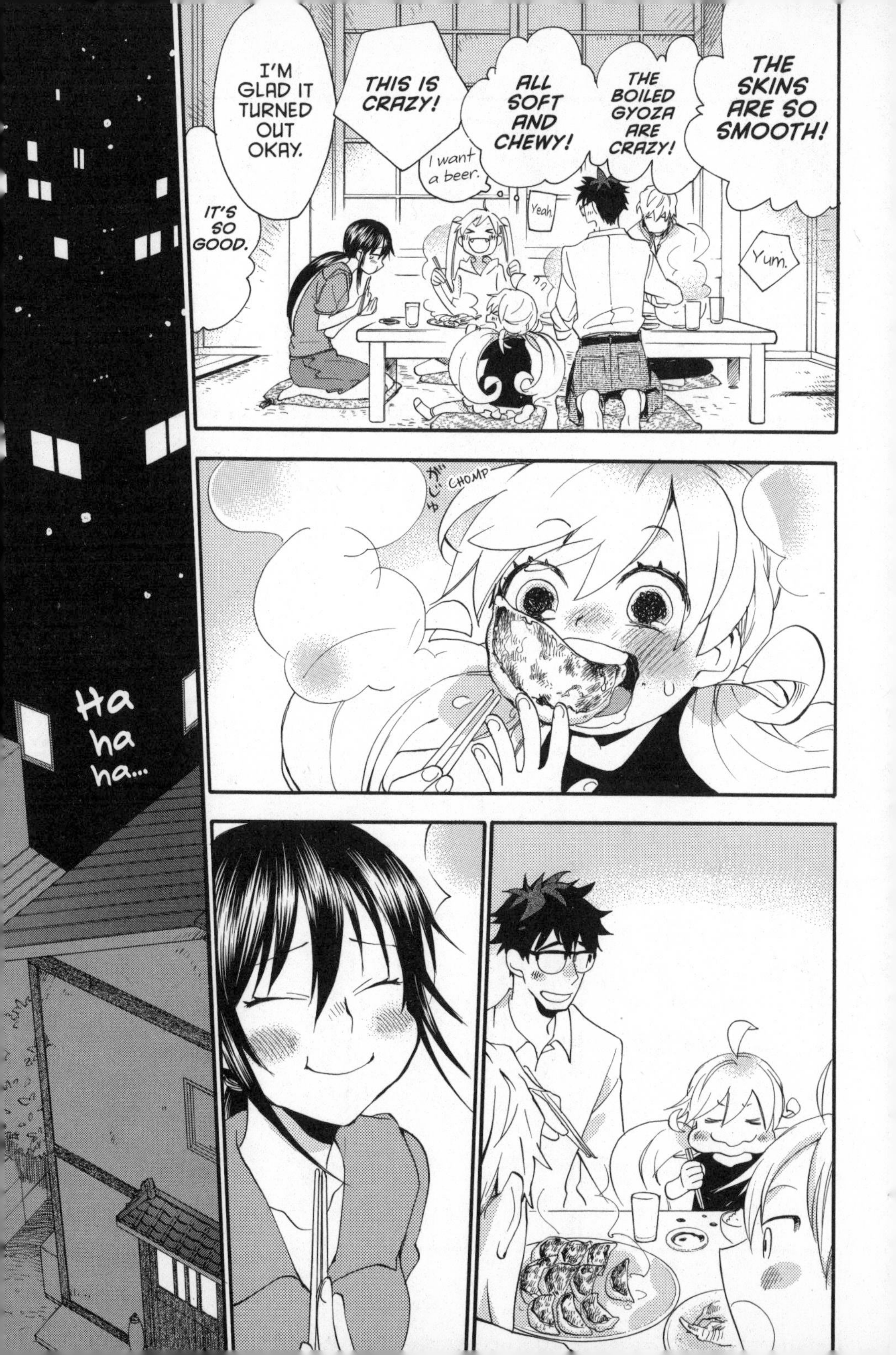
THE SKINS ARE SO SMOOTH!
THE BOILED GYOZA ARE CRAZY!
ALL SOFT AND CHEWY!
THIS IS CRAZY!
I'M GLAD IT TURNED OUT OKAY.
I want a beer.
Yeah.
Yum.
IT'S SO GOOD.
CHOMP
Ha ha ha...

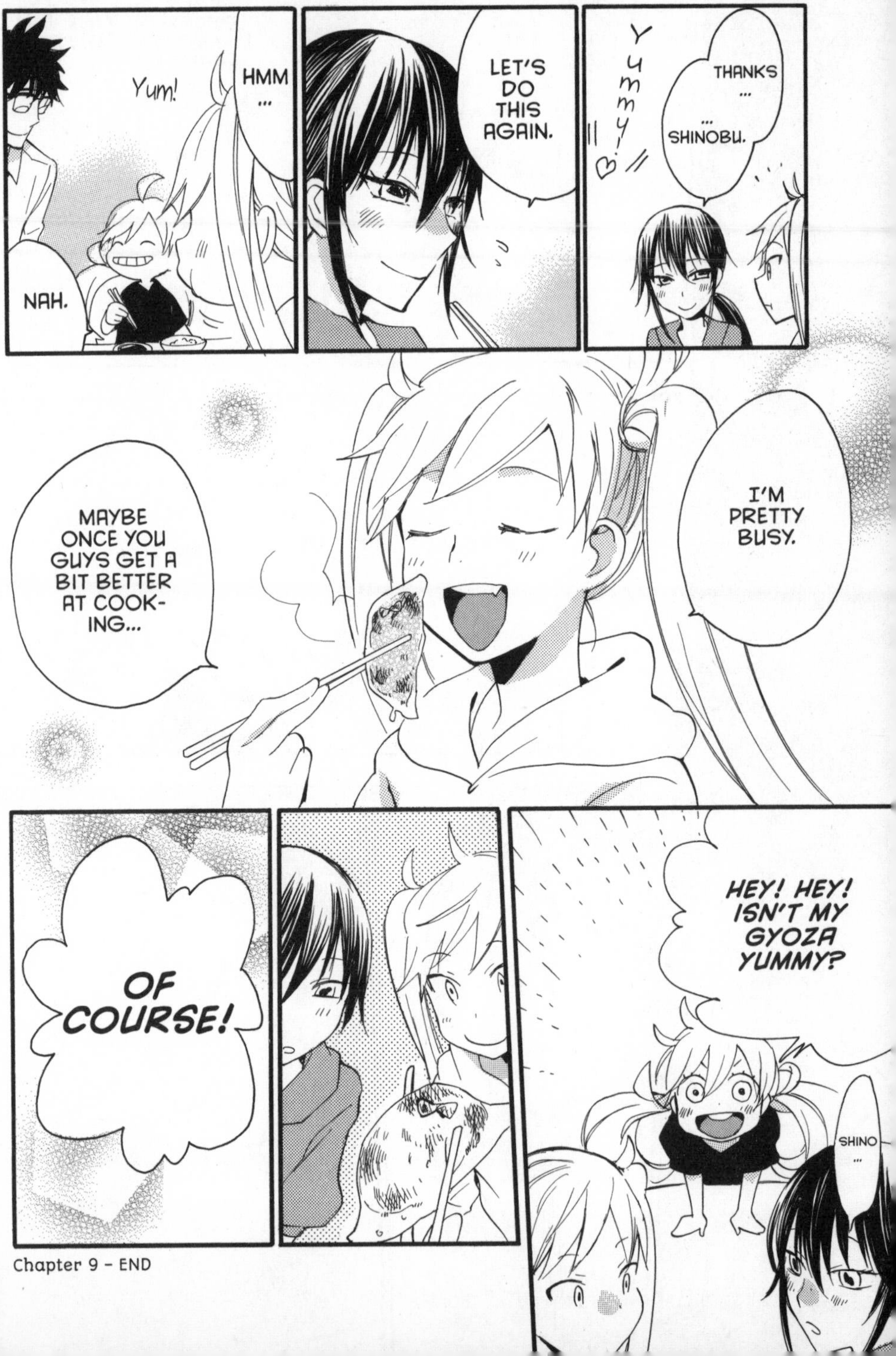
Yummy
THANKS... ...SHINOBU.
LET'S DO THIS AGAIN.
HMM...
Yum!
NAH.
I'M PRETTY BUSY.
MAYBE ONCE YOU GUYS GET A BIT BETTER AT COOKING...
HEY! HEY! ISN'T MY GYOZA YUMMY?
SHINO...
OF COURSE!

Chapter 9 - END

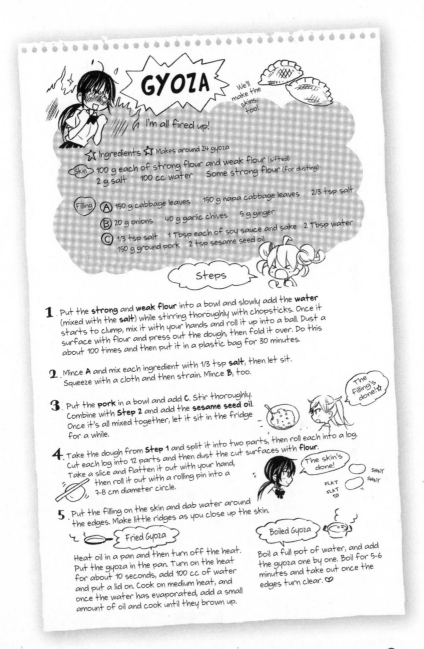

GYOZA

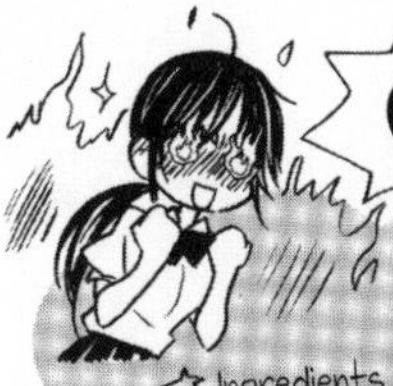
I'm all fired up!

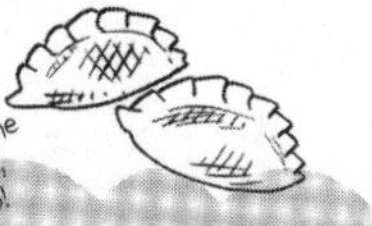
We'll make the skins, too!

☆ Ingredients ☆ Makes around 24 gyoza

(Skin) 100 g each of strong flour and weak flour (sifted) Some strong flour (for dusting)
2 g salt 100 cc water

(Filling) Ⓐ 150 g cabbage leaves 150 g napa cabbage leaves 2/3 tsp salt

Ⓑ 20 g onions 40 g garlic chives 5 g ginger

Ⓒ 1/3 tsp salt 1 Tbsp each of soy sauce and sake 2 Tbsp water
150 g ground pork 2 tsp sesame seed oil

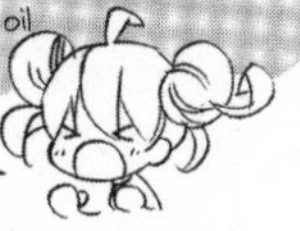

Steps

1. Put the **strong** and **weak flour** into a bowl and slowly add the **water** (mixed with the **salt**) while stirring thoroughly with chopsticks. Once it starts to clump, mix it with your hands and roll it up into a ball. Dust a surface with flour and press out the dough, then fold it over. Do this about 100 times and then put it in a plastic bag for 30 minutes.

2. Mince **A** and mix each ingredient with 1/3 tsp **salt**, then let sit. Squeeze with a cloth and then strain. Mince **B**, too.

3. Put the **pork** in a bowl and add **C**. Stir thoroughly. Combine with **Step 2** and add the **sesame seed oil**. Once it's all mixed together, let it sit in the fridge for a while.

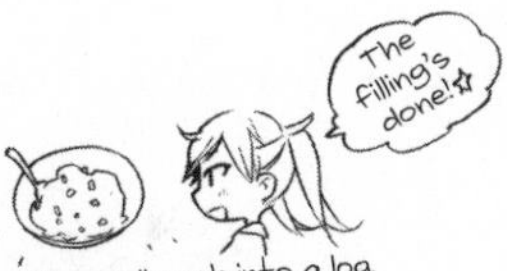
The filling's done!☆

4. Take the dough from **Step 1** and split it into two parts, then roll each into a log. Cut each log into 12 parts and then dust the cut surfaces with **flour**. Take a slice and flatten it out with your hand, then roll it out with a rolling pin into a 7-8 cm diameter circle.

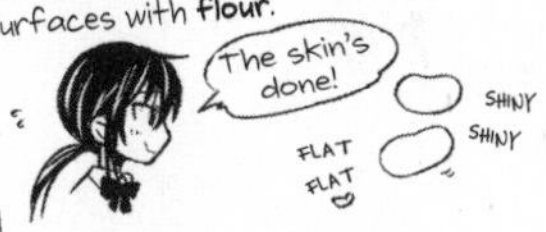
The skin's done!
SHINY
SHINY
FLAT
FLAT

5. Put the filling on the skin and dab water around the edges. Make little ridges as you close up the skin.

Fried Gyoza

Heat oil in a pan and then turn off the heat. Put the gyoza in the pan. Turn on the heat for about 10 seconds, add 100 cc of water and put a lid on. Cook on medium heat, and once the water has evaporated, add a small amount of oil and cook until they brown up.

Boiled Gyoza

Boil a full pot of water, and add the gyoza one by one. Boil for 5-6 minutes and take out once the edges turn clear. ♡

CONVERSION NOTES:
100 G SIFTED FLOUR = ABOUT1 CUP, 2 G SALT = ABOUT 3/4 TSP, 100 CC WATER = 6 3/4 TBSP, 150 G CABBAGE = ABOUT 1 1/2 CUPS CHOPPED, 20 G ONION = ABOUT 1/4 CUP CHOPPED, 40 G CHIVES = ABOUT 1/2 CUP CHOPPED, 5 G GINGER = ABOUT 1 TSP, 150 G PORK = ABOUT 1/3 LB

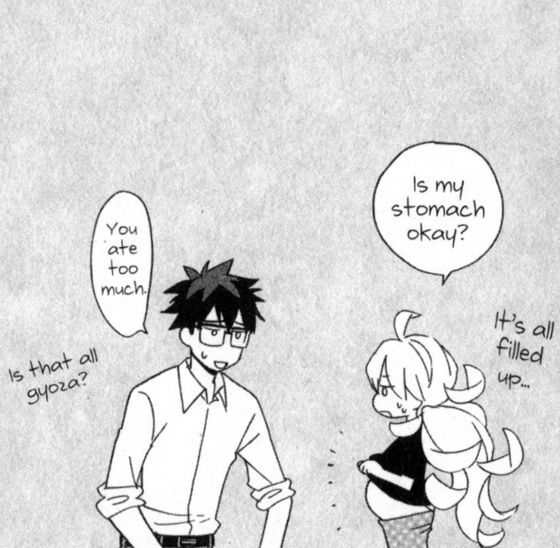
Is my stomach okay?
It's all filled up...
You ate too much.
Is that all gyoza?

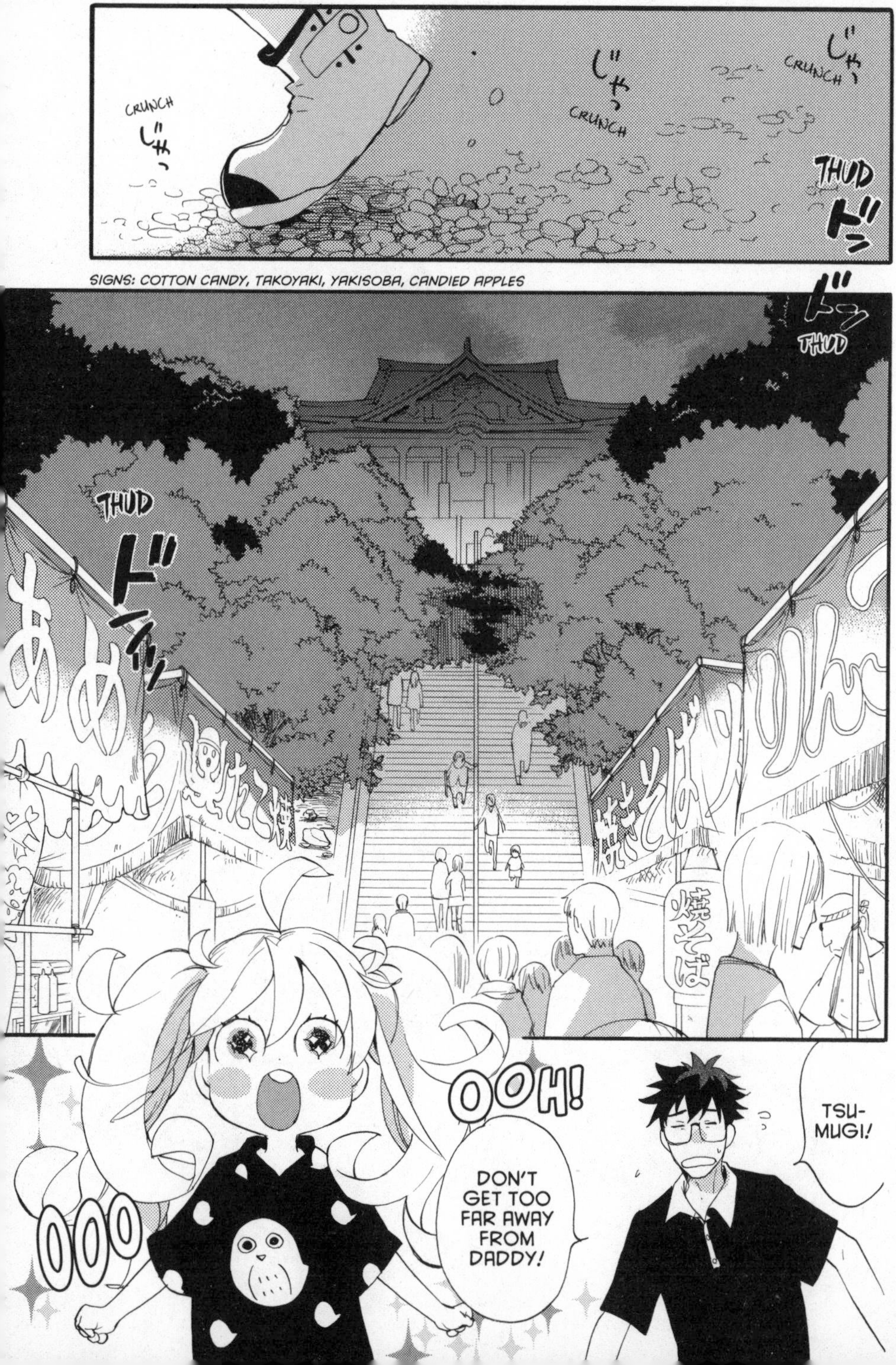
じゃっ
CRUNCH
じゃっ
CRUNCH
CRUNCH
じゃっ
THUD
ドッ
SIGNS: COTTON CANDY, TAKOYAKI, YAKISOBA, CANDIED APPLES
ドッ
THUD
THUD
ドンッ
焼そば
TSU-MUGI!
DON'T GET TOO FAR AWAY FROM DADDY!
OOH!
OOO

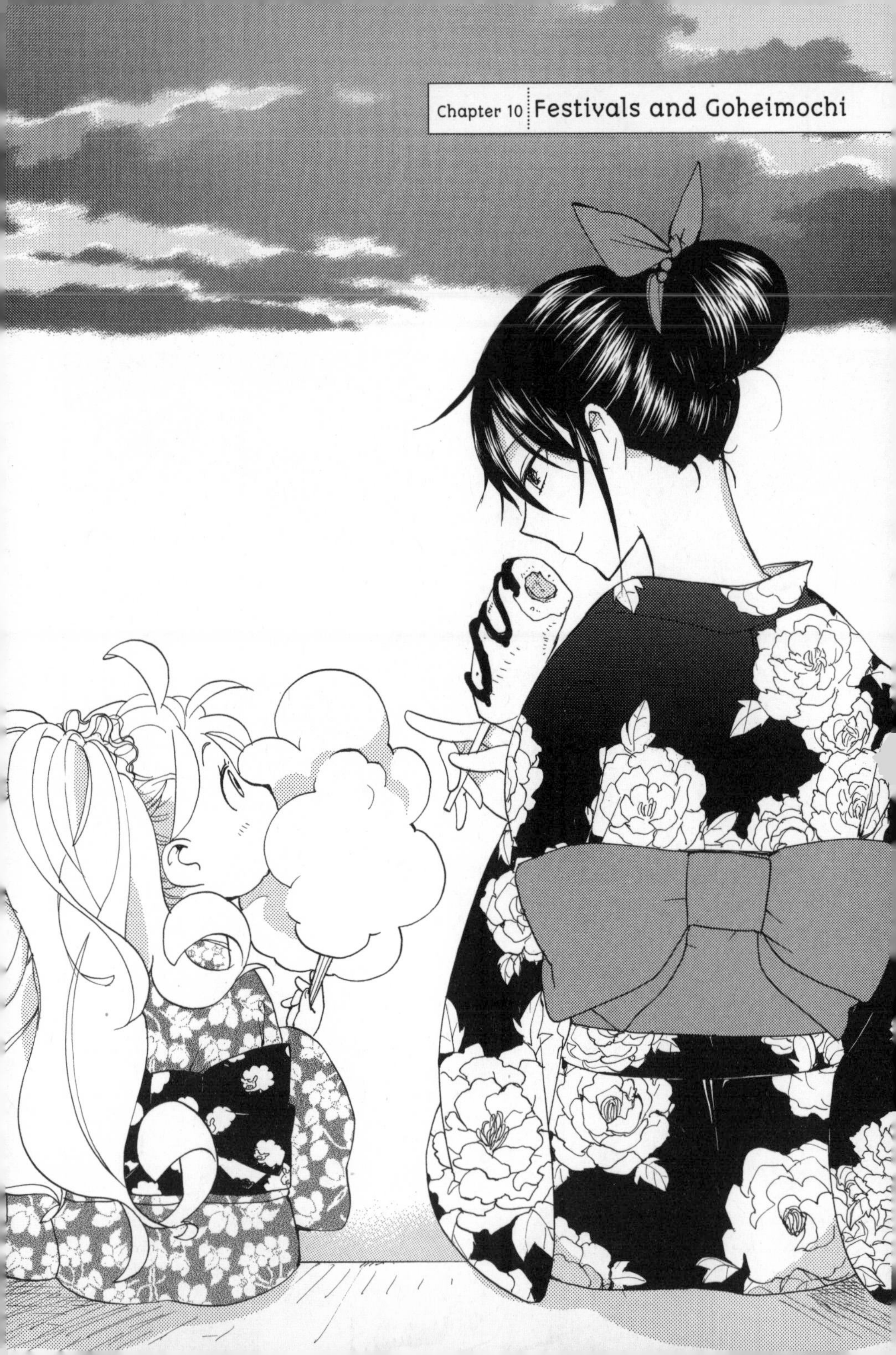
Chapter 10 Festivals and Goheimochi

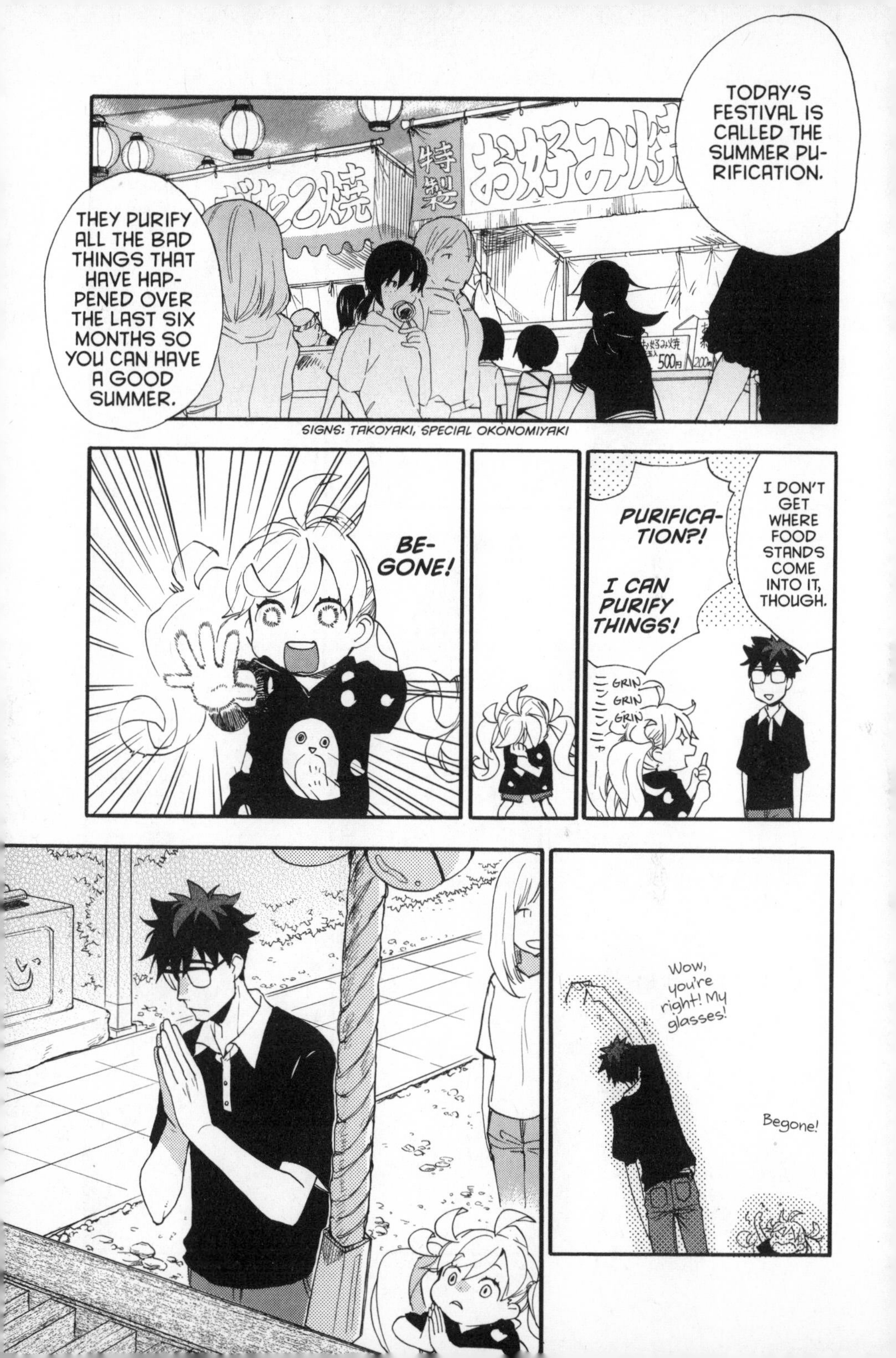
TODAY'S FESTIVAL IS CALLED THE SUMMER PU-RIFICATION.
THEY PURIFY ALL THE BAD THINGS THAT HAVE HAP-PENED OVER THE LAST SIX MONTHS SO YOU CAN HAVE A GOOD SUMMER.
SIGNS: TAKOYAKI, SPECIAL OKONOMIYAKI
I DON'T GET WHERE FOOD STANDS COME INTO IT, THOUGH.
PURIFICA-TION?!
I CAN PURIFY THINGS!
GRIN GRIN GRIN
BE-GONE!
Wow, you're right! My glasses!
Begone!

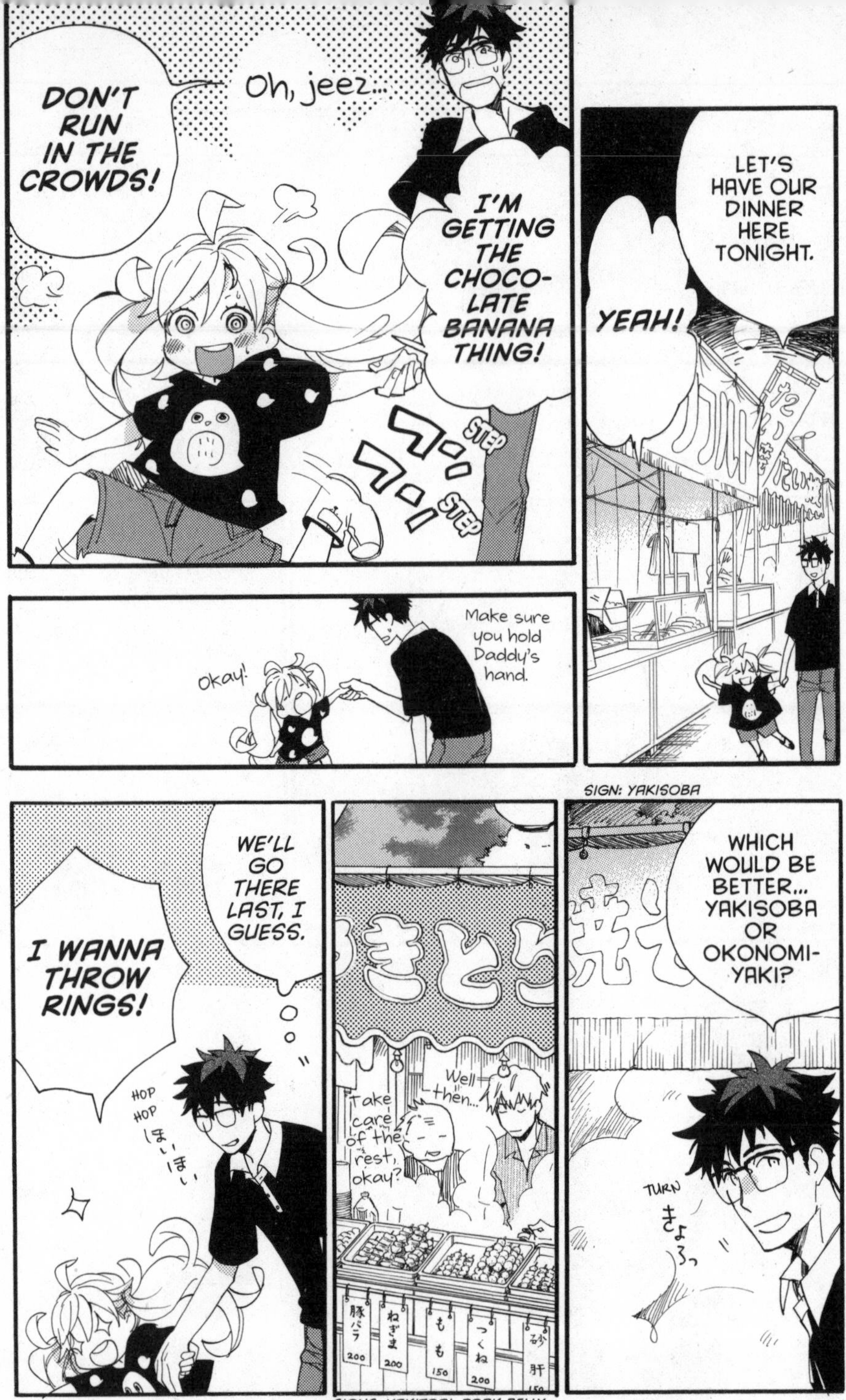
LET'S HAVE OUR DINNER HERE TONIGHT.
YEAH!
Oh, jeez...
DON'T RUN IN THE CROWDS!
I'M GETTING THE CHOCOLATE BANANA THING!
STEP
STEP
Make sure you hold Daddy's hand.
Okay!
WHICH WOULD BE BETTER... YAKISOBA OR OKONOMIYAKI?
TURN
Well then...
Take care of the rest, okay?
WE'LL GO THERE LAST, I GUESS.
I WANNA THROW RINGS!
HOP HOP

SIGN: YAKISOBA

SIGNS: YAKITORI; PORK BELLY, CHICKEN AND ONION, THIGH, CHICKEN MEATBALLS, GIZZARD

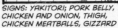

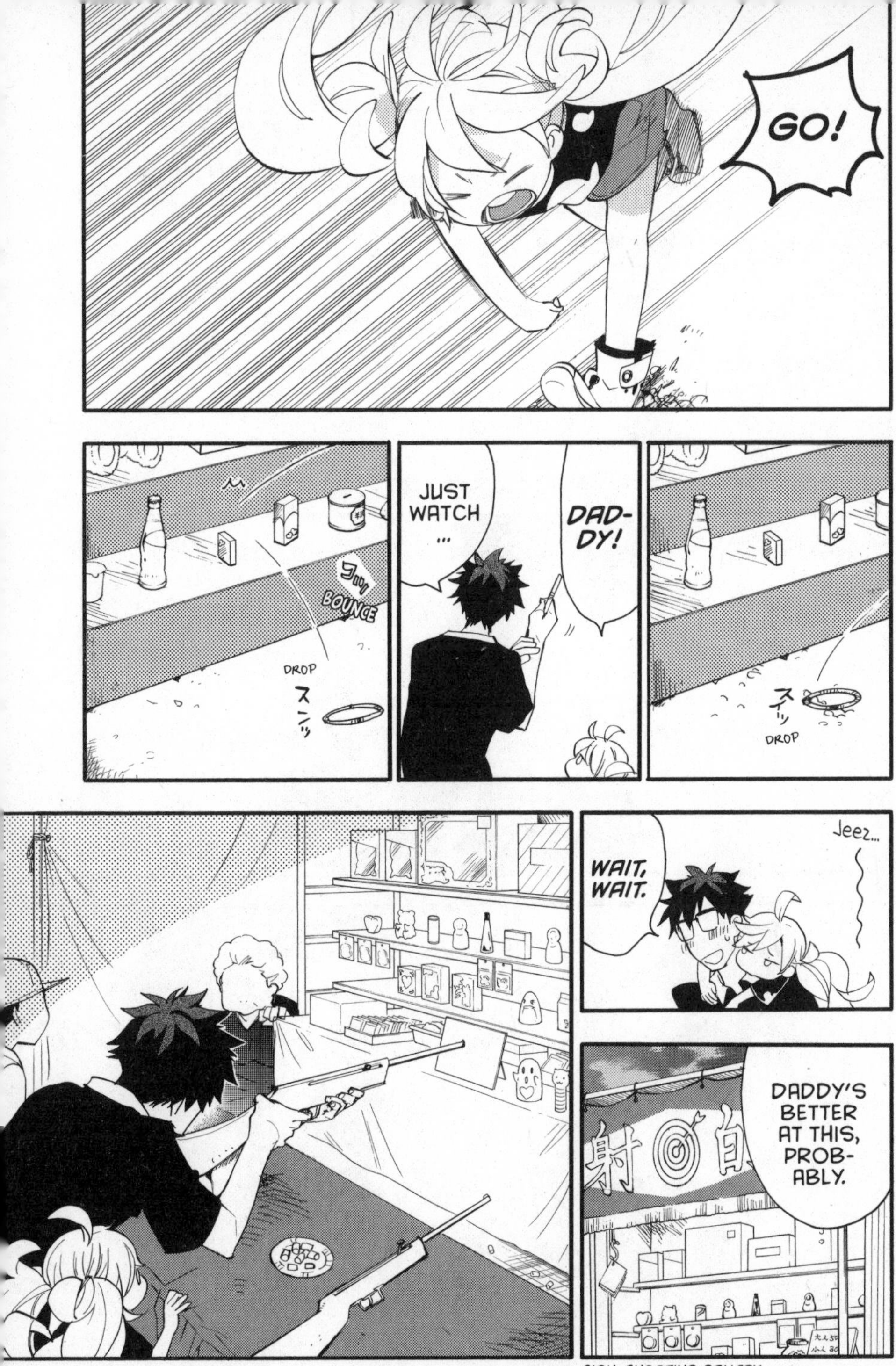
GO!
スイッ
DROP
DADDY!
JUST WATCH...
フワッ
BOUNCE
DROP
スンッ
Jeez...
WAIT, WAIT.
DADDY'S BETTER AT THIS, PROBABLY.
射的
SIGN: SHOOTING GALLERY

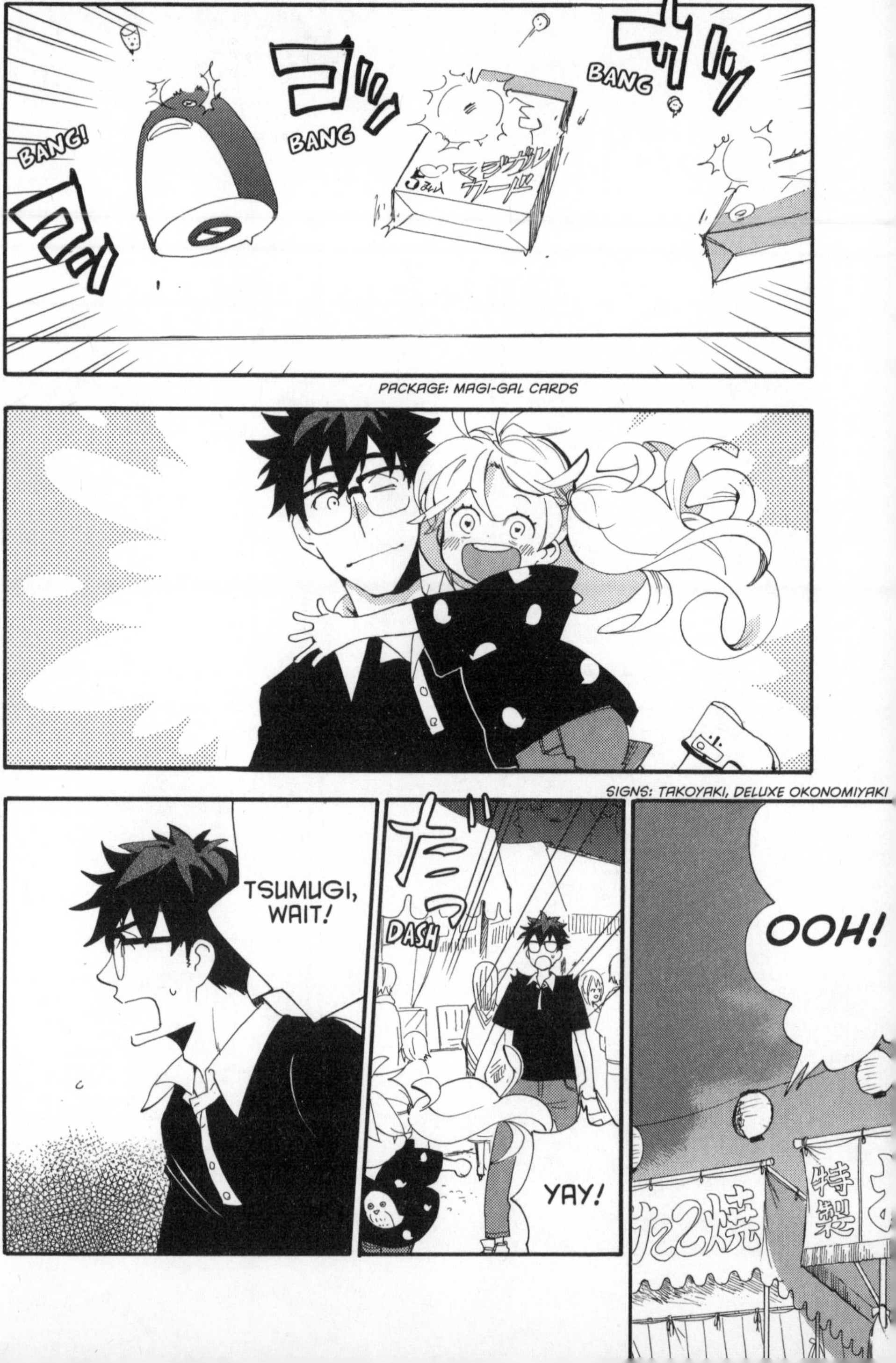
BANG
BANG
BANG!
PACKAGE: MAGI-GAL CARDS
SIGNS: TAKOYAKI, DELUXE OKONOMIYAKI
OOH!
DASH
YAY!
TSUMUGI, WAIT!

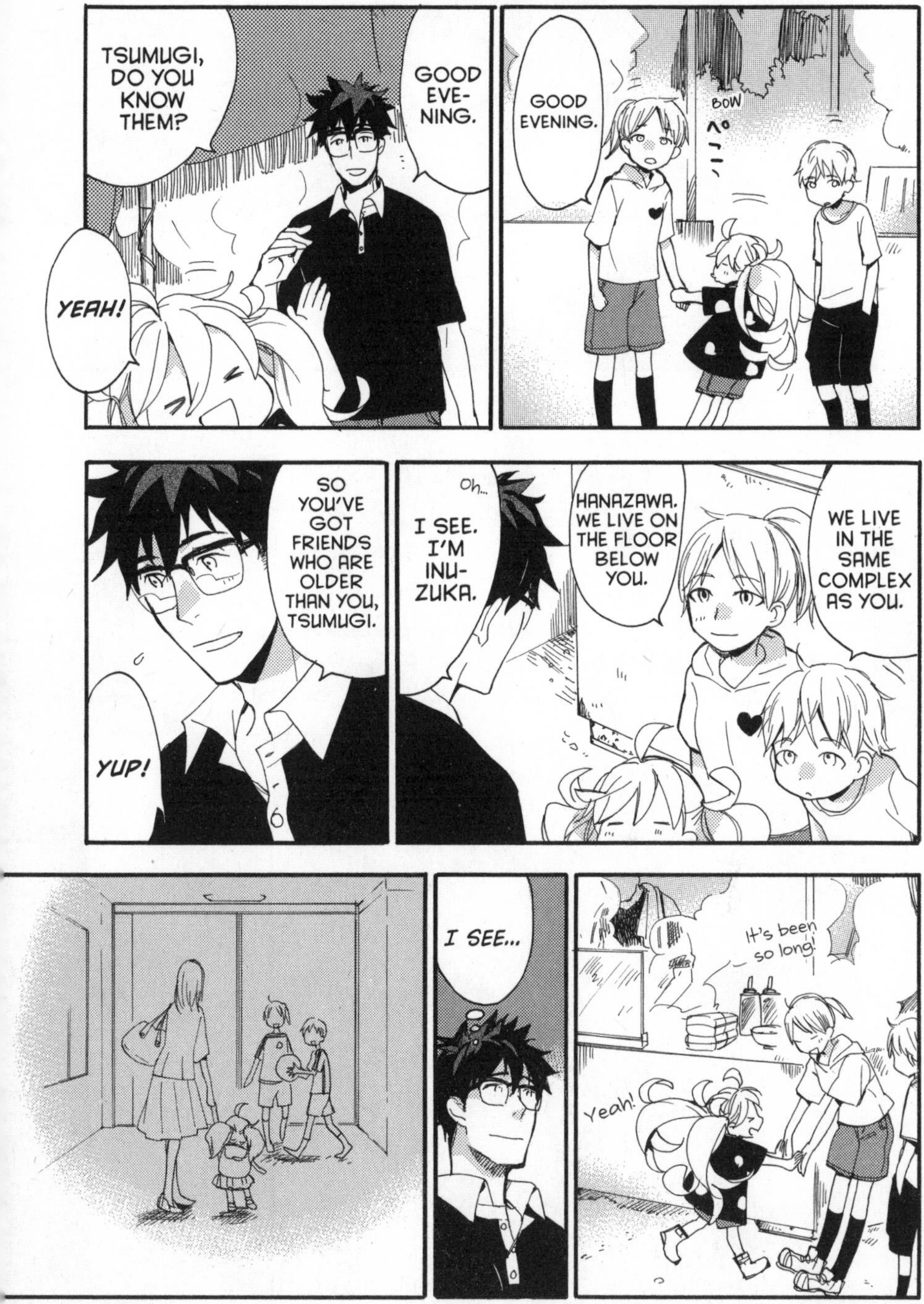
GOOD EVENING.
BOW
ぺこ
GOOD EVE-NING.
TSUMUGI, DO YOU KNOW THEM?
YEAH!
WE LIVE IN THE SAME COMPLEX AS YOU.
HANAZAWA. WE LIVE ON THE FLOOR BELOW YOU.
Oh...
I SEE. I'M INU-ZUKA.
SO YOU'VE GOT FRIENDS WHO ARE OLDER THAN YOU, TSUMUGI.
YUP!
It's been so long!
Yeah!
I SEE...

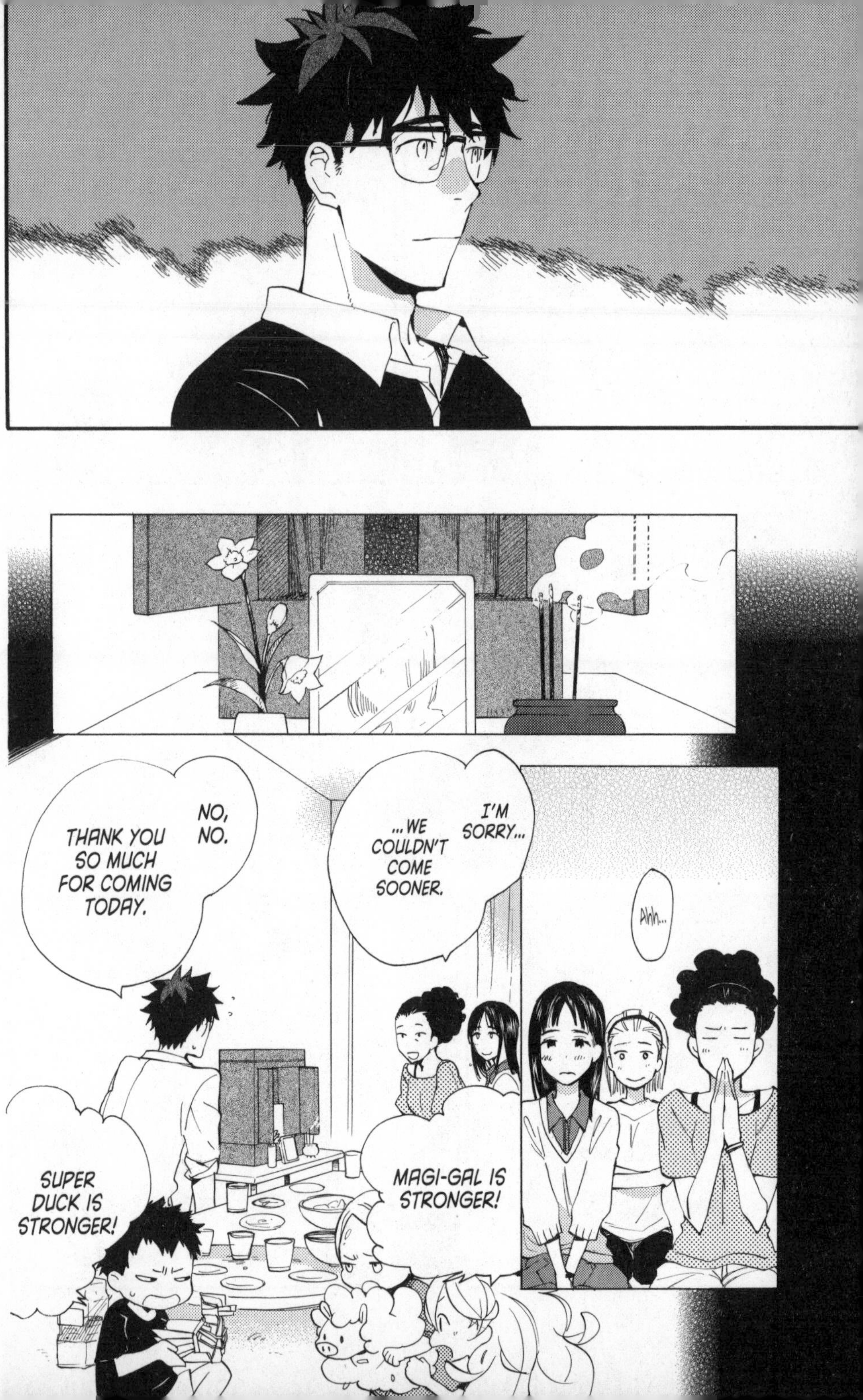

Ahh...
I'M SORRY... ...WE COULDN'T COME SOONER.
NO, NO. THANK YOU SO MUCH FOR COMING TODAY.
MAGI-GAL IS STRONGER!
SUPER DUCK IS STRONGER!

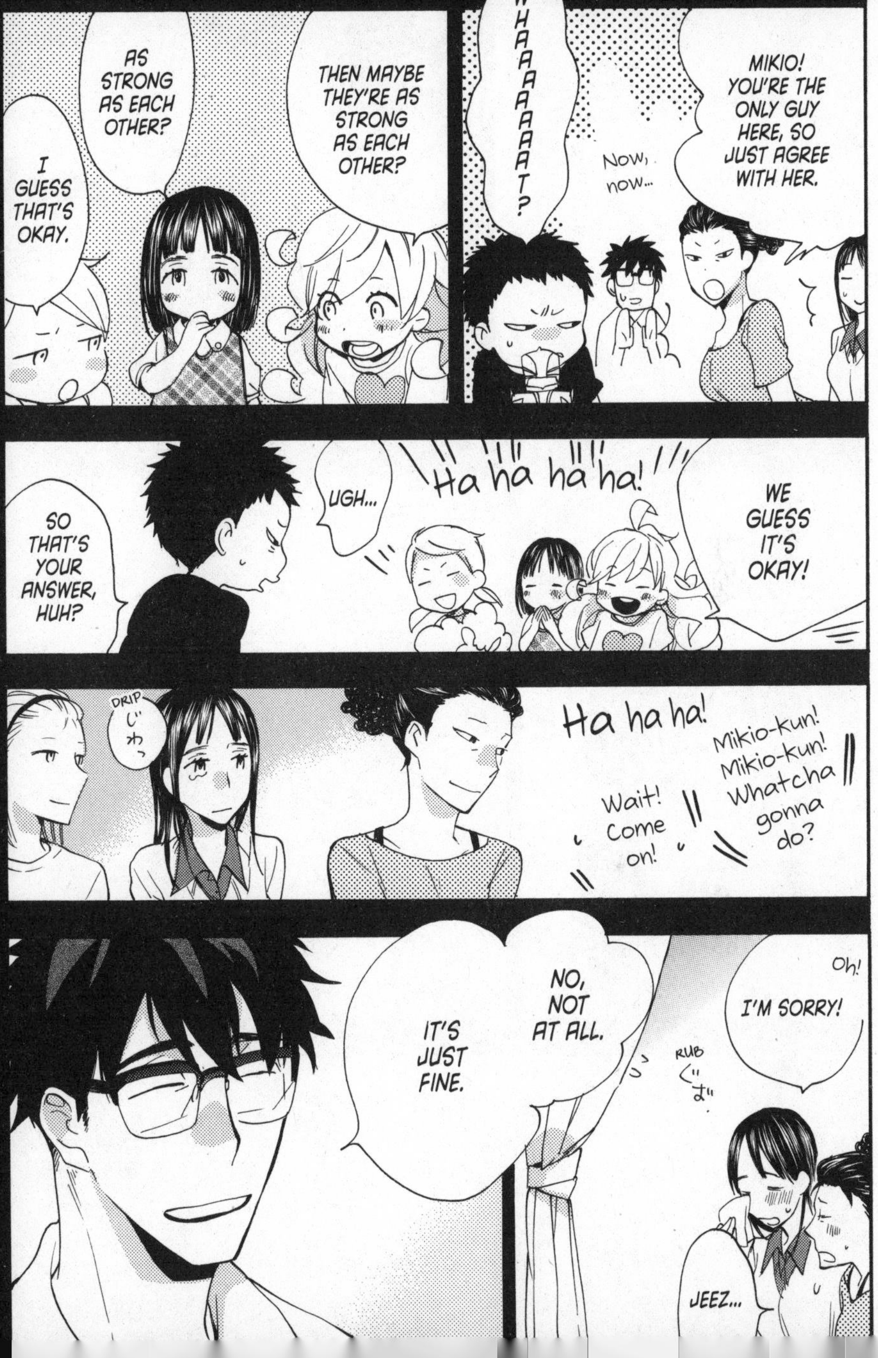
MIKIO! YOU'RE THE ONLY GUY HERE, SO JUST AGREE WITH HER.
Now, now...
WHAAAAAAAT?
THEN MAYBE THEY'RE AS STRONG AS EACH OTHER?
AS STRONG AS EACH OTHER?
I GUESS THAT'S OKAY.
WE GUESS IT'S OKAY!
Ha ha ha ha!
UGH...
SO THAT'S YOUR ANSWER, HUH?
Mikio-kun! Mikio-kun! Whatcha gonna do?
Wait! Come on!
Ha ha ha!
DRIP
じわっ
Oh!
I'M SORRY!
RUB
JEEZ...
NO, NOT AT ALL.
IT'S JUST FINE.

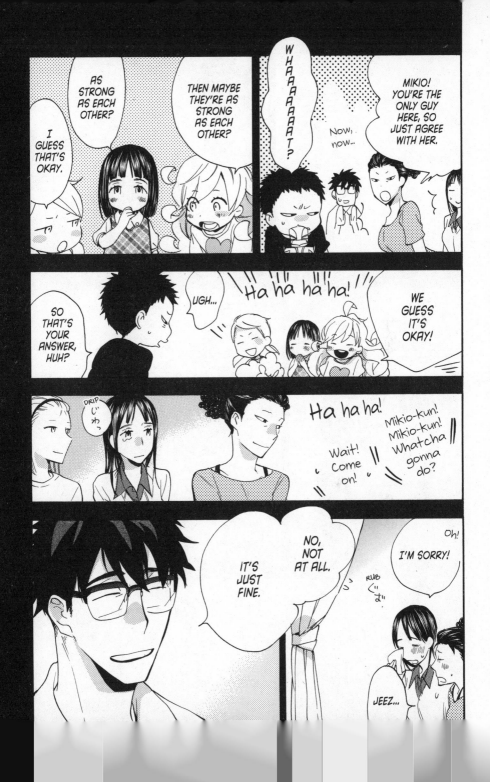

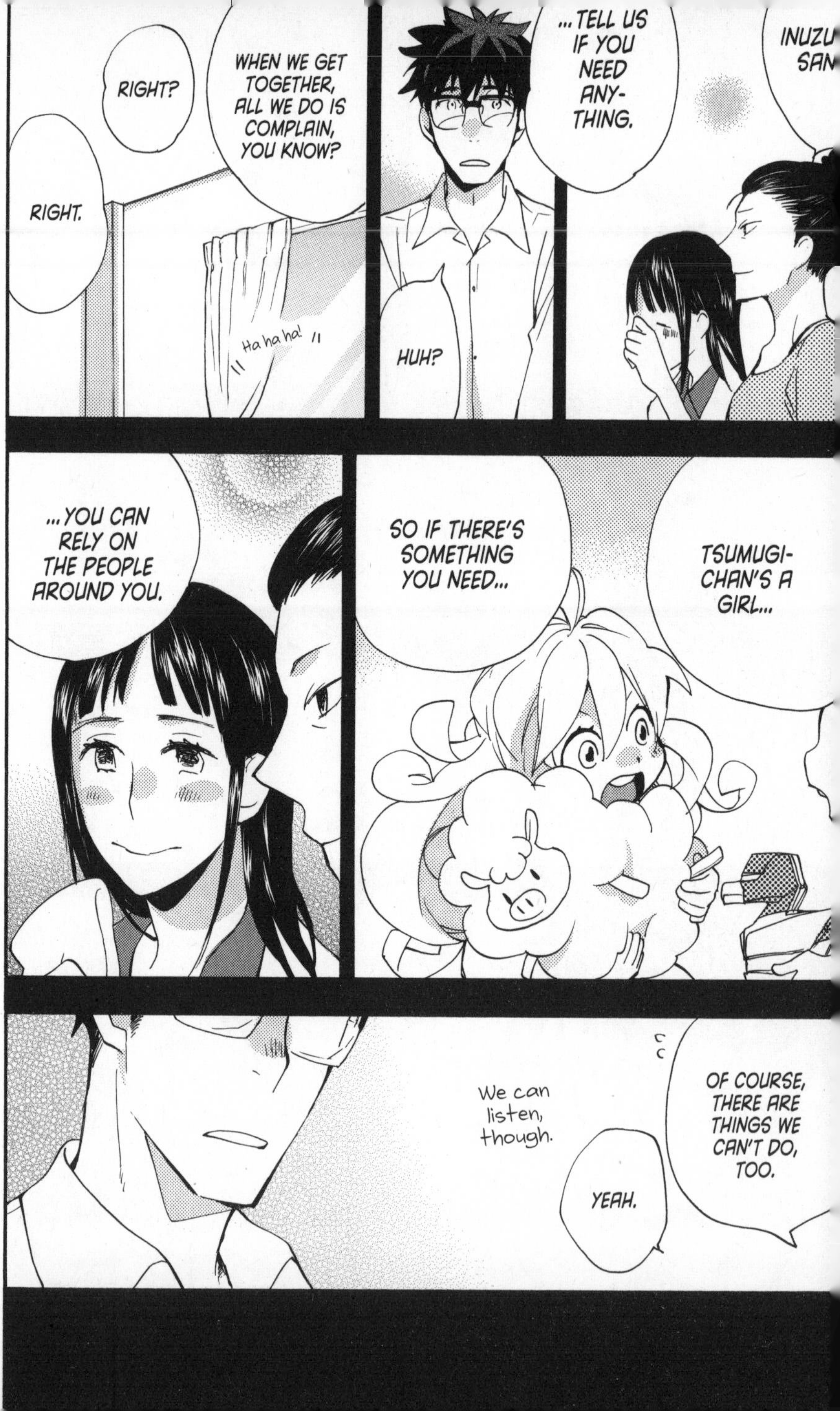
INUZU
SAN
...TELL US IF YOU NEED ANYTHING.
HUH?
WHEN WE GET TOGETHER, ALL WE DO IS COMPLAIN, YOU KNOW?
Ha ha ha!
RIGHT?
RIGHT.
TSUMUGI-CHAN'S A GIRL...
SO IF THERE'S SOMETHING YOU NEED...
...YOU CAN RELY ON THE PEOPLE AROUND YOU.
OF COURSE, THERE ARE THINGS WE CAN'T DO, TOO.
YEAH.
We can listen, though.

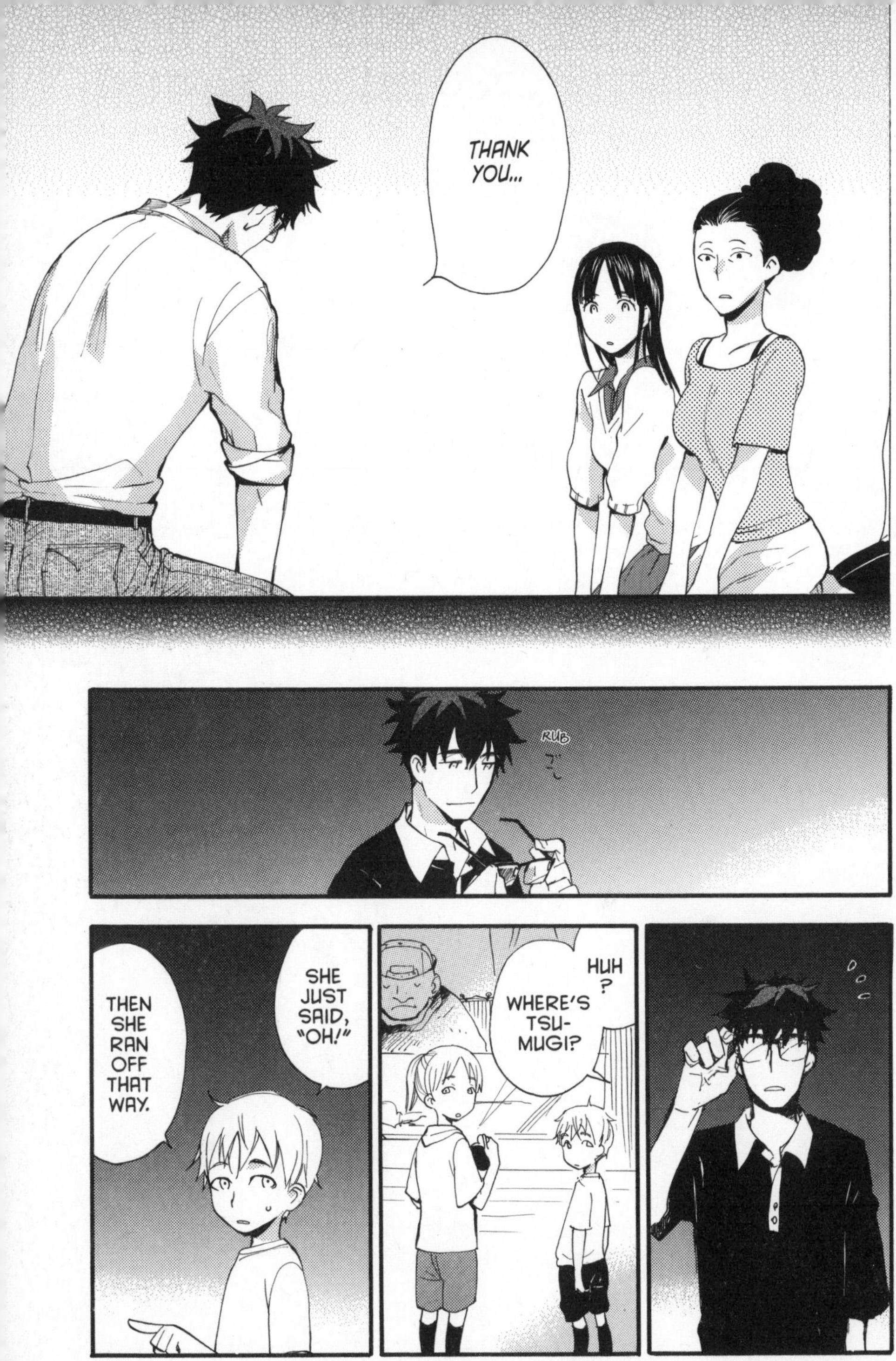
THANK YOU...
RUB
ごし
HUH?
WHERE'S TSU-MUGI?
SHE JUST SAID, "OH!"
THEN SHE RAN OFF THAT WAY.

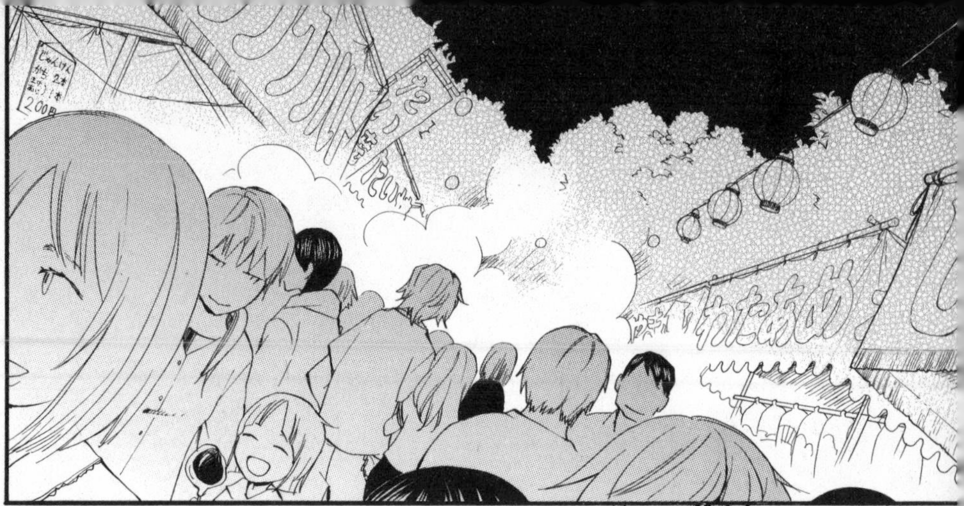
200円

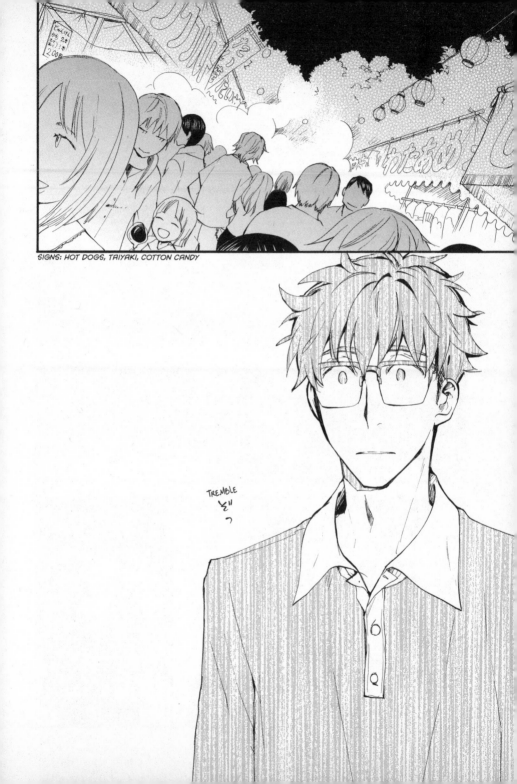

SIGNS: HOT DOGS, TAIYAKI, COTTON CANDY

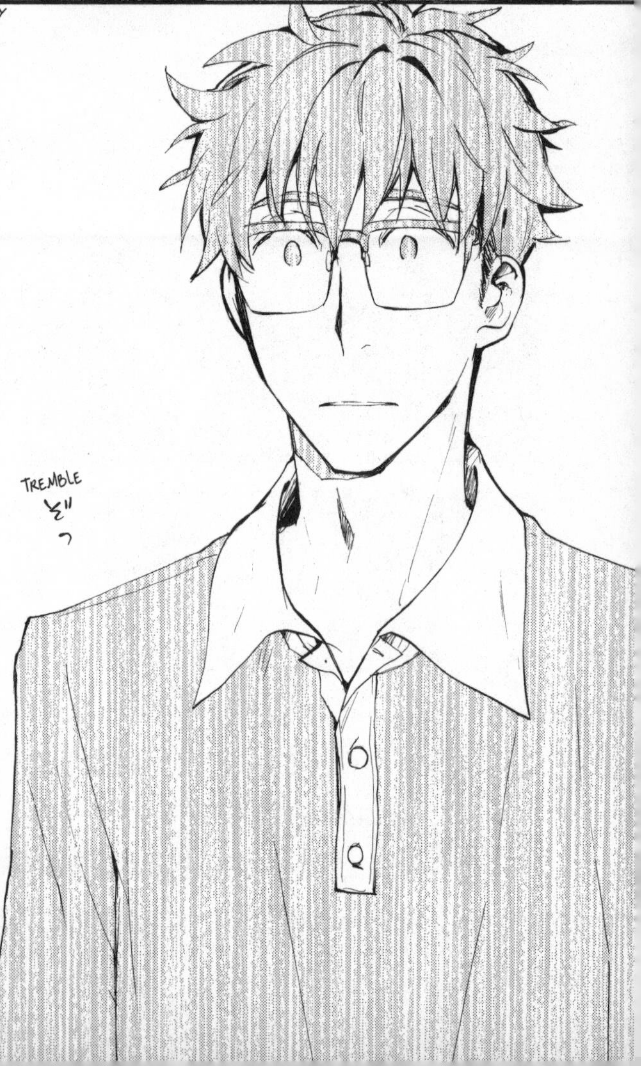
TREMBLE

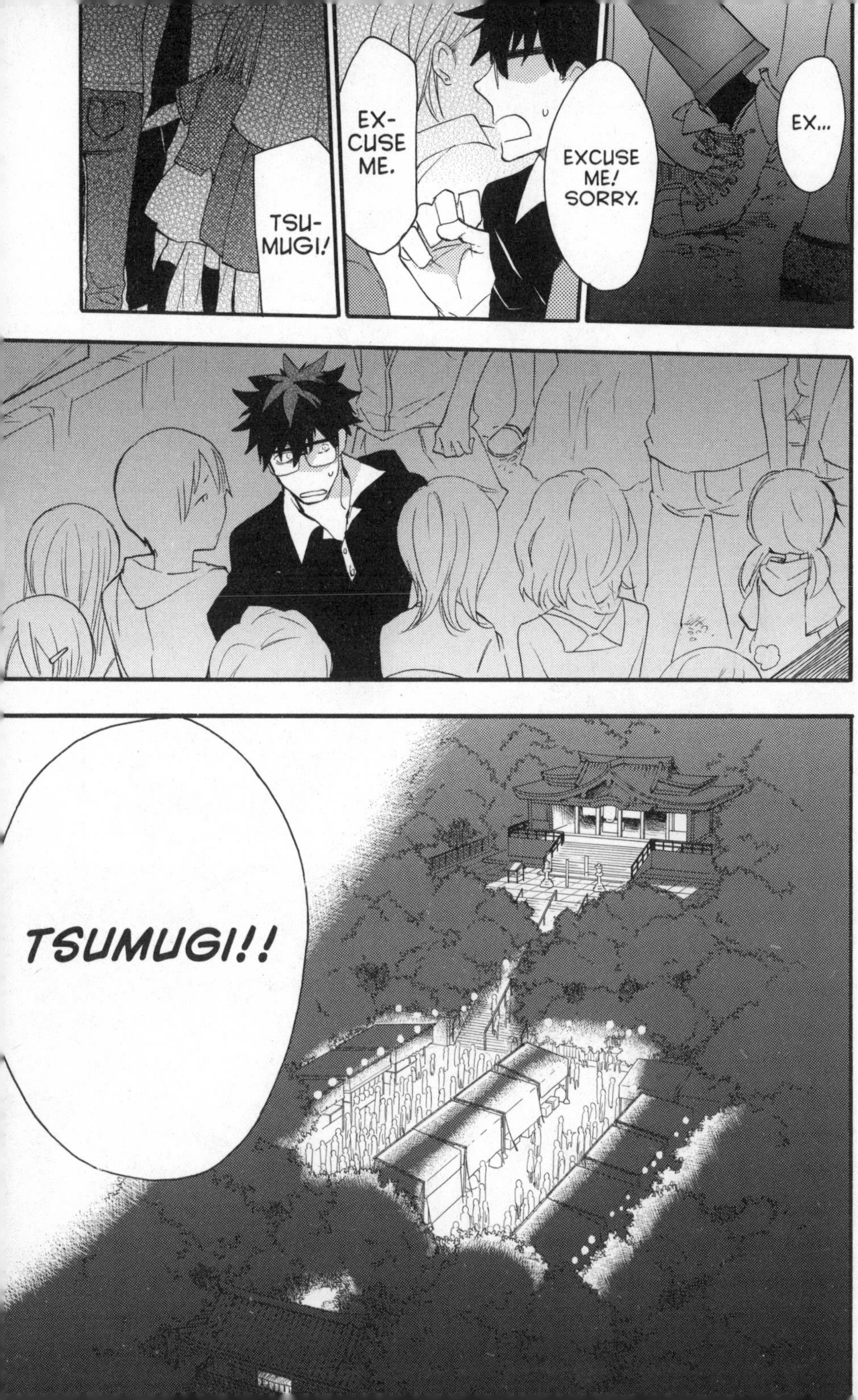
EX...
EXCUSE ME! SORRY.
EX-CUSE ME.
TSU-MUGI!
TSUMUGI!!

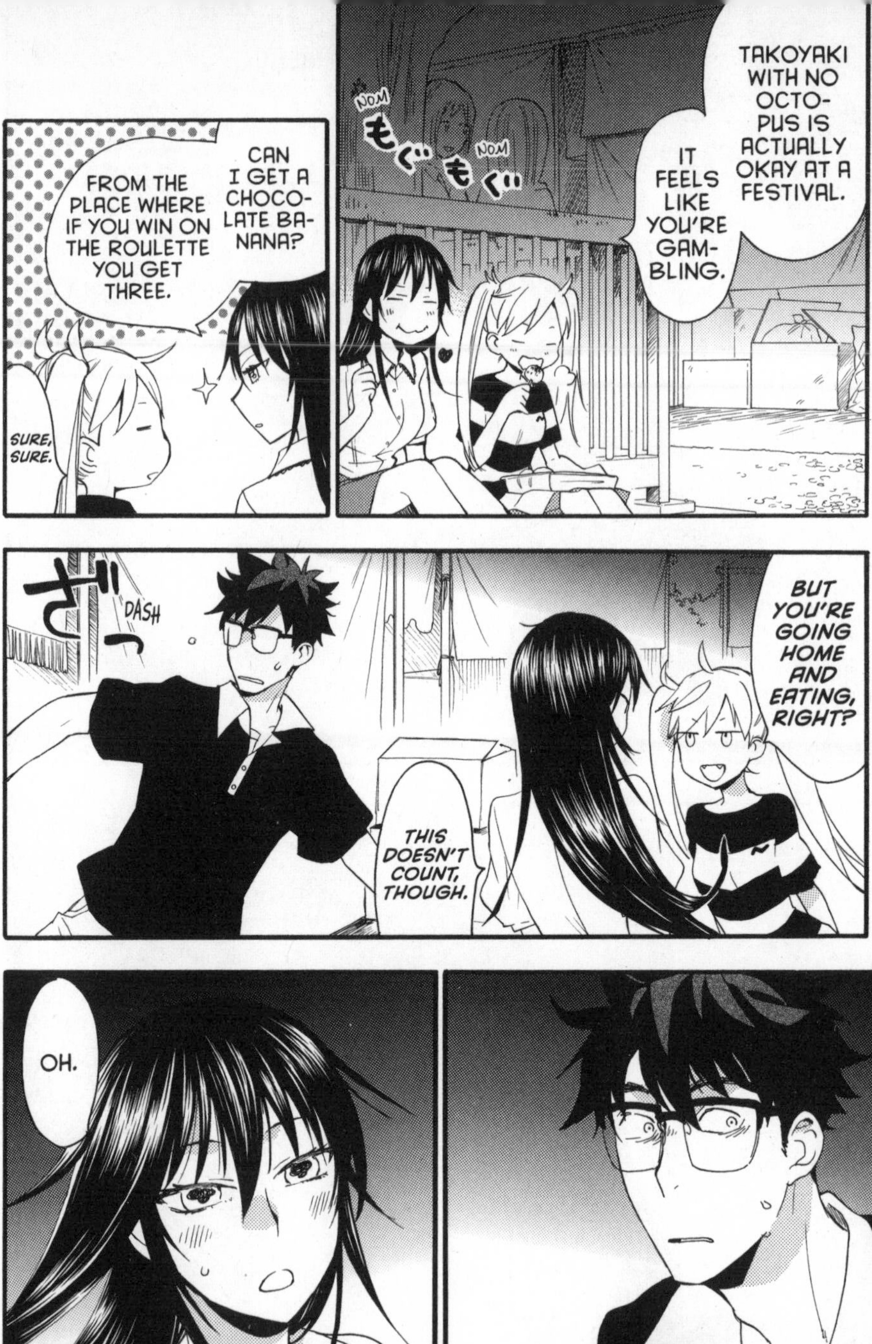
TAKOYAKI WITH NO OCTOPUS IS ACTUALLY OKAY AT A FESTIVAL.
IT FEELS LIKE YOU'RE GAMBLING.
NOM
もぐ
NOM
もぐ
CAN I GET A CHOCOLATE BANANA?
FROM THE PLACE WHERE IF YOU WIN ON THE ROULETTE YOU GET THREE.
SURE, SURE.
BUT YOU'RE GOING HOME AND EATING, RIGHT?
THIS DOESN'T COUNT, THOUGH.
ざー
DASH
OH.

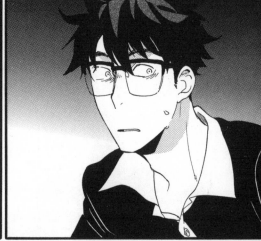

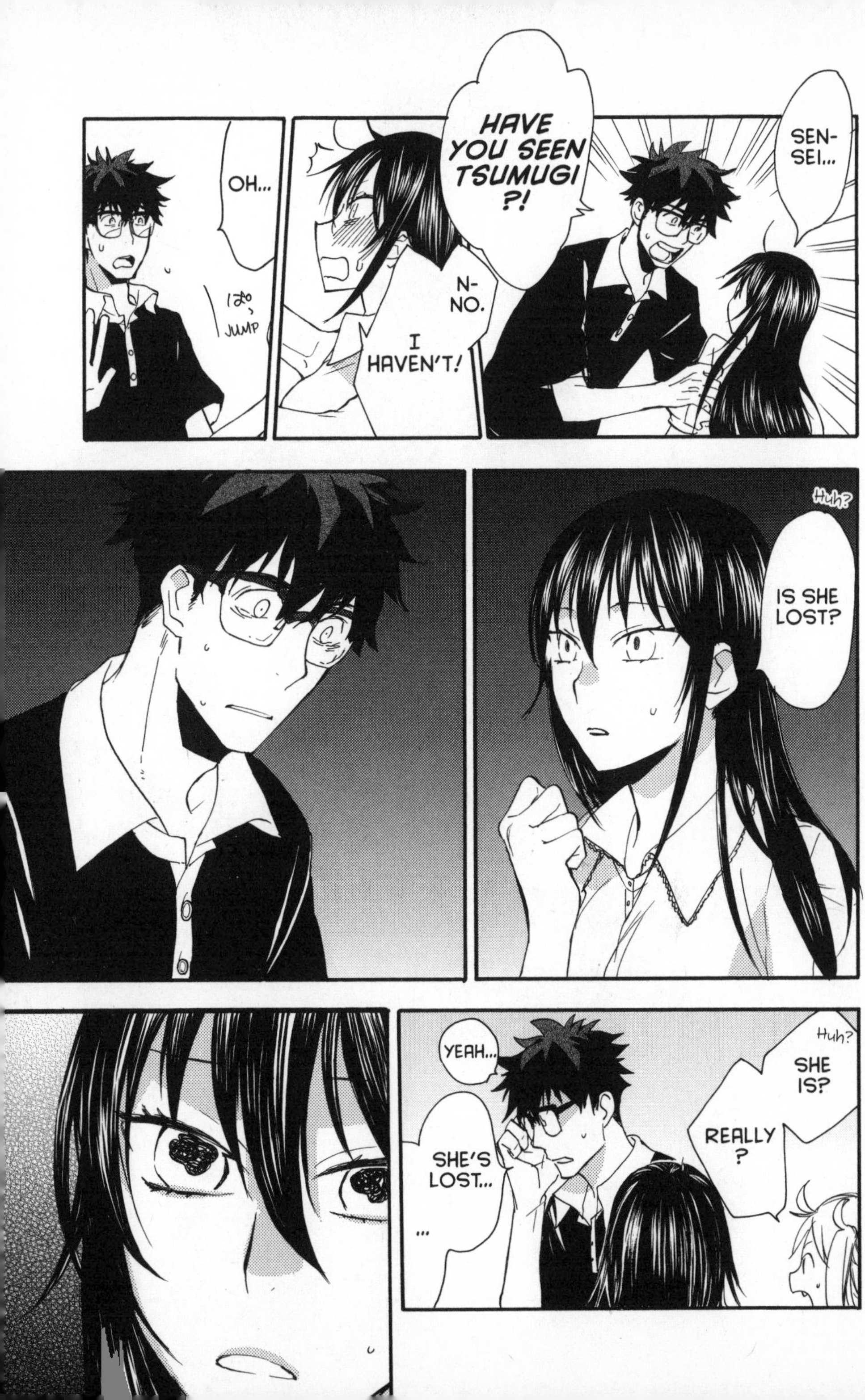
SEN-SEI...
HAVE YOU SEEN TSUMUGI?!
N-NO.
I HAVEN'T!
OH...
ぱっ
JUMP
Huh?
IS SHE LOST?
Huh?
SHE IS?
REALLY?
YEAH...
SHE'S LOST...
...

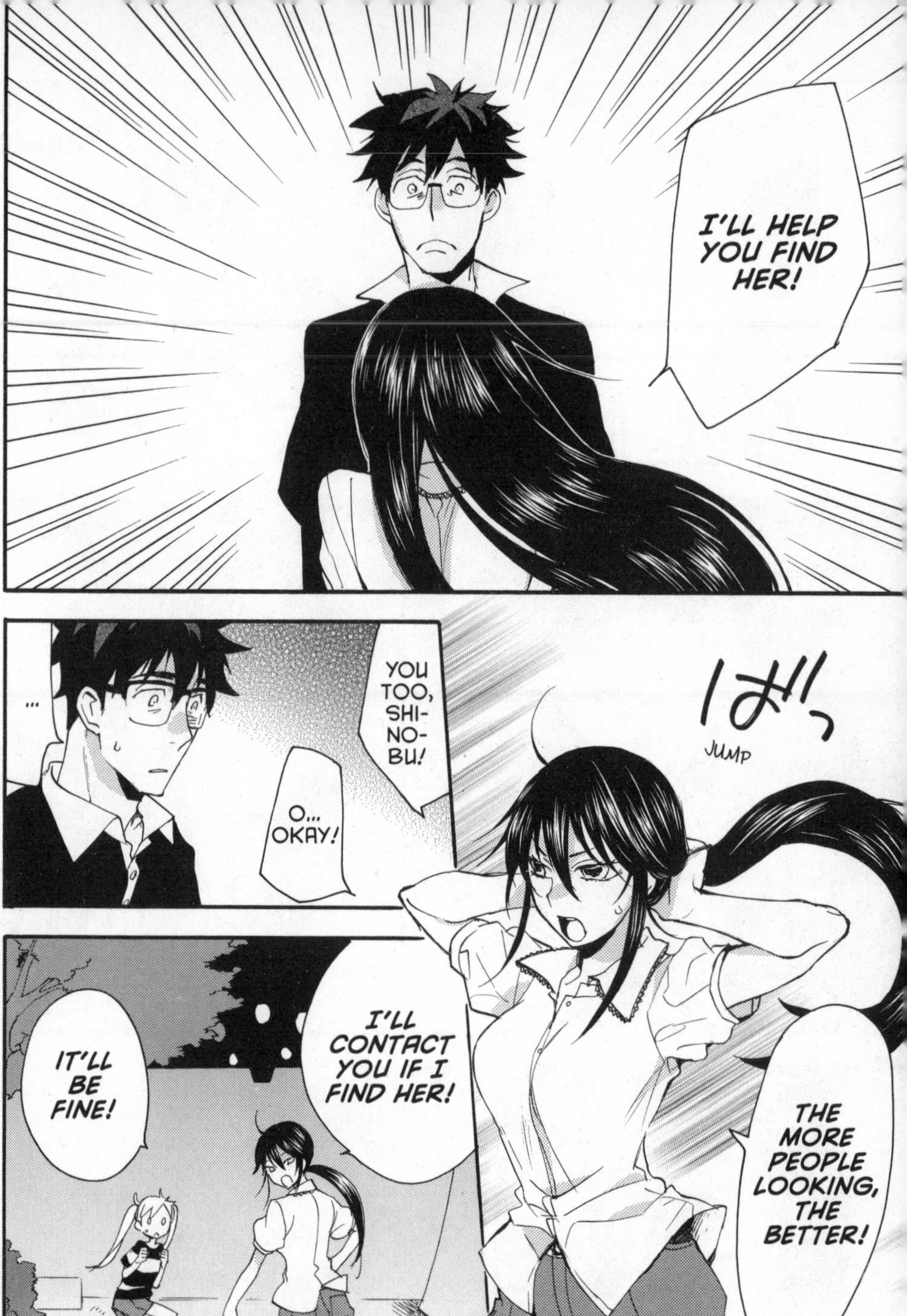
I'LL HELP YOU FIND HER!
ぱっ
JUMP
THE MORE PEOPLE LOOKING, THE BETTER!
YOU TOO, SHI-NO-BU!
O... OKAY!
...
I'LL CONTACT YOU IF I FIND HER!
IT'LL BE FINE!

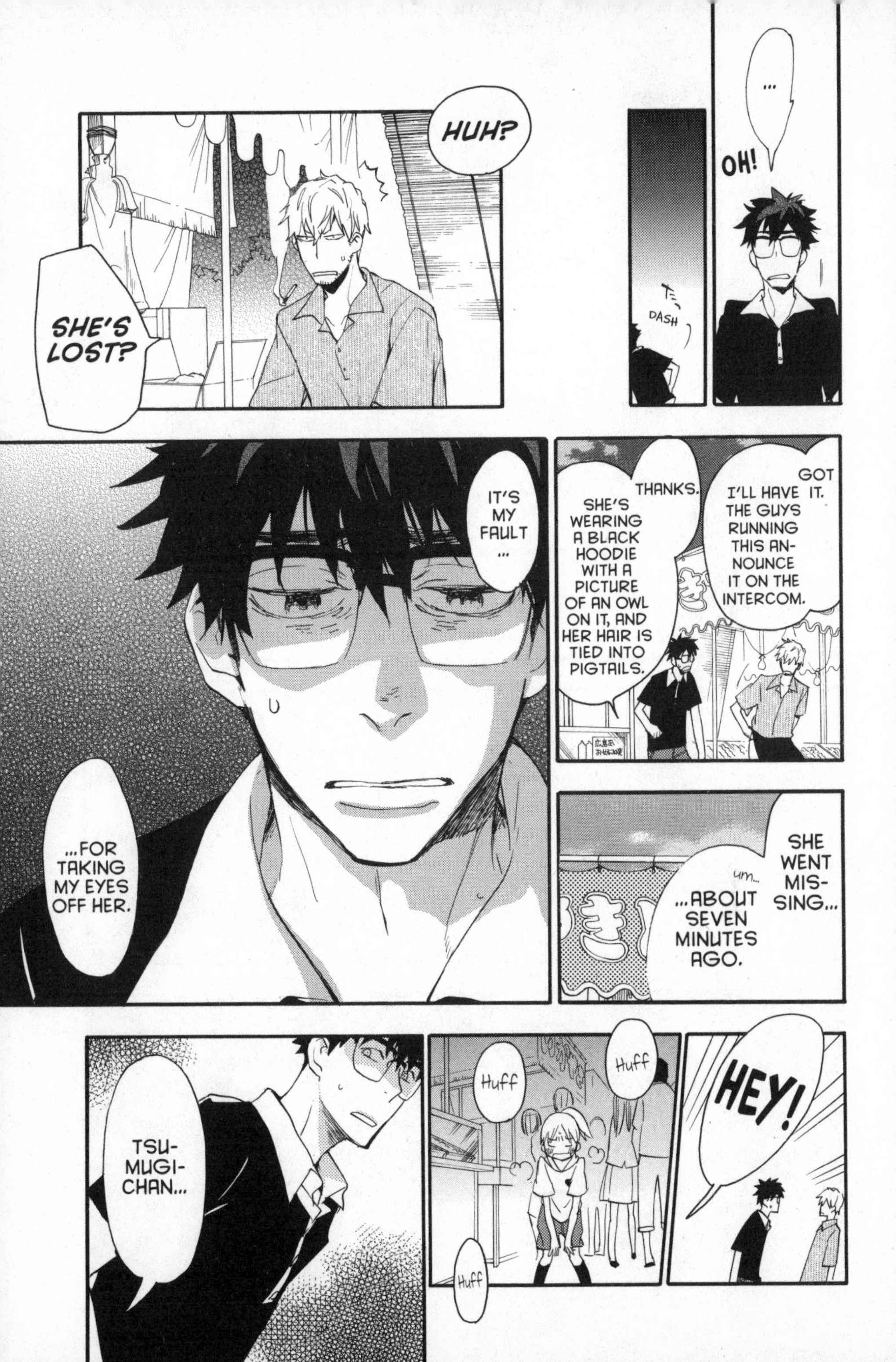
...
OH!
DASH
HUH?
SHE'S LOST?
GOT IT. I'LL HAVE THE GUYS RUNNING THIS ANNOUNCE IT ON THE INTERCOM.
THANKS. SHE'S WEARING A BLACK HOODIE WITH A PICTURE OF AN OWL ON IT, AND HER HAIR IS TIED INTO PIGTAILS.
SHE WENT MISSING...
um...
...ABOUT SEVEN MINUTES AGO.
IT'S MY FAULT ...
...FOR TAKING MY EYES OFF HER.
HEY!
Huff
Huff
Huff
TSUMUGI-CHAN...

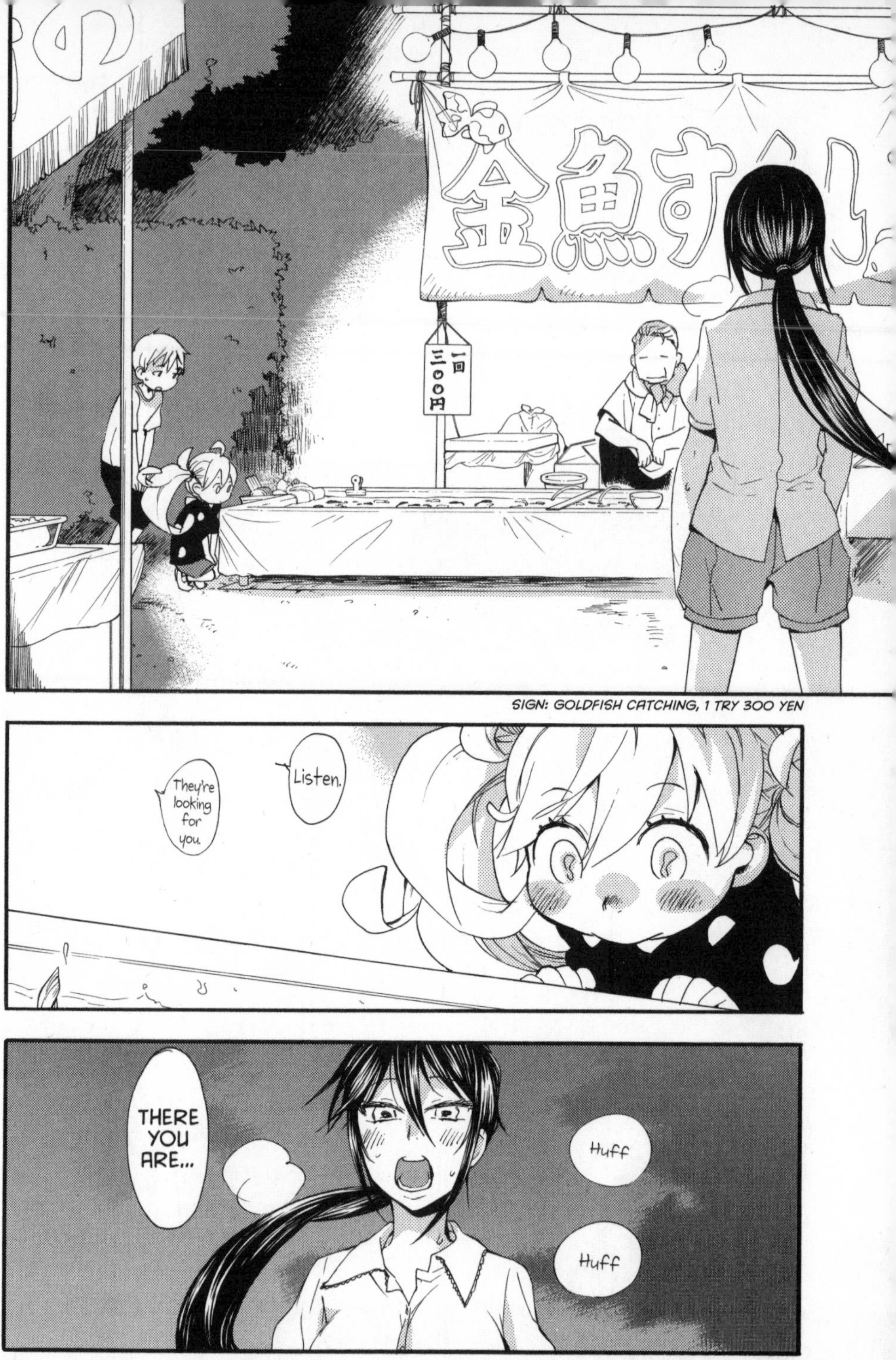
金魚す
一回 三〇〇円
SIGN: GOLDFISH CATCHING, 1 TRY 300 YEN
Listen.
They're looking for you.
Huff
Huff
THERE YOU ARE...

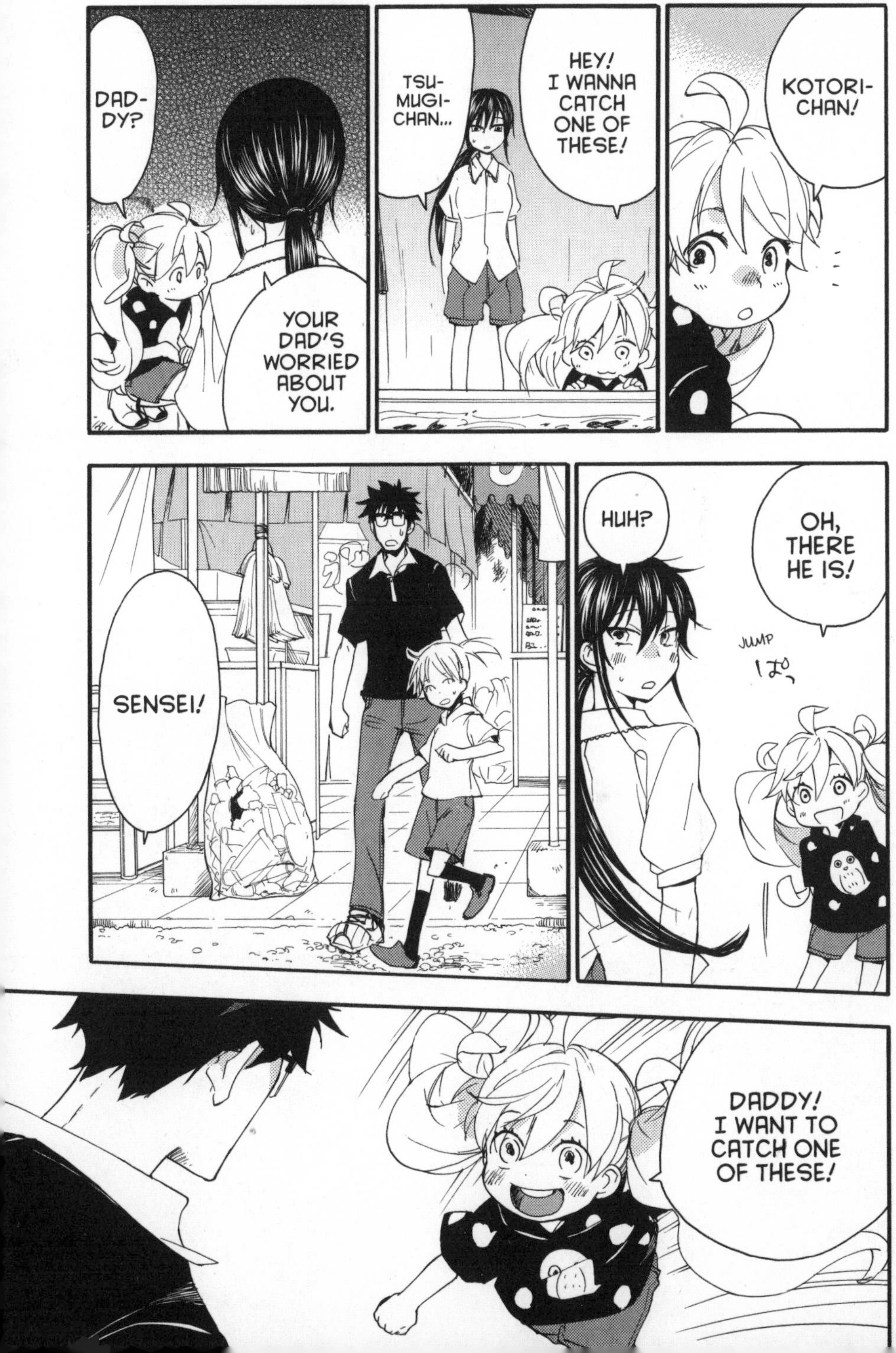
KOTORI-CHAN!
HEY! I WANNA CATCH ONE OF THESE!
TSU-MUGI-CHAN...
DAD-DY?
YOUR DAD'S WORRIED ABOUT YOU.
OH, THERE HE IS!
HUH?
JUMP
ぱっ
SENSEI!
DADDY! I WANT TO CATCH ONE OF THESE!

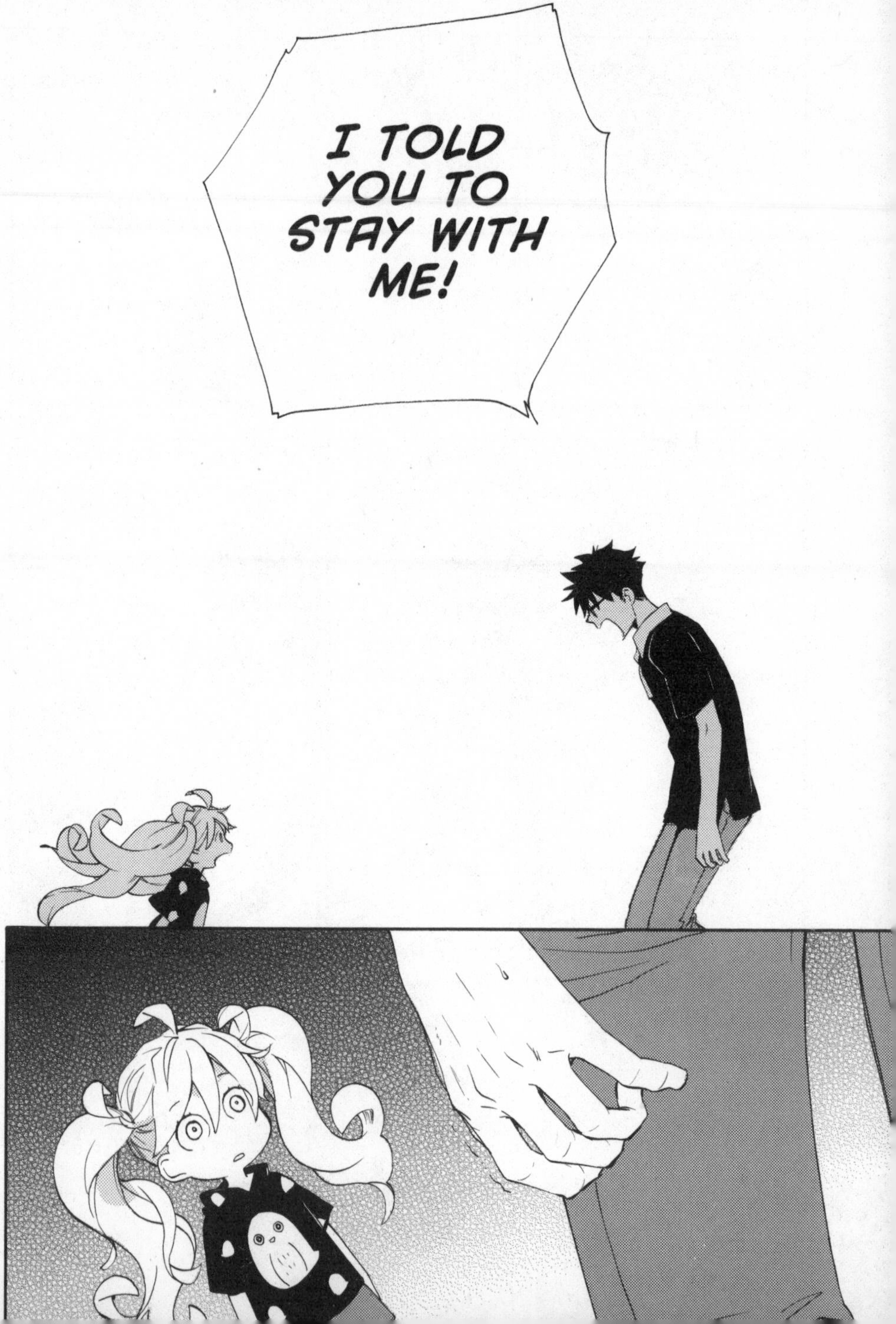
I TOLD YOU TO STAY WITH ME!

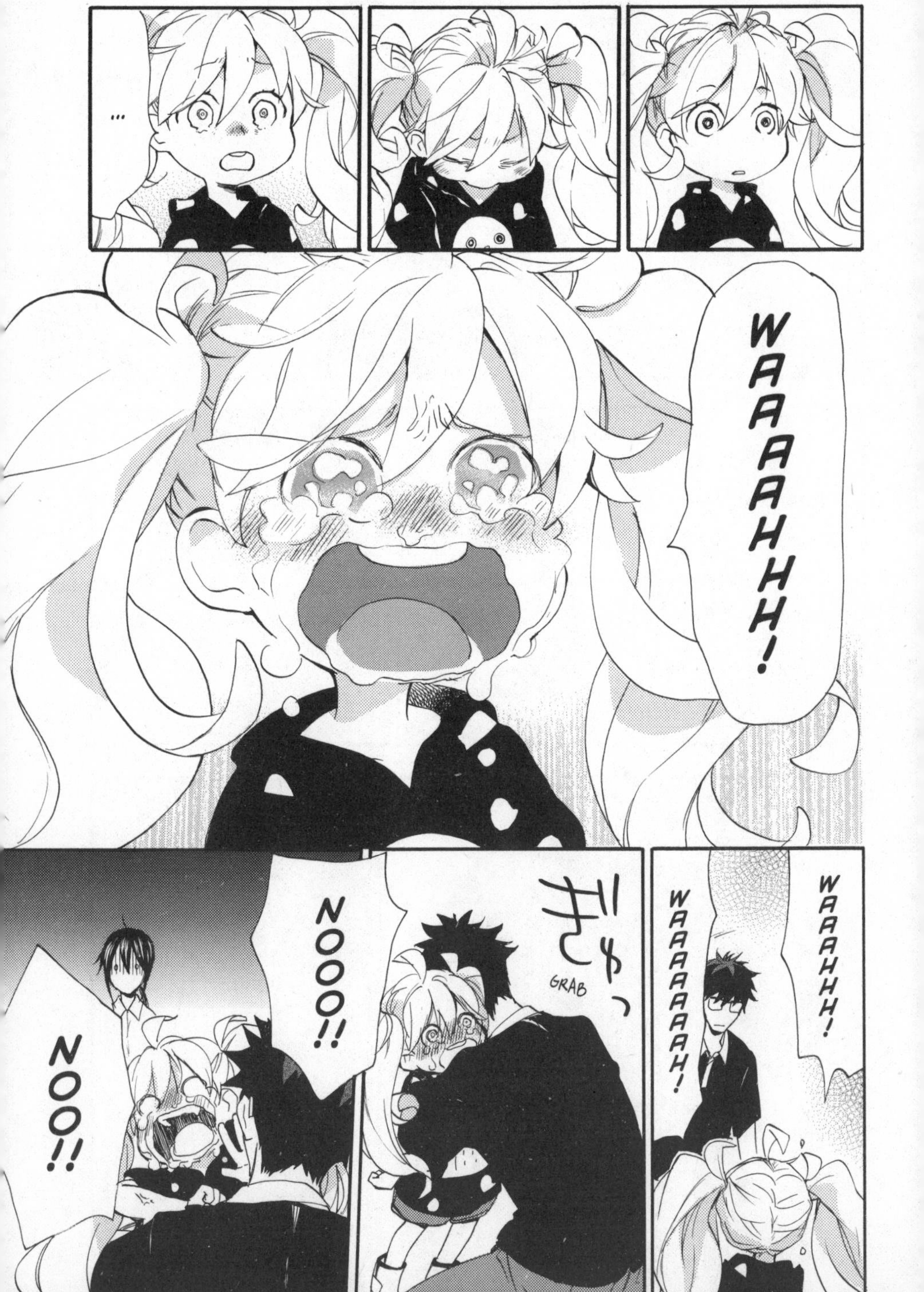
...
WAAAAAHHHH!
WAAAHHHH!
WAAAAAAAAAH!
NOOOO!!
ぎゅっ
GRAB
NOO!!

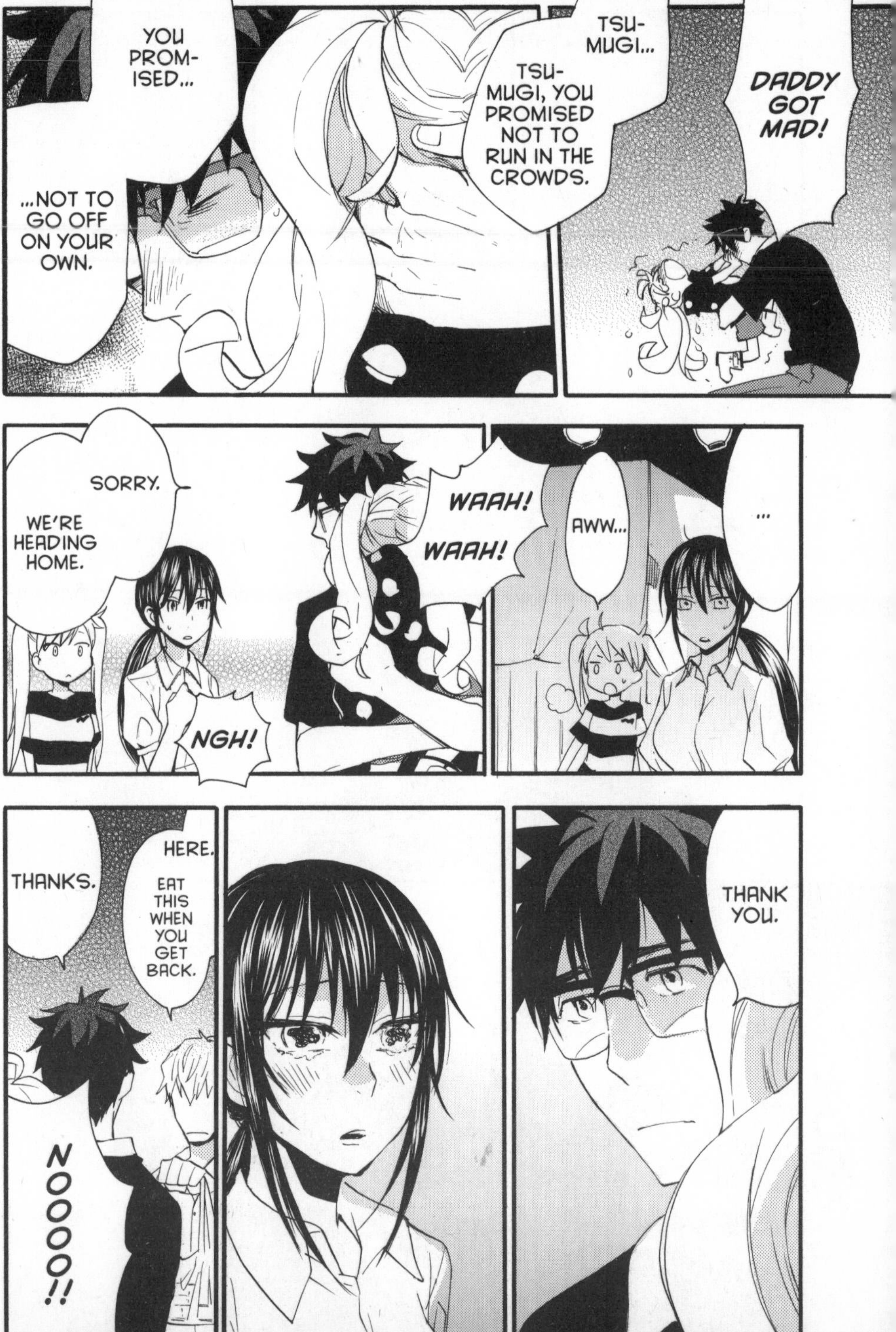
DADDY GOT MAD!
TSU-MUGI...
TSU-MUGI, YOU PROMISED NOT TO RUN IN THE CROWDS.
YOU PROMISED...
...NOT TO GO OFF ON YOUR OWN.
...
AWW...
WAAH!
WAAH!
SORRY.
WE'RE HEADING HOME.
NGH!
THANK YOU.
HERE.
EAT THIS WHEN YOU GET BACK.
THANKS.
NOOOOO!!

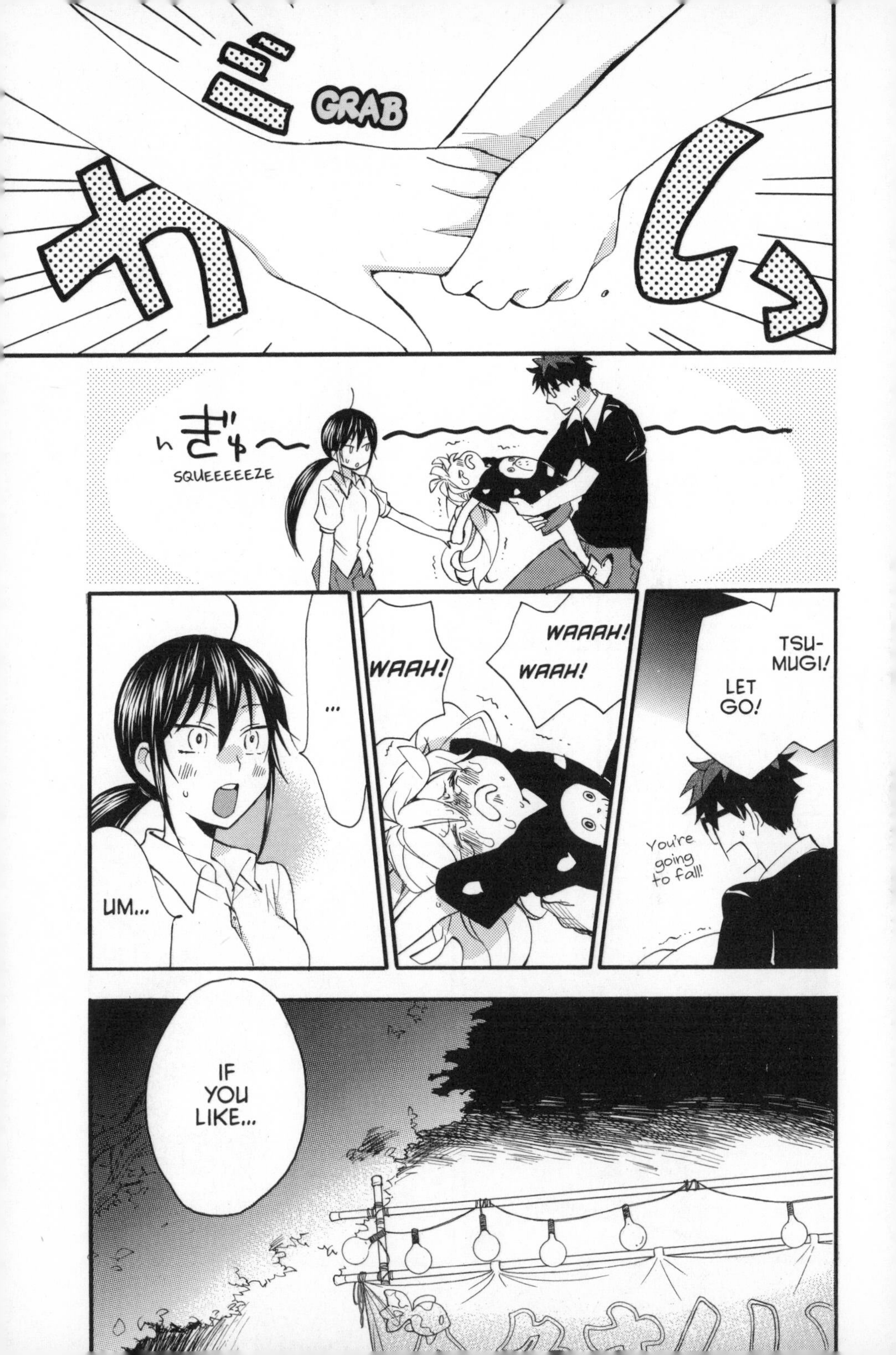
ガしっ
GRAB
んぎゅ〜〜〜
SQUEEEEEEZE
TSU-MUGI!
LET GO!
You're going to fall!
WAAAH!
WAAH!
WAAH!
...
UM...
IF YOU LIKE...

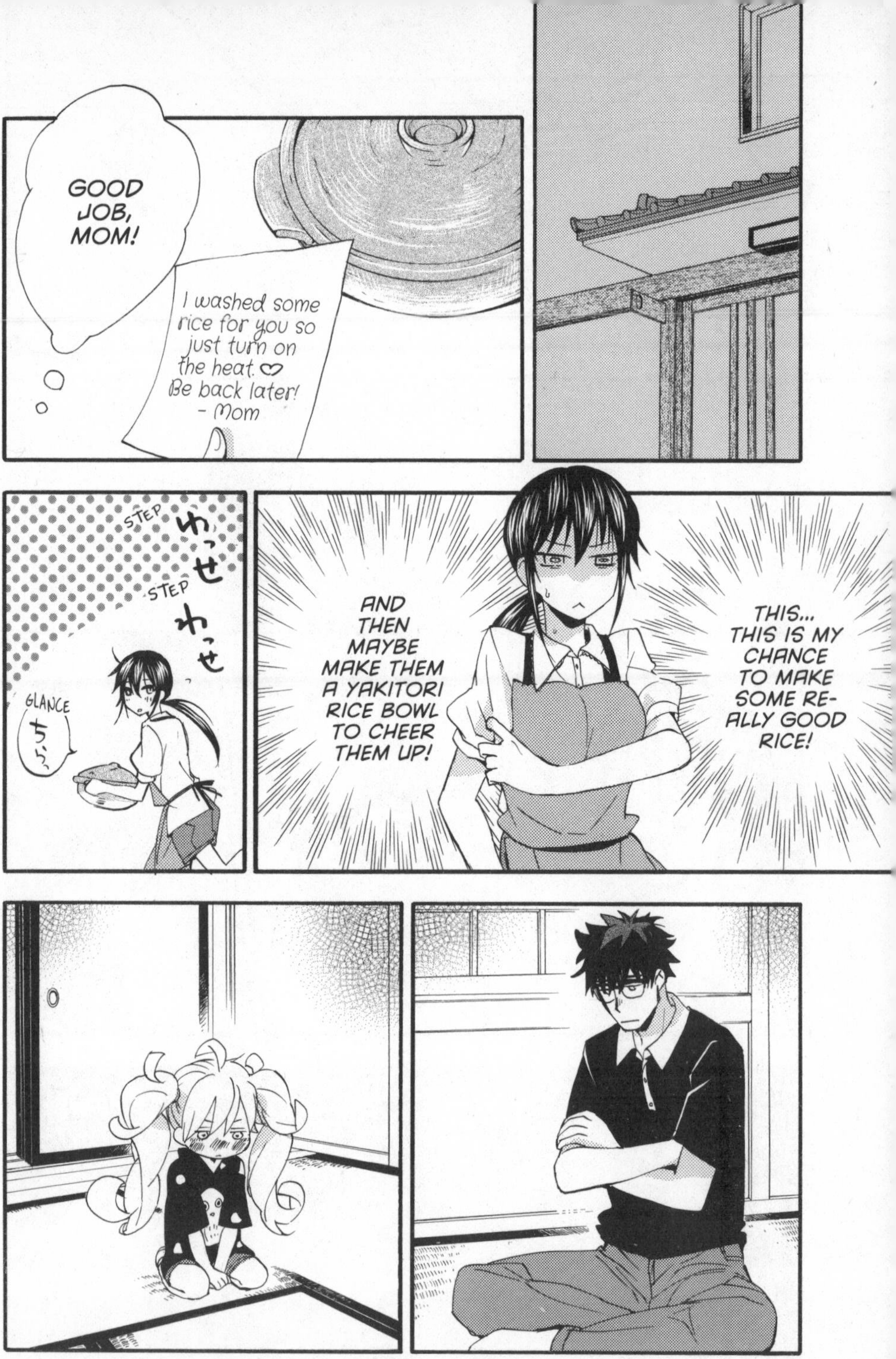
I washed some rice for you so just turn on the heat. Be back later! - Mom
GOOD JOB, MOM!
THIS... THIS IS MY CHANCE TO MAKE SOME RE-ALLY GOOD RICE!
AND THEN MAYBE MAKE THEM A YAKITORI RICE BOWL TO CHEER THEM UP!
わっせ
STEP
わっせ
STEP
ちら
GLANCE

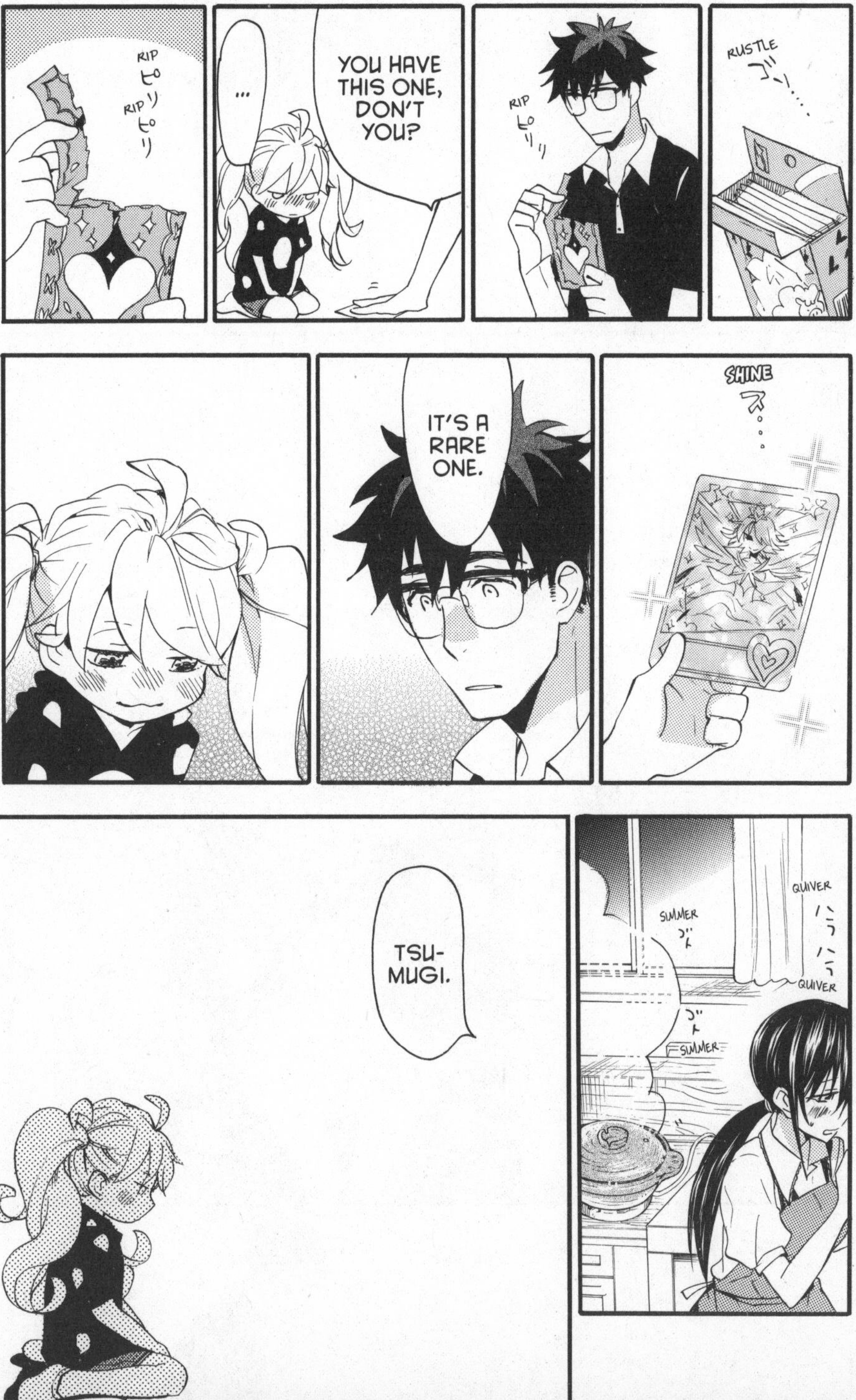
RUSTLE
ゴソ…
RIP
ピリリ
YOU HAVE THIS ONE, DON'T YOU?
…
RIP
ピリ
RIP
ピリ
SHINE
ス…
IT'S A RARE ONE.
QUIVER
ハラ
ハラ
QUIVER
SIMMER
ゴト
ゴト
SIMMER
TSU-MUGI.

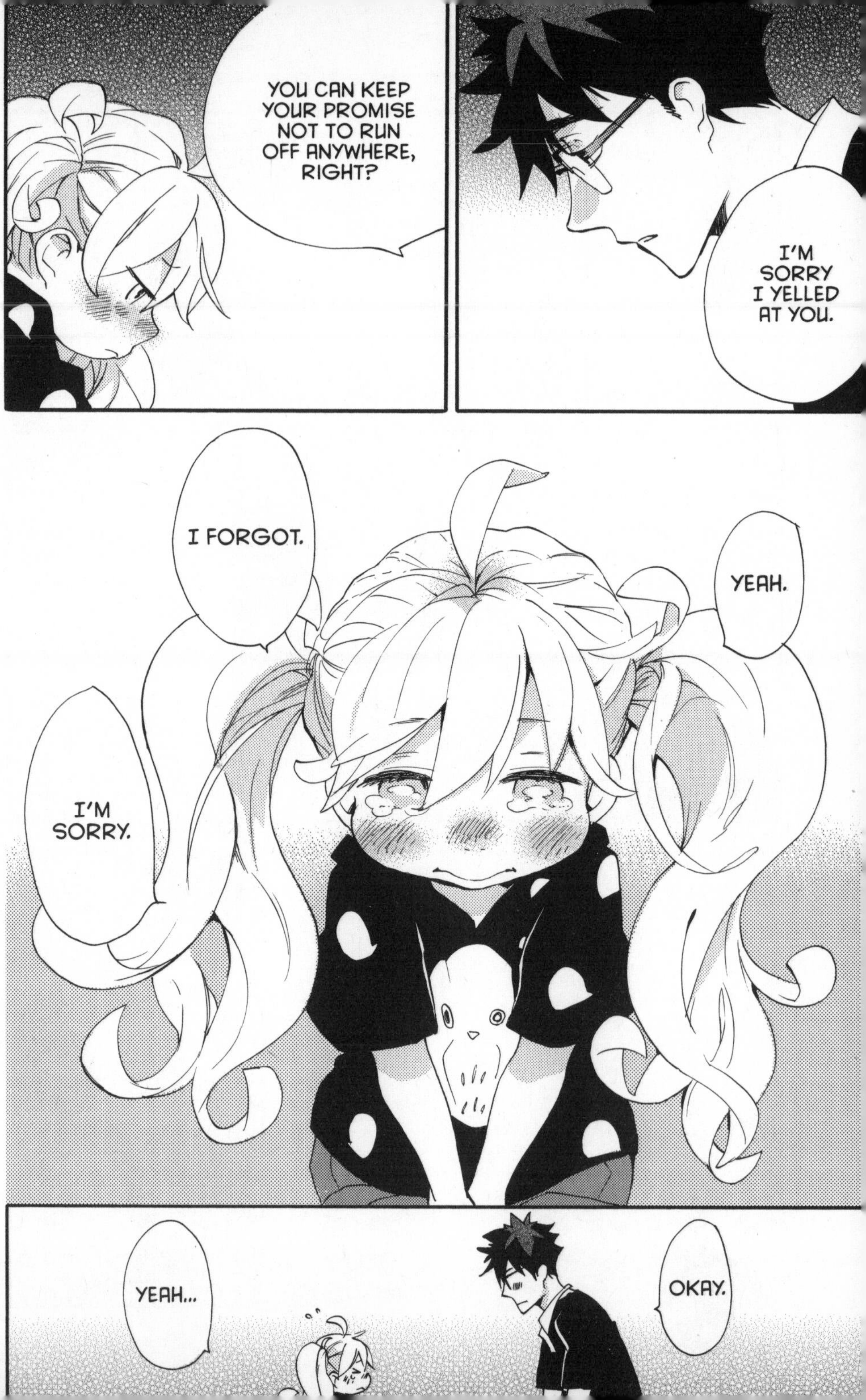
I'M SORRY I YELLED AT YOU.
YOU CAN KEEP YOUR PROMISE NOT TO RUN OFF ANYWHERE, RIGHT?
YEAH.
I FORGOT.
I'M SORRY.
OKAY.
YEAH...

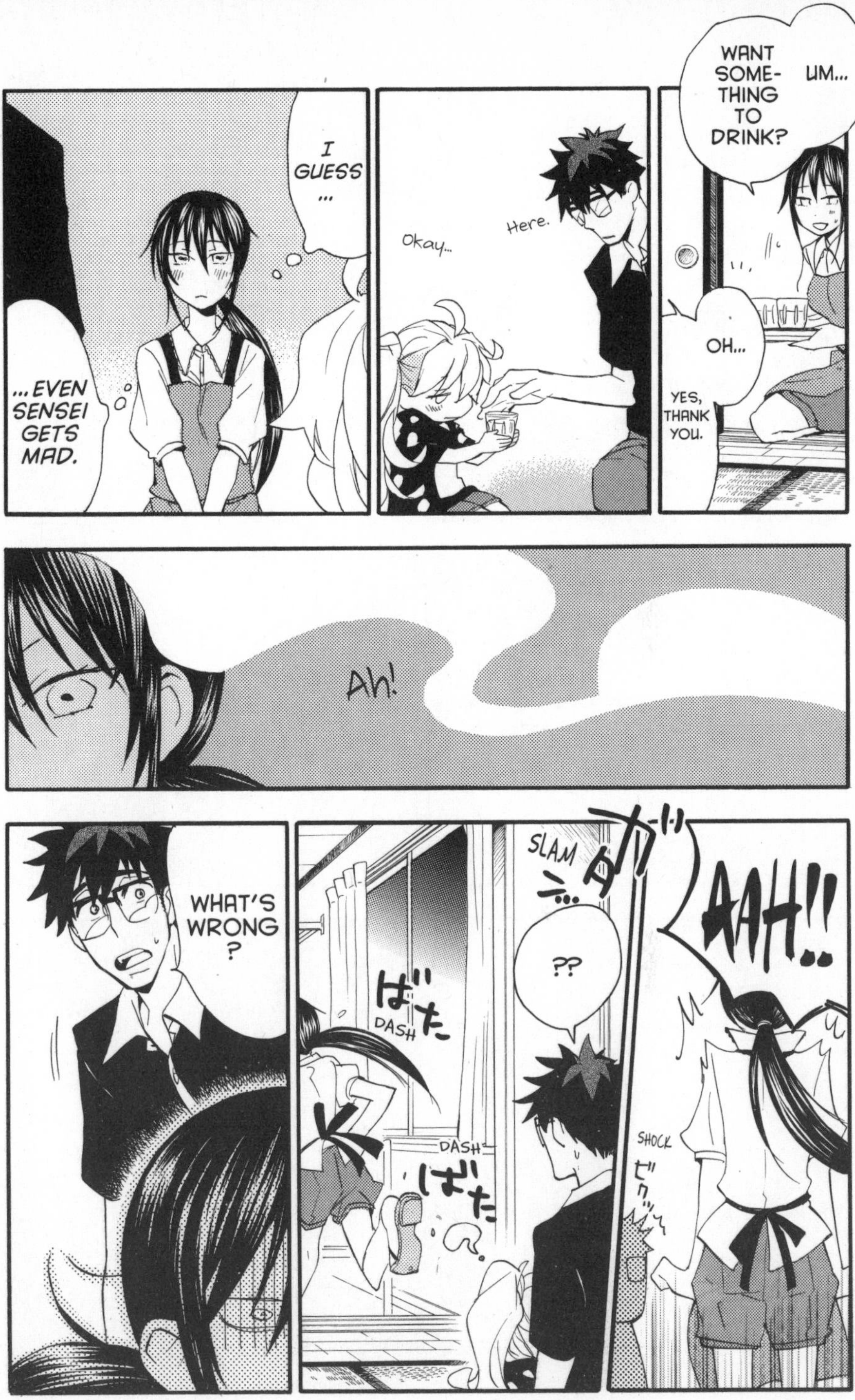
UM...
WANT SOME-THING TO DRINK?
OH...
YES, THANK YOU.
Here.
Okay...
I GUESS ...
...EVEN SENSEI GETS MAD.
Ah!
AAH!!
ガーー
SLAM
SHOCK
ビクッ
??
ばた
DASH
DASH
ばた
WHAT'S WRONG ?

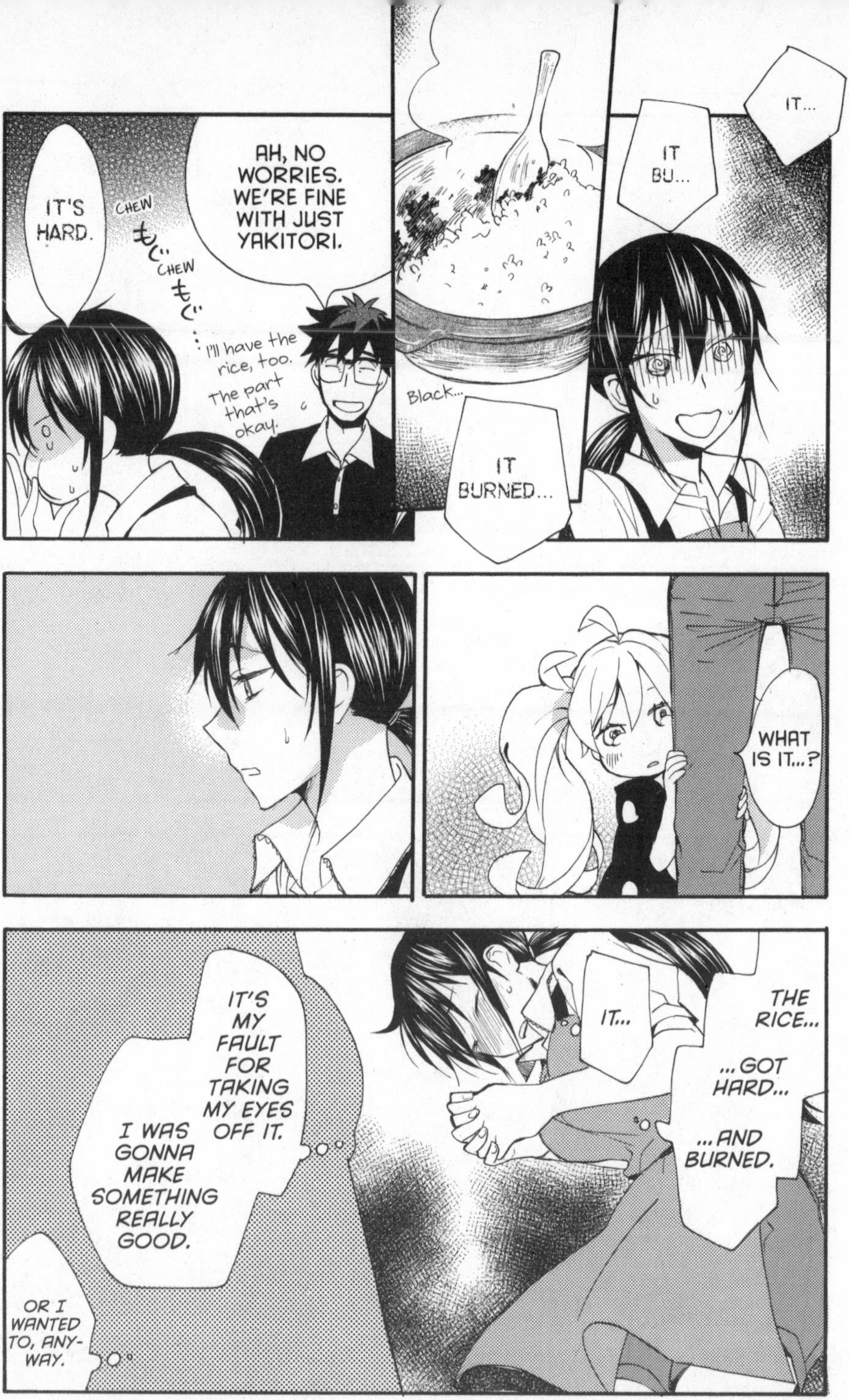
IT...
IT BU...
Black...
IT BURNED...
AH, NO WORRIES. WE'RE FINE WITH JUST YAKITORI.
CHEW もぐ CHEW もぐ...
IT'S HARD.
I'll have the rice, too. The part that's okay.
WHAT IS IT...?
IT...
THE RICE...
...GOT HARD...
...AND BURNED.
IT'S MY FAULT FOR TAKING MY EYES OFF IT.
I WAS GONNA MAKE SOMETHING REALLY GOOD.
OR I WANTED TO, ANYWAY.

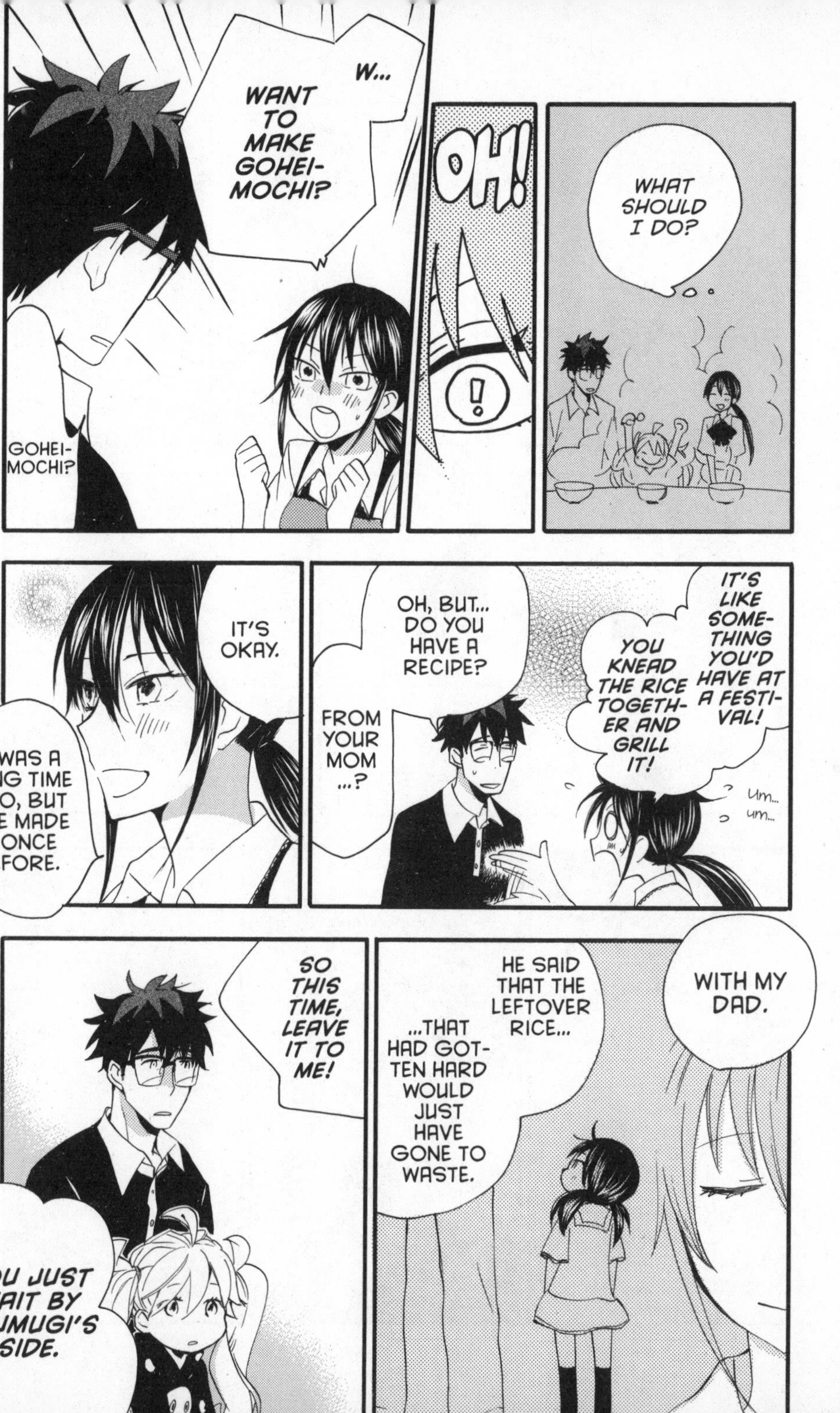
WHAT SHOULD I DO?
OH!
!
W...
WANT TO MAKE GOHEI-MOCHI?
GOHEI-MOCHI?
IT'S LIKE SOMETHING YOU'D HAVE AT A FESTIVAL!
YOU KNEAD THE RICE TOGETHER AND GRILL IT!
OH, BUT... DO YOU HAVE A RECIPE?
Um... um...
FROM YOUR MOM ...?
IT'S OKAY.
IT WAS A LONG TIME AGO, BUT I'VE MADE IT ONCE BEFORE.
WITH MY DAD.
HE SAID THAT THE LEFTOVER RICE...
...THAT HAD GOTTEN HARD WOULD JUST HAVE GONE TO WASTE.
SO THIS TIME, LEAVE IT TO ME!
YOU JUST WAIT BY TSUMUGI'S SIDE.

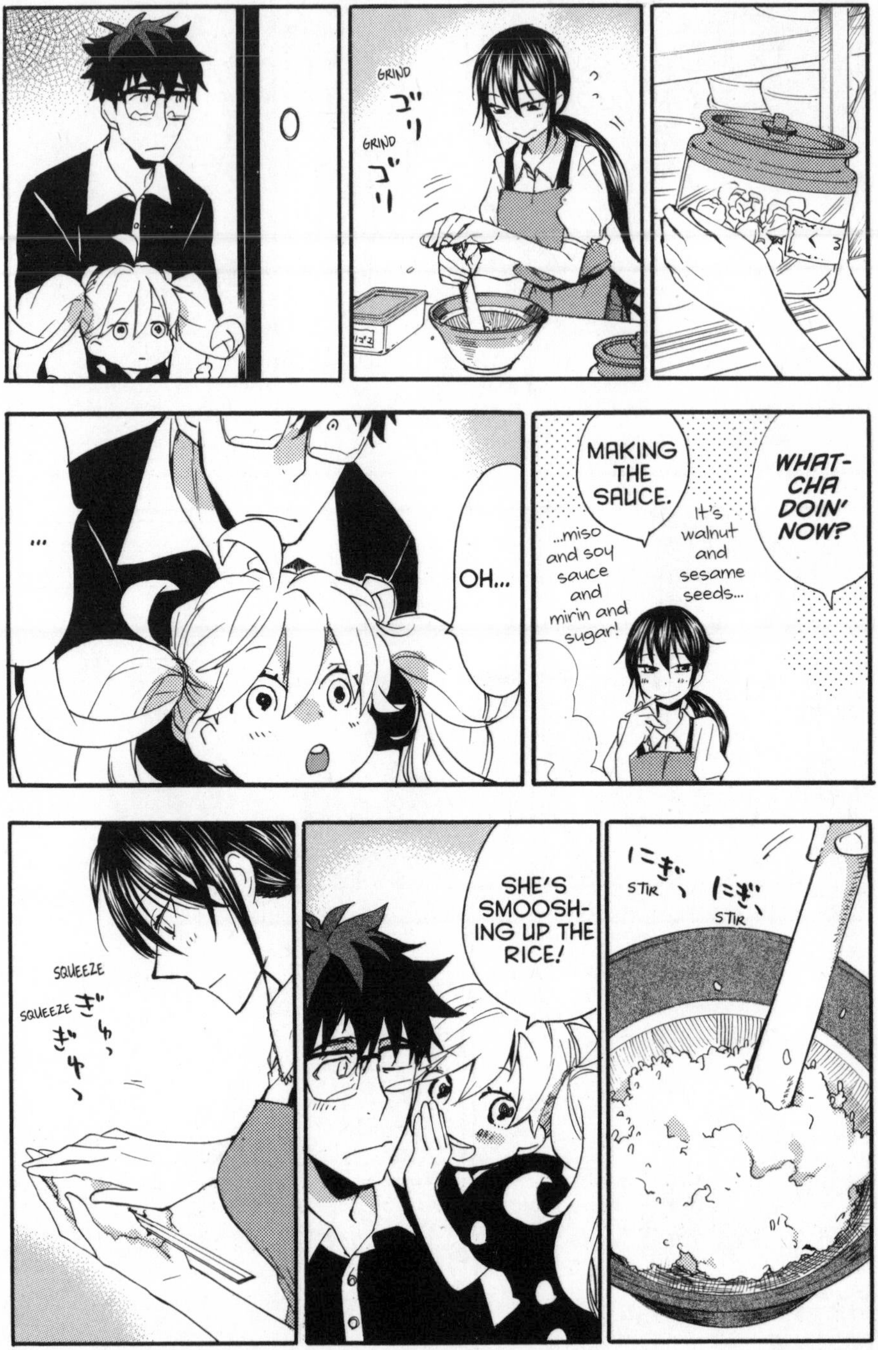
GRIND
ゴリ
GRIND
ゴリ
WHAT-CHA DOIN' NOW?
MAKING THE SAUCE.
It's walnut and sesame seeds...
...miso and soy sauce and mirin and sugar!
OH...
...
にぎ、
STIR
にぎ、
STIR
SHE'S SMOOSH-ING UP THE RICE!
SQUEEZE
ぎゅっ
SQUEEZE
ぎゅっ

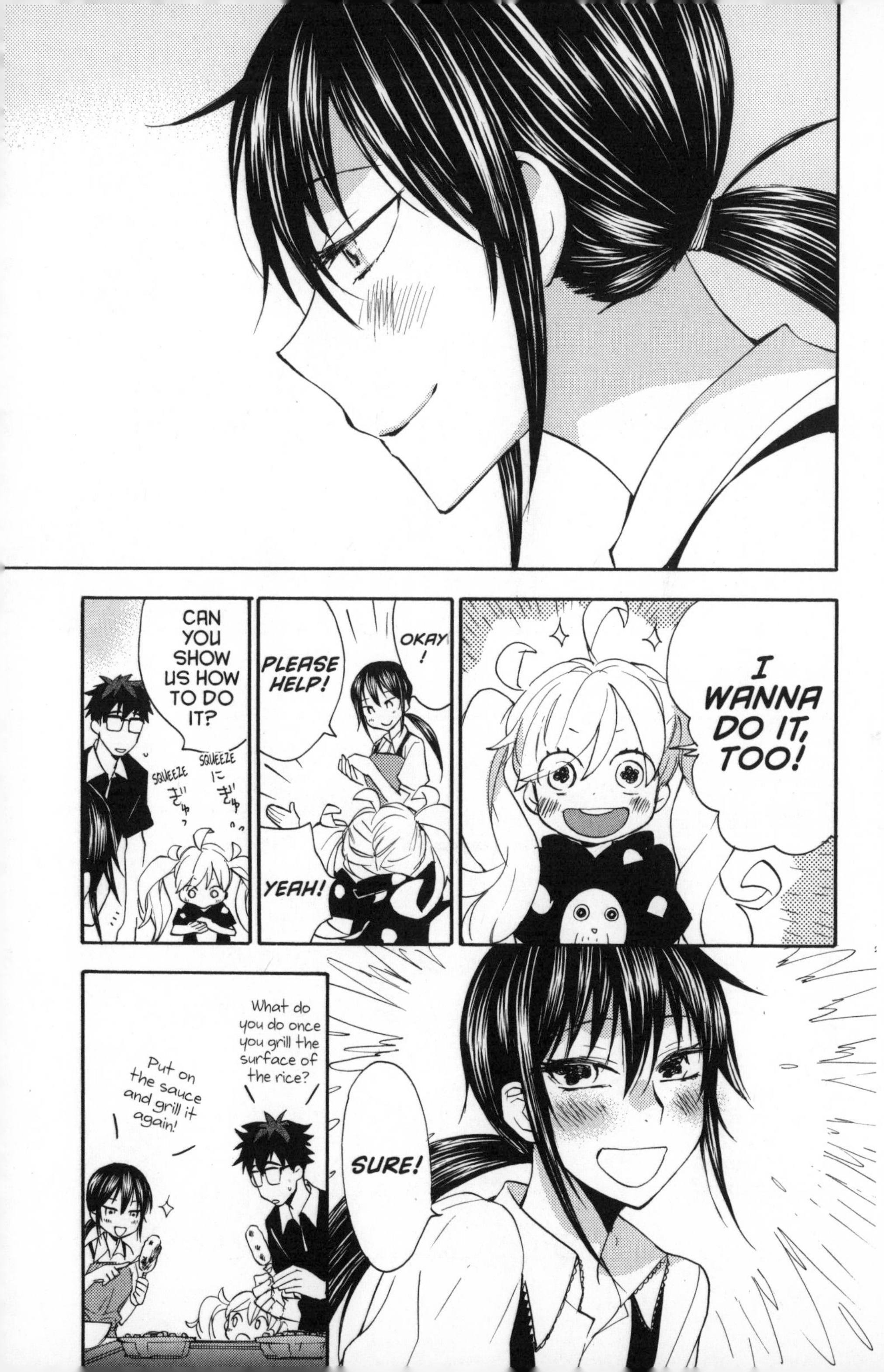
I WANNA DO IT, TOO!
OKAY!
PLEASE HELP!
YEAH!
CAN YOU SHOW US HOW TO DO IT?
SQUEEZE
にぎゅっ
SQUEEZE
ぎゅっ
SURE!
What do you do once you grill the surface of the rice?
Put on the sauce and grill it again!

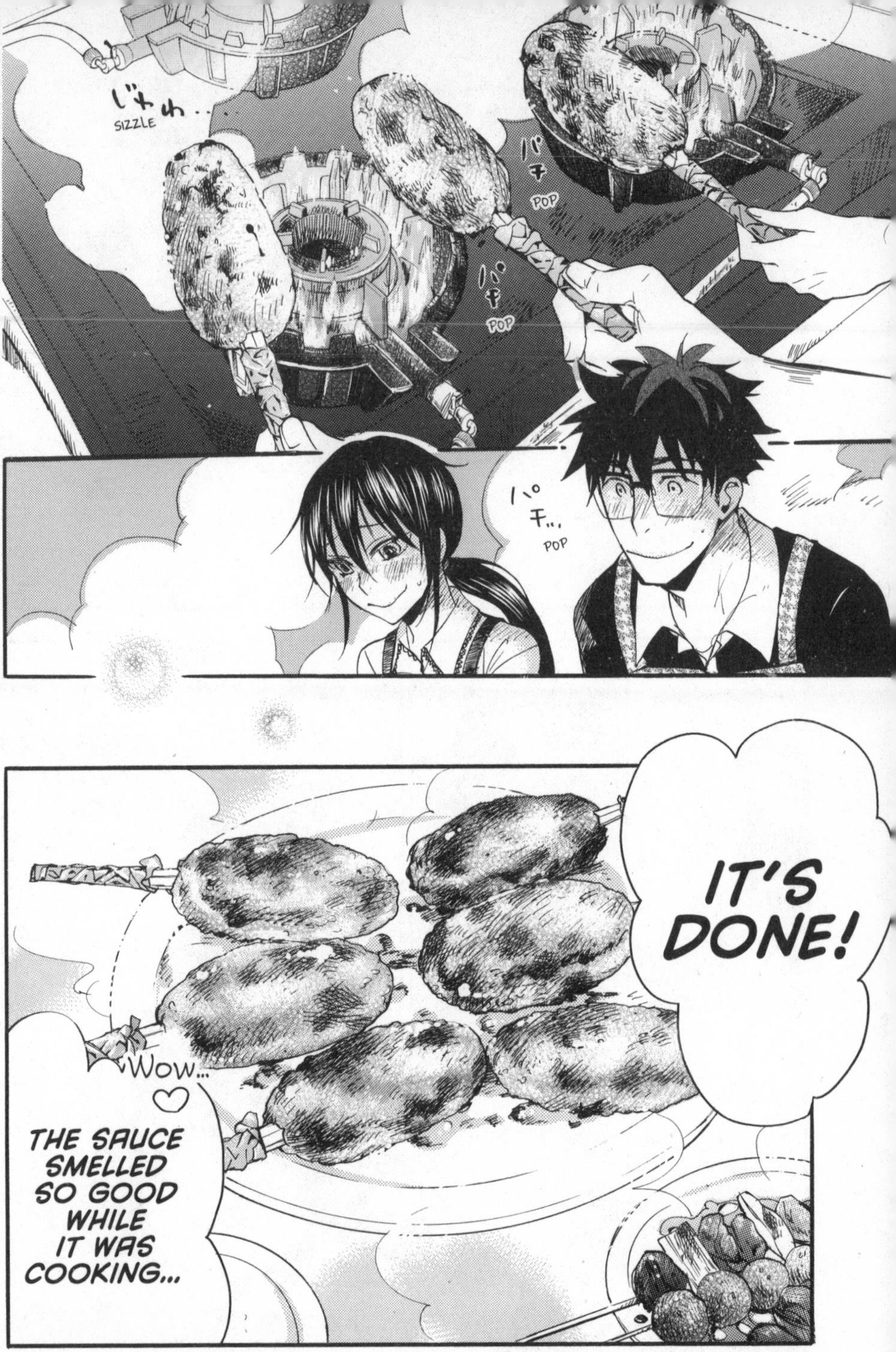
じわわ…
SIZZLE
パチ
POP
パチ
POP
パチ…
POP
IT'S DONE!
Wow… ♡
THE SAUCE SMELLED SO GOOD WHILE IT WAS COOKING…

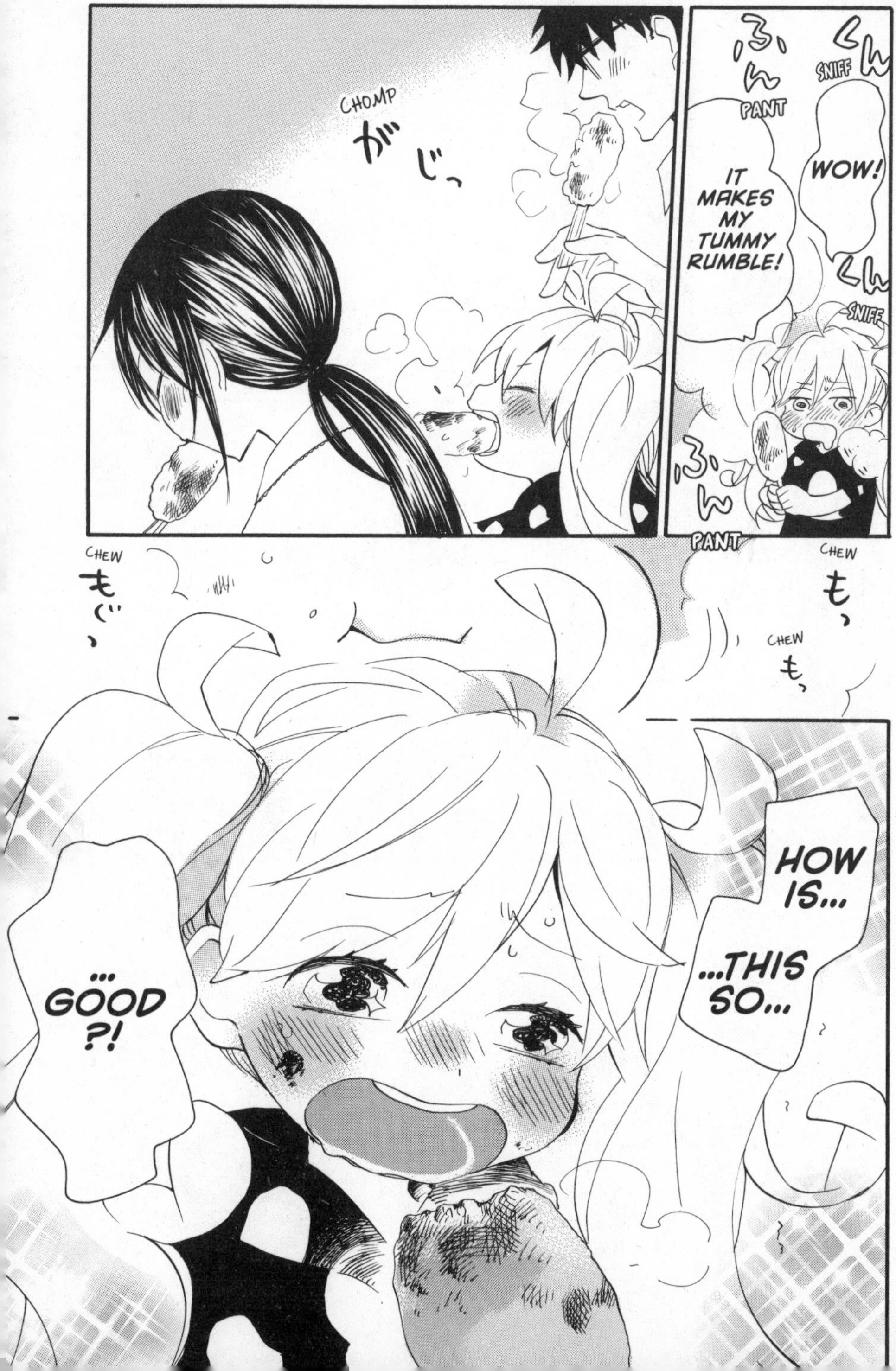
くん
SNIFF
WOW!
ふん
PANT
IT MAKES MY TUMMY RUMBLE!
くん
SNIFF
ふん
PANT
がじっ
CHOMP
も、
CHEW
も、
CHEW
もぐ、
CHEW
HOW IS...
...THIS SO...
...GOOD?!

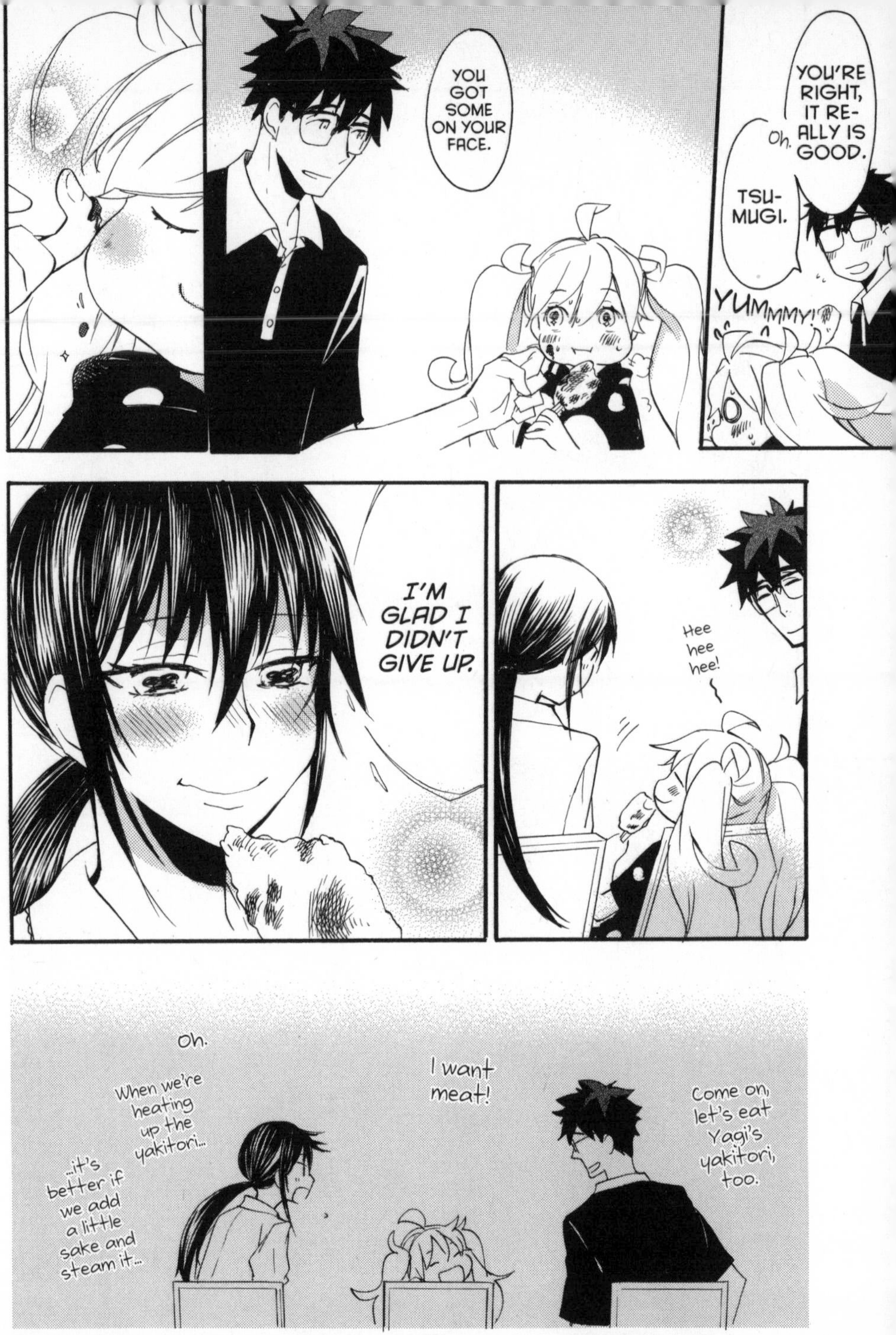
YOU'RE RIGHT, IT REALLY IS GOOD.
Oh.
TSUMUGI.
YUMMMY!
YOU GOT SOME ON YOUR FACE.
Hee hee hee!
I'M GLAD I DIDN'T GIVE UP.
Come on, let's eat Yagi's yakitori, too.
I want meat!
Oh.
When we're heating up the yakitori...
...it's better if we add a little sake and steam it...

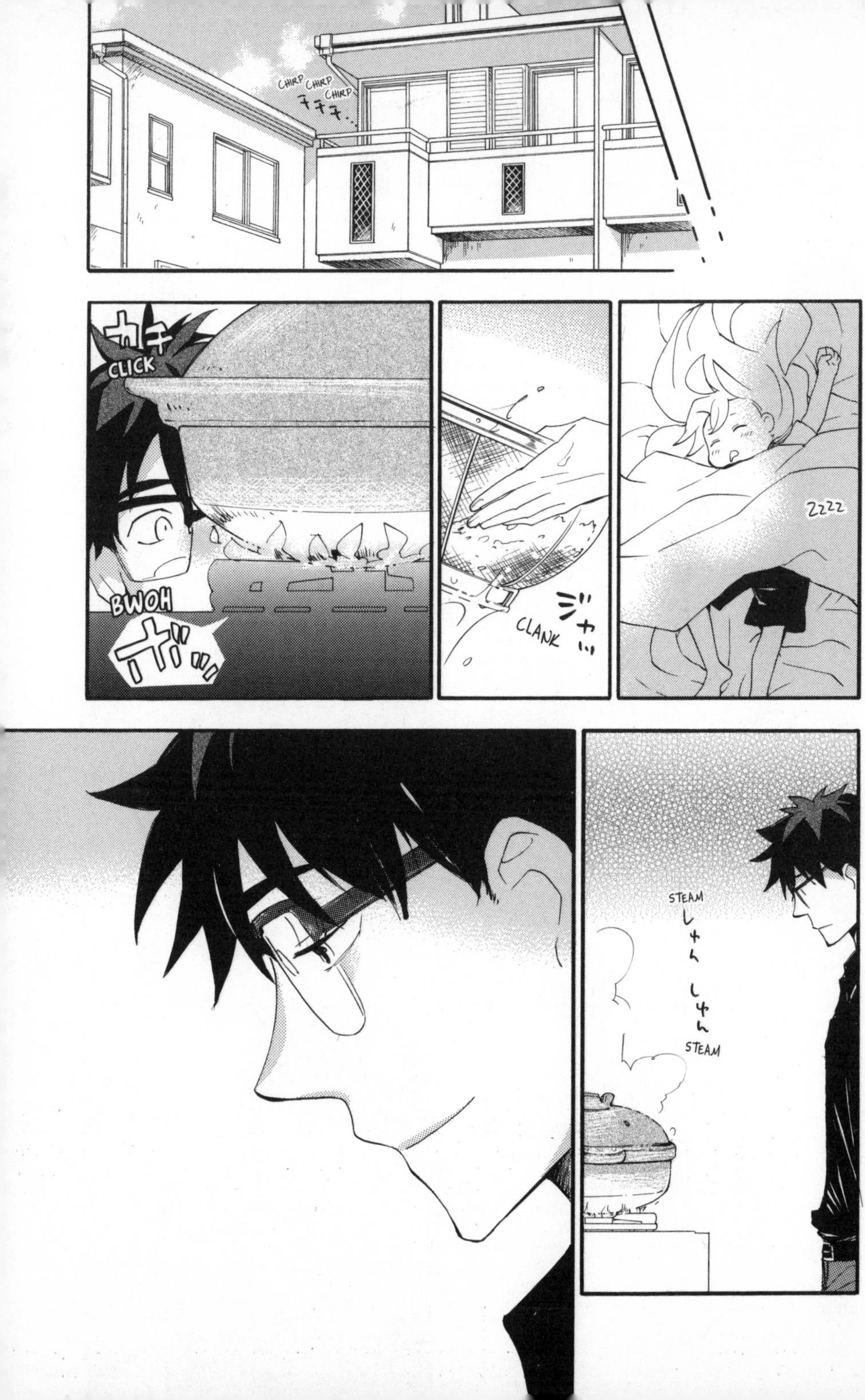
CHIRP CHIRP CHIRP
チチチ…
Zzzz
ジャッ
CLANK
カチ
CLICK
BWOH
ボッ
STEAM
しゅん しゅん
STEAM

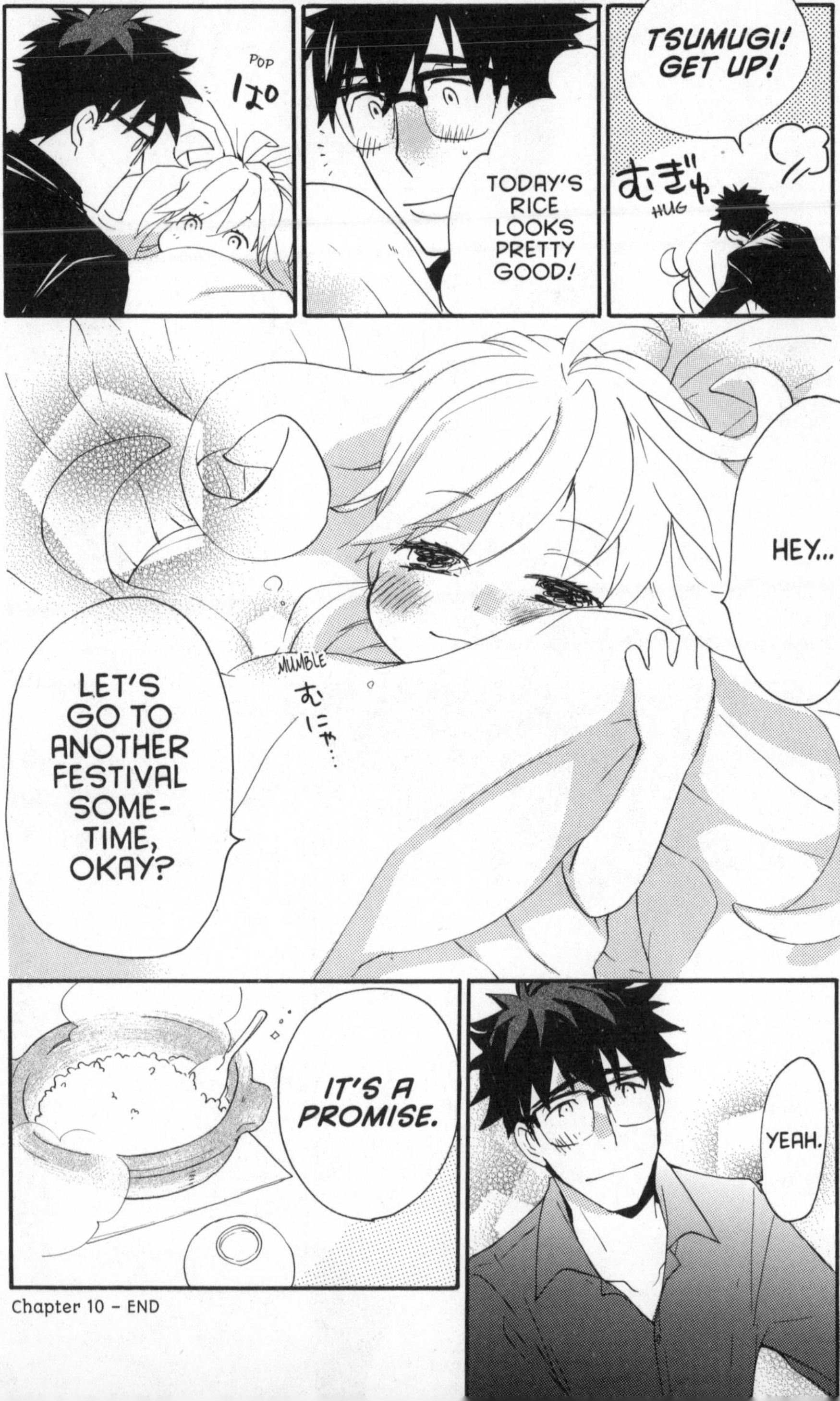
TSUMUGI! GET UP!
むぎゅ
HUG
TODAY'S RICE LOOKS PRETTY GOOD!
POP
HEY...
LET'S GO TO ANOTHER FESTIVAL SOME-TIME, OKAY?
MUMBLE
むにゃ…
YEAH.
IT'S A PROMISE.

Chapter 10 – END

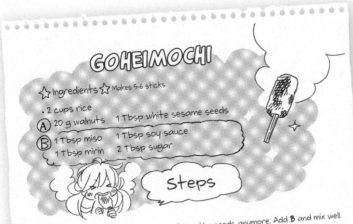

GOHEIMOCHI

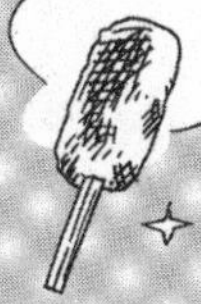

☆Ingredients☆ Makes 5-6 sticks

- 2 cups rice

Ⓐ 20 g walnuts 1 Tbsp white sesame seeds

Ⓑ 1 Tbsp miso 1 Tbsp soy sauce
1 Tbsp mirin 2 Tbsp sugar

Steps

1. Grind **A** in a mortar until you can't see the seeds anymore. Add **B** and mix well.
2. Make firm rice and grind in mortar. Taking enough to make one goheimochi stick, flatten and mold with your hands, then skewer with a disposable chopstick.

POINT Stick the wider end of the chopsticks in. Wrap aluminum foil around the pointed end of chopstick so it doesn't burn while grilling.

3. Place over direct heat for 2 minutes on each side, grilling enough to slightly char it.
4. Spread the mixture from **Step 1** on both sides and then cook for 2 minutes over direct heat. Once it's slightly charred, it's done.

POINT It burns easily, so move it around and keep it a good distance away from the flame.

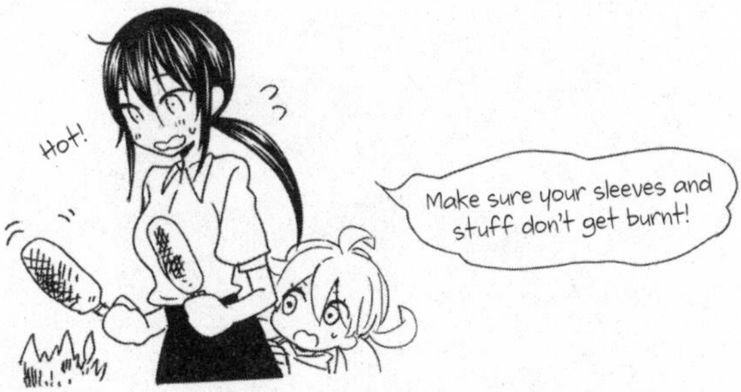
Hot!
Make sure your sleeves and stuff don't get burnt!

Sweetness & Lightning Recipe — 10

CONVERSION NOTES:
360 ML RICE = ABOUT 1 1/2 CUPS UNCOOKED, 20 G WALNUTS = ABOUT 2 TBSP CHOPPED

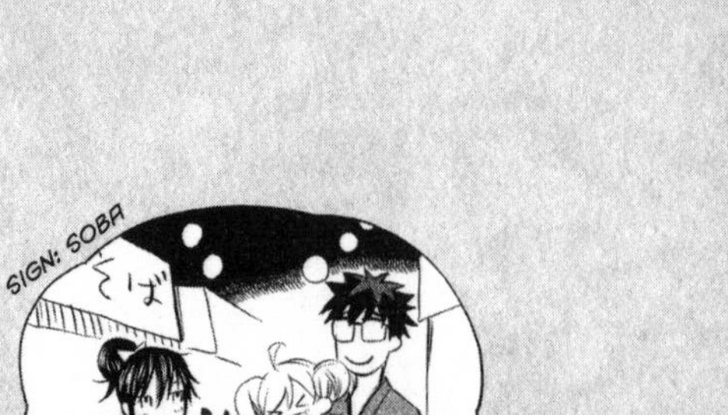
SIGN: SOBA
そば
Zzz...

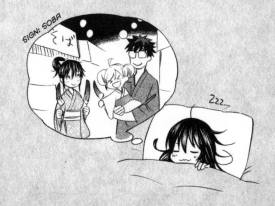

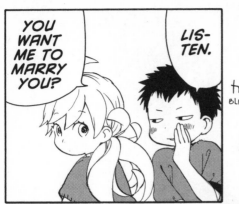

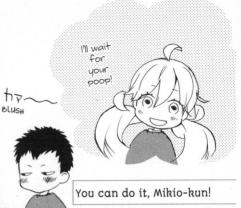

I'll wait for your poop!
カァ~~
BLUSH
You can do it, Mikio-kun!
LIS-TEN.
YOU WANT ME TO MARRY YOU?
NO...
...WAY!
'CAUSE YOU'RE A MEANIE!
U-UH... AM I?
I don't wanna marry you!
Ha ha ha...
AWW, YOU GOT RE-JECTED, HUH?
Ha ha ha!
SOB
さめざめ
SOB
Pffft.
SORRY, SORRY.
FROM NOW ON, BE NICE.
SHE MIGHT START TO LIKE YOU!

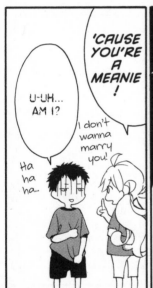

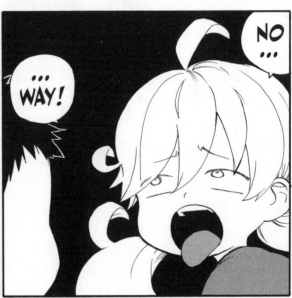

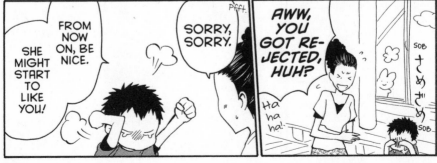

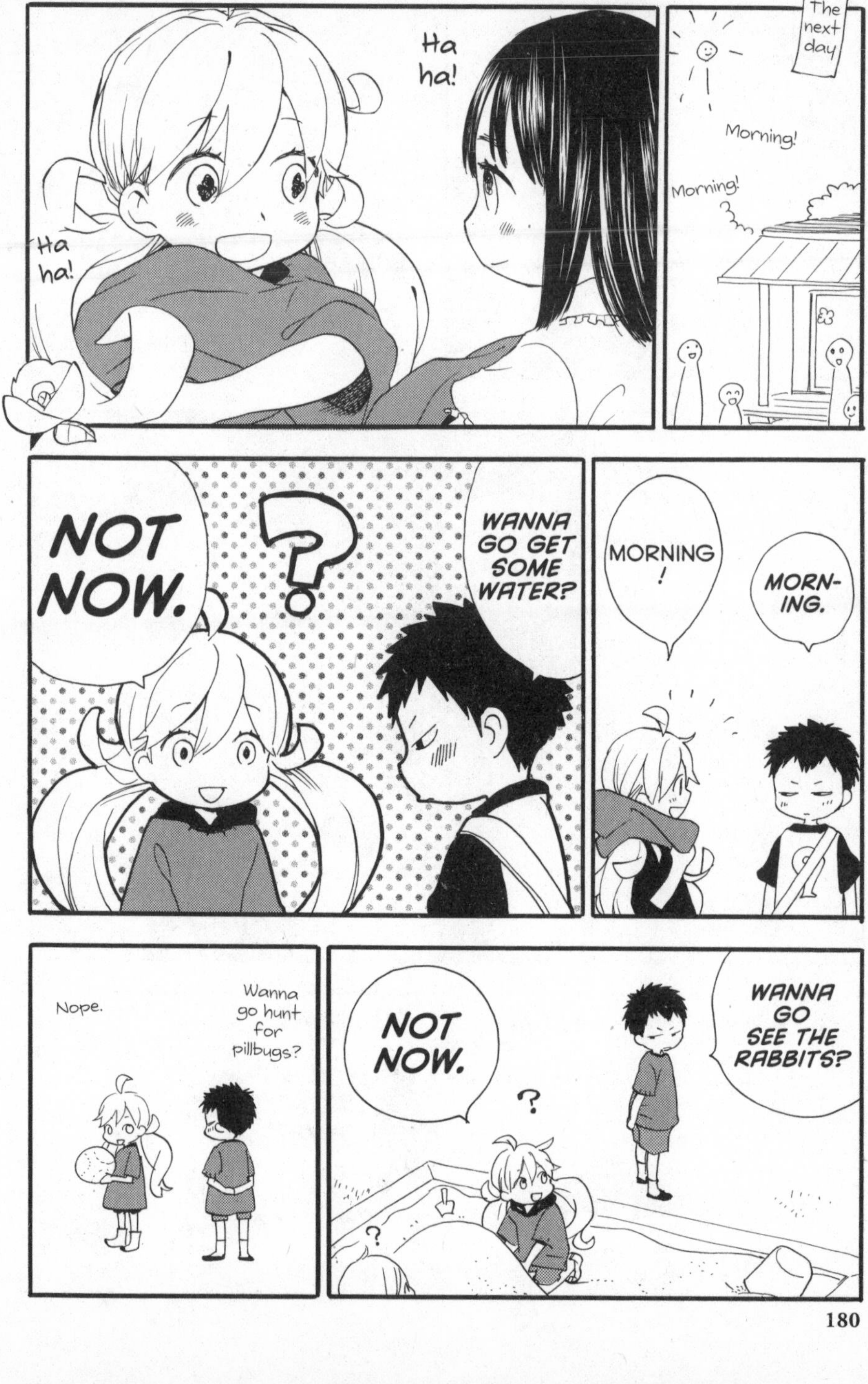
The next day
Morning!
Morning!
Ha ha!
Ha ha!
MORNING!
MORN-ING.
WANNA GO GET SOME WATER?
?
NOT NOW.
WANNA GO SEE THE RABBITS?
?
NOT NOW.
?
Wanna go hunt for pillbugs?
Nope.

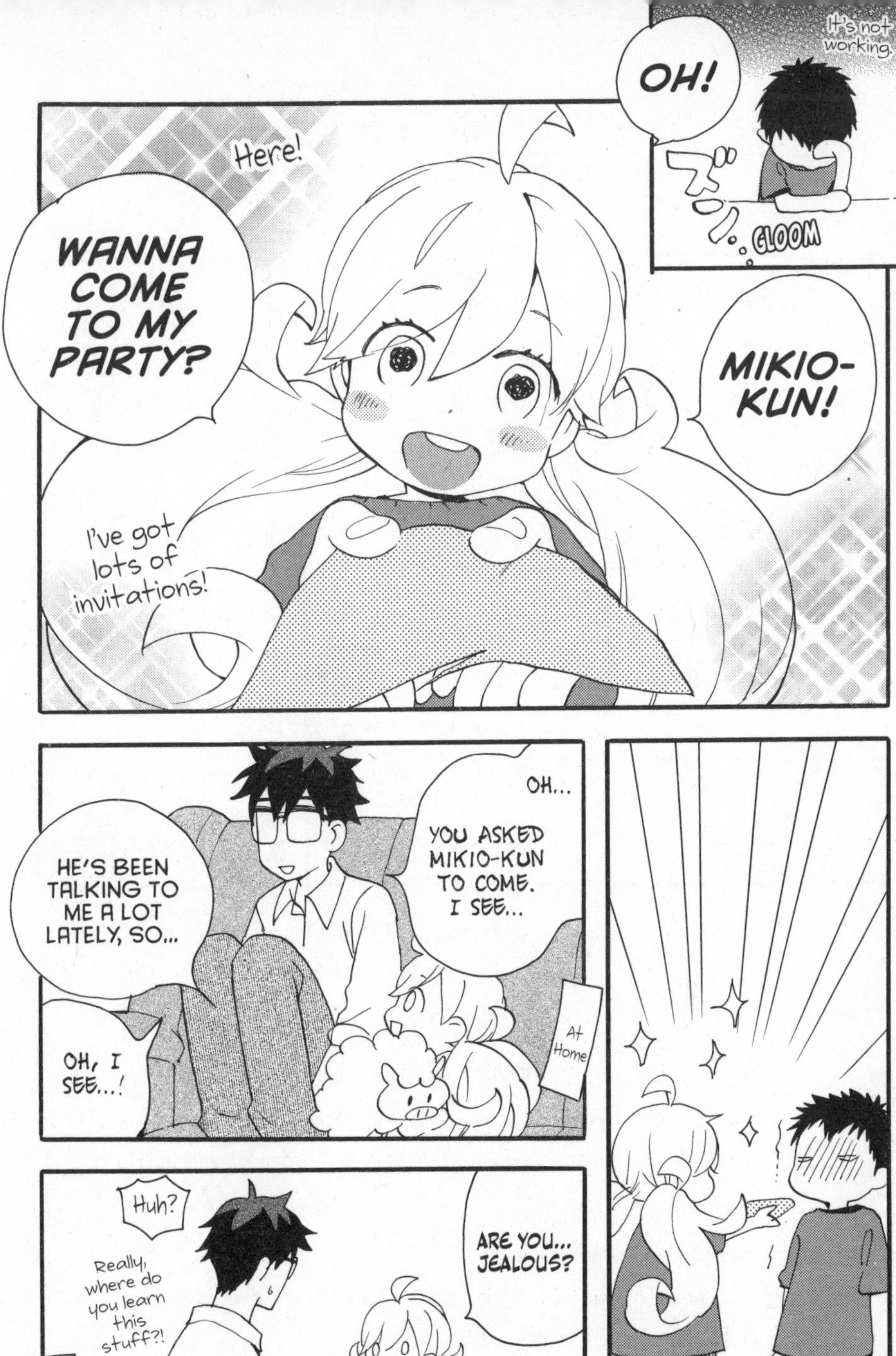
OH!
It's not working.
GLOOM
Here!
MIKIO-KUN!
WANNA COME TO MY PARTY?
I've got lots of invitations!
OH... YOU ASKED MIKIO-KUN TO COME. I SEE...
HE'S BEEN TALKING TO ME A LOT LATELY, SO...
At Home
OH, I SEE...!
ARE YOU... JEALOUS?
Huh?
Really, where do you learn this stuff?!
The End

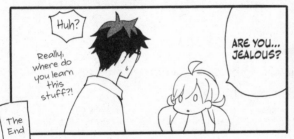

Afterword

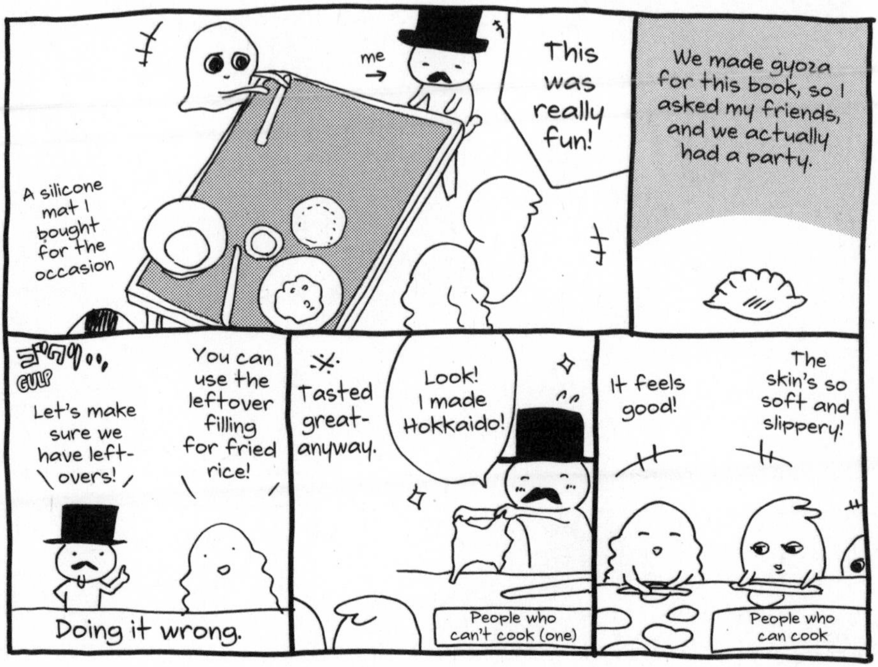
We made gyoza for this book, so I asked my friends, and we actually had a party.
This was really fun!
me
A silicone mat I bought for the occasion
The skin's so soft and slippery!
It feels good!
People who can cook
Look! I made Hokkaido!
Tasted great-anyway.
People who can't cook (one)
You can use the leftover filling for fried rice!
GULP
Let's make sure we have left-overs!
Doing it wrong.

See you next volume!

雨隠ギド
Gido Amagakure

Thank you!

Koz-tan, Gon-chan, Tsuru-san, Wakayama-san
M-chan, E-chan, S-chan, Y-san, Ten-chan, Kou-chan

T-shiro-sama, Jun Abe-sama
Research Cooperation: Tabegoto-ya Norabou-sama
Cooking Advisor: Yo Tatewaki-sama

And thank you to everyone else who helped!

Translation Notes

Weak flour, page 23: Flour with a lower gluten content. May be called "cake flour" in the US.

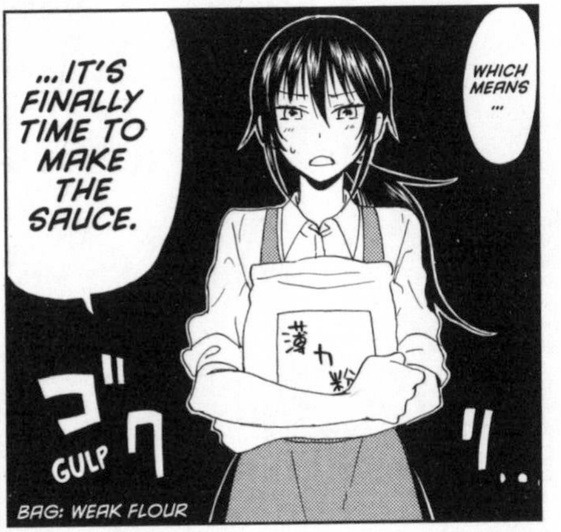
WHICH MEANS ...
...IT'S FINALLY TIME TO MAKE THE SAUCE.
薄力粉
ゴクリ..
GULP
BAG: WEAK FLOUR

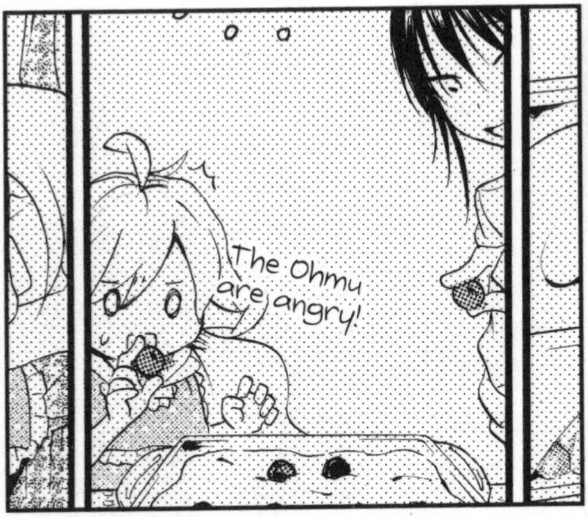
The Ohmu are angry!

Ohmu, page 28: A reference to the enormous telepathic arthropods in Hayao Miyazaki's 1984 film *Nausicaä of the Valley of the Wind.*

Strong flour, page 52: Flour with a high gluten content. May be called "bread flour" in the US.

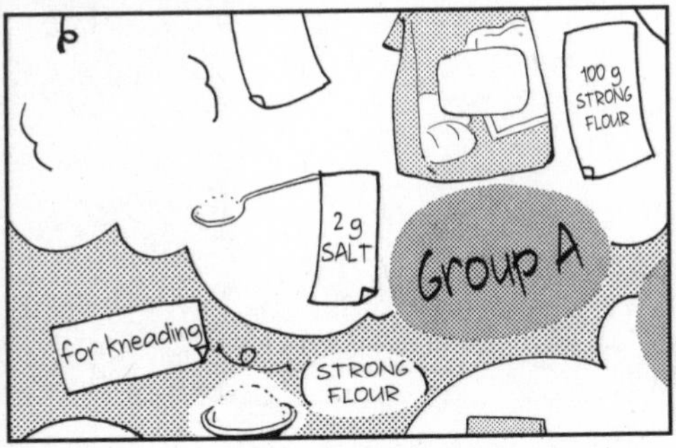
100 g STRONG FLOUR
2 g SALT
Group A
for kneading
STRONG FLOUR

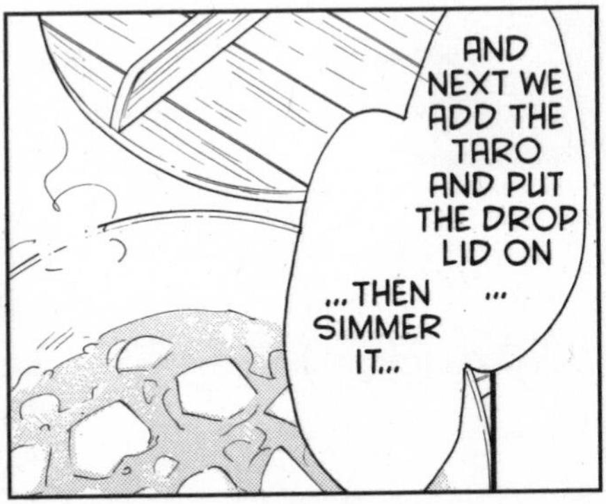
AND NEXT WE ADD THE TARO AND PUT THE DROP LID ON ...
...THEN SIMMER IT...

Drop lid, page 94: Called an *otoshi-buta* lid in Japanese, a small wooden lid that fits inside the pot, resting on the simmering liquid to ensure even distribution of heat.

Next Issue

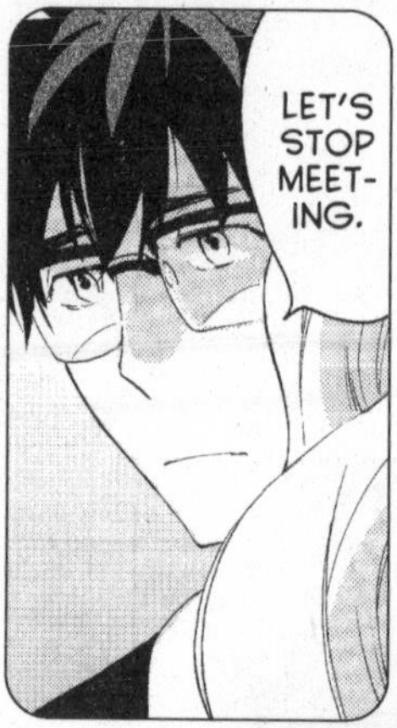
LET'S STOP MEET-ING.

A sudden declaration that it's over!

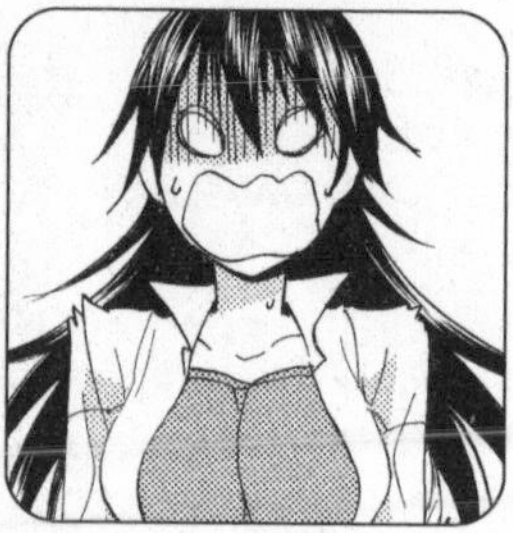

Kotori is shocked.

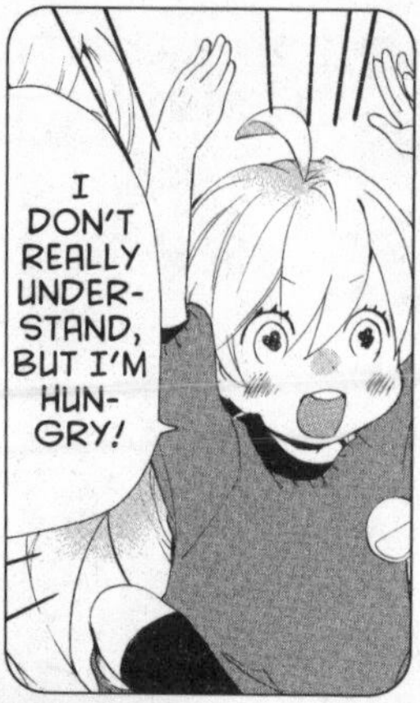
I DON'T REALLY UNDER-STAND, BUT I'M HUN-GRY!

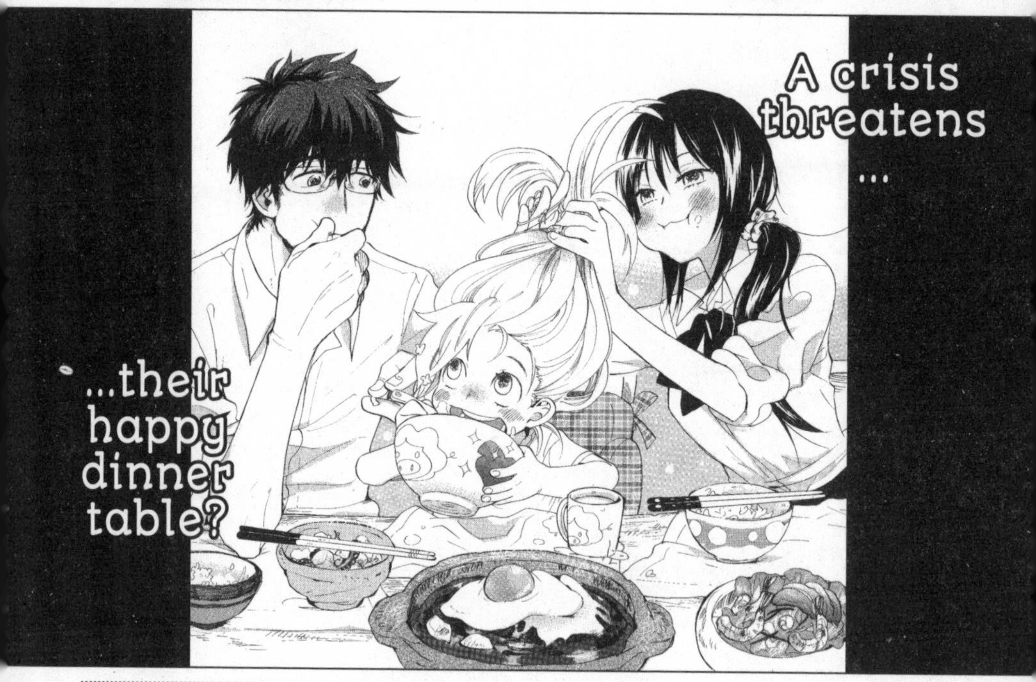
A crisis threatens ...
...their happy dinner table?

sweetness & lightning 3

a Silent Voice

KC
KODANSHA
COMICS

"The word heartwarming was made for manga like this." –Manga Bookshelf

"A harsh and biting social commentary... delivers in its depth of character and emotional strength." -Comics Bulletin

"A very powerful story about being different and the consequences of childhood bullying... Read it." –Anime News Network

Shoya is a bully. When Shoko, a girl who can't hear, enters his elementary school class, she becomes their favorite target, and Shoya and his friends goad each other into devising new tortures for her. But the children's cruelty goes too far. Shoko is forced to leave the school, and Shoya ends up shouldering all the blame. Six years later, the two meet again. Can Shoya make up for his past mistakes, or is it too late?

Available now in print and digitally!

My Little Monster

OPPOSITES ATTRACT...MAYBE?

Haru Yoshida is feared as an unstable and violent "monster." Mizutani Shizuku is a grade-obsessed student with no friends. Fate brings these two together to form the most unlikely pair. Haru firmly believes he's in love with Mizutani and she firmly believes he's insane.

KC
KODANSHA
COMICS

Yamada-kun AND THE Seven Witches

SWAPPED WITH A KISS?!

Class troublemaker Ryu Yamada is already having a bad day when he stumbles down a staircase along with star student Urara Shiraishi. When he wakes up, he realizes they have switched bodies—and that Ryu has the power to trade places with anyone just by kissing them! Ryu and Urara take full advantage of the situation to improve their lives, but with such an oddly amazing power, just how long will they be able to keep their secret under wraps?

Available now in print and digitally!

Praise for the anime:

"The show provides a pleasant window on the highs and lows of young love with two young people who are first timers at the real thing."

-The Fandom Post

"Always it is smarter, more poetic, more touching, just plain better than you think it is going to be."

-Anime News Network

Mei Tachibana has no friends — and says she doesn't need them!

But everything changes when she accidentally roundhouse kicks the most popular boy in school! However, Yamato Kurosawa isn't angry in the slightest— in fact, he thinks his ordinary life could use an unusual girl like Mei. But winning Mei's trust will be a tough task. How long will she refuse to say, "I love you"?

María
THE VIRGIN WITCH

"María's brand of righteous justice, passion and plain talking make for one of the freshest manga series of 2015. I dare any other book to top it."
—UK Anime Network

PURITY AND POWER

As a war to determine the rightful ruler of medieval France ravages the land, the witch María decides she will not stand idly by as men kill each other in the name of God and glory. Using her powerful magic, she summons various beasts and demons —even going as far as using a succubus to seduce soldiers into submission under the veil of night— all to stop the needless slaughter. However, after the Archangel Michael puts an end to her meddling, he curses her to lose her powers if she ever gives up her virginity. Will she forgo the forbidden fruit of adulthood in order to bring an end to the merciless machine of war?
Available now in print and digitally!

KC
KODANSHA
COMICS

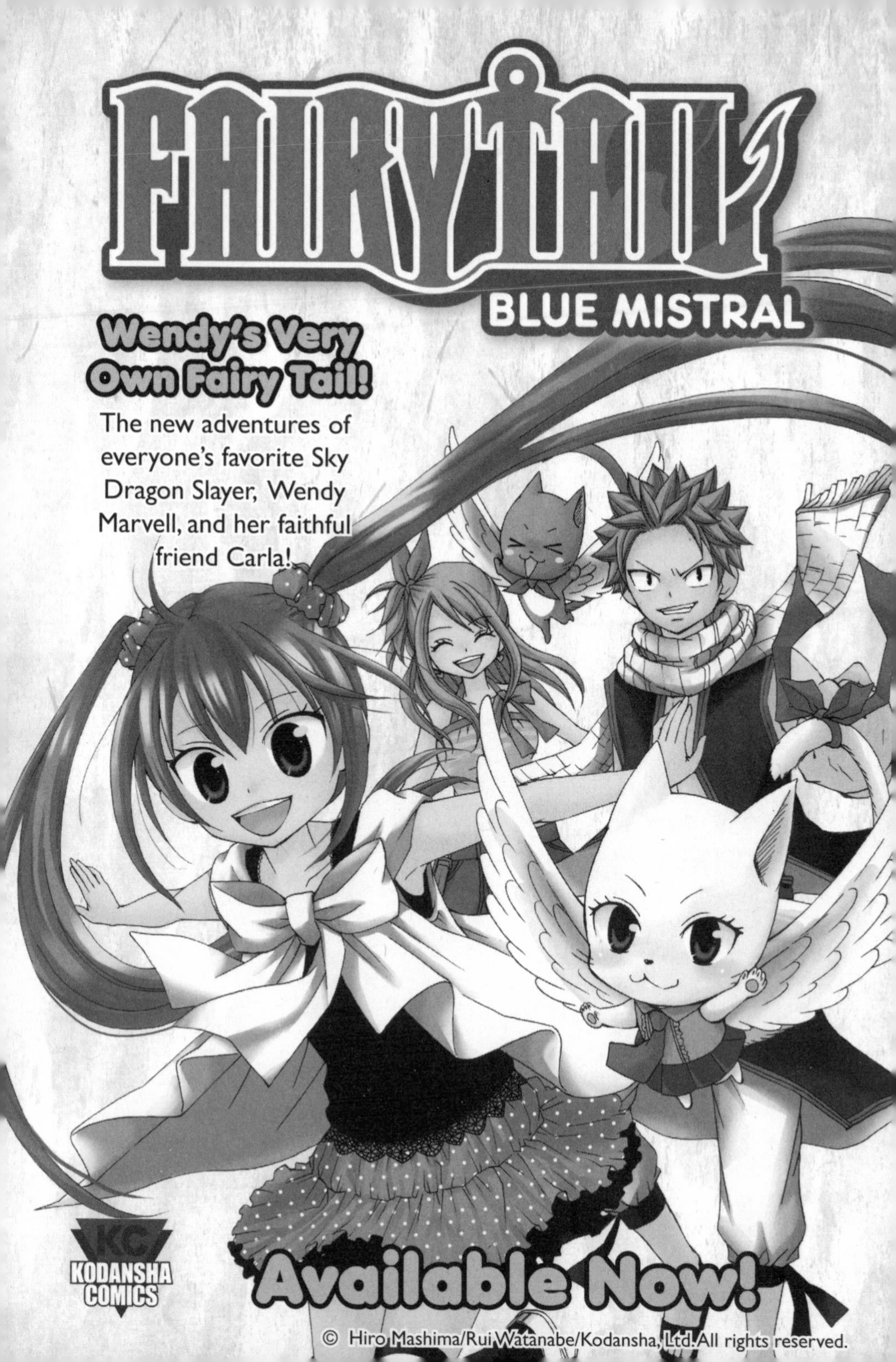

A Kodansha Comics Trade Paperback Original.

Published in the United States by Kodansha Comics,
an imprint of Kodansha USA Publishing, LLC, New York.

Publication rights for this English edition arranged through Kodansha Ltd., Tokyo.

First published in Japan in 2014 by Kodansha Ltd., Tokyo, as *Ama-ama to Inadzuma* volume 2.

ISBN 978-1-63236-370-1

Printed in Mexico.

www.kodansha.us

9 8 7 6 5 4 3

Translation: Adam Lensenmayer
Lettering: Lys Blakeslee
Editing: Paul Starr
Kodansha Comics edition cover design: Phil Balsman